A Signal War

A Canadian Soldier's Memoir
of the Liberation of the Netherlands

John Raycroft

Babblefish Press

Prescott

copyright © 2002 by Babblefish Press

All rights reserved. No part of this publication may be stored in a retrieval system, translated or reproduced in any form or by any means without written permission of the publisher.

Canadian Cataloguing in Publishing Data

Raycroft, John
A Signal War
A Canadian Soldier's Memoir of the Liberation of the Netherlands
Includes biographical references and index

ISBN: 0-9730058-0-7

1. Raycroft, John. 1923-. 2. Netherlands—History—German occupation—1940-45. 3. World War, 1939-45—Personal narratives, Canadian. 4. Canada. Canadian Army, Canadian Division, 3rd—Biography. I. Title

D811.R394 2002   940.54'21492'092   C2002-901335-6

Babblefish Press
Box 633
Prescott, Ontario
K0E 1T0
Tel: (613) 925-0078
www.babblefishpress.ca

Printed and bound in Canada

AGMV Marquis, Montreal, PQ

Cover photos by Donald I. Grant /National Archives of Canada

Contents

Prologue ix

1 Signing Up 1

2 Training 10

3 From Halifax to Borden to Ostend 27

4 The Schelde Pocket 42

5 The Five Days of Gent 56

6 The Nijmegan Salient 65

7 The Ardennes Setback 82

8 The Rhineland: Part I 101

9 The Rhineland: Part II 115

10 The Rhineland: Part III 125

11 The Rhineland: Part IV 138
   Photos 156-167

12 Preparing to Cross 168

13 The Rhine Is Crossed 186

14 From Emmerich to Zutphen 204
   Photos 220-231

15 From Zutphen to Gorredijk 232

16 Into North Germany 243

17 The Last Days 258

18 The War Is Over 269

19 The Canadian Army of Occupation: Part I 293

20 The Canadian Army of Occupation: Part II 310

21 The Countdown To Home 334

22 Epilogue 355

   Endnotes 367

   Bibliography 380

   Index 384

To Jean
my wife of 48 years
who did not live to see the work
completed.

A Word of Thanks

It has been said that a writer who tries to produce something for publication is his or her own fault. True, it is hard to blame others for shutting oneself in a den for long, seemingly unsocial periods of time. Nevertheless, the blame has to be shared.

Steve Wormington served as adviser, editor and general factotum. Mike Paradis and and my son Brent gave the manuscript their scholarly scrutiny. David Halpin-Byrne, with his exceptional knowledge of matters military and grammatical, was always available to answer questions. Essential expertise in the mysteries of modern print technology was supplied by Robin Morris. In spite of such assistance, there will be mistakes, of course, but they'll be because I didn't listen. To all of you who shared the blame, I am grateful, and offer my sincere thanks.

A Word about Spelling

For the proper spelling of names of persons, I turned to biographical dictionaries. Checking the spelling of hamlets, towns, cities, rivers and bodies of water, however is not so straightforward. It seems sensible to me to respect the spelling used by the country in question unless established usage presents compelling reason not to. "The Hague," for instance, has become well-established and recognized in the English world, which is understandable when considering that the official Dutch name is "'s-Gravenhage."

I have respected the Dutch letter "ij," capitalizing both parts of it whenever it begins a word requiring a capital, as in Ijssel.

In Belgium, where there is the choice of either Flermish or Walloon spelling, I use "Gent," "Antwerp," and "Ostend"

A Signal War

Prologue

An old adage says that no one has a good enough memory to be a successful liar. A corollary to the adage might be that after a certain amount of time has passed no one has a good enough memory to tell the difference between truth and fiction. Imagination blurs the line. We old World War II veterans are usually left unembarrassed, even by fellow veterans, when we have told three different versions of the same event. Ronald Reagan, who had never left the U.S. in those years, went so far as actually to create for himself a role in the War, a remarkable suspension of reality, yet no less remarkable than his repertoire of suspensions throughout his presidency.[1]

Certainly there were survivors of the war's "sharp end" who would have difficulty exaggerating the ugliness and horror of their experiences and of those who died beside them. But within Canada's World War II overseas army of some quarter of a million, the numbers of these men, relatively speaking, were extremely small. We in the field artillery regiments, although still frontline soldiers, were back a bit from the sharp end; yet we, too, were a small number. Only about one in eight soldiers was associated with the front line. Only one in 11 air force people ever flew in combat. It takes the other 90 or so percent to handle the immense and indispensable job of supplying those few.

Prologue

All of us were paid to risk our lives. Even crossing the ocean was a risk. Bombs, V-1s and V-2s killed soldiers and civilians alike, and at distances far from the front lines. The duty of all in the armed forces was ultimately to help kill the enemy. But those whose job was to kill directly were those who died directly, and in infinitely greater numbers than the rest of us. Back from the sharp end — artillerymen, engineers, medics, stretcher-bearers and the like — the risk was lower. It drops to normal civilian level somewhere farther back — and long before reaching, say, the training-camp barber. In broader terms, out of Canada's total armed forces of 468,000, our five divisions and two armoured brigades contained only 90,000 men, and only a percentage of those stood on the front line.

Those of us in training for artillery signals were told that our job was to maintain communications and to kill anyone who tried to stop us. Although one of our artillery officers did, no signaller in our unit, to my knowledge, ever directly killed anyone. Indirectly, of course, we all did. That was a condition of the job.

I mention those odds and percentages out of deference to those who were at the extreme front line. I was close enough to see their suffering, friend and foe alike, and eventually to perceive in a broader analysis the relative innocence of both, and the madness and guilt of those who set them upon one another. The army's death rate in World War II is recorded to be about 3.6 percent. In consideration of where the dying is done, the figure is wildly misleading. That point, I think, comes out in the story.

Military historians, such as Colonel C.P. Stacey, stress that the only evidence to be trusted regarding military actions is that which was written down at the time, preferably the entries in a unit's operations log. All else is suspect and, if used, should be checked against other sources. Historian A.J.P. Taylor is quoted as saying, rather harshly, that putting together reminiscences after 30 or 40 years might end up as nothing more than "old men drooling over their youth" and substituting myth for truth long forgotten.

To set down a war memoir after 55 years might well provoke pity from Taylor, rather than his sneer. Nevertheless, here it is; and for reasons I will outline shortly, I think it is successful in what it attempts. But first, a glance at the basics of the memoir! It is one soldier's considered account of his war years, half a century later — a re-examination of all the recorded events and experiences, with a determination to keep distortion and exaggeration from tainting the truth. My total army career was three months short of three years, hardly a long one compared to the five-year boys. As a replacement who entered the War in north Belgium, my time in action was about four months less than those who landed on D-Day. Casualties, however, were heavier during these final months than they had been in France, including the landing. From this span of time and events the story is mainly formed.

To go on little but memory after such a lapse of time would certainly produce, with or without the drool, a tale with only a weak resemblance to reality. But, as mentioned, this is a reconsidered account. People do grow in perception — something Taylor seems not to expect.

My memory has had a lot of verifying and reinforcing help. First of all, I kept a diary in the war, a punishable military offence, by the way. (I have been an unwavering recorder of events since the spring of 1935, at age 12.) During pauses at the front, I wrote brief entries on folds of paper and stuffed them into my pockets. Whenever I was back to the battery where my gear was, I would transfer these notes to a little book which I kept in my big pack — or else just leave the loose scraps in it, to be transferred later when there was more time. My plan was to eat them if I were captured, so I wanted to get them out of my pockets as soon as possible. (In fear, I probably would have choked, drawn attention to myself and been forced to throw up.) These notations were made for the most part within the day of the events and, although not detailed, would tend to satisfy Colonel Stacey's criterion for the most reliable evidence. Also, with the help of the National Archives of Canada, I drew once or twice on the very logs of which Stacey speaks.

Especially for verification of the time and place and purpose of daily actions in which I was involved, I turned to the regimental history books of my own regiment and of the infantry with which I was

Prologue

mostly associated. Visits and correspondence over the years with Dutch and German civilians living in the relevant former war zones, and with a dear veteran friend and partner in the war, Elmer Whittington, verified and awakened memories as well.

There were no hometown boys in my outfit, but I met about a dozen of them in various places overseas, in holding units or on leave. In talking with many of them since the war, I found a few with good recollection and a few with very little. Some had wild ideas about where we had met, and others had no memory of seeing me at all. And I would have had no memory of seeing many of them had it not been for my diary.

Post-war visits in 1956, 1980 and 1995 to those previous war zones in the Netherlands and Germany have been a big help in fine-tuning recollections. Because of the number of requests for information that were for a time showing up in the Legion magazine, placed there by Dutch citizens and occasionally by Dutch immigrants, I decided in 1991 to write one common letter that would outline my complete relationship with their country, and then send out a copy in answer to each request. I enjoyed the project so much that it expanded into a 50-page open letter. It was translated and widely distributed, with a portion of it published over six instalments in a small Dutch weekly. Relevant here is the fact that these citizens found two mistakes which came out of my diary: one involved the date of an event and the other involved a five- or six-kilometre shift in the location of an action. A third mistake, discovered by a fellow veteran, also involved a location — a change of under a kilometre this time. It was not discovered for 50 years. I'll explain that within the story. So, three mistakes is still a pretty good record, surely. There are bound to be other, minor, ones, but I doubt that they would alter the story much.

My mother saved all my letters to her. Those written immediately after the war, when censorship was lifted, were treasures. They went back over everything. And the souvenirs I sent home occasionally yielded something. Part of the adjustment of coming home was the long periods of time I spent in my room, incorporating into my diary what those letters and souvenirs brought to mind again, but had not been originally recorded. I expanded my original notes in the process, to include more detail now that there was time for it. Memory was still fresh. After all, it had not been quite two years since landing in Europe, and a matter of two or three months since returning.

As for the larger picture of the war and the strategy of the military force in north-west Europe after the middle of 1944, which enclosed my microscopic speck of involvement, I turned to the heavier historical tomes in order to get it right. Giving a parallel running account, in brief form, of the immense overall action helps make my movement through it more understandable, although at the time none of us in the bottom ranks of our unit, or surely of any unit, were aware of much of what was going on beyond our own actions and those of the infantry brigade we were supporting. It was not until I enrolled in a modern history course some 10 years after the War that I began to do any serious reading on the topic.

There you have what I believe qualifies me to write my war memoir after 55 years. A fair question is, "Why bother?" Well, there's always a measure of self-assertion involved. What actually started me was the thought that the three offspring of my partner Jean and myself might appreciate a more considered account than the exaggerated fragments they had heard. The thought, too, that our grandchildren might some day be curious, especially if by that time the government has removed history studies from schools and replaced them with indoctrination courses on trans-national corporations.

My effort was not to be too ambitious; but then, after gathering some stuff together and starting, I realized that my experiences, my reading and my 55 years of having considerations settle into place, had given me things to tell about that are obscured in military accounts. I don't see war in the way that I think most veterans do, and as a result have included considerations and events that are not commonly known or have been flashed only briefly before the eyes of the public. The reader will find that I interrupt my personal story frequently with these considerations, which include background material from military histories, anecdotes about others, and references dated before the conflict and long after it — all in an attempt to

Prologue

emphasize the nature of war and its damaging effect on human understanding, as one old veteran sees it.

The damage is portrayed today by the entertainment media's seeming effort to keep alive the savagery in humankind. Back when this tendency in entertainment was warming up, the drama critic Pauline Kael in her review of *A Clockwork Orange* said, "How can people go on talking about the dazzling brilliance of movies and not notice that the directors are sucking up to the thugs in the audience?"[2]

Violence tends to make thugs of us all. Media drama thrives on its depiction because with new technology it is easy to do, and lucrative. Dramatic depiction of war, with notable exceptions, becomes not a study of causes and morality and degradation of perception, but simply a display of ever more thrill-satisfying gratuitous violence which tends further to damage a culture already flawed – "sucking up" to the lowest common denominator. Usually there is almost no concern for understanding human relationships or human suffering.

It had not been a deliberate plan on my part to wait this long before revisiting my diary and setting it down as a memoir, but I'm glad I did. Having to withdraw an earlier version and acknowledge its weaknesses would have been embarrassing. Facing my exaggerated oral anecdotes is bad enough as it is. The writer of an earlier memoir would have been quite a different person from the writer of today's. Ironically, in seeming contradiction of what Taylor suggests, the early account would have been the inaccurate one.

1

Signing Up

"Thank the Lord you children won't have to go," Mrs. Rooke said as she passed me in the yard on her way into our house to talk to my mother, most likely about the war news of the last couple of days. She made the remark through tears. The First World War would be on her mind. Mr. and Mrs. Rooke were neighbours of ours on Russell Street. Mrs. Rooke was a friend of my mother, but older by enough years that my mother, who was 40, never used her first name. It was always Mrs. Rooke.

When she came by me, I was busy with something in our yard. The year was 1939, in September, perhaps on Monday the 11th after school, but I'm guessing. As a result of the German and Russian invasion of Poland on September 1, Britain and France two days later had declared war on Germany. Canada had done the same on the 10th. Hardly a child in the literal sense, I was 16 years old, the oldest of the three boys and one girl in our family. It was for this, our young age, that Mrs. Rooke was suggesting that the Lord should be thanked. I had returned to high school that month to begin grade ten.

In May of that year a special train out of our CPR station had taken us students and our teachers to Ottawa to see King George VI and Queen Elizabeth pass by our designated spot along the route of their royal carriage — the first reigning British monarchs ever to visit Canada. We students were each given a little flag to wave, and also a

Chapter one

badge which spelled out the name of our town. In this tour, which went from coast to coast, loyalties were being reaffirmed for a conflict that was seen to be inevitable. An unpleasant number of us who were students on that special train would be killed by what this royal visit had foreshadowed.

Mrs. Rooke, along with most people, had not dared to think that the war would last over half a decade. After all, there was the impregnable Maginot Line this time, in front of an immense French army of 84 divisions, which had more tanks than Germany. And Britain had an expeditionary force in France ready to help. Then, in December Canada's 1st Division sailed for Britain to be available if needed. For six months after the dividing and devouring of Poland in September, there was an ominous lull. The press started to speak of the "Phoney War." The lull suddenly ended in April of 1940. Germany invaded Denmark and Norway. In May it invaded the Netherlands, Luxembourg, Belgium and France. The story of that British expeditionary force's tattered retreat from Dunkirk is well known.

Lesser known, however — and of much less consequence — is a close call of the 1st Brigade of Canada's 1st Division. Through some incredible military nonsense, its men and equipment were sent into France in May from Plymouth on a French passenger ship. From Brest by train they went inland about 300 kilometres. As Farley Mowat tells it, the station-master at one of the stops questioned the sanity of the affair, and was amazed that they did not know that Paris was surrounded and that Panzers were getting closer by the minute. The brigade retreated to Brest and miraculously got out, but left behind almost all its equipment. One man was killed, in an accident. To indicate the brigade's questionable seriousness in taking this romp, the men of one of its regiments had brought with them their mascot, a 227-kilo statue of a cigar-store Indian, which they had to leave there, buried in a ditch.[3]

By the end of May, French resistance had ended, and the country officially surrendered in June. Here at home that month my father became ill and had to quit work. Things became tight for the family. Grocery debts piled up. My brothers and sister and I were eventually

Signing Up

out for our school's summer holidays. We had a big garden, which helped out. My father's illness was severe rheumatic fever, misdiagnosed until it was too late. He died on July 4, at the age of 42. I turned 17 the next day, and floundered in ignorant teenage sullenness and confusion for a couple of weeks after the funeral. My mother and well-meaning relatives kept trying to tell me that I had to go to work. Facing the truth was hard for me. What I think finally did it — although it enraged me at that moment — was what I heard an uncle of mine say to the others on an occasion when I stalked out of the room: "When is that boy going to grow up?"

That same uncle found a job for me with the International Cooperage Company in the village of Cardinal barrel-making shop, a few kilometres east of Prescott, at $15 a week. Eventually, after learning the trade, I would go on piece-rate. With a stubbornness that possibly owed a lot to that enraging question of his, I took the job in spite of its hard work and dreadful working conditions. Maybe I wanted to show him a thing or two about who's grown up. The big wooden barn of a building had no insulation and no heat beyond the two shavings-burning stoves designed to cook and slightly char the barrels' interiors. There were three of us on the job, and occasionally four in busy times. A line shaft driven by a heavy motor ran the length of the shop. Belts ran off it to the noisy machines, one of which was a riveter that pounded constantly. The air hung with smoke and dust. There was no sink, no toilet — no plumbing whatsoever. We carried drinking water from the Canada Starch plant about 200 metres away, in a pail that would freeze and burst overnight in the winter if it were not emptied. We walked over there also if we seriously had to use a toilet. The older fellows did, anyway. Except when the ground was frozen, I dug a hole in the earth underneath the building which was up on pillars on the south side and wide open. For simple urination we used the shop's back door. It opened out onto the factory's dump several metres below. An east wind made the act messy, but we had a can for those occasions.

Chapter one

All jobs for unskilled, uneducated workers were not necessarily this bad, but most were, and very few escaped having something of this texture to them.

My father, as a motor mechanic in the 'dirty'30s, worked six days a week and every third Sunday from 7 o'clock in the morning until six in the evening — and every second evening after supper until 10. Cars were repaired and spray-painted in the same enclosed area, with little ventilation. There were no sick benefits or other forms of social insurance. One has to grasp this to understand a significant feature that helped give the National Socialist German Workers' Party (NAZI Party) its strength — month-long paid holidays, workers cruise ships, a 48-hour week, health care, clean factories. Of course, the young Canadian and American immigrants who returned to Germany in the 1930s for employment would never have suspected that some day their bodies might lie frozen at the gates of Stalingrad.

To mobilize for the war and keep track of its citizens, our federal government designated three days in August of 1940 for the national registration of every Canadian over age 16. Our town set up registration centres in wards, similar to its organization for voting.

In the war in Europe during that month, the Battle of Britain began, a decisive struggle in the air against fighter-escorted Luftwaffe bombers on their way to London and other British cities. Opposing them were limited numbers of fighter pilots in Hurricanes and Spitfires. Earlier enemy bombing had been focussed on military targets, with a success that was becoming worrisome. But one night a German plane got off course and unintentionally dropped its load on London. Germany apologized for the mistake, but the British War Office saw it as an opportunity to retaliate and, it was hoped, stimulate Hitler into irrational action. So the RAF bombed Berlin. It worked. The enraged Hitler, beginning three weeks later, unleashed his bombers on London night after night. The battle lasted into the next year, ending in victory for the RAF. Churchill is reputed to have said that the British sacrificed London to help win the war. The Luftwaffe had exhausted itself, thereby lessening the serious threat of a German invasion. In addition, the failure drove the vengeful Hitler

Signing Up

to give top priority to the manufacturing of bombers, instead of the fighter planes the Luftwaffe desperately needed.

Also in 1940, Hitler's ally, Mussolini, invaded Egypt, and was not only defeated in that attempt but also lost all his North African territory to a British force containing Australians and New Zealanders. Having learned little, apparently, he decided later in the year to invade Greece — through Albania, which he had annexed earlier — and was stopped cold. German troops eventually had to subdue the country for him in the spring of 1941, overrunning Yugoslavia on the way down. These troops then landed in North Africa, to begin the struggle-turned-legend between the British Desert Rats and Rommel's Afrika Korps.

A carload of us on our way to work in Cardinal one cold January morning in 1941 was stopped at a road-block set up by the Mounties at the top of Windmill Hill. It was still quite dark. They studied our faces with flashlights, checked our identities, and asked whether we had seen anyone along the road. As we learned later, they were hunting for the German Luftwaffe ace, Franz von Werra, who in the Battle of Britain had been shot down, shipped to Canada and escaped from a trainload of prisoners-of-war by jumping out a window into the snow as the train was moving along near Smiths Falls. Somehow through that biting January night he covered 70 to 80 kilometres to the St. Lawrence River somewhere between where we had been stopped and Johnstown, another kilometre or two farther east. Here he stole a boat (the ice was broken up) and paddled across to the neutral United States. By way of the German legation in the United States and by a route through several South American countries, he eventually got back and flew again for his country. He is said to be the only escaped Luftwaffe prisoner in the entire war to do so. In October of that same year he crashed off the coast of the Netherlands. His body was never found.

Hitler's invasion of the Soviet Union on June 22 of 1941 was possibly the first good news for the British War Office. Seventy-five percent of the German forces went in on a 3,000-kilometre front. It is

Chapter one

hard to believe that their actions on the Western Front were being carried out with the remaining 25 percent.

It was a big year, 1941. Pearl Harbour on December 7 was the next news uplift for Britain. The United States was now involved. And it was also the year of the tragic and inexcusable blunder of sending 2,000 Canadian soldiers to Hong Kong, an act that resembled a ritual sacrifice. The men themselves apparently sensed that they were caught up in military ignorance or indifference. Fifty-one of them deserted before they left. Another 30 to 40 men jumped ship and got down into the dock area sheds, but were rounded up and forced on board.[4] Their vehicles, especially the precious water-trucks, never arrived at the dock until a couple of days after the ship sailed, even though there was room on board for some 20 of them. In November their vehicles, over 200 altogether, were sent on an American carrier; but they never arrived, for the navy diverted the ship and eventually used the vehicles in the fighting in the Philippines.[5]

There were 550 of those men who did not come home, who either died in the pointless fight for the colony or because of the treatment they received as prisoners-of-war for three and a half years. Many of the returned survivors died young from the effects of malnutrition and poor medical care. A few years after the war, I worked for Ontario Hydro with one of these veterans, Carl Innis. Malnutrition and ill-treatment had left him damaged. He managed to reach middle age.

War's blunders, like those that can occur in any major undertaking, have people who will deny, even defy, the evidence. The investigation later over the Hong Kong affair was demonstrated to be fraudulent, and one critic charged that to involve the police in this fraud was "shameful prostitution" of the RCMP. Canada's official war historian, C.P. Stacey, condemns the suggestion that the sacrifice served to disturb significantly the Japanese course of the war as "an egregious absurdity."[6]

The fact that Canada before the war had insisted — to please the Americans, apparently — that Britain break the Anglo-Japanese Alliance was not an act that would encourage better treatment of the

Signing Up

Hong Kong prisoners. Nor would Canada's internment of its Japanese-Canadian citizens.

Meanwhile, German blunders progressed. In August of 1942 its forces reached Stalingrad and began a disastrous siege of the city, which lasted through the winter, an event that is widely accepted as marking the turning point of the war. Germany had 150,000 men killed or wounded and 90,000 taken prisoner, of whom fewer than 6,000 survived Stalin's terrible vengeance.

In my little world in 1942 I became 18 and a half years old. Draft age! My mother was receiving some sort of an allowance as a widow with children. The details have long left me, but I remember her showing me figures that seemed hardly enough to keep the family in footwear. Also, one of my brothers was now 16, which may have taken him off the allowance.

Nevertheless, I wanted him and my other two siblings to finish high school. My employer listed me as a breadwinner and also as a tradesman supplying an essential service, inasmuch as our barrels were used to ship starch, powdered milk and soap. All this, combined with the plea that coopers were as rare as dodo birds, added up to what was called a deferment, which exempted me from the draft. But I was getting restless, because for one thing the work was getting to me. I had taken the foreman's job, after watching the previous one slowly go mad. It was not pleasant. He was living alone, and apparently no one paid much attention. A relative of his whom I told and who went to his house to check became rapidly convinced, and had him committed at once. The job was not to blame, although it was hardly therapeutic.

Canadian soldiers and airmen were arriving in greater numbers in Britain. In the summer of 1943, with Montgomery victorious in North Africa, the 1st Canadian Division was sent from Britain to help British troops in the invasion of Sicily, which began the Italian Campaign. In December, on the Italian mainland, the 1st Division was joined by a part of the Canadian 5th Division.

I had long paid off the family debts and was making a relatively high wage now on a piece-rate. But the hard work and the working

Chapter one

conditions were making it more difficult to get up each morning. In September of 1943, now 20 years old, I quit, after three years, one month, three weeks and one day on the job. My employer was not pleased. Out went my deferment status, of course.. My first venture was to Ottawa to join the air force to train as a mechanic in the ground crew, for I was not brave enough to fly. A lot of the Prescott boys were; and, in numbers disproportionate to other services, had already paid the supreme sacrifice because of it. With those two years of high school, I could read the papers.

Even though I had some of the enlistment routine completed, the recruiting staff told me that a new restriction stopped all recruitment for ground crew positions. I was so pathetically naive in this attempt that I told a friend that having available my father's old motor-mechanic tools might help me get in.

After cutting a supply of winter wood for the family and helping my grandfather dig his crop of potatoes, I went to Kingston to Fort Frontenac, Military District 3 (MD3), on October 12, 1943 and joined the army. Until the big political conscription fiasco near the end of the war when, replacements overseas were badly needed, the draft was for home defence only. The army pushed its recruits, though, to volunteer for active service overseas. This I did, as I think most did. The reasons would be varied: pressure from the military staff, a pittance more money for each day overseas, prestige, dismissal of a pending jail sentence, special privileges, adventure, even patriotism. Whatever the reason, soldiers quite naturally accepted the image of patriotism and courage — and, if I should be an example, actually came to believe it over time, whether it was the original motive of not. It was understood that after a period of honourable overseas service we would receive what was called the Canadian Volunteer Service Medal and Clasp. As an immediate distinguishing mark, we got a small circle of fabric about 2 centimetres in diameter, containing the letters 'GS,' which stood for "General Service" and was to be sewn on one of our sleeves at a specified distance above the cuff.

I must admit, though, that possibly the strongest influence on me was my belief in what the press was saying: that the war would quite

Signing Up

possibly be over by Christmas of 1944. Also, as a volunteer I had the privilege of choosing from a limited number of branches and of jobs within them. I eventually grasped that they were choices because they represented areas where a lot of maiming and dying was taking place. I chose artillery signals training, with the hope that the training would take a long time.

Years later, on an occasion of light-hearted correspondence with a dear friend, Dave McIntosh, author of several books on the war and an RCAF veteran who had been awarded the Distinguished Flying Cross, I suggested that he probably signed up to get off welfare, whereas I did so through the mature and reasoned decision that the Hun had to be routed and the world made safe for democracy. We both knew the truth about one another. He had told me that he signed up because near the close of his last university year the university waived its final examinations and granted the degree automatically to any student who volunteered for active service and was accepted.

The day after I signed up, the government of Italy under King Victor Emmanuel and Marshal Badoglio, both by that time behind Allied lines in Italy, declared war on Germany. Not that it mattered to the war, for the Germans had already disarmed the Italian forces. Back in April the King and his supporters in a quiet coup had removed and imprisoned Mussolini, but he was rescued in a daring escapade executed by Otto Skorzeny, the famous German rescue expert. The Germans then set up the Duce as head of a puppet Italian government in north Italy. About a month before its declaration of war the Badoglio government had signed an armistice with the Allies. A reigning optimism held that these events were quickly bringing the war to an end.

2

Training

My introductory night in a barracks required no diary note to remember. Being among the first through the door, I took a bottom bunk.

Later, when the choices were narrowed, a fellow recruit coming in asked me if I would mind taking the upper, for he had a sinus and nasal condition that gave him trouble when lying down and often required him to get up and clear his head. I traded. When we settled in for the night, he opened up a thickness of newspaper beside his bed. Not long after the lights went out, he started noisily to suction out his sinuses through a vacuuming effort with his lungs that came close each time to clearing his stomach as well. Then would come the gob of phlegm striking the newspaper. Other fellows shifted in their bunks and uttered expletives. It was not a good night. He disappeared after the medicals the next day.

The doctor who checked my feet asked me whether I did much walking. A lot, I told him. Your feet are almost flat, he said, but you'll be alright. I have a measure of colour-blindness known as Daltonism, but if the army's optometrist found it, he didn't say anything. Years later I learned it through those Japanese circles with the coloured dots that form numerals. Owing to the need for casualty replacements, medical requirements, it was said, were getting more lenient by this time — which inevitably led to stories such as the one about the fel-

Training

low they reluctantly had to turn down on discovering that his guide dog had flat feet.

Because I signed over a designated amount of my army pay to my mother, she received an extra allowance which I believe was the equivalent of a marital status amount, inasmuch as I was the breadwinner to a family with children in school. The only other document that I remember being guided through and signing was my will. I still have it. A strange feeling hung to that piece of paper, but certainly not because it was complicated. To my mother I did "give, devise and bequeath . . ." and then, out in a big open space, in block letters, were the words, "ALL I OWN." It wasn't much.

Altogether, the indoctrinating process took four days, including the tedious initiation to parade square drill, which at the time seemed quite idiotic to me. I eventually came to see its basic purpose: the development of blind obedience, combined with a way of keeping track of and moving large numbers of people here and there efficiently on foot. I hated it on the very first day and never grew any more fond of it. Shortening down my tall-man's longer strides made my legs ache. The interspersed lectures were a relief.

Now that we were ensnared and uniformed, the fortress command gave us four day's leave. When we returned, the drilling continued and the lectures and films increased. The ones on venereal diseases were a shock to me. They took the edge off my warm, erotic memories of secretly leafing through my uncle's booklet of hard-core cartoons. When another fellow and I took a walk outside the Fort one evening and were gently addressed by a prostitute, I pictured her as a barely human slattern with a mess of running sores underneath somewhere. The whole business damaged my image of Claire Trevor in the movie, *Dead End*. The sergeant who was in charge of this phase of our enlightenment showed us a film that was not to entertain us but, it would seem, to make sexual abstinence appear to be an appealing option.

Also a shock was the tough sergeant's blunt follow-up on the film. Although I quickly became accustomed to the language of soldiers, probably the most disgusting of any organized collection of human

Chapter 2

beings, I never swore or used foul language in my entire army career — no doubt because of my religious mother's influence. I began to indulge in it only years later when the pain of arthritis broke me. So when the sergeant scattered some condoms on the table — he called them French safes — and employed rough language to drive the point home about using them, my mind shifted uneasily. Purchasing condoms was a surreptitious undertaking before the war, and for too long after. Not all drugstores carried them, and they were certainly not on display. Asking for them was an embarrassment. In the 1950s, I bought mine in a men's clothing store. At the right moment, out of earshot of others, the proprietor would say, in a disarmingly casual manner: "Oh, by the way, my store carries prophylactics, if you would like a box while you're here." ("Good! I'll just drop them in here with your socks.") Prophylactics! That was the polite term used then.

The sergeant had some crude and frightening things to say about any soldier who would go in "bare pole" as he called it, especially when the "safes" were free. He also expanded into a variety of safe-sex procedures that would have impressed the most forward-thinking campaigners some 40 years later at the outbreak of HIV — although they would have winced at the, to say the least, politically incorrect terminology. I would learn eventually that he was not exaggerating all that much the problem of VD in the military.

On the afternoon of November 4 a contingent of us was marched to the train station on Kingston's Division Street and departed for the artillery's training camp at Petawawa, on the Ottawa River just north of Renfrew. It was a desolate place — sand and black flies in the summer, dreaded cold in the winter. My time there for the most part was a miserable and depressing experience. Roll call in the morning darkness was on the parade square. We stood in rows in great coats and even in balaclavas in the more vicious temperatures that dipped as low as -36 degrees centigrade. It was not the stuff of cherished memories. Much of the basic training in infantry tactics was carried out in the snow. The drafty wooden barracks were heated by coal stoves in the middle of the aisles, to which we were assigned in shifts to feed and

Training

look after, with the threat of being put on charge if one of them should go out.

There is a theory that some sinus problems come from an unfavourable emotional state. I believe it. Even though I never had the condition before or since, I suffered blocked sinuses off and on for much of that winter. My symptoms seemed to be different from that fellow's in the Kingston barracks. At least I didn't make his noises. I just had a stuffed nose and across my forehead a gnawing pain which at times became excruciating when I bent over. But I wouldn't go on sick parade because so many fellows were getting bawled out for malingering. My emotional state in that camp was something less than stable. I hated both the place and the army. The pure wool of military clothes and blankets was a gnawing irritation in itself. Wool next to my hide, even in small percentages in a fabric, was a tormenting experience for me. To pull on those heavy socks each morning required determination. I had to screw up courage to wear the balaclava. And being homesick made all these things worse.

Our introduction to the camp, delivered to us on the parade square shortly after our arrival, certainly had nothing in it to warm the heart — although warmth was intended when we were told that we would leave some day as well-trained soldiers. It was not uplifting either to be warned about thieves who can cut a money-belt off you with a razor blade while you sleep. The officer's advice on dealing with the problem was not for the ears of civil rights advocates. But he knew that the thieves were listening; they were standing there among us. He did warn us though, with telling subtlety, that if they were caught in the act they should at least be alive when eventually turned over to the military police.

A vaccination and a schedule of inoculations began rather quickly. Being excused from duty for up to 48 hours with each painful shot had at least some consolation when it fell on one of those days with a face-numbing wind coming down the river valley. The most dreaded of these needles were the ones called the T.A.B.T. shots. I have forgotten what diseases or evil spirits the initials stood for, but they could put you onto your bunk all day and maybe two. We received a total of

Chapter 2

three of these, a month apart, followed by three spaced typhus shots. That ended the needles until we got overseas.

Weapons training began with a .22-calibre rifle, and then on to the .303 calibre. Later came extensive training on the Bren gun, which included repeatedly assembling and disassembling it until it could be done in a particular length of time. Becoming familiar with the Sten gun was certainly no morale-builder. Even the instructors couldn't conceal their dislike of it. It jammed discouragingly often. On the other weapons, we had to achieve a certain tightness of grouping on the target at various distances to qualify. The Sten was so inaccurate, as the story goes, that we qualified if we could get all our rounds to perforate only our own target.

We practised the stiff-arm throwing of unarmed #36 hand-grenades, eventually graduating to live ones when the instructor was convinced that we weren't going to drive it into the side of the trench a metre away and then stand there paralysed, looking at it. The instructors had incredible stories of how trainees could foul up the simple act of throwing this object forward, even after many dry runs. For safety during the live throws, we were all crouched in a zigzagged trench, and then came out into a wider spot, the throwing area, one at a time. After telling us to pick up a grenade and observing that we were holding it properly, the instructor retired behind a barrier.

Seven years after the war, my intended, Jean, and I were invited to break bread with a war amputee and his family, who lived next door to Jean's parents. The man's name was Allen Piper. He had been an instructor early in the war. In his attempt to save the life of one of the trainees who, against all training, released the firing pin on a grenade in his hand and then froze. In trying to save the man's life by getting the grenade away from him, Piper lost both his hands when it exploded.

What he had become able to do with his two mechanical hooks was phenomenal. He managed everything during the meal. Later he drew a cigar from his pocket, took off the cellophane, removed a match from a matchbox, lit it, fired up and sat back for a smoke as we

Training

talked. For a number of years he was head of the War Amputees Organization.

My group, however, managed its throws without incident. In gas-attack training, after repeated drills with the mask and several dry-run attacks, we eventually were hit with tear gas, which was a painful and nauseating affair for a couple in the group who fumbled too long with the mask. We were all equipped with gas capes as well, and had drills in getting prepared for chlorine gas and mustard gas attacks. We saw gruesome films and listened to lectures on these substances, but its falling on our capes was left to the imagination.

Bayonet warfare made no sense to many, if not most, of us trainees — certainly not to me. Some argued that a show of steel demoralized the enemy. Yet the Canadian bayonet had been reduced to nothing more than a 15-centimetre (six-inch) round spike — and without a handle or cutting edge, which left it with no auxiliary uses beyond a tent peg and something to poke a hole in a can of juice. Our bayonet instructor brooked no critical views. The bayonet was very effective in World War I, he said (simply not so, as I read years later), and the spike was less cumbersome and easier to get out of a body. But it would get stuck occasionally, he admitted, in which case we were to stomp the victim hard with our boot where the bayonet went in, and at the same time yank back on our rifle. A method of last resort was to fire a round and let the recoil snap it out.

In bull sessions in the barracks and over canteen beers, we found this last-resort method particularly hysterical. Why not fire the round in the first place and save all the hassle? It all seemed insane. A bayonet attack against machine-guns? A bayonet battle arranged with the enemy, each side promising not to shoot? To attack when out of ammunition? Wouldn't that be suicidal? To flatten the enemy's truck tires? It is amazing that the sword concept could hang on so long after the development of repeating firearms.

In bayonet training, we faced suspended straw dummies shaped like humans. To help us get the hang of the procedure the instructing sergeant set up a rhythm by repeating three commands: "Point! Withdraw! On guard! Point! Withdraw! On guard!" The comedian

Chapter 2

in our basic training group broke the rhythm in one of our sessions. On the command "Point!, the order to drive the bayonet home, he obeyed on cue. But, ignoring "Withdraw!", he held his rifle by the butt with one hand and pointed to the adjacent dummy, his next victim-to-be, and asked the sergeant, "While I'm doing this, what is he going to be doing?" His question, and our snickering appreciation of it, brought us a tirade from the sergeant which included a depressing prediction about our survival without his training. As we rhythmically jabbed away, he would shout with ferocious assurance such things as: "Either you kill him or he kills you." I felt wrong somehow in being part of it — nothing heavier than simple cowardice, probably. To maintain inertia in the circle of madness, a German soldier somewhere in Europe may have been practising on a dummy that represented me.

We were, after all, in the Royal Canadian Artillery, so the likes of bayonets and small-arms had to give way to cannons sooner or later. Those of us destined to be in signals with the "field artillery," as it was called, with its 25-pounder guns, had to learn how to manhandle these weapons into firing position so that we could help in emergencies. Through lectures and performance, the basic outline of range setting, loading and firing was given to us; but none of us who were destined for signals ever fired a 25-pounder that I know of. I certainly didn't. The more serious working of the weapon was left to those gunners who would become thoroughly drilled in all of it.

During our training in the heavy labour of wrestling around the 25-pounder, I worked all one day alongside a North American Indian. As well as performing his own role, his sense of knowing what I was doing or supposed to be doing alongside him surprised me. His anticipation of my next move was as though we had always worked together, and yet we were strangers. At breaks, he stayed near me, but I don't remember a word out of him all day. I assumed that he considered me to be below standard as a partner and was angry with me. That night as I sat reading on the edge of my bunk — probably the Reader's Digest, my source of worldly knowledge then, — I became aware of someone standing in front of me. I looked up. It was my day's silent

Training

partner. "Let's go to the show!" he said. I was so pleased that I leaped up, grabbed my greatcoat and started to prattle nervously — in true white-man's fashion, he may have thought. "Good idea . . . When's it start? Hope it's in colour . . . Bette Davis is my favourite . . . A beer later? .." He did talk, but little beyond answering my questions. After that phase of training, which may have been one more day, I never saw him again. He was in a different hut and no doubt in a different training program.

Playing hockey on a camp team gave me the only hours of joy that I can chalk up to that winter. And those hours included for me an outstanding experience in the game that could only come about by a war's cold necessity of scattering people's lives and then grouping them indiscriminately: I actually played hockey with Turk Broda and Connie Brown, both from the National Hockey League. Broda was goal-tender for the Toronto Maple Leafs and Brown was a Detroit Red Wings forward. Both men were on Stanley Cup teams either before or after the war. But for this winter they were on the Petawawa camp team, in a league that included cities down the valley. They played with us lesser mortals between their games in this league. When my types managed to get a shot on Broda, he occasionally left his one arm cocked up on the back of the net; and as he kicked the puck aside he would say: "It won't go in if you keep shooting it at me." He got serious only when Brown approached.

By coincidence I met Connie Brown years later, when he had retired from the NHL. I still recognized him. He was travelling for a liquor company. It was not until some 30 years after the war, when my hometown's retired Boston Bruins star, Leo Boivin, would come out and play with us local old-timers, that I was ever to experience again the skill and grace which make those fellows something very special.

The military draft by 1943 was surely picking up a different kind of person. There would be, for instance, no unemployed to draw on by this time. We had a saxophone player, who practised into the night in the washroom, as it was more remote, had better acoustics and was the only place where the lights remained on. He was a professional, caught in the draft, his friends said.

Chapter 2

Possibly another professional was the fellow who asked that question in bayonet practice. He developed comedy at every opportunity, and seemed to be at home with it. In the mess hall one day after he cut open an apple, he stood up on the bench while he held aloft half the apple in one hand and a seed of it in the other hand, and sang the one line: "Oh sweet mystery of life at last I've found you!" and sat back down as though nothing had happened. At the mess-hall cafeteria counter he had to duck the swing of a cook's ladle occasionally. I once heard him ask whether the animal for the stew de jour had been killed for us to eat or were we eating it because it had died. On another occasion after a ration was dumped into his mess tin, he broke into gales of laughter, then straightened himself up and said: "OK, you've had your joke. Now where's dinner?" His comedy act of getting into a top bunk was worthy of Buster Keaton or Danny Kaye, and was surely not something he had just developed in the army. In today's terms his stuff seems pretty silly, I suppose; but to many of us he was a blessing in that desolate place.

A quiet-spoken fellow whom I got to know rather well had a bunk opposite mine. He was nearly a head shorter than I was, and had no extra weight on him. We often talked in the evening, running down the army and sharing events in our lives. He was from Matachewan, he said, near Kirkland Lake, and worked in the mines there. I remember his telling me about a town in that area called Swastika, and how some outsiders decided that for patriotic reasons the name should be changed — and how the townspeople told them that they had the name first and were keeping it; and if there was any conflict, then ask the Nazi Party to do the changing.

He told me that miners, too, had had deferments because of their essential service, but it had been dropped for single men, and that is why he was here, and disgusted. One night into our hut came a big fellow shouting out something like: "Arm-wrestling, ten dollars!" and sat down on the bench at one of the tables in the centre aisle. That was a big amount then. My friend got up from his bunk and commented that he could use that money. I thought he was kidding.

"That guy's a gorilla. You can't take him. "

Training

"Oh, I think so," he said quietly. "Come on!"

It wasn't much of a contest. He picked up the twenty dollars and we came back to our bunks. I questioned him about his confidence, and he explained to me about "hard-rock mining" as he called it — about swinging one of those big jack-hammers up into a horizontal position to drill into a mine face all day. And then there were the beer-hall contests among those miners, which were part of mining culture. I had to try him after that, just to be able to say I had twisted with the best. I was as outclassed as I was in trying to take the puck away from Connie Brown.

In the middle of December, I began to feel terrible, and got a sore throat so bad that I knew I couldn't be accused of malingering. The doctor would just have to see something down there. He did: streptococcus infection, for which he put me into the camp hospital and fed me great quantities of sulfanilamide pills for eight sick and groggy days. In the camp there was a fellow who at every bull session would bring up a wild concept that his religious sect believed in. It had to do with some bogus history which allegedly proved that Christ was not a Jew but something akin to an Anglo-Saxon. His sect apparently felt more comfortable with an Anglo-Saxon Christ, to be killed by the Jews. His reasoning had something to do with the migration of the Biblical house of Dan up through Europe, which is traceable in terms like Danube and Danzig and, in Danish, "Danmark." I mention the incident here, for I realized many years later, when responsibility for the Holocaust became a topic, that this incident — although I hardly knew what it was about — was possibly my first brush with anti-Semitism. The second came in that army hospital.

Another patient in the ward, who was there when I arrived, became obnoxious whenever a particular nurse came on shift. He let us all know she was Jewish, but never explained his diagnosis. To me she didn't stand out in any way from the other nurses. Each time she came near him, he uttered some vulgar stupidity. He asked her in various crude ways how she felt being around white men. He spoke to her occasionally in French, for she was bilingual. She seemed to ignore his remarks and tended to him as she did the rest of us. I was

Chapter 2

flat-out sick, and the nurses were goddesses to me. None among us in the room of patients indicated any agreement with him that I can recall, but I believe it can be said that, although we might have been repulsed by his crudeness and cruelty, we accepted his low-brow awareness of what was considered to be an unsatisfactory element in our society. Our racial and religious prejudices were a firm part of our culture. I remember no exposure to racial rants among my school friends or family members or fellow coopers, yet the distortion was there. The tower of Babel warning! Anglo-Saxon superiority with its Christian tolerance! The perversion of interracial marriage! The Chinese family who have the laundry "can't help the way they look." After hearing that George Gershwin was a Jew, I can remember thinking that maybe that's why his music seems so awful — that deduction from a youth whose musical taste ran to "cowboy" at that point.

The day before Christmas I was discharged from the hospital, with some convalescent time, and on December 30 was given a week's leave. It was a joyous experience to shed the uniform, to have a game of hockey on the river with the gang and to tell them about playing with those NHL fellows. On New Year's Day the whole family of us had a joyous dinner and supper at my grandparent's — like earlier times, with roast goose for one meal and turkey for the other. I had been in the army less than three months, but my loathing of military life had painfully drawn the time out. I discovered from her letters later that I brought home to my mother not only my laundry, but also streptococcus bacteria. She believed she caught it from the steam when pressing my uniform to return. I learned much later that she would not go to the doctor and suffered dreadfully with it, giving credit for the cure to Buckley's Cough Mixture. She said that each time that stuff went down her throat the pain was something terrible. To her generation the pain was evidence that the concoction was working. I felt responsible for it all.

After two weeks of further training, 46 of us were sent from Petawawa to Woodstock, Ontario, to a motor-mechanics and driving school, where for six weeks army life was less unpleasant, even though quite intense from morning till night — and even into the night

Training

in driving practice. All signals gunners were to know how to drive most army vehicles and to know how to do reasonable repairs on them. The cut-away vehicle components, the instructions, the practical work — all were very impressive. In preparation for Britain the vehicles were right-hand drive, which took some getting used to. My left hand for awhile was lost with the gearshift, and the double-clutching routine didn't help any. I remember once revving up a big truck in low gear and then shifting into what I thought was second but was something close to the top. As the poor motor vibrated itself up to speed, the instructor in a tone of quiet forbearance said, "Saves a lot of work, doesn't it? But we would prefer you to go through them all. So let's try it again"

The meals there were remarkably better — all the fresh eggs for breakfast that you could eat, in contrast to Petawawa's scoop of soggy powdered ones. And the camp's setting was more pleasant. Downtown Woodstock was only a short walk. Map-reading and driving practice, especially convoy practice, acquainted us with much of the surrounding area. We each got two weekend passes in the six weeks. On one of them another fellow and I saw Niagara Falls for the first time in our lives. In the romance of it all we picked up two girls from one of the services, but kept the honeymoon script to pretension only. On the second weekend I went to Brantford and to the town of Paris, nestled attractively at the bottom of a valley, a place that seemed fascinating to me at the time.

Four days after arriving back in Petawawa — 17 hours travelling, my diary says — 15 of us were off again, this time to Vimy camp at Barriefield outside of Kingston, to take the wireless operating course. The date was March 9. I enjoyed all the train rides in my army career. Other than those taking me on leave, I never wanted to get off. As Will Rogers might have said, I never met a train ride I didn't like.

In these troop movements I always felt a slight twinge of loneliness whenever getting out and watching a train move on. What with the train's movements, some sort of womb complex may have been involved. As well as in cramped seats, I have slept in pull-down

Chapter 2

bunks, up in luggage racks, on the floor — and mostly in the foetal position.

The camp commander at Vimy was a bit of a martinet. He wanted to make sure, it seemed, that the sedentary aspect of our long hours at Morse code practice, lamp-reading, coded wireless procedure and the like did not get us out of shape. In the three months that we were there, we had routine drill periods on the parade square; and on a couple of occasions had the entire camp on the square in full gear for a formal inspection and a ceremonial procedure involving the band and strange manoeuvres that were performed for high-ranking dignitaries. One of the stupefying gavottes that seemed to excite his narrowed military mind had in it the command, "Advance in review order!" Meaning? I have no idea.

The longest route march in my army career was not in Petawawa basic training but out of this camp, all day in full pack. And the camp commander himself led it, also in full pack. I had to admire him for that. Something I remember about the march aside from being tired and having my ankles chewed raw with those stiff army boots, was seeing Turk Broda sitting with his back against a fence, no more than a kilometre outside the camp gate, where he had dropped out under some pretence. We gave him a cheer as our column went by, and he waved and smiled. This is the first I'd seen him since we left Petawawa. He was stocky and a bit overweight, hardly designed for route marches. The military was obviously letting him go through the motions, but I don't remember seeing him again around the camp.

The commander apparently thought also that we might be getting a little rusty on gas attacks. So on the parade square one day as we stood waiting for the next command, a voice shouted, "Gas!" as tear-gas canisters came from behind and rolled among our feet. With some fast scuffling, we all made it without having to stagger out of the ranks.

The military had deliberately mixed in among us a unit of the reserve forces — men who had been drafted but who had refused to sign up for active service. These forces as a whole were commonly referred to as the NRMA people, although the initials were of the con-

Training

scription act itself, the National Reserves Mobilization Act. Less politely they were called "Zombies." The army no doubt mixed us together in the hope that we would help entice them to go active. And maybe we were expected to be antagonistic toward them. If so, the tactic failed. They were a good bunch and we got along well together.

Military authority, however, saw to it that their life was unpleasant. First of all they had been shipped down from western Canada, which meant that they would have little hope of seeing home until the end of training. There were training camps in the west to which they could have been sent. Then, whenever we got a weekend pass, we left them sitting on the edge of their bunks, for they got none. We felt sorry for them. They told us that on those weekends, officers came into the huts for talks and with enticements such as a long leave in exchange for a signature. I doubt that any of it worked. In our conversations in the evenings, they would tell us about their reasons for not signing up. Some asked what the slaughter of the First World War had solved, and pointed to the plight of that war's unemployed veterans. Some had been children in the hungry families during the wave of strikes across the West in 1919, and had had their parents beaten by city-hired thugs, and threatened by the rifles and machine-guns of the army in the streets of Winnipeg — the same army that was now asking them to use those weapons in Europe, in a war that was none of our business. Others had been teenagers in the fruitless hunger march on Ottawa in 1935 and had felt the clubs of the Mounties. All agreed that they should and would fight if our country was invaded.

Prescott was less than 100 kilometres away. With a weekend pass, I would walk into Kingston and go back Montreal Street to the train station. That's where it was then. The Toronto-to-Montreal "Flyer," as it used to be called, came through around 8 o'clock in the evening. It didn't stop at Prescott. No flyer did. I think its first stop out of Kingston was Brockville, and the next was Cornwall. The 12 miles home from Brockville was an easy hitchhike. On weekends when nothing was scheduled in camp, there was no roll-call before Monday morning. I wanted to go home at such times, but to be outside of the

Chapter 2

Kingston area without a pass was dangerous. The MPs — military police, that is — could pick you up. So, while going home on the Flyer on my first pass, I watched to see where they were. The danger spot was at Brockville station, probably because it was a terminal, connecting with a train to Ottawa. It was a place to avoid.

And there was a way. The Flyer's locomotive took on water at Brockville. The water tank was a short distance west of the station. The train stopped there, had its long drink and then pulled on in to the station platform. While it was drinking, I went out through a door on the south side, the opposite side to the station and struck down through town to #2 Highway. I did it a lot of times while at Vimy and never got caught. I usually took a bus or hitchhiked back. Only for a couple of weekends was the little subterfuge thwarted; out hut was quarantined because two of our bunk-mates came down with scarlet fever.

Once when coming home on a pass, I caught a train that was designated to stop at Prescott if there was anyone to get off or on. For this anecdote I'll put down the dialogue as I recorded it many years ago.

"Looks like you're the only one for Prescott," the conductor said as he reached across and picked his marker out of the window blind. He looked irritated, the demeanor that most conductors routinely displayed back then. With about a kilometre to go, I slung my pack and moved out between the cars. No slackening of speed! The conductor happened to be moving through just as the cattle-loading ramp flashed by — about 200 metres from the station.

"I thought you were stopping at Prescott," I remarked.

"That's what I said," the conductor snapped back.

"Well, that was Prescott," I pointed out as the town flashed by. He jumped to the window and muttered a curse as he grabbed the cord. We snubbed down about a kilometre east.

"I live in the east end," I said. "Just let me out here!"

"You stay right there! He's going to stop at the station just as I told him to." Those fellows were as ugly with one another as they were with the passengers.

Training

We slowly started to back up. When the conductor moved on, I swung open the big door and latched it back. Without lifting the steel plate to get down to the steps, I jumped off the edge of it onto the cinders and struck off through the pines that were at the north end of the commons pasture for the town. The engineer must surely have seen me jump. I pictured the possible scene back at the station when no one got off — an irritated conductor, a snickering engineer and a confused station agent.

Today as I read in my diary what I did when home on those leaves, I see a symbolism of shedding the iniquities of the outside world and of attempting to draw back to innocence. I shed my uniform and all was well again. Don Kirkby and I take the dog and go for a hike in the woods. I attend church Easter morning with my mother! My brother and I go fishing at Johnstown Creek, catch 14 sunfish, and we have them for supper!

In Vimy camp on June 1 and 2, we in the Petawawa group went before the trade board to take our trades test. Three of us passed and were given a two-day leave. We helped the others in review and practice to prepare them for the test again. On June 6, D-Day, everyone was gathered around radios. We joked about how we may have all trained for nothing, and may be discharged by Christmas.

On June 8, the unit of us returned to Petawawa, and on the same day my next oldest brother, Glenn, joined the army. For another two weeks in the heat in our short-pant uniforms and silly First World War puttees, we signallers continued with reviews of our training. On June 25 a unit of us received a two-week embarkation leave. I got around to bid all my relatives good-bye, especially my grandparents and uncles. The town's east-end gang of us, including Tip Webb, who was home on leave from the air force, spent many of those hot July days in the St. Lawrence, our beloved river that was still clean then, and clear. Glenn came home on a two-day pass, the last time home before being shipped to Yarmouth, Nova Scotia, and the last we would see one another until after the war.

Mother and youngest brother, Donnie, and I went to early church on the Sunday of July 9, and I left for Petawawa on the train out of

Chapter 2

Brockville that evening. In the next few days in camp, we had kit inspection, "short-arm" inspection, replacement of worn items (no joke intended), and on July 17 the dreadful experience of a final parade in full gear, to be formally inspected and congratulated and bid good-bye and told how wonderfully trained we were—by a person who was probably the camp commander. The heat that day was unmerciful. And we were in battle dress, with our summer stuff returned to stores. I decided to suffer with the wool of my pants rather than wear long underwear and perhaps pass out on the square. Suffer was the word. When not walking, I tried to hold my legs in a position that allowed the minimum contact with the pants. It was agony. After the parade I rushed almost in a panic to get inside and get my pants off.

Early the next morning at 0445 hrs, I left with a draft for Halifax, arriving on July 20. We boarded the Dutch liner, Niew Amsterdam, and left Halifax harbour at 2020 hrs.

On that day in Germany, an assassination attempt on Hitler almost succeeded. The accounts of the number of the plot's conspirators rounded up and killed by the Gestapo on the charge of treason vary between 6,000 and 11,000. Many died by torture. On Hitler's orders, some were hanged by piano wire strung from meat hooks so that death would be prolonged and agonizing. It came out after the war that these slow strangulations were filmed and were viewed by Hitler numerous times.

3

From Halifax to Borden to Ostend

The sun was going down as the harbour entrance and coastline slowly dropped away. The *Niew Amsterdam* must not have been at home when the Netherlands fell, for she carried troops for the Allies throughout the war. On this trip 6,800 of us were on board, 200 short of her usual load. I did not know it at the time, but at least three more hometown boys were passengers.[7] The ship, in her days of peace and joy, carried 1,275 — which gives an idea of life on a troop-ship.

Our hammock was the focal point for each of us, with our gear hanging above it, and the time spent in it beyond eight or nine hours was generally a measure of how sick we felt. The contraption had one benefit if it was suspended lengthwise, as they were in my area: the elimination of feeling the ship's side-to-side roll. To stare at the ceiling or a wall, though, could cancel a lot of this blessing.

My stomach felt the effect of the first swell and all swells thereafter, but never bad enough to lose any food nor to miss a single feeding, although I did not feel well for the entire trip. An ocean voyage would be one of my last choices for a holiday. Keeping food down possibly had more to do with stubbornness and parsimony than with anything else. The waste would have bothered me. We were fed twice a day, in units at different times, identified by a colour-coded card that we were given on boarding. The intercom called out the times for the colours. Years after the war, my brother-in-law told me about how well he ate on his troop-ship voyage. He was assigned to help some outfit bring on its equipment, and consequently boarded early with

Chapter 3

them. He got in line for one of the outfit's coded meal tickets as well, then came back on with his own unit and picked up his rightful one. He said he had a pleasant trip, enjoying three or four meals a day and never threw up one of them.

By sections we had a head-count and roll-call every day, usually by a different NCO each time. On one occasion, a sergeant-major who, after I answered to my name, stopped and shouted out: "Are you from Cardinal?" I thought of the cooper shop, so I said: "That's right." On he went. I never saw him again.

One of the contingents, possibly the first to arrive on board, had been assigned police duty. They guarded restricted areas, checked mess line-ups and wandered the decks with their armbands and short clubs. I was curious to know what it was like down deep in the lower levels. The guards keeping watch on forbidden doors eventually became a bit sloppy, which allowed me to slip by. Down in the ship's bowels was no place to be if one had claustrophobia. With each deeper level the pounding and vibration became more pronounced. I opened a door near me and was startled to look into another world — short, black people, scurrying about, naked to the waist, in bare feet, working at tables piled with something. The heat coming out of the room felt tropical. The area may have been the kitchen scullery. I said something impressive and diplomatic to bridge our cultures, like, "Hi there!", but those dark piercing eyes just burned into this bleached fellow in heavy clothing who was not supposed to be there. I closed the door and came briskly back up. They must have been from the Dutch colonies in the East or West Indies. What would be the life of these people? When and where would they go ashore, if they ever did? I never saw them on deck. To come up they would certainly have needed more clothes.

Shortly after setting steam, we were briefed on our life-jacket and life-boat procedure and then went through the drill while the ship's unnerving alarm, which we had been warned about, shrieked at us to prepare to abandon ship. We got the idea. And we were told that the next one could be real or, with no forewarning, be another practise drill. Later, somewhere in mid-ocean, the alarm was much more

From Halifax to Borden to Ostend

frightening when it suddenly cut loose with its dreaded order. To add to the tension, the ship's Bofors gun on the upper deck fired a series of rounds. We rolled out of our bunks and bounced off one another occasionally in the nervous excitement of getting out and to the correct stations. We knew that we were on the northern route, which is above the Gulf Stream and hence quite cold even in July. The first real scare of the war was complete as I shivered at the railing in a cold Arctic blast, with my Mae West on, and looked down with the thought of having to go into that water. I wondered whether an approaching torpedo made a visible streak. It was a practice alarm, and we returned to our quarters. By mid –1944, the U-boat scare in the Atlantic was all but over, but that had not seriously registered with many of us.[8]

Nevertheless, a danger still lurked as our troopship was cutting through the cold north Atlantic water. The captain warned us over the public address system not to be throwing overboard orange peelings, cigarette packages and the like, because they left a trail for submarines, the newest types of which, running on the surface, he said, had a slight edge in speed over the Niew Amsterdam. That seemed hard to believe, but no one wanted to argue.

Perhaps he had been briefed on the new design of sub that the Germans had been working on earlier. It was said to have an engine that burned hydrogen and oxygen, obtained by breaking water into its two elements. With the use of a "schnorchel," as the Germans called it (which at that point gave English the word "snorkel") to stick up for air, its underwater time was alleged to be limited only by the endurance of the crew. Also, its surface was reported to be coated with an anti-ping material to avoid sonar detection. I have not read that it ever went into production.

The fact that no troopship was sunk, or very few ships of any kind were lost in the Atlantic crossings if they made the trip alone and unescorted, is a point used by some armchair strategists in proposing that losses would have been very much less if every ship had been on its own, leaving at different times on an assortment of routes. When one U-boat finds one ship, his maximum achievement is to sink one ship. Not so when he finds a convoy, a convoy whose departure was

Chapter 3

much harder to keep a secret, and its size much easier to spot. One writer gives a statistic that is perhaps more interesting than it is useful as evidence. Apparently Norway turned over a thousand merchant ships to the Allies for the Atlantic convoys, and lost over half of them. Yet one old Norwegian freighter crossed back and forth for six years of the war and never encountered the enemy.

The only other craft we saw on the crossing was one empty lifeboat, which we strained to follow with our eyes until out of view. It was not going to tell us anything. It left us to make up stories if we chose, Porpoises put on a fine show for a number of days, and land birds came out to tell us that we were passing the southern tip of Greenland. It was never in sight, though. The first view of land was the north-east coast of Ireland on the morning of July 26, as we passed through the North Channel. By 1630 hrs we had entered the Clyde River in Scotland and anchored off the town of Greenock. Six days! The *Queen Elizabeth* was anchored near us. Until we beheld her dimensions, we thought our ship was big.

A Scotsman and I became friends on the way over. Mackay was a nice fellow, with the mild manners and diction of a clergyman. And he oozed innocence. He was romantically, even chauvinistically, enthralled with the image he had of the Scottish people and of Scotland, apparently the birthplace of one or both of his parents. I had the feeling that his Scottish brogue was consciously maintained. The Scots were, he insisted, upright and proud, with a strength of character which just had to be the envy of other nations. Inasmuch as my name was of English origin, by way of Ireland, I suggested that the English might be just as good. He thought, however, that there were certain things about the English that could stand improvement. I left Ireland out of it because one of my elementary school teachers had stressed the point that if any of us in the class were Irish we should not be proud of it. That teacher had problems. Also in those school days we giggled, along with the Catholics in our gang, at the Orangemen's parades on the 12th of July, and waved to our schoolmates who were obediently marching along with their parents. And we suggested, less than charitably, that none of those schoolmates

From Halifax to Borden to Ostend

stood anywhere near the head of the class. Of course, that's not the way we expressed it.

My friend was anxious to meet and mingle with a number of these Scottish stalwarts. "You'll see," he would tell me. Both of us thought somehow that there would be opportunities after landing. We were another day and a half onboard, during which time tugs gently placed our liner against a dock at Greenock. We disembarked at 0700 hrs on July 28, and marched with hardly a hesitation directly onto a waiting train. But Mackay did get his opportunity to meet a few of his beloved Scots, as did the rest of us. He was dismayed and embarrassed. I kept quiet, but others who had listened to him rubbed it in with glee. Scotsmen and Scotswomen who worked in the rail yards and at the station came along the platform, and down on the tracks on the other side, to beg and yell for cigarettes and chocolate and whatever candy we might have. Mackay was trying in the hubbub to tell them how disgraceful their behaviour was, and was getting some unpleasantness for his efforts. Some soldiers threw stuff out to watch them scramble for it.

The man gave up some of his innocence on that early morning. I suggested that the same thing would be happening at English ports where well-supplied Canadian or U.S. troops were coming ashore among a tightly rationed people. He was sullen for awhile, but the beautiful countryside eventually loosened him up. The night would close around us, though, before we reached Borden in south England, 18 hours later. The British trains fascinated us. It was as though we were on a trolley, which would be taking us to the real train somewhere. I thought that the method of opening and closing a train window by lowering it down and pulling it up by a strip of leather belt was a great idea. Most thought it was primitive. As it grew dark, we were told about the black-out curtains. What Luftwaffe still existed would be busy opposing the invasion, so our odds of being attacked were pretty small. Rules were still in force, nevertheless. It was eerie to pass through a town or city and see just a silhouette of black buildings, and to realize that there were people in them.

Chapter 3

The Luftwaffe may have quit, but V-1s were now coming into London. The first one had landed in the outskirts on June 13, a week after D-Day. The citizens were once more under the gun, and would be for about three months. If the practice firing of the Bofors on the ship is not counted, then the first sound of the war reached us during our slow movement through London in the darkness that night. We heard and felt at least one explosion that I can remember. The air-raid siren was wailing.

In Borden camp, our responsibility at dusk was to put in place, in the frame of the windows on the inside, a heavy black-out board structure meant to slow down flying window glass as well as keep the light in. We eventually got used to it all, but for a time we newcomers found a fascination in moving about the blackened streets of towns and cities and then coming through the two-door entrance (shut the one behind you first) of a pub and into warm lights and merriment. A mug (possibly a pint) of beer in England was "one and four" (a shilling and four pence), or 32 cents. Pepsi Cola was three pence, or six cents. As a contrast I noted in my diary what grapes cost: "23 and 6," or $5.74 a pound, a price that was then a day and a half's wages in Canada. Grapes for the wealthy!

Because we had come into camp shortly after midnight, the military left us alone for the rest of the day, so my Scottish friend and I went for a walk through the countryside. So much of the landscape was like a beautiful garden to us, and everything seemed so settled, so comfortably permanent, with narrow winding roads and hedges and hedgerows and glossy-leafed rhododendrons. We wondered why four or five years of soldiers at the camp had not trampled everything flat. We learned the next day why not: all military training activity took place in areas long ago set out for that purpose. Nearby Salisbury Plain was one of them.

A training schedule began the next day, with a quick recap of the basics. One machine-gun is about the same as another, but map-reading was a bit different, because of the tightness of everything and the less mathematical layout of roads. A heavy emphasis was put on aeroplane identification. All this was over after one intense week. To cel-

From Halifax to Borden to Ostend

ebrate, I and a North Bay boy by the name of Ken Holman went to a movie in Borden. It was *Lost Angel*. My Scots friend had disappeared on some other course.

Our next step was over to the driving wing. With only a break now and then for a review of mechanical skills, we drove night after day for two weeks in order to become accustomed to staying on the left-hand side of the road — even though, as I thought of it years later, the military must have known that the threat of an invasion was by then virtually non-existent, and that the moment we landed on the continent, we would be back on the right side again. In the middle of August I received my first letter from home. My mother said that my letter to her took seven days, which was just what hers took to get to me. On-board ship in the Clyde River we were told that for a certain fee — the amount has left me — we could send a telegram home with a standard message of safe arrival. I was one who did. It took six days, my mother said, one day faster than a letter. A scam!

We finished driving school, and were now more prepared to fight off the German invasion. This time my North Bay friend and I took a bus to Aldershot and saw *Brother Orchid*. The next day those of us who were in signals launched into a review of our training. On August 22, the BBC told us that Romania had surrendered. A day or so later a V-1 came down a couple of kilometres away, but still rattled our barracks. It was the first — and, to my memory, the only — V-1 to land in this area in our time there. Another interested person and I went down to Farnborough one Sunday to the airport and experimental station there. We wanted to get in, but could only look through the fence at the array of German planes being studied and tested.

In September I got a letter from Don Kirkby, my good pal and next-door neighbour on Russell Street. I still have the letter, and cherish it. And the first parcel from my mother arrived, which had a trip of one month and six days, but it hung together.

Our first air-raid alarm in a month in Borden was on September 24. Something came down well outside the town and camp, but shook both wide awake with the biggest explosion any of us had heard. We were told that it had been a piggy-back type of bomb made from an

33

Chapter 3

old Heinkel bomber loaded with explosives and propelled by a fighter plane which cut loose and let it glide. The next day we signallers, having finished training, went to Aldershot to take the trades test that the additional overseas training called for. Maybe I can blame it on that old Heinkel, but something made me shaky when sending a message by Morse code in a moving truck, so I failed. The next day I went back and got it.

Our training was now completed — for both sides of the road — and we were given a nine-day pass on September 28. I planned to visit my uncle's parents in Devonshire, near Exeter, but the first stop had to be London to see all those famous places I had heard about. After getting a room at the Union Jack Club and picking up a map, I went into the underground, the "tube," and with the excellent diagrams they have down there, I began the voyage of a young ignorant tourist backed by the enlightenment of his high school's grade 10 history course. Bombed-out homeless families were living in the tubes, sleeping in rows of bunk-beds along the station walls. It was strange to get off a train and see people dressing, undressing and paying no attention to the rush of traffic. After the first week in September, the V-1 menace on the city was virtually over, although the first of a more terrifying weapon had landed on September 8: the V-2. They were more sporadic because their launching sites were being persistently bombed or overrun by the Allied advance. I don't recall any coming down during this London visit.

I went to see at least two films at the Regent theatre on Piccadilly, but didn't note them in my diary — strangely, for that sort of thing seemed important to me then. I probably put the names in a letter to someone. The theatre charged more for the better seats, something we never heard of in our small-town theatres at home. So, on the first occasion I bought the most expensive and then hung onto the stub. The lady who tore your ticket in two was not the same lady who showed you to your seat, so I palmed the cheap stub, substituted the expensive one on other occasions, and was guided to the best. I tucked the precious stub away. Perhaps because of wartime austerity, the rolls and colours were not often changed. For a soldier, the price differ-

From Halifax to Borden to Ostend

ences were not trivial, as I recall. My only diary note on price is that the cheapest movie seat "on Picadilly" was four and six, well above the average at the time.

The movie theatre has brought to mind those flashlights — or torches, as the British call them — which got their power not from a battery, but from a small generator that was spun at high speed by rapidly squeezing and releasing a plunger on the flashlight. They were invariably used by theatre ushers, who operated them while showing patrons to their seats. The operating ratchet and the squeal of the little generator made up a familiar theatre sound: kazeee, kazeee, kazeee . . ..

In the hours of light on that day and until the afternoon of the next, I managed to find Buckingham Palace, Westminster Abbey, Piccadilly, Trafalgar Square, the Houses of Parliament and the Tower of London. Although the pubs in London's Soho district were the really crowded places, I was surprised at the number of soldiers that were doing the same thing I was. And those pamphlets at the Union Jack Club weren't kidding. There really were guides at the Abbey and the Tower who gave us in each place what to me seemed to be a great tour and history lesson.

There were guides of a kind at Picadilly Circus, too, female guides, but they weren't on the government payroll — not the British government payroll, anyway. I just had to see them so that I could nod knowingly at the barrack bull sessions, when others talked of their exploits which began at the Circus — what they got for what price. After that sergeant's VD lessons at Kingston, my only move was to talk silly with one of them for a couple of minutes. An image that stayed with me was of streaks running down the legs of one girl. There was a fine rain in the air when I came up out of the tube. Knowledgeable boys in the barracks told me that rivulets of water had cut those stripes in her painted-on imitation stockings. This cosmetic feature was new to me. So was most of the whole vicious structure. One author speaks of an Englishman's lament. The price for a "piece of ass" was a shilling before the Canadians came and started to pay two. Then came "the God-damned Yanks" who paid as much as a

Chapter 3

pound. I think I saw it all as a matter of good and evil — in religious terms, I suspect. The injustice of it was not getting through to me. It's just the way things were — good and bad people, clear lines clearly cut.

That evening an American corporal and I and two uniformed British girls of the Auxiliary Territorial Services — ATS girls, who served as truck-drivers, depot workers and the like — giddily circulated between spots in the city that exuded music, merriment and drink. Around midnight, we saw the girls off at a station for their return to camp. That night was actually a big deal for me.

After lunch the next day, I took a train to Exeter, got a room at the YMCA, went to a show, got up after a good night's sleep and walked around the city. I don't know how to describe it, but the feeling of freedom to do these sorts of things — here, London or wherever — is quite powerful in contrast to the discipline and restrictions of military life. But I was not free, of course. The very military life that gave this amazing level of hedonistic freedom had me tightly in its grip — a contract with the Devil.

In the morning, I continued on by train south along the River Exe to a little fishing village called Lympstone. After leaving London and other cities, everything seemed to be in miniature. A little train ran little distances between little places. Lympstone, a small fishing village, was the home of the parents of my Uncle Frank Horsford, by marriage, the uncle who had wondered when I was going to grow up and who had gotten me the job in the cooper shop. I can't remember their faces today, of course, but do remember recognizing the Devon accent that my uncle was never to lose.

They were a kindly couple, bursting with questions, wanting an expansion on all the things their son wrote about in his letters. He had told them I would be visiting. They seemed genuine in wanting me to stay with them for the remainder of my leave, and suggested what I should see along the coast in short day trips. When I told them I had ration cards for my full leave, that solidly clinched the matter.

The ceilings in their small home were low, and I ducked to go through doorways. A small back yard ran to the river, where their sail-

From Halifax to Borden to Ostend

boat was moored at the dock. The yard also had an outhouse; and to the best of my memory, it was their home's only such facility — as it was at my grandparents' farm and many small communities at home. So it was no culture shock to me. What was a culture shock hit me when my host and hostess a night or two later took me out to be introduced to their friends — in a pub, as it turned out. To see Mrs. Horsford walk into that establishment was for me the equivalent of seeing my mother walk into a beer hall back home. Experience in English pubs had already shown me their cultural contrast with our Canadian macho hovels. Women were in every English pub I had been in, even working behind the bar and as waitresses; but they were somehow different, usually younger and not someone referred to as "Mrs."

Those ration cards were another part of the army's Faustian deal. Sometime later, I was given advice by the boys who had been over longer on how to have a really good time with those cards. It seems that a large number of young single women worked in the factories in the cities of Leeds and Bradford — clothing factories, I think — and lived in small rooms with housekeeping facilities. These experienced fellows said that if you go up there with your ration cards and chocolate and a parcel from home, you can shack up for your entire leave and have a wonderful time. You can do the pubs during the day while she's working. It sounded great, but my innocence, or timid apprehensiveness, hadn't been sufficiently dissolved yet.

After listening to some of our older soldiers who were instructors or on camp staff, or any of the troops who had been here since 1940, I came to suspect that they were more settled and at home in Britain than they had been in Canada. They handled with ease the currency system which we fresh soldiers found complicated; and many mentioned that they had more money here than they ever had at home. Being in the army, rationing didn't bother them. More than a few had married, and considerably more than a few had nestled in comfortably with a girlfriend. Later, on the Continent, a fellow I got to know referred to his leaves to Britain as going home. He and his wife, who had come over as a nurse and whom he had married in England, had

Chapter 3

a baby and had had a comfortable apartment for three years. It would be easy for men in these situations to forget Canada, especially if they had jumped off a freight train in 1938 and, in resignation, decided to sign up.

I walked along the shore of the Exe River before supper on that evening of my arrival. Swans were something new to me. They were big white ones, and seemed to symbolize the tranquillity of the place. My hosts and I talked long that evening, around the soft light of a lamp as I remember. The next day, Sunday, I walked into Exmouth after breakfast. It wasn't far. As I was passing a church, a sweet woman on her way in invited me to join her, and took my arm to help me in deciding. It worked. The title of the sermon, "We will give God no rest," disturbed a couple of my simple religious concepts. I was not satisfied that God could get tired on the one hand, and, on the other hand, that He would not be irritated by all the nagging. After church , I checked on historic sites that the woman directed me to, and, for reasons my diary says nothing about, came back to the city the next day and also on Wednesday.

On Tuesday, I sailed with Mr. Horsford out to the mouth of the River Exe to gather winkles and mussels off the shoals at low tide. The lives of fishermen are governed by the tides, of course. He had it timed so that we would be on the shoals as the water began to recede. First the keel hits and then the boat lies down slowly on its side. He had equipped me with rubber boots and we went to work with two containers each. It was a fascinating day for me, even including the dreadful job of picking and gathering. It was my first experience at sailing. We also caught 19 flatfish (my penchant again for exact recording) as the boat slowly righted itself and we correspondingly righted our full containers and set sail to come back up the river with the wind and returning tide.

Plymouth was my experience on Thursday, with a visit to its museum and with a quiet, sunny couple of hours sitting in the park high up on the bluffs overlooking Plymouth Hoe, watching the water traffic below, especially the big four-motored Short-Sunderland water-borne cargo planes taking off and landing. The city had been

From Halifax to Borden to Ostend

bombed for two hours earlier in the war. It was a strict secret at the time, but over 40 years later the story came out in the press of the war's worst training catastrophe, which occurred off this Devon coast on the night of April 28, five months before my leave and just a little over a month before D-Day. Operation Tiger, as it was called, a U.S. military practice exercise for the Normandy landing, was taking place when a German submarine patrol discovered it and sent torpedoes and shells crashing into the landing-ships loaded with tanks. In the confusion and darkness, ships fired on one another, mistaking them for the enemy. At least 750 men died as their ships, tanks and other equipment went to the bottom. The U.S. military that night suffered three times more casualties than it did at Utah Beach landing on D-Day.

Morale was a significant factor in the war, responsible for more secrets than that one. What would the effect on morale have been, soldier and civilian alike, had it been known that, while the invasion was taking place, every jail and detention compound throughout England, even up into Scotland, was crowded with British, U.S. and Canadian deserters?[9]

My leave was up the next day, Friday, October 6. Mrs. Horsford cooked me a big feed of mussels for breakfast, a delightful meal. (She had me try the winkles earlier — snails to me. They were good, but too much fiddling work.) I caught the morning train to London, changing for Aldershot at Waterloo Station. Not wanting to surrender until the last minute, I went to a movie in Aldershot. It was called *Murder on Thornton Square*, which for some reason was called *Gaslight* in North America. With every hour used up, I checked into Borden camp just after midnight.

For the next fortnight we had spare time between each of the numerous activities to prepare us for a draft across the Channel. I got many letters away, and also my laundry caught up. Under open-sided shelters the camp had tubs of water on wood-stoves with an open front to feed the fires. There was soap with fixed scrub boards and scrub brushes. It didn't strike me at the time as being primitive. Stoking a fire seemed natural. In the reading-rooms, there were copies of the Canadian armed forces magazine called the *Maple Leaf* which pub-

39

Chapter 3

lished in each issue a recent list of Canadian casualties. We scanned through column after column for people we might know, but I remember having a more peculiar twitch of anxiety as I moved through the "Rs" of the artillery branch, expecting perhaps some sort of time-warp surrealism that would cause my name to flash there for a moment. The listing was of questionable psychology for us replacements, it seemed to me, on thinking about it years later.

Surrealism, too, might come to mind when considering objectively the scene of an open-air "short-arm" inspection. Doctors must surely take a good gulp of whiskey before and after their stint of sitting on a chair while an interminably long line of exposed penises moves across in front of them, each man in turn skinning back and stripping forward as the chairperson checks for chancres and pus. Maybe the doctors draw straws to see who gets the typhus shot assignment, with its more picturesque bare-arm line-up.

Having been duly sorted for good health and believed to be fully trained, we were paraded to turn in our rifles in exchange for Sten guns and ammunition — a disappointment for us, because the replacements going to Italy were given .45-calibre American Thompson submachine-guns, the "Chicago Piano." We had all seen at least one movie with the St. Valentine's Day Massacre in it. Maybe the boys for Italy got them because Al Capone was born in Naples. We weren't made any happier either by a news report that this same gun was being dropped to Tito, the Yugoslav communist, who was carrying on guerilla warfare against the Germans.

Another equipment issue was the leather jerkin, an armless, collarless vest-like jacket that just covered one's backside, and had four large buttons. It was hardly a piece of Dior design, but it did keep the torso warm when the tunic was not enough and the greatcoat was too much. Somewhere, and it may have been at this time, we were issued with the new design of helmet, to replace that dreadful Great War piece of equipment known disparagingly as the piss-pot, but better described as a large, shallow soup dish, which sat on top of the head above the ears. The design seemed to symbolize the indifference to human life in World War I, yet it was still stamped out for World War

From Halifax to Borden to Ostend

II. The fact that the relic offered considerably less protection than the American helmet, and most certainly the German model, was insultingly obvious. The German design is widely used by armies today.

On October 16 our draft left Borden, proceeded to Southampton on the Channel coast and camped there miserably overnight in tents in a mist that made everything damp. Black British African troops were there as well, in British uniforms, all bundled in their greatcoats, but still feeling the cold as they huddled around a couple of fires burning in oil drums. A good guess is that they had come up for a special form of training and were now waiting for a ship back to a Mediterranean British front. I forget what issue firearm they carried, but do remember how the big ugly-looking knife that some of them drew out of their clothing to splinter wood for the drums gave them a scary appearance. They were the only black troops I saw in Europe. But black troops were somewhere about, as part of the U.S. force. And the U.S., true to its interpretation of enlightenment, kept them segregated and in service jobs for the most part. These black British troops may have been segregated too, in a way, but they certainly did not appear to be segregated from the soldierly function of killing.

Our draft embarked around noon and left Southampton shortly after. My stomach objected once again, especially on reaching the more open seas beyond the Isle of Wight. My only pleasant experience on-board was the discovery of a hometown boy, Graham Seeley, who was going back into the war, perhaps off leave or out of hospital. He was a couple of years ahead of me in school and consequently didn't know me.

Around noon on October 18, after a 24-hour trip on the English Channel and through the Strait of Dover, our vessel docked at Ostend, in Belgium. Just 45 kilometres along the coast to the south is Dunkirk, from where the retreating British expeditionary force escaped nearly four and a half years earlier. Just about the same distance to the northeast at the moment was the Canadian front line. This had to be the right place.

4

The Schelde Pocket

Our draft of reinforcements disembarked onto one of Ostend's docks and marched directly to a former German barracks, vacated by the original owners about two months previous. In a matter of hours we were then transported about 60 kilometres to an old high-walled, stone Belgian barracks on St. Peter's Square in Gent, which, of course, had also been used by the German occupying forces. Its massive buildings inside the wall went up three and four floors. The fortress-like structure probably has historical significance to the Belgians. Maybe Napoleon's men had once marched through that massive front gate.

A strange feature of the place which I remember was the design of its toilets. Each facility consisted of a room with a cement floor — perhaps ceramic in places — in which were formed several pairs of raised footprints, with shallow water swirling through between each pair. The soldier placed his feet on an inviting pair and then, with pants appropriately adjusted, squatted down. That's pretty basic — bivouac field conditions brought into the barracks, one might say.

We were warned to be careful in the darkened streets, for there was a Belgian faction in Gent whose sympathies lay with the Germans, and who felt strongly enough about it to have stabbed a couple of our troops. That evening a number of us went to a stage show in a Gent theatre. Full of bravado, we pretended to hope that a

The Schelde Pocket

knifer would leap out of a black alley and meet his doom at our hands. In the morning we learned that somewhere else in the city that night the stabber did strike again. The soldier lived, we were told. In our short time there I found two more Prescott boys: Louie Peterson and Johnny Smith. Louie and I bravely went to the show the next evening, knowing that there would be plenty of us in the street on the way back to barracks. The story was that those who had been stabbed had been walking alone.

As part of our quickening approach to the front line, a draft of us was trucked from this fortress to the 3rd Canadian Infantry Division's holding unit, where we moved into tents. The distant sound of war was now upon us. How often we were shifted farther forward in this area I can't remember; but somewhere short of the front, my first experience with serious noise is quite vivid.

Some heavy guns had moved into a nearby field. They appeared big, even from a distance. I had never seen a gun of this size in any part of my training. It was no 25-pounder. I walked over to take a closer look at the nearest one. Those old World War I books with their pictures of big canons came to mind. As I was getting close, approaching the barrel from the side, it fired. The concussion staggered me backward. I felt as though I had lost consciousness for a second. My eyeballs seemed jarred out of co-ordination. But the ego thing was still working; I tried to turn and stroll away casually, as though it were all routine with me. The seasoned gun-crew, at the less concussive breech end, and with their ear-plugs in, probably found it funny. I walked back with the feeling of being under water until my hearing returned somewhat. The guns were called 60-pounders, as I learned later — named for the weight of the projectile that they could hurl up to 15 kilometres. That required a powerful explosion with a lot of noise.

Noise is surely the first shattering feature of war that a raw replacement encounters at the front, although more unpleasantness won't be far behind. The volume and intensity of the noise is beyond anything experienced in training or lightning flashes or fireworks displays.

Chapter 4

We were destined to be replacements for the dead and wounded in the three Canadian divisions north of us. The Canadian 2nd and 4th (armoured) divisions were fighting alongside British forces to clear the east end and north side of the Schelde Estuary in the Netherlands. The 3rd Division was assigned the task of clearing the south shore — of tightening in on a pocket of the German army, which had the water of the Schelde at its back. The Schelde Pocket some called it; others, the Breskens Pocket, after a German-occupied town within the encirclement and on the water's edge. Antwerp, which had been captured by the British in September, was useless as a port until both sides of its long entrance to the sea through the estuary were cleared of their powerful gun emplacements, and the estuary's waters swept of mines.

Some of us were in the holding unit only for 24 hours. Throughout the night those 60-pounders that had moved in fired every few minutes. The noise and the shaking earth allowed only a fitful sleep. This is probably nothing, I thought, to what is up ahead. How does a soldier at the front get the sleep he needs? I would eventually learn what fatigue can do. By next morning we had become personnel of the 3rd Division's 13th Field Regiment, Royal Canadian Artillery, and were consequently shipped to its wagon lines. A big quartermaster, Bud Carter, with his clipboard could hesitate only long enough to bark out to others to put us to work. We were among the buildings and the chewed-up yard of a shattered farm, with trucks grinding in low gear in the squidging mud, jockeying into position to load and unload. Some of us were assigned to lug heavy boxes of artillery ammunition out of trucks and stack them in piles. Although used to bull-work, I was dragging by the end of the day, with wet feet and boots heavy with mud. Whatever it was that the cook slapped into my mess-tins went down with appreciation.

I got my first rum ration that night. It surprised me to be on the check-list. The army always seemed to know about you. Somewhere among the rubble and ruins someone was running a typewriter. Everything looked like recordless chaos, but it wasn't.

The tradition of the rum ration mustn't be underestimated. To the armed forces in action it offered an uplifting moment in many miser-

The Schelde Pocket

able, depressing nights. I was not accustomed to belts of hard liquor before this night's introduction. A bottle of beer at training camp canteens had been my speed. So, while the glow tranquillized my sore muscles, I buried into some hay with my blanket clutched about me, circled a bit as a dog does to get all the stems lying down or running in the same direction, then dropped off into snatches of sleep. The sounds and vibrations now were more mixed and intense. Through gaping holes in the barn, I could see the jagged flashes reflecting off the clouds.

The bull-work with those heavy boxes continued the next morning after breakfast and first light; but shortly the quartermaster told us to get our gear and ourselves into a couple of trucks that were going up with supplies to the Regiment's battery locations. A few of us were dropped off at the 44th Battery gun position — and into the miserable conditions of the battle to clear the Schelde.

It was October 29. The fight for the south shore would last only another week, a fight that began in the early morning of October 6. The German defence line was set up behind a well-chosen barrier: the Leopold Canal, which ran from the coast in Belgium just south of Heyst to a point near the Schelde's Braakman inlet. It formed the north-east side of the Pocket. On that morning a tenuous bridgehead across the canal was established by the 7th Brigade behind a wall of fire that preceded them across — a searing wall created by the spewing of 27 "Wasps," as the Bren carrier flame-throwers were called. On the 7th,, the Brigade formed a second crossing, which also barely held on, taking heavy losses. Both bridgeheads were roughly north of the Belgian city of Maldegem. The situation was saved by the 9th Brigade which went around the canal defences and crossed the Braakman Inlet in "Buffaloes," an amphibious troop-carrier, which could transport about 25 men. On October 11 the North Shore Regiment, which I would eventually come to know rather well, were ferried across the canal. Over three more days the whole 3rd Division was across and into the Pocket _ an area at its most extreme width and depth was about 35 by 20 kilometres, almost all of it in the Netherlands.

Chapter 4

A war-created marine phenomenon occurred in Braakman Inlet, perhaps the first of its kind in the annals of war. Preparations for the crossing of the inlet by a platoon of the Algonquin Regiment of the 4th Division were struck and scattered by a nearly two-metre tidal wave. Apparently an exceptionally heavy bombing raid on the coastal gun positions on the far side of the Schelde created a large swell in the water, which, when it entered the funnel-shaped Inlet on the south side, became increasingly higher because of the Inlet's narrowing effect, as in the Bay of Fundy tidal bore.

I appreciated missing these early events in the tightening of the pocket, but developed a deep respect for those who did not. What they told me about it in quieter moments from time to time made the struggle more vivid when I read about it after the war. The fighting conditions for control of the Schelde were, to use Montgomery's term, "appalling." Frequent rain turned the flat, sea-level polders into ankle-deep mud. The land was laced with ditches, canals and low dikes, all to the advantage of the defender. Anything on the roads on top of dikes was exposed to a variety of fire, including that of the "88," quite possibly the most outstanding field gun of the war — surely the most feared. Activity could also draw the attention of big coastal guns from the north side of the Schelde, until they were eventually silenced. Booby-traps took their toll; they were everywhere, including on the dead. Mines were in the roadbeds and in other strategic spots. Some of the more devastating ones were said to have been converted marine rockets.

As an added touch, the enemy troops being faced here were not just some last-ditch conscripts; the German 64th Division contained many Russian front veterans, but fortunately were heavily outnumbered in men and equipment, and had no air support. Occasionally, though, they got help from our own strafing and rocketing air force, which in the turmoil could not always distinguish between friend and foe. A Captain Thompson of our Regiment was one of those wounded by these mistakes, I was told.

In the last seven days of the battle, I got at least a taste of what it had been like during those previous 24 days. When we were dropped

The Schelde Pocket

off that morning, it sounded as though all eight of the 44th Battery's 25-pounder field guns were firing — again, a gun named after the weight of its projectile. Its maximum range was 11 kilometres. I was resigned now to the noise; but the closeness and intensity of it here at the gun position gave me some involuntary motions of fright, for I didn't know what was going out and what was coming in. The difference would eventually get through to me.

The others who arrived with me — we were all signallers, I believe — were absorbed by different parts of the Battery. The Battery signal-sergeant told me to throw my gear into a particular trailer that he pointed out. It had a tied-down tarpaulin on the top. Storing my gear there meant I had already been placed, but I didn't know that yet. The trailer held the equipment of D-Troop signals. ("Dog Troop" was the phonetic term used.) We may speak of someone as being a person "of few words." The signals sergeant was a man of almost no words.

In the late afternoon the guns fell silent. Men who knew what they were doing began to carry stuff from dug-outs and the remains of buildings, manoeuvre vehicles into place, load them, tie equipment on the sides of them, hook onto guns and trailers, and be ready to move into convoy. I found plenty to do to help but had no idea of my exact job yet. Soon we were following the Battery's Recce (reconnaissance) party, who had already surveyed the new location. The Regiment was on the move.

The new position was south of Oostburg. There were many more enemy dead here than at the other location. I was to find that in the haste of action, removing the dead of the enemy had a low priority unless they were somehow in the way. There would be a detail along sometime later. No part of training prepares a soldier for the sight — mud splattered corpses, with some of the mud on the faces, with no hand about to come up to brush it away. Our dead, as I would eventually learn, were looked after quickly, as soon as possible after the wounded were evacuated. It was all very orderly, as I once observed much later — padre, burial detail, dog-tags checked, pocket contents bagged, forms filled out.

Chapter 4

Perhaps the discipline of the training that is for the purpose of creating deaths is supposed to condition us to accept what we have created; and I guess it does, for I began to accept the corpses as part of the debris. An important phase of the acceptance came that late afternoon when the signals sergeant, in a sentence or two that were impressively void of verbiage, gave me my first specific job. I now had a specific role to play in the carnage. It would not be much — just be part of the communications that fires artillery shells up ahead to destroy people and things. His order was about this brief: "Let the Dog-troop command post signaller know where you're sleeping! Relieve that signaller at so and so hundred hours!" It was one of the first two hours of the early morning.

With little if any sleep — I was checking my watch constantly — no one needed to awaken me. I crawled into the cramped command post, accepted some all-too-bare instructions from the departing signaller, who dissolved into the darkness while assuring me it was a quiet night. There had been no heavy return fire coming in for the last couple of days. The fight was winding down. So, the command post was not seriously dug in and banked, but was just a make-shift shelter in the corner of a ruined building. A canvas flap at the entrance kept the light in. A kerosene lamp hung over something serving as a table, with the officer's map board at one end and a telephone at the other. The phone was my job. Tense with the dread that I might foul up fire orders somehow and cause the officer to plot incorrectly, I hoped that the enemy stayed hidden and quiet all night and, hence, keep that phone from ringing — an unmilitary wish, I suppose.

It did ring once, but the call was not for fire-power. It was from battery command post, which quickly rattled off to me a bunch of figures with plus and minus values, then "click"... silence. They made no sense to me. I passed what I had written to the officer, but the jumble was not salvageable. He called back and copied it down himself, correctly. My first message reception in action and I failed it! The officer explained later what it was all about. It had to do with plus and minus adjustments that were necessary to make when plotting the guns for firing, adjustments based on current wind velocity and direc-

The Schelde Pocket

tion. He was a good man. On realizing how green I was, he explained a lot of things to me that night about what could be expected to come over that phone line, things occasionally quite different from what was in our training manual drill. But I was quite happy not to have experienced the difference that night: not a shot was fired. It must have been about daybreak when my relief came in.

After breakfast we packed up and moved again with the regiment to another muddy location just north of Zuidzande. While I was helping to close in the new command post, the signals sergeant, Buswell by name, came into the area on his Harley-Davidson motorcycle, spewing mud with its attempts to get traction. After he shut it down, he motioned me over to a particular vehicle nearby. It was what the army officially called a Carrier, Universal Mk II, but more commonly called a "Bren carrier," or just "carrier." It was a small open-top, tracked vehicle with a centrally-placed Ford V8 engine. It normally held a crew of four. A lance-bombardier, the artillery name for lance-corporal, had just climbed out of it. Calling him by name, the sergeant said something terse that amounted to "Here's your new man." Then he was gone. I had a new job. My previous job in the early morning hours of that day turned out to be my first and last command post shift — although there would be an untold number of times when I wished I had been left there.

Artillery field guns, being back three to 11 kilometres, would be virtually useless, of course, if it were not for someone to give them the precise location of targets. That person is known as the forward observation officer, generally referred to as the FOO — and so pronounced. His location at the front, the observation post, is abbreviated to OP and, in our regiment at least, was pronounced O-Pee. Absolutely essential, then, is a communication between the FOO and the guns. This was the job of the crew I was assigned to: the forward line crew, as it was called. There was additional communication work as well, shared by other crews of the regiment: a line from the battery to regimental headquarters, for example.

Each troop of four guns had a forward line crew and an OP crew, operating out of Bren carriers. In contrast to usual army structure, we

Chapter 4

of the line crew were, I was to discover, given a fair amount of independence — which made sense in the light of efficiency. When lines were cut or blown up, only the crew that laid the lines would know their often-strange routes. This carrier, and also the OP carrier, had a radio transmitter, used only in emergencies and in that period of an infantry advance when a phone line cannot yet be laid to the FOO. The radio was convenient but required a pair of wet-cell batteries and a noisy charger. Also, the enemy could listen, and often find its position.

The boss of the crew, the lance-bombardier, was Oliver Shaw, a tough, shrewd hunter and trapper from the wilds of northern Saskatchewan, a few years my senior. I had no particular fondness for the military mentality, and consequently was lucky to be assigned to him, for he was not a basic military type either. It was hard to picture his ever marching in a parade, in step, with those long swinging strides of one who was very familiar with snowshoes. The army came to know, however, what kind of man he was.

Just several days earlier, before my arrival, he was awarded the Military Medal for a particular act of bravery. An advancing company of the North Shore Regiment had been stopped and pinned down. The artillery FOO with the company had worked his way into position to call down fire on the mortar and machine-gun positions that were pounding and sweeping the area. But there was a catch: His sputtering portable radio, known as the Number 18 Set, went completely dead. Shaw took it upon himself to take up batteries and spare radio components. He used a carrier until blocked by two knocked-out vehicles. He then took off running and crawling over a scarred landscape that was being further scarred by mortars and raked by machine-guns. Snipers would also be trying to pick him off. He made it and fixed the set. Behind heavy artillery fire, the company took its objective as a result of his achievement.

When hearing of the feat, my first thought was the wish that there would be no more such opportunities come along that he might hear about and expect one of his crew members to take a turn at. The "total disregard for . . . personal safety" that his citation mentions is an infi-

The Schelde Pocket

nitely higher level of disregard than I could ever imagine crossing my mind.

The abbreviation MM for "Military Medal" was also the abbreviation for "motor mechanic." When an officer first told Shaw that he had been recommended for an MM, it said something either about Shaw's sense of humour or about his indifference to the military that he answered, "I don't understand. I can hardly drive these things let alone fix them." I tend to think it was the latter. He sincerely enjoyed humour, but wasn't one to make a joke.

The four men who occupied the carrier consisted of the driver, the lance-bombardier and two signallers. But Shaw had two more signallers, who served as relief. Except for a short time with the OP crew at the end of the war, I remained with Shaw for the duration. Another fellow was with him almost as long, the old man of the crew, Elmer Whittington, who was 28 at the time. I was 21, the youngest, at least for awhile.

Whittington came in about a month before I did. Several days previous, Shaw's line carrier became exposed to fire as it crossed an open area. The rush for cover resulted in a track dropping into a hole, flipping the carrier over and killing one of the crew by cutting him nearly in half. Whittington always believed that he directly replaced that man, but indirectly it could have been the signaller who was killed at the OP or the one killed while repairing a cut phone line; for all three died on that same day. No one of us in the truckload of the regiment's replacements I arrived with could ever claim to be replacing any particular dead or wounded soldier.

Nine days before we arrived, an outfit that was transferring a shipment of TNT while parked near Regimental Headquarters made a slip. The explosion levelled a large area, causing some 200 casualties, including a number of Dutch civilians. Before that, on October 17, the 78th Battery lost an entire line crew, carrier and all. The next advance in the area revealed that the crew had taken a wrong turn and had laid a phone line right up to a German dugout. One member was killed; the body was still there. The other three were taken prisoners. In three days of October ending with the 22nd, four men were wounded when

51

Chapter 4

a shell landed near a gun of the 44th Battery; and three FOO signallers were hit at the regiment's various OP positions. On the 28th another FOO signaller was wounded—who, by the way, may be among the very few soldiers in the war to come under a doctor's care at or near the front. Some boys of the North Shore Regiment picked him up in a blanket and carried him to the German medical officer whom they had captured and were keeping to look after their wounded.

October was a rough month for the 13th Field Regiment, in casualties and in rounds fired; and it had a bit of work to do yet. On this day of my assignment to the line crew, the regiment's guns were placed in support of the 9th Brigade. They fired all night long. I was out during the previous afternoon, my first experience in the carrier. We had little work, as the guns were under the control of 9th Brigade observers. Firing stopped around first light of the 31st, and the gunners through the rest of the day had a break they sorely needed.

Early the next morning, November 1, the North Shore Regiment attacked the town of Sluis, which had received an unmerciful beating sometime earlier by bombing raids and finally by our artillery during the night and directly in support of the attack in the morning. There were a lot of dead civilians in Sluis. Years later, I read that about a hundred were killed. I have read nothing, though, on why the population was not evacuated — or whether we knew that.

There was no return mortar or artillery fire as our carrier came along behind, with our radio on and phone line ready if needed. If there had been any small-arms firing by the North Shore, it had now stopped. The attack was apparently over. I had been walking up ahead for some reason, trying to step always in well-trampled places, having already developed a respect for mines. I may have been looking in the scattered debris for one of the German portable field telephones that I had been told to keep an eye out for. They were much superior to ours.

The defenders must have given a surrender signal. I was close enough now to see German soldiers coming out of openings in various places along a low dike. My first view of the enemy, alive! It gave me a peculiar feeling. I moved along quickly for a closer look, and ended up near a low bunker door where they were still coming

The Schelde Pocket

out. I happened to see one of them, stooped over, half shielded by the fellow ahead and in the darkness of the opening, unsnap and drop his belt with a pistol on it just before he put his hands up, and then force it out of sight with his boot in the ankle-deep, soupy mud, hardly changing stride. I fixed the spot in my mind and then turned to see if anyone else appeared to have noticed. No one had. They were lining up the prisoners, searching them and shouting orders. As a junior, I imagined that I would have no chance at all in claiming the prize, especially if someone of rank had seen it. Anyway, I thought, maybe it's just an empty holster. Trying to appear nonchalant, I walked over to the spot. Casually, as though I had just found an old boot, I fished the prize out of the mud and headed back toward the carrier at a constantly quickening pace. Something was inside; for it had weight.

As the crew gathered around, I cleaned the mud off the belt and holster, and then opened it as though it were Christmas and I were 10 years old again. It was a Luger. Very little mud or moisture had gotten inside. "It's complete," Ab Harrison our driver said after he looked it over. He had one with a part missing. I learned that often before surrender the owners would remove an essential part, throw it away in one direction and the weapon in another. The calibre of my find, I soon discovered, was 7.65 millimetres, quite unusual. Most Lugers were 9 millimetres, the common calibre at the front. The only ammunition I had, with no prospects of more, was what came with it. I heard that a fellow on one of our gun crews had a P-38, which was the other common issue of pistol in the German armed forces; and they were 9 mm. He wanted a Luger, regardless of its calibre, so we traded. The P-38 was a new design of pistol, with several important new features, one of those being an exposed hammer, which allowed a round to be in the chamber, ready, without the pistol's being cocked. The design made it, unlike the Luger, easy to clean and maintain under military conditions. It was considered one of the finest of sidearms, and was used for a long time after the war by German police forces.

After the success at Sluis, the North Shores advanced on a little town nearby called St. Anna ter Muiden. Following some heavy fire from our guns, the defenders surrendered to the infantry. The OP was

Chapter 4

using radio. We had little to do but stay close and be ready to relay with our carrier radio if necessary. It was the last objective for the North Shores in the Schelde. I remember the way in which I was looking at the surrendered Germans as they were marching back. Propaganda had gotten through to me. They would all be atheists, church-burners and zealots because of an evil indoctrination, all of which made them morally inferior to Allied troops, but very good fighters because of their cruel fanaticism. I imagined that their food would be of a crude sort, much of it possibly we wouldn't eat. To have fallen for this way of thinking made me feel a little embarrassed later on.

Our regiment on November 2 moved to the edge of Knocke-sur-Mer, which meant that we were back in Belgium. Heavy firing took place the next morning in support of attacks on Zeebrugge and Heyst. Infantry of the 8th Brigade were not involved. The garrison of both places surrendered with little opposition, but there obviously had been heavy fighting in the area we advanced through. The dead of the enemy were strewn everywhere as though caught in heavy shelling. The carnage around Knocke-sur-Mer, the regiment's last gun position of the Schelde campaign, produced a special mention in my diary. It was in this area that General Kurt Eberding, Commander of the German 64th Division, defenders of the Schelde Pocket, surrendered to the North Nova Scotia Highlanders of the 9th Brigade.

It says something about the character of the Dutch that as soon as the guns fell silent, families began to move back into the area — onto farms and land unmercifully destroyed — to begin the heartbreaking cleanup. They were warned about the possibility of overlooked mines, so they stayed in our vehicle tracks as a precaution. I heard the North Shore boys talking about one family who were bringing along a cow on a long piece of rope tied behind a wagon. The meandering animal stepped on a mine, a big one, the boys figured, judging by the area exposed to pieces of cow and roadbed. The sadness of it was not getting to any of us, of course. Just the humour! I had learned already that this was the way it was done. Did any child who might have been

The Schelde Pocket

on the back of the wagon lose a leg or die from shrapnel wounds? I doubt that such questions would ever come up.

Certainly not on these happy days! The job of the 3rd Division in this area of land, known in abbreviated form as the Schelde, was over. The Pocket was cleared. Orders came down to take our guns out of action. For the first time in a month the gunners could get a good night's sleep — in some dry spot above ground, because no shells would be coming back at them. The next day, November 4, the regiment packed up and moved in convoy toward Gent, where the entire 3rd Division would have a five-day rest.

5

The Five Days of Gent

The clearing of the Schelde River's banks, which was the severe assignment given to the Canadian 2nd and 3rd Divisions, and the equally mean assignment given to the 4th Division to secure the south Netherlands area east of the Schelde north of Antwerp, including Woensdrecht, were now completed. The date of the ceasefire, at least for the 3rd Division, was November 3.

These successes left only the island of Walcheren, on the north side. Actually it is not an island, but a wider piece of land at the end of the Beveland Peninsula, a long, slim peninsula for the most part (which had been the 2nd Division's task), making a formation with the general shape of a tennis racquet — all of which forms the north side of the Schelde and its estuary. At any rate, the ugly task was completed by the British, which involved coming ashore against an opposition, one war historian contends, that was more taxing than on D-Day. But they did it, and had the entire area secured by November 8. All land opposition to block entry to the Schelde was finally destroyed. The rest was now up to the navy with its minesweepers.[10]

When the battle for the Schelde first began, we troops must have been told about the significance of that river, and no doubt the enemy troops were told the same thing. An individual soldier has more basic thoughts, though, about what is significant. It was not until after the war that anything registered with me about what the situation was in

The Five Days of Gent

the fall of 1944. The Allies needed the port of Antwerp desperately. Overland supply lines from ports to the south were intolerably long and inadequate. Antwerp, on the other hand, had 10 square miles of docks, with over 900 berths. The first convoy, consisting of 18 ships, arrived on November 28, led by the Canadian-built Fort Cataraqui. She was met with bands, dignitaries, speeches, and representatives of all appropriate groups and authorities. Well, not quite all! Somehow representatives of the 1st Canadian Army were not invited.

Surely it was an oversight. The records show that in their part in clearing the Schelde and south-east Netherlands, Canadians suffered over 6,000 casualties. As a general rule, about a third of army casualties were deaths. (In the air force, the figure is said to be close to 90 percent.)

As costly as it was, clearing the Schelde into Antwerp was a major success. Earlier in this area, however, a major blunder took place, in the opinion of some military historians.

After the fall of Antwerp back on September 4, it is the contention that the Allies should have concentrated all their efforts in advancing to Woensdrecht, less than 40 kilometres farther north, at which point a narrow strip of land leading to the Beveland peninsula could have been cut off to trap the German 15th Army. Instead, beginning on about September 6, this army, the army of General Gustav von Zangen, which had been caught in the Schelde Pocket, escaped with some 65,000 men and a lot of equipment, by ferrying across the Schelde River from Breskens to Walcheren Island, a five-kilometre run, then moving by road along the peninsula to Woensdrecht and home free, so to speak — to continue to give the Allies trouble for the rest of the war. The 64th Division of that army, which had been left behind to block the Schelde as long as possible, was what our 3rd Division had to fight in the Pocket.

As mentioned, our 13th Field Regiment on November 4 moved with the division along the 50 kilometres or so toward Gent. The battery half-track was pulling the signals trailer, bulging above its sides but tightly battened down with its tarpaulin, ready to sit for five days in the wagon-lines compound, holding most of our personal kit,

Chapter 5

including weapons, except enough for guard duty, as we were officially out of action.

The light was fading by the time we entered the city. And shortly to fade also was the plan to get the 13th Field Regiment settled in quickly before dark.

A couple of things went wrong, including a missed rendezvous with the guides that were to lead us to all our assigned places. The rest of the division had apparently already been placed throughout other parts of this medieval city of some 200,000 people. As we crept slowly along winding streets, having no idea where we were going, a rumour spread along the convoy that we would be taken right on through and clear of the city. With that rumour in mind and with the temptations in one section of a street beckoning — literally beckoning — one of the lead gun crews faked an accident by jack-knifing its vehicle and gun, which blocked the street and stalled a long section of the column. Many of the men quickly piled out and disappeared into taverns and upstairs rooms. Vehicles farther back that could move out of the jam began to hunt for similarly saturnalian locations of their own.

Guides and regimental convenors had by now gotten together. The rest of the night consisted of enraged officers and NCOs racing around in jeeps, threatening soldiers out of taverns and out of the arms of women. Accompanied with images of penal servitude, the gist of the order was: "Get in those vehicles, get them to the now-known compound, get introduced to your billets, and then you can come back and go crazy."

As dawn broke over the city, most of the original arrangements had finally been completed — as they were supposed to have been about eight hours earlier. Only a couple of vehicles and a few men were still unaccounted for. In his reference to the affair, one can feel the disgust of Lieutenant W.W. Barrett in his history of the Regiment. He gives it only six lines, which include the remark, "one of the greatest snafus in the regiment's history."

Our crew and the rest of the signallers stayed put in the carrier and battery half-track during the snafu. There was a "compo-pack" of

The Five Days of Gent

food in the carrier — a strapped wooden box of canned food a little bigger than a 24-beer case — so we were not hungry. Vehicles with crews that were not always able to catch the battery mess calls carried one of these. Our staying put paid off, for we eventually were guided to our street of billets relatively early, around midnight.

At the time I had no idea what the snafu was all about, only that we sat or moved slowly for hours in darkened streets between heavy dark buildings. No tavern doors with their shaft of tempting light flew open in our section — which may have saved us from the premature plunge into sin that befell some of the others.

My diary on our days in Gent contained only the bare notes on my part in it all, which I fleshed out after the war ended. The full story of the night of our arrival in Gent I first learned in 1970 in Prince Albert, Saskatchewan, from a former 13th Field Regiment artillery officer as we sat talking in his business office. I got another slant on it at a regimental reunion in 1988 in Red Deer, Alberta, this time from a lower rank, the 44th Battery quartermaster sergeant. Their versions were essentially the same, a phenomenon not all that common among veterans.

Actually, the army's organization of the whole affair was impressive once it was finally in place. The kitchen and mess hall area were central, and were a focal point. Orders and information were posted here. All our billets were within easy walking distance. The city was our oyster. There were no out-of-bounds areas. The streetcars were free, and were constantly bulging out at the doors with soldiers. We junior people had to do shifts of guard duty at the kitchen and at the equipment compound, but the shifts were thinly distributed among us.

It was on one of these kitchen shifts that I received my first and last serious bawling-out in the army. Early in the evening some curious children had gathered around where I was standing, with the rifle that was assigned to the post and passed along in turn to each shift. In a mixture of French, English and body language, a boy conveyed the idea that he wanted to hold the rifle. So I kept hold of it up at the barrel end and let him carry the weight for a couple of seconds while he gripped it in the middle. Of course, others then wanted the same priv-

Chapter 5

ilege. The joy of the children distracted me from watching over my shoulder. Suddenly a startling blast from an approaching officer frightened the children into scattering and me into rigid attention. He outlined, loudly and at very close range, the selection of punishments for me that he could choose from. Fortunately, he chose just a withering tongue-lashing.

After the first couple of days, the whole regiment got a scolding. We were told that complaints were coming in about our behaviour; and that if we didn't straighten up, we would be pulled out early. Because of what we had been led to imagine about the behaviour of the enemy in the streets of occupied cities, some of us were more than a little surprised to be told that the German soldier had conducted himself well in Gent, and the citizens expected no less from us. Years later, when reading about wars' propaganda and its methods of fomenting hate, I wondered about the wisdom — from the point of view of propaganda, that is — of our officers' telling us this about the enemy. To maintain hate and still deliver the message, they could have said something like, "Do you as liberators want to have the name of conducting yourselves as disgustingly on the street as the enemy soldiers did?" This revelation about civilized enemy conduct affected me enough to make a diary note of it.

Although the generation of hate is surely the biggest feature in shaping a killing soldier's mind, other parts of his mind are attended to by more delicate approaches. Will R. Bird in his North Shore Regimental History mentions that one of the regiment's officers received a clipping from a Hollywood screen magazine which portrayed several actresses, each associated with a Canadian regiment's crest that had been superimposed on the page. There in all her stardom was Faye Emerson, associated with the North Shore crest and with a statement that she had chosen "this famous New Brunswick Regiment as her unit." Setting up these pages for the thousands of regiments, buying rights and so on, was probably a big business, so somebody had to pay — our government perhaps. Maybe it actually worked as a morale-builder. Were we soldiers at the bottom actually

The Five Days of Gent

that naive? I never saw one of these pages, but like to believe that I would have considered it an insulting charade.[11]

Yes, we did tone down our behaviour after the threat — or perhaps it was just dissipation setting in. An example of what might disturb the average citizen is the story of the jam-packed streetcar slowly moving across a low trestle over a canal. A Canadian out on the step was hanging on, hooting and waving. His friends — all of them drunk out of their minds — tripped his fingers off the bar that he was hanging on to and let him drop into the water. Even though his friends and some citizens (with a pike-pole, it was said) helped him out, the victim's terrible language and drunken attempts to inflict damage on his companions was not a good image.

One morning at breakfast a woman, appearing quite frightened, came running into the mess hall claiming that she had just found her billeted Canadian lying unconscious in a heap at the bottom of the stairs leading to her apartment. A couple of the boys went back with her, made a diagnosis, carried him up and dumped him on the bed.

In a crowded drinking-hole one evening, a bleary-eyed member of our battery came in, sat down, took off his boots, plunked them on the bar in front of the attendant, pointed to a bottle in exchange, clutched it by the neck and walked out the door in his sock feet. I had heard about it at the time; but that quartermaster sergeant in Red Deer in 1988 brought it up as one of the many incidents of the Gent rest that he could recall. The end of the incident as the quartermaster told it, went something like this: "In a pair of civilian slippers, he came to me when we were about ready to leave and asked for an issue of new boots, with the wild story about how the other pair had rotted off him in the Schelde mud or had been blown off him by an incoming mortar. He didn't realize I was in the bar that night."

He wasn't the only barterer. Articles of clothing, chocolate, cigarettes (my favourite, as a non-smoker), army issue jack-knives, all were quite marketable. Somewhere along the way we must have been issued Belgian Francs in a "pay parade," as it was called, but I have no recollection of it. We had them, though. Some of us spent more heavily and quickly than others, hence the need for barter.

Chapter 5

There may have been some financial arrangement between the Gent city council or perhaps the Belgian government and the Canadian military to take care of billeting and general wear and tear on the city. If not, then the gesture on the part of the Belgian people of Gent was truly outstanding. All of us on the carrier crew, and others in discussions, were quite moved by the way we were treated. We were not just billeted; we were one of the family. Some of us corresponded long after. Shaw fell in love at his billet. He and a young lady in the household corresponded intensely throughout the rest of the war, and perhaps long after. In my war scrapbook is the front of an envelope from one of her letters to him, saved because of the beauty of her handwriting. Whenever the mail caught up with us, he would get several letters from her. He let us smell the perfume and admire the envelope, but we could enjoy only vicariously the romance he radiated while reading them and holding them tenderly in those big, moose-skinner's hands — reading sometimes in ghastly surroundings.

Soldiers in blacked-out Gent occasionally had to do some enquiring to find their billets again after a night of carousing, or perhaps even when sober. The rows of attached buildings confused us. Also the names of the streets and the people could be daunting. For instance, the names of my host and hostess and their street address were Mr. and Mrs. Hector Hardijus, Ondernemerstraat 70 — not something to be trying to read, with impaired faculties, from a scrap of paper in a dark street.

I went back to the military barracks on St. Peter's Square where we replacements had been sent after disembarking at Ostend. It seemed like the thing to do, although I had been here just two and a half weeks ago. It felt a great deal longer.[12]

After such a short time in action, I didn't deserve these five days, but the men who went through the Schelde campaign deserved every minute of them. As well as the general threat to life at the front, the gunners had stretches of back-breaking work that is hard to appreciate without having watched the lifting, carrying and ramming of that heavy ammunition in the process of feeding those guns. And the noise! Always the noise! The regimental records show that in one

The Five Days of Gent

eight-day period its 24 guns fired 1,146 rounds per gun. In a short period, while the infantry were poised for the attack on Oostburg, they fired 250 rounds per gun, an intensity not known, it says, since the days before Caen in France. Those fellows were in remarkable physical shape. But the army knows they must have a break, or something else will break.

Also, a soldier cannot be faced with death too often without being taken out of action. Television and movies have done terrible things to the truth of human endurance in the face of mortal danger, and to the truth of the effect of killing. The routine terror of an infantryman's job must especially have its relief. And terrible moments can strike in bizarre ways. For instance, a driver with a 60-hundredweight (three-ton) truck loaded with "jerry-tins" of gasolene took the wrong turn on a Schelde dike road and came into the distant sights of what was later determined to have been a 20-millimetre anti-aircraft gun. Instead of jumping out and getting clear when the first couple of shells ripped through his truck, he managed to wrestle the gasolene soaked vehicle around and bring it back — saved because neither he nor the engine was hit and the gas did not ignite. A large number of the cans were found to have been punctured.

From these conditions there must be a release, an escape, a measure of compensation. The army, of course, knew this, knew that it was essential in keeping a healthy force. That's why there were leaves and leave centres with writing paper and reading material, and why there were chaplains and church parades and no shortage of beer and free condoms.

The Commander of the U.S. China Air Task Force, General Claire Chennault, knew that the success of his " Flying Tigers" in China depended on the rest and relaxation (R&R) that his men received. In his early attacks on the Japanese he had serious trouble keeping his planes in the air because of rampant venereal disease among his pilots and ground crew, who were getting their R&R in a Chinese city district known as "slit alley." So he did what the armed forces of many countries (not Canada, that I know of) have always done: he set up a whorehouse. He flew in a collection of medically-certified prostitutes,

Chapter 5

"an anthology of prose," from India. When his superior, General Joseph Stilwell, who was overall commander of the Far East, heard about it, he went ballistic and ordered it shut down.[13]

In Gent, those five days were essential to keep the Canadian 3rd Division viable for the fighting it had yet to do. And lapses in what is called civilized behaviour during those days must at least be accepted, if they can't be understood. For five days we were, in a sense, licensed libertines. No, not all of us by any means chose to exercise the licence. Whittington had a wife and child at home. Another signaller was also married. I was still a mother's boy, I suppose, with an equivalent of a married person's percentage of my army pay signed over to her to help with the household. When listening later to those two married fellows, I learned that my behavior during those days had much in common with theirs and apparently quite a number of others: buying presents of food and drink for our hosts and hostesses, accepting invitations to their great meals, writing many letters and generally enjoying the atmosphere of home. Whittington stayed clear of alcohol, a most uncommon trait in the army. I didn't; but managed to avoid the contradiction of drinking to oblivion and then suffering for it.

On November 10, following orders, we reported to the wagon lines. The conditioning of military discipline is impressive. One might think that after such a five-day licence, men would be missing. Maybe a few were, but I heard no mention of it. Our group of signallers was complete.

The plan apparently was to get an early start, before the city got entirely awake. I don't believe that it was fully light yet when we moved into our place in the long procession of curling exhausts in the cool morning air and began a 16-hour journey north to our next front in the Netherlands, near the Dutch-German border — in the Nijmegen Salient, as it was called.

6

The Nijmegan Salient

When our convoy reached Antwerp, we knew we were back in the war. V-1s and V-2s were coming down on the city. Hitler lost the port, but he was going to make it as difficult as possible to use it.

These two weapons are mostly thought of in terms of their strikes on London. Of the 10,500 or so V-1s that Germany launched during the war, England did get the most of them, almost 7,000. More than 2,400 fell on London, about the same number that dropped on Antwerp. They were dreadfully effective. In London, beginning with the first one in June of 1944, arriving at 120 a day for a time, they killed 6,000 people and badly injured 18,000. Carrying a warhead of 850 kilograms, the cigar-shaped weapon was eight metres long and had a wingspan of 5.7 metres. It flew at almost 700 kilometres an hour. Its rocket-type engine was noisy, so you could hear it coming, which gave you a chance to prepare to dive for cover. When it was over the target for which it was programmed, its motor cut out and it plunged earthward. That sudden silence was your cue to make what arrangements you could.

The V-2, on the other hand, gave no notice. It arrived at an incredible speed calculated to be 5,750 kilometres an hour, many times faster than sound. There was no warning. In its 14-metre length and 1.65-metre diameter, it carried one tonne of explosives. To us who were working our way through the city well clear of its centre, one or

Chapter 6

the other of these two types of killers seemed to be coming in every few minutes. The report I read on them years later said that the first one arrived in the city on October 13, 1944, and the last in March of the next year. The last two sent to England arrived on March 27. One of those landed in London and killed 134 people.

When a V-1 — or "buzz bomb," as they were often called — came over, we were poised, ready to get down fast if it should fall silent before getting clear of us. But nothing much could be done to prepare for the V-2, except to try to ignore in your mind the thought of sudden oblivion or at least some missing body parts. Our regiment moved through and continued on, however, with no casualties.

The only casualty I know of in this long convoy to the new front was in the North Shore Regiment. On one of our stops along the way, a private jumped from a vehicle and was killed by his own Sten gun, which was hanging on his back by its strap. The jolt of his landing caused the weapon to fire, the result of one design flaw from among several for which the weapon was noted.

Our route into the Nijmegen Salient was the one carved out by Operation Market-Garden on September 17, a story well told by Cornelius Ryan in his book, *A Bridge too Far.* The plan of Market-Garden was to seize and hold a series of bridges north for about 110 kilometres through Holland so that the British 2nd Army could get over water barriers and strike into Germany by skirting around the north end of the Siegfried Line, to end the war before winter. With the exception of the final one at Arnhem, which a large British airborne force was to capture, the bridges were to be taken by the U.S. 82nd and 101st Airborne Divisions. This they did, but the overall scheme failed, however, and the war would see another winter. I was ignorant then of the geography of Market-Garden events other than the knowledge that although the bridge at Nijmegen had been taken, something had gone terribly wrong at Arnhem.[14]

Just after midnight, in the opening hour of November 11, we spread out into our new positions south-east of Nijmegen about halfway to Groesbeek, relieving a British regiment that had been supporting the U.S. 82nd Airborne, who were now relieved in this sector by

The Nijmegan Salient

our 8th Brigade infantry. Our 44th Battery headquarters set up in a house on a farm on the eastern edge of a small forest called the Dekkers Wald, with C- and D-troop guns in fields close by. We, in D-troop line crew, tried to get some rest in shifts. Little sleep had been possible in those jolting 16 hours, but line had now to be laid quickly.

Already earlier that day, some infantry along with the 22nd Battery's OP crew and line crew stepped onto German soil, which was on our side of the front line where a small projection of Germany extends into Holland, thereby claiming themselves to being the first Canadians to enter Germany. It could well be true. Certainly true was that on this November 11th — Armistice Day, as I believe it was called then, in memory of the end of World War I, "the war to end all wars"— the regiment fired its first shells into Germany.

Green replacements like myself were not shunned, but quite clearly there was the feeling that they were not part of this regiment that came into existence in Shilo, Manitoba, in October of 1940, that arrived in Britain on November I, 1941 and that landed on D-day. When Shaw directed the carrier into the barnyard in that early morning, a couple of the crew members looked for a place to dump our excess equipment — a place which could be staked out as belonging to the crew. No one had taken the chicken-house, so we dropped our stuff into it among the roosts and nests. Coming back in the evening after an exhausting day, it was decided that five could get a cramped sleep in there, but not six. I took my bedroll and found another spot. Whittington, the next newest replacement, told me back in the Schelde how long it was before he felt like one of the group. Gun crews, line crews, OP crews, headquarters staff — all were a cliquish bunch. They would know there had to be replacements, but it didn't mean that the newcomer's ignorance and lack of experience had to be embraced right away. After all, I had been overseas only four months, and with the regiment only two weeks. I was careful not to be pushy.

Shortly after our arrival, something happened that drew attention to my greenness and, ironically, may have stepped up my acceptance: our position took a shelling. I had picked up the habit already, in the

Chapter 6

Schelde, of noting where the holes and trenches were. But when that first round came in, I dove in a panic through the opening in the building beside me and flattened against its cement foundation on the inside, which, as I noted later, was about 40 centimetres high. The shelling was quite brief but I was terrified. It was my first such experience. When it was over and the fright dropped out of my neck enough to let my head turn, I could see nothing but walls and a ceiling of shattered glass, pieces of which were resting on me. I was in a hothouse — and never got a scratch. For awhile, a few comrades-in-arms found amusement in pointing out the new guy the who thought that flying glass wasn't all that harmful. [15]

Sometime during the next day as we strung line, Shaw casually remarked that the crew had decided there was room for one more in the chicken-house, now that roosts and nests had been thrown out. The crew had figured, he said, that someone with my kind of luck should be kept close by. Also I would be easier to find for those repair runs in the night.

About 25 years after the war, an infection laid me low. Whittington and I had kept in touch. I must have told him in a letter that the doctor was putting me in the hospital, for I got a note from him during my stay. It read: "Anyone who can take cover in a glass house from a shelling and come out without a scratch doesn't have to worry about a little thing like an infection. He's got it made." I think that note helped defeat the infection.

The chicken-house turned out to be as good as any spot on the farm. When the chicken manure was cleaned out, the floor was discovered to be concrete, which was recessed below ground level by about 40 centimetres. And the concrete foundation walls extended a bit above the surface — all in all, not bad protection. In 1956, I took pictures of the exterior of the place but didn't take measurements. It appears to be about three metres by four metres, with headroom at the high end of the lean-to roof, dropping to stooping level at the low end. Over the first couple of weeks we had scrounged enough material to put together six bunks, that is, two along each of the three clear walls. With three years of barrel-making behind me back home, I was the

The Nijmegan Salient

nearest thing to a carpenter in the crew. The bunks were crude, small, with minimum clearance, and just wide enough to bend up your knees without their hanging over. We looted some shelves ready-made. These, with some spikes to serve as hooks, kept much of our equipment up out of the road.

While we were doing these renovations in the first week or so, we would return from some job in the night and spread out our bedrolls among the bunk construction material and the disorganized mess of our equipment — so tired that we would hardly notice the smell of the chicken manure that still lingered. A new military position demands the setting up of a basic communications network as fast as possible. But here, Shaw said, they were asking for more lines than usual, an indication that we were not moving again soon. They wanted the convenience of more direct phone contact — fewer party lines, so to speak. Maintaining this expanded network was difficult, with Jeeps and carriers and supply trucks grinding out their own roads. We would occasionally just get to sleep when our laconic signals sergeant, who never seemed to sleep, would swing the door open with the words, "Let's go!" followed by the name of the line that was out. The line we feared to hear him say — I did, anyway — was the one to the OP.

Eventually, things settled down a bit and we became less rushed. We would take time to stop what we were doing whenever we heard a V-1 coming, and try to catch a good look at it. Our location was obviously under a flight path to somewhere; and the launching sites must not have been too far away, for they came over quite low. We assumed that the enemy would not waste them on us, so we weren't as nervous as when on the receiving end of them while passing through Antwerp.

One did give us a tense moment, though. An anti-aircraft (ack-ack) gunner happened to nick it or somehow disturb its mechanism with a near miss. It circled around and came back toward our area like a wounded angry animal. We scrambled for protection, but it hit well short of us. [16]

The cynical belief was that the ack-ack gunners in the Salient from then on deliberately missed. At any rate, those that we saw go over our

Chapter 6

position after that event kept right on going; although by the sound of the firing, no gunner was neglecting to put up a show. But the charge is unfair. Anti-aircraft people had no warning beyond a moment or two of that distinctive coarse, sharp-edged throbbing — hardly time to get onto their gun seats. And as I say, they were coming at us low. Gunners farther on would have a much better chance, for they would surely be warned of the approach and of the flight path, as would fighter planes.

The best outcome, of course, was to get them to explode in the air, which was much better than irritating them into more lethal behaviour. I have read that the best V-1 killer among planes was the two-motored, two-seated, plywood-constructed Mosquito. Of the 97 V-1s shot down by planes, the Mosquito was responsible for 82 of them. It could apparently catch them by coming in at a long slant from above, but it then had to fire at a range no closer than about 200 metres in order to avoid a kamikaze result.

A V-2 launching site must have been close as well. Beginning at dusk we often saw the smoke and the fire of the rocket's propulsion exhaust. We would watch the fire until it was just a speck among the stars, still climbing. We seemed to be watching longer than a minute; but it couldn't have been any longer, for I understand that the propulsion stopped after 60 seconds. Our amazement at experiencing these two scientific marvels may not be fully understood in a world that has today advanced this technology to the moon and beyond.

As the sky greyed slightly toward dawn on that first morning in this area, our crew were at one point cautiously laying line along the edge of a field, toward some forward position around the town of Groesbeek. What appeared to be a vast, ghostly junkyard for aeroplanes — on their backs, on their noses, a wing missing, rammed into one another — was at first silhouetted in black form and then, later, came into the light. They were gliders, scattered as far as we could see. We couldn't stop then, but we came back now and then later on when the pressure was off.

Probing through the twisted frames gave uncomfortable scraps of evidence of what those men must have experienced. The odds on a

The Nijmegan Salient

safe landing in a glider can't be encouraging. If a pilot saw no room where he was coming in, there was no going around for another try. With no armour at all, they were an easy target, and could not fight back until they landed. The skin on them appeared to be no more than tightly stretched canvas soaked with several coats of paint. Bits of equipment were scattered about.

I found a bayonet and scabbard, which I carried for the rest of the war and still have as a souvenir. The Canadian bayonet, discussed earlier, was nothing but a spike. The German one had a conventional double-edged shape with the so-called blood groove, but was dull except for the point. The American bayonet, or at least this particular model, had one sharp edge and a flat back that could be pushed on or pounded on to split wood. And there was nothing about it to hinder the standard uses of probing for booby-traps, prying things open, cutting out the top of cans, lifting a coffee pot off the fire.

The amount of wreckage and equipment was enormous — field after field of it, continuing on to the west beyond our regiment's section of the front. The figures tell the story. In the U.S. 82nd Airborne's four lifts from September 17 to 23 onto this high ground south-east of Nijmegen, nearly 10,000 men, over 100 tons of supplies, 60 artillery pieces and 177 Jeeps dropped out of the air by parachute or came down in better than 400 gliders, the twisted remains of which were in those fields. Fields around other bridges would be littered as well, for the number of gliders that came into Holland in the Operation is said to have been 2,500. And losses occurred well before the drop zones. On the flights to Nijmegen alone, close to 100 gliders crashed between leaving England and reaching their destination. [17]

Halfway out of a glider in the landing area just west of us was a Jeep, clearly visible from both lines. The fact that the 82nd Airborne had left it there made everyone suspicious. Binoculars, we were told, revealed no flat tires or other damage. After a few weeks the temptation became unbearable. One night, taking all precautions, a small patrol from some regiment took on the challenge. The morning light revealed the Jeep in the same position. According to the story, the

Chapter 6

patrol never returned, for the Germans had used the Jeep as bait to capture prisoners.

There were four abandoned communities near the front in our area: Ubbergen, Beek, Berg en Dal and Groesbeek. The last was almost surrounded by the 82nd regiments' drop-zone. In the Schelde, towns in the path of war had been reduced to rubble by our shelling and bombing. Here they were relatively untouched. The drop, of course, was to be unannounced. Street fighting did occur, but the bulk of the action was around the perimeter of the drop-zone, as the first of the airborne troops to land fought to keep the zone clear for further arrivals. Spasmodic enemy shelling did take place, but more damage to these towns was done by soldiers — Americans, British and now us — not by fighting the enemy directly, but simply by various abuses. When civilians were evacuated from all this area of Holland south of Nijmegen, they left behind much of their furniture and other belongings.

There were evenings in November when a stillness would come over the front. It was a haunting experience if we happened to be in a field of those mute glider ghosts or in a house in a quiet street of one of those empty communities, from which people once rushed to watch in amazement at what was coming out of their sky. Even in the coarseness of war, I was affected by it — by the cameo of the setting, without a sound and motionless, which was now accepting our trespass. But the business of war, the sputter of a machine somewhere, invariably started time again.

This whole area of relatively high hills must have been a particularly beautiful section of the Netherlands before the war. Groesbeek was to the south by about five kilometres from the other three communities, which were nestled close to one another, and were connected by a trolley which came out of the city of Nijmegen and wound its way through the attractive groves and climbed the soft hills of these places. We crossed over or proceeded along its narrow-gauge tracks quite often. Commuters would have been the main traffic to and from these predominantly bedroom communities; but on pleasant Sunday afternoons citizens of the city, dressed in their finery, may have taken

The Nijmegan Salient

the ride just to enjoy the beauty of the setting. War had now sullied the beauty, however, as wars will.

Because the opposition seemed light after the 82nd Airborne's first lift landed on September 17th, its men marched into Nijmegen and attempted to take the bridge, their purpose for landing here; but they failed, and then had to rush back because the enemy, now getting organized, was putting pressure on the landing zone. British ground troops eventually arrived to help maintain the bridgehead. However, the well-established German force held the main Nijmegen bridge along with the adjacent railroad bridge until the evening of the 20th, when the two were taken by an attack on both ends after a small force of the 82nd, suffering a terrible slaughter in flimsy boats, managed to cross the river downstream. It was all too late, nevertheless, to save the British airborne troops holding the Arnhem bridge to the north. The attempt to proceed to Arnhem over the single elevated road was disastrous. On September 21, the first four tanks were quickly knocked out by one German gun, effectively blocking the road for any further advance.

Such is the immediate history that brought about the front into which our regiment moved during that first morning hour of November 11. Various hints and clues — those extra phone lines, for starters — told us of the rank and file that we were not going on the offensive, at least not for a time. Regimental headquarters personnel set themselves up in a large comfortable building on the outskirts of Nijmegen, and gave every indication of intending to live there for awhile. Our battery headquarters people acted the same way in the farm house they took over — now and then asking us on the line crew to keep an eye open for certain non-battlefield amenities, such as dinner plates, when we were scrounging in those deserted communities.

Officers ordered trenches dug at convenient spots. Line crews had to be careful, for infantry were dug in at road junctions — a defensive action, Shaw said. Our gun crews went underground, taking time to be quite elaborate, with household furnishings looted from Groesbeek. In the Schelde, when men had their meals dumped into their mess-tins, they ate wherever they could find a place to sit or squat. Here on the

73

Chapter 6

farm, they cleaned out the pigpen, looted some tables, benches and chairs, and set up a mess hall. Conveniently, it was just across from the kitchen, which was in the cow stable attached to the back of the house. No, it would seem that our offensive was not going anywhere for awhile.

Scrounging! Looting! Soldiers did indeed use those abandoned communities badly. The street fighting between the American Aitborne and German troops probably caused the least of the damage. While we were altering the interior design of our chicken-house, our carrier seldom came back from a run to Groesbeek without a load of material. Some things, like a saw, nails and a hammer took a more serious hunt. Doors were a big item. We alone used six for our bunks. We found a little stove with some pipe. Also, after the bunks and shelves and hooks, we discovered that we now had enough floor space for a table. It was an attractive oak one.

Earlier, we had found a beehive set up in the corner of a field on the farm. When the news spread, every frame was eventually yanked out when the weather was cold enough to keep the bees sluggish. They would now starve to death, of course. Looting occurred occasionally even on operating farms back near Nijmegen. Later, when snow was on the ground in January, a farmer reported having seen a two- or three-man German patrol in white camouflage near his barn. A force was sent out to track them down. It was a North Shore patrol getting some chickens to augment their diet.

Damage occurred, however, that was less excusable. Things were pulled out of cupboards and scattered about. Furniture was smashed. Drapes yanked down. In now-waterless washrooms, one of the more subnormal gestures was the repeated defecation in toilets, to a point where the last dozen or so users could not possibly have sat down.

A Dutch citizen living on the outskirts of Nijmegen once asked me why some of the Airborne troops behaved so badly. He had watched the gliders come in; and even though the citizens were out waving with glee, troopers entered houses, refused offers of greeting and proceeded to ransack through personal belongings. When a trooper in his house tried to open a roll-top desk, he handed the fellow the key. But

The Nijmegan Salient

he refused it and smashed his rifle butt repeatedly through the slats to get in. Being young and part of it all — and ignorant — I was not the best person to ask. The threat of death in the young is not a stabilizing experience. Those who are conditioned to kill others are bound to set aside other aspects of civilized behaviour as well, in spite of the effort of military discipline to keep it from occurring. The best I could tell the citizen was that those Airborne soldiers, landing here near the German border, and under tremendous stress to stay alive, may have thought that they were in Germany — not that the mistake would excuse such behaviour, but the explanation would at least give the hope that they would not deliberately treat their friends that way.

Bottom-rank soldiers often did not know where they were. And soldiers of all armies looted, depending on the degree and direction of the discipline they were under, personal and military. Canadian soldiers tended to use the word "liberated" rather than "looted." When looting an object in Holland or Belgium, it was common to hear the remark that the owner was probably a collaborator.

Although we had time now to do the scrounging to get more comfortable, the war stayed with us. Our OP apparently saw something along the line one evening that called for one of our 25-pounders to be brought up into a sniping position for pinpoint accuracy. I was the signaller assigned to the operation to maintain communications. Under darkness, the battery half-track took the gun and personnel up as quietly as possible to a position previously surveyed beside a trench that had probably been dug by the U.S. Airborne. The gunners manhandled their weapon into the best position. We laid low for awhile after everything was ready. I told the signaller who was with the artillery officer in the trench where I would be if the phone went dead, and then I climbed into the back of the half-track to get some rest.

Eventually we fired; how effectively I don't know, but it at least irritated the opposition. In almost no time came the scream of mortars. I was the only one of us above ground, but safe at least from smaller pieces of shrapnel — if not from the concussion and from the reverberations of those steel sides on the half-track. When the barrage stopped, I answered my fellow signaller who was inquiring about my

Chapter 6

health; and then, on the officer's orders, obeyed with inspired haste, we packed up, hooked on the gun and got out of there. They had narrowed in on our location rather quickly. If we had fired another round, they could well have achieved the pinpoint accuracy on us that we were trying to achieve on something of theirs.

That was on November 19. Three days later, we carrier crew were ordered to set up a forward exchange in Beek. The exchange was a small portable variety of what would be seen in any telephone office at home, with its jacks and cords for patching through calls, and with perhaps a capacity for less than a dozen subscribers. It allowed contact between forward units without having an entanglement of individual lines to one another. Into the carrier we loaded the instrument, along with our bedrolls and a compo pack, and took off — four of us, which left two men in the chicken-house, available for D-troop signaller duties. In Beek, we picked a place on the outskirts, a good sturdy building that had been a light-bulb factory. Beek was on the road to the bristling German fortress town of Wyler, but five kilometres back from it, fortunately, and also hidden from it by trees and hills. We were to stay there until further notice, installing and maintaining lines, and patching through calls. We established ourselves in a small front room, an area which still had all its windows intact. The exchange fit nicely on a counter.

Behind us to the south-west, those attractive hills began immediately to rise gently toward Berg en Dal. To the north-east, immediately in front of us by about 50 metres, was the Wyler Meer, a width of water that a Canadian would call a creek. It came into Holland at Wyler and ran to the Rhine at Nijmegen. Beyond and stretching to the Rhine was an expanse of flat, low Dutch and German farmland with a cluster of farm buildings here and there, most of them badly damaged. Huddled in the remains of a farmhouse out on that flat land, with some of the North Shore men, were our OP crew. The only way to reach them was by a Bailey bridge over the Wyler Meer. The bridge couldn't have been much over 100 metres from us, toward Nijmegen. No doubt that expanse of flat land in front of us was once a sea, which washed against a shoreline on which Beek now sat.

The Nijmegan Salient

By far the most dangerous piece of the front in this sector was along the road from Beek toward Wyler. After it skirted the tree-covered hills, it cut across flat farmland. To hesitate in the open at this point was to be dead. According to a prisoner, the Germans called the area "Hell's Corner" because of the intensity of the fire in both directions. The North Shores who were dug in there were satisfied with the name. It was a strategic piece of real estate, a roadway into Germany on relatively high land. Machine guns and mortars in Wyler cut loose at anything that even twitched out in front of them. We were pleased that our OP was where it was. Wyler was watched by an OP on the high land to the west.

On November 26, the Luftwaffe dropped several bombs on Nijmegen. They killed a number of soldiers and civilians, one historian says. On that same day, the sound of more machine-gun fire than usual coming from the direction of Wyler caused Whittington and me to grab our weapons and come outside the door of our Beek residence. We were the only ones home at that moment. A Focke-Wulf 190, flying at low level, was coming from the south-east above the Wyler Meer. He was carrying a good-sized bomb underneath, which was visible as he approached. Was he after the Bailey bridge? The bridge was slightly obscured by a row of trees, but we craned our necks, expecting to see it blown to bits as the plane went by and then banked away. The bridge was safer than we were. The bomb fell short, and the explosion staggered us backward. Some debris smashed into the wall beside us, but left us untouched. The bomb striking into the soft bank at the water's edge below our line of sight is no doubt what kept us from career-ending disfigurement. Our phone contact with the OP did not fare as well. The Luftwaffe wouldn't have been pleased to know that the only damage from its effort was the annihilation of a span of wire which crossed near the bridge.

Whittington and I uncomfortably realized in a moment or two that neither of us had fired a single shot — as useless as 9 mm rounds from short barrels would have been during those five to ten seconds of opportunity. Nevertheless, it would have been something to brag about, and we blew it. It did inspire us to loosen up our weapons now

Chapter 6

and then with some practice. The isolation in the woods and hills made it a good spot. I neglected my official Sten, but not my P-38. Whittington limbered up his Schmeisser in an interior room in the factory. Outside, someone might hear its easily identified sound, and get nervous.

Repairing that line to the OP was always an edgy experience, especially the sections we had strung along those table-flat fields. There was no question that from one of those distant church steeples a good Ernst Leitz binocular was sweeping the landscape. Even with no magnifying assistance it was possible for us, from the higher land at Beek, to see across that area for possibly three kilometres. One day just before dusk we noticed a Bren carrier out there, barely visible. As it drew closer, the riders who were standing — three, I think — appeared to stick up unusually high. Soon, the reason became clear: they were wearing high top hats. When this apparition came over the bridge and drove by us, we saw that the driver also had on a top hat and that each of the other three was wearing a long-tailed formal jacket over his uniform. Somewhere in their travels, more than likely in a funeral parlour or a theatre storeroom, they had looted the garb and had possibly planned this mad-hatter entry into their regimental headquarters compound. This sort of nonsense was not uncommon. Better comic relief, surely, than furniture-smashing relief!

Back at the gun position one morning, the sergeant of our nearest gun stepped out of his dugout in full fencing gear: the big padded torso protector, shin protectors, face mask and foil. He did some deep-knee bends and a wide variety of calisthenics, interspersed all the while with thrusts and parries and lashes that ripped the air. Gunners were coming out of their holes now and going by with their mess-tins to breakfast. With a typical sergeant-like bellow, he moved them on with the rhetorical question, "Well, whata ya all starin' at?" He had found the gear in the back of a closet, no doubt, in a house in a once quiet street in Groesbeek or Beek or Berg en Dal.

Relief had other expressions. Several of the North Shore boys — drivers of supply trucks, I believe — occasionally brought in women guests from somewhere and set up housekeeping in the back end of

The Nijmegan Salient

our building. Big doors allowed them to get their vehicles in out of sight. Their actions indicated they preferred to be quiet about it all, so we left them alone. Occasionally, others of the North Shore regiment, more talkative, would drop in at our side of the building on noticing the carrier parked outside. Soldiers are always checking with other groups to see if they have anything to drink — even a cup of tea as a last resort.

A few of them on a visit one day were talking about the word from the higher ranks that a photographer was coming up to get some "action shots" for a newspaper. They had heard similar reports before, and were making cynical comments about how the pictures were usually of road signs, a knocked-out vehicle and some movement around brigade headquarters. One seasoned infantryman, who had not been saying much and who had probably seen more than enough "action shots" for a lifetime, offered his suggestion: "Send him up the road to Wyler! That'll develop his goddamned negatives."

We were relieved on the exchange by the signallers of another troop on November 29, and had just gotten our gear thrown into the chicken-house when we heard the sound of a plane in trouble. A Tempest fighter, barely hanging in the air with a sputtering motor, came in low over our position at tree level. The pilot had his canopy back, and was throwing out whatever was loose, possibly to lighten his load to keep him in the air long enough to find a landing spot. He did get clear of the farm, and perhaps another two hundred metres, skidding into an open area that had tall brush at the end. Whittington and I had started to run after him; for we could see that he was getting still lower. When we got there, the infantry had the pilot out, and were putting him in a Jeep to get him to an aid station. His face, a mess of blood, looked badly smashed, yet he was conscious and sitting up as the Jeep left. He had cut down a quantity of brush before some larger trees stopped him abruptly — abruptly enough so that the motor tore loose and went bouncing and gouging for an amazing distance. I remember blood on some object on the cockpit panel, and we assumed his face hit it each time he sheared off a piece of the vegetation.[18]

Chapter 6

If he had had enough power to clear some taller trees just ahead, and had survived, he would have become a prisoner of war behind the very piece of front he was strafing. Our D-troop gunners at the farm said he had made a couple of gun-blazing dives before being hit. The air force was apparently being called on more often now in the Wyler area. Typhoons struck quite regularly. The Typhoon was a single-engine plane carrying four rockets — a devastating instrument, but not always too accurate. The Luftwaffe was getting more active in the area as well. Like the bomb at the Bailey bridge, another bomb at a different spot took out our OP line shortly after we got back from the Tempest crash site. That run kept us out until after dark.[19]

December brought in weather more uncomfortable, but a long way from a typical Canadian December. The first snow fell on the ninth, but was gone in two days. On a regular basis now, "liberty trucks," as they were called, had been taking groups of off-duty men into Nijmegen for an evening. Beer by way of army canteens and sex by way of private enterprise were the key attractions. Whittington and I stayed at home in the chicken-house, fired up the little stove, wrote letters by lantern-light at the oak table and shared our food parcels.

We did catch the truck to all the "bath parades" that our battery was allotted. They were shower parades, actually, but the facility was called a "mobile bath unit;" and one of them had set up in a big tent outside Nijmegen. I can remember the catwalks of boards running under rows of showerheads, and those pans of disinfectant that we walked through, but have no recollection of towels. After running around naked from one area to another to get in line for fresh clothes, we had probably dried off. As mentioned elsewhere, I wore cotton underwear, or long-johns, because wool next to my hide was torture. I had brought a number from home, which were kept replenished by ones that my mother, well aware of my condition, padded canned goods with in her parcels. Having a surplus allowed me to discard dirty ones when washing them out wasn't an option.

All the while, as November slid into December, it was obvious that a formidable force was slowly building in the salient. Heavy armour was coming in, including a lot of Churchill tanks. They were

The Nijmegan Salient

nestling away in various camouflaged positions. On each successive run that took us near Nijmegen, we would find more groves and shaded farm areas filled with them. One thing was certain about the plan for them, however: they would not be heading north. On December 2, the Germans opened the dykes along the Neder Rhine and turned the area between Arnhem and Nijmegen into a large lake.

On December 13, the North Shore Regiment was relieved in that flat country toward the Rhine and took over a section of the front in the Groesbeek area. The southern edge of the town looked out on the front line. Our FOO decided to set up his observation post in the attic of one of the houses there. He worked loose a tile in the roof, enough for a binocular. The most common type of house roof in Europe at that time was constructed out of interlocking reddish tiles, hooked on strips of wood aligned across the roof rafters. They were held in place by the interlock and by gravity. This new location set our crew to work making changes in communications. We brought in the OP phone by approaching the house from the north, through the empty town — a ghost town, so to speak, a little worrisome at night because it was a good place for enemy patrols to hide, but much more pleasant than those low fields out from Beek, which were turning ugly with mud in the fall rains.

7

The Ardennes Setback

On December 16, a German army with over 20 divisions launched an attack against U.S. forces in the Ardennes Forest in south-east Belgium, with the aim of reaching Antwerp and cutting the Allied forces in two. Their armoured units penetrated 80 kilometres.

The force that had been building up in our area now reversed its course and began to leave us, heading south to help the U.S. troops in stemming the breakthrough. With column after column of those slow, clanking Churchill tanks at 40 tons each, moving out, hour after hour, it was easy to imagine that the departure could be heard in the German lines. Although all that armour was nowhere near our gun position, which was only 1,400 metres from the front, we had talked among ourselves about how it was going to lead the way in our big attack soon, and make it easier for us and the infantry. Some of our D-day veterans, including Shaw, found this dream amusing. Not if the Germans have a half-dozen Tiger tanks over there, they cynically suggested. We who would survive the months ahead — and read about the war's campaigns in the years to follow — would come to know what those fellows meant.

Something in our area drew the attention of Luftwaffe fighters on December 17. They may have been sent to catch Typhoons which at intervals had been rocketing enemy positions along our front. A small ack-ack gun had been with our battery since we arrived in the Salient

The Ardennes Setback

over a month earlier. If its gunner ever had any activity, it must have been when M3 and its crew were out. His job was a lonely one. At any rate, three F-W 190s on this date came over our position quite low, trailing one another by a few seconds. Whittington and I were out by the carrier with our mouths hanging open. They were flying level, as though just looking around. The only harm they did was to the mental stability of the ack-ack gunner who, in a frenzied fashion, was swinging his gun around wildly but without firing a single shot. Moments after the three passed, his extreme profanity and stomping about indicated great frustration. It seems that in his excitement, and perhaps lack of experience, he forgot about the gun's safety device, some sort of foot-trip, which has to be held down or the gun will not fire.

The rage of his sergeant when he arrived was not a pretty sight. To add to the frustration, it was reputed that ack-ack crews were promised a leave if they shot down a plane. A couple of the old-timers in our battery recalled an incident back in France when two or three German ME-109 fighter planes came in on strafing runs, one after the other in quick order. An excited ack-ack gunner missed them all except the last plane. It was a Spitfire, obviously trying to get onto the tail of the last ME-109. The tragedy of war has no limits.

That night, we happened to be out checking a line along the side of a road. The drone of a plane was coming from somewhere. Abruptly, search-lights from the Nijmegen area jabbed shafts of light into the black sky. One of the lights as it swept about caught a glint of steel, and snapped back to fix on it — a plane of the other persuasion, possibly a ME-110 night-fighter, who may have wandered carelessly over blacked-out Nijmegen on his way to a formation of our bombers approaching the coast. All the other lights swung to focus on him. An impressive quantity of ack-ack guns cut loose, filling the sky with tracers and explosions.

To avoid what appeared inevitable in his position, he dove almost straight down — aimed, it seemed, at a point ahead of us, where he would either crash or smear himself and us across the landscape in his attempt to level out. As he screamed closer, beautifully lit in the cross-

83

Chapter 7

ing point of a dozen beams of light, we ran across the road into a field and tumbled into shell depressions. The firing stopped. He was below the lights, and pulling up hard. We stopped breathing. Suddenly, his black form filled the night sky in front of us for a split second as he flashed by just above the silhouette of our carrier. He couldn't have had much to spare. When we were able to talk again, one of us suggested that he must have grass burns on his backside. At breakfast at the gun position the next morning, the event had been embellished to include how Shaw's helmet had left a mark along the bottom of the fuselage.

On December 19, our battery, the 44th, with its eight guns was ordered to move to a position at the edge of Nijmegen, about five kilometres back. Officers were tight-lipped about the reason. The most unreasonable rumour was that the move formed part of the strategy for our big offensive, which was about to begin. Begin with what? The build-up was leaving us. The more believable rumour, which fits one historical account I have read, suggested it was a defensive move because of some scare of a breakthrough or a sweeping raid. Some guns did refresh their drill for anti-tank firing, over open sights. If a threat had been perceived, new intelligence must have played it down, for the battery was ordered forward to its old position after three days.

We regular troops knew next to nothing about the details, but felt certain that we would sooner or later attack over the border and through what we were told was the northern end of the Siegfried Line. From a junior officer, who would occasionally on a quiet night drop into the chicken-house for a cup of our tea and sit around the oak table, we learned that the Ardennes attack was going to lengthen our stay in the Salient, even though the German offensive had been brought to a halt after a week. In short, the line-crew's lease on the chicken-house had been extended. A military report that I read after the war said that the date of our attack south into the Rhineland was to have been January 7, over frozen ground, a favourable condition for armour, and that the delay was not because of the Ardennes breakthrough, but because of the rancorous squabbling in the high command.

The Ardennes Setback

Christmas Day was eerie. The weather was still and overcast, with just the odd flake of snow now and then, but none on the ground. The front was silent from both sides. As was usually the case when we were all in residence for a complete night, I was the first one up in the morning. With the bit of wood put together the night before, I started our little stove, heated some water to wash from a dish on a small bench just outside the door. There was no room inside. This day I shaved as well, with a looted mirror hanging on a nail. It was a special day. Perhaps a subconscious religious ablution ritual was at work. I took off my shirt for a more advanced wash, but had no urge to thrash myself with a cluster of brush. The freezing temperature was enough. The battery laid on a truck for church parade for those so inclined, and a driver who knew where the various denominational services were being held. Whittington and I had decided to go Church of England. We climbed into the truck, which was far from loaded, and were dropped off at a big house on the outskirts of Nijmegen.

The accoutrements were familiar, set up at the end of what appeared to be a large dining room. An attempt at a hymn would have been a catastrophe, as no doubt the minister perceived, looking out at his congregation, crowded mostly at the back as though the front were a minefield. He had an appropriate sermon, which avoided rabid pacifism, and also the sixth Commandment with its objection to one person terminating the life of another.

When the time came for Holy Communion, no one moved across that minefield. The minister refreshed our memories about the order of events at this point in the service , and then stood quietly with the wafers to wait us out. Perhaps no one wanted to take Communion or simply did not want to be first. There were no officers present, a chance factor, or maybe segregation applied before God as well. Neither Whittington nor I were true church-goers at home; we had discussed the topic that morning at breakfast. After a few uncomfortable seconds we looked at one another, raised our eyebrows to express mutual agreement and went up. A few others then followed. I think we both wanted to tell our mothers. He had a wife to tell as well; but

Chapter 7

church attendance goes back to mothers. And the experience felt good. We agreed on that.

The two of us walked back rather than wait for the truck. We were still impressed by the silence of the day, the stillness. Years later, in one of our get-togethers, that Christmas came up in our reminiscing. Neither of us could remember whether any V-1s had come over. We decided no; for the sacrilege would have been impressed on us. Sacrilege did come to mind on the walk back that day, when I realized I had knelt at the Communion rail with a P-38 resting against my ribs in my inside tunic pocket.

The crew members had all been receiving parcels. Mine were bunched, having received three since December 20, one each from my mother, an aunt and my grandparents. My dear grandmother had hermetically sealed a cooked turkey leg in a jar, but it didn't work. The leg had been taken over by an ominous-looking organism that seemed to have it suspended in the container.

The battery cook had nothing special planned, because the army's official Christmas dinner for us was to be on a later date, in Nijmegen. So we traded a few parcel items with him, for bread and butter mostly, and that evening created a feast for ourselves out of all the goods we had saved up and pooled for the occasion — possibly four different kinds of meat, served hot, cold, on bread, on toast, with olives and homemade pickles and cranberries. Because of what our families thought we would most long for in food, our oak table spread was heavy on desserts: chocolate bars, baked goods and canned fruits. There was condensed milk and evaporated milk for our coffee. The excess heat from our little stove, which was kept hopping to cook and boil for us, brought out of the foundation of our little hovel a clear reminder that the cement and its cracks still held something of the chicken manure

We were, as the military put it, "in a state of readiness" between Christmas and New Years, a state I had assumed we were always in; but apparently it means that even units out of the line must not unwind enough to be unable to return very quickly. We in the line were warned to be extra cautious. In certain land configurations considered

The Ardennes Setback

vulnerable, some infantry had been ordered to dig in near our regiment's guns. The OP carrier driver and signaller were sitting with us in the chicken-house one night shortly after Christmas. The OP crew had been relieved. Both of them had gotten into a good measure of Yuletide liquor somewhere. The signaller, Smitty, by far the drunkest, was convinced that we were not being cautious enough, given the warning that was going around. Our weapons should be right beside us, he said, and after dark we should have a trip-wire outside to give a warning. We told him the infantry had men posted all over, and that our weapons, which were hanging or standing near our bunks, were loaded and ready.

He interrupted his lecture to weave his way out for a leak. We heard a carrier motor start, and something hit near the door. The OP driver jumped up and opened the door — to look straight into the barrel of the Browning machine gun on our line-crew carrier. We froze. Smitty continued his lecture with proposals like: "I'm the enemy. You're all dead." Then had a few rhetorical questions, such as: "Where is your state of readiness now? Where are your weapons?" We put up our hands in surrender and repeated frantically, "You're right. You"ve won. We were wrong," and we begged him to rest that breech down. He did, after a couple of scary moments and then took an awful bawling out. He was falling asleep while Shaw was still threatening him. The matter went no further up.

Incidents of comedy in war are generally only a hair-trigger away from tragedy. An OP was in the attic of the house in Groesbeek. For some reason the Germans did not seriously shell the town, not even the southern street of houses that looked out at them. Consequently, the attic was not without comfortable furniture and other amenities, where the FOO's crew would lounge and take turns at the hole in the roof. To spread around the experience, the officers were changed at the OP frequently. For one of them it was his initial experience, and he was a nervous type, as well. He had a trip-wire rigged up outside the house, which if disturbed would cause noisy things to take place with some empty cans. In the still hours of one night, he was perched up on the high stool at the hole. His aide and

Chapter 7

driver and signaller were curled up here and there in the room. An infantryman, as it was later learned, hit the trip-wire. A loud clatter of cans broke the stillness.

As the driver described it to us in the morning, the officer fell off the stool, dumping over a table loaded with maps, phones, wires and the radio remote system, a mess in which he floundered while trying excitedly to get his pistol drawn. When he finally got to his feet, the driver said, there was a tense moment while he swung his pistol around wildly, as everyone else crouched, frozen, hoping that he wouldn't start firing in the dim light. He didn't, fortunately.

The army's official Christmas dinner was distributed over the evenings of the last half of December, so that no major part of the division would be out of action at the same time. Our regiment was allotted the 29th. A big hall in Nijmegen was festively decorated. Some 700 men of the regiment sat down to turkey, dressing, vegetables, plum pudding, at least a double rum ration — and one orange each. It was never explained, but German cigars were passed around at the end of the meal to go with the rum. Someone must have found a cache of them. I was not a smoker, but puffed on one anyway. I loved the smell of cigars, and still do. The aroma that night reminded me of childhood Christmas dinners at my grandparents', when the men would sit back, light up and examine the brandy in their glasses.

The padre led us in prayer. The brass of the regiment made speeches of encouragement and praise. We were assured that our next Christmas would be with our loved ones; and this one might have been, as well, but for the Arnhem disaster. The evening's feature entertainment was a boxing match between the regimental sergeant-major and his brother, who was one of our D-troop gun sergeants. Both of them had boxed in civilian life. It was in keeping with the circumstances somehow — a Christmas entertainment that kept to violence, lest any unwise softening should occur.

Perhaps a V-1 launching site had been shifted. At any rate, a note I made two days after our plum pudding says that the buzz-bombs, as they were commonly called, were now going over us at close to one

The Ardennes Setback

an hour. Antwerp may have been getting more as a gesture of Hitler's frustration over Rundstedt's failure to reach it.

Maybe to get a better view of a V-1 passing over, I walked for a distance from our guns in the Groesbeek area just at dusk one evening. It was quiet except for the occasional "scrump" of a distant mortar landing somewhere, or a burst of harassing fire from one of our machine-gunners. I couldn't have been seen for any great distance, yet a bullet went by my ear, dropping me to the ground as fast as gravity would oblige. In a shelling or an attack, the noise and concussion are so powerful that the sound of the shrapnel and bullets that are flying everywhere is masked. This single bullet made a sharp split-second 'rip,' so impressive that I couldn't even remember hearing a rifle shot. It was probably a German in an advanced listening post, celebrating the year end with a bottle of Schnapps and some blind shots toward those Canadians over there. I would come to experience much more stuff flying around before the war was over, and be a lot more scared; but because of the stillness and the isolation of this event, it stuck in my mind.

As the old year narrowed to a half hour or so, the front became completely silent, ghostly. The crew of us had come back to the chicken-house, but were still up, and more than likely munching on something picked from our latest package from home — a routine treat after a night excursion. Shaw had gone down into D-troop's underground command post. We commented on the stillness, but none of us, as I remember, were attaching any significance to what night it was, and may not have known the time. All of a sudden the entire front on the German side came alive with gunfire, filling the sky with a startling display of tracers, rockets and flares. It took us an uncomfortable moment to realize what it was all about: the birth of 1945, and a nice touch of psychological warfare on the enemy's part, reminding us of the high spirits and the force we would soon meet.

I received a letter years later from Ainsley Barley, who happened to be the FOO that night at the OP in Groesbeek. He wrote of the things he still remembered clearly about those war days. One of the them — and I'll quote from his letter, because he puts it so well —

89

Chapter 7

was: "the phone call I received at the Groesbeek OP on New Year's Eve, having just witnessed through the viewing hole in the roof what turned out to be a feu-de-joie from the Jerries, but what in my mind was the start of their 1945 counter-offensive , only to hear Ollie Shaw's cheery 'Happy New Year, sir!', a greeting I'll never forget."

Obviously, Shaw was well aware of what particular midnight was approaching, and he went down into the command post deliberately to be right by the phone to the OP when his watch said midnight. He would not know of the display that was about to go up, of course, and would not know of the total effect his wishes would have on the OP officer.

After a rum ration and a good sleep, we found the rest of New Year's Day to be quiet. I can't remember whether or not the V-1 launching crews took the day off. Not likely! The day's mail included a parcel from my mother. Because I didn't smoke, her shipments were virtually solid food.

Our tranquillity in the Nijmegen salient, however, was far from being shared on this day by the Allied air force on the continent. Starting at about 0900 hours, some 700 planes of the Luftwaffe simultaneously struck at Allied airfields from France to the Netherlands and destroyed about 400 aircraft, almost all as they sat on the runways. It was a very successful operation — and on a well-picked day, when Allied pilots would be nourishing hang-overs — but, as Luftwaffe General Adolf Galland has written, his force — already close to extinction — lost heavily to achieve it.

The first snow to come and stay in our area dropped during the night of January 8. I was up first, as usual, and made a fire. I stepped outside into a remarkable scene. Everything was white with a sticky snow that blended objects together. A motorcycle looked like a snow sculpture. The torn and gouged landscape was repaired with a soft ivory fleece. There had been no firing in the night; all four of our D-troop gun positions in the field seemed to have vanished.

On the way back from the battery outhouse, I stopped again to take in the impressive transition. As I watched, a black spot appeared on the white surface some distance away, and a head came out. Then

The Ardennes Setback

another black spot, and another, as more doors to underground quarters flopped open and gun crews came out into the morning light.

On the afternoon of that day, any beauty that remained was thoroughly sullied by a planned raid into the enemy lines for prisoners and information. It was the most ambitious 3rd division sweep ever conducted in the Salient. In support of a North Shore company, dressed in white overalls, the artillery supplied the fire-power of two other field regiments besides ours, one medium regiment, ack-ack with low-level airburst shells, and some tank fire. The plan in general was to destroy the heavier defensive positions and to create a wall of intense bombardment in a semi-circle behind enemy lines in order to prevent reinforcements coming in or escape out, while the infantry raided the isolated section.

The affair was partially successful, our regiment's history book says. A few prisoners were taken. Shaw had told us earlier that we were to be one of the line crews for the two OPs on the raid, but our carrier broke down a day or two earlier. Shaw may have been disappointed, but there was clearly no such emotion in the rest of us. In the crews that were given the job, three signallers were wounded while repairing lines. Our crew had a safer job; we were assigned to the battery half-track to position ourselves to relay orders on its radio when necessary during the raid.

The next night a German patrol was reported to have gotten through as far as the regiment's gun positions, perhaps in retaliation for the day before. On top of that, a rumour of white-clad parachutists circulated. Gun crews and battery personnel checked over their personal weapons and moved them a little closer. There was no question that someone or something cut phone lines; and shells didn't do it, for none had come in that night. With that picture in our minds, we moved out into the night. The procedure is to run the line through your hand until you come to the break, with the carrier creeping along a few metres back. Usually we would spread out and each take a section to save time, but it was better to stay together in conditions like this. I gladly did most of the finger-numbing work of splicing, with knees soaked in the snow, knowing that Whittington with his Schmeisser

Chapter 7

and Shaw with his 30-calibre carbine were crouched close by. Patrols that have crossed through will not shoot you unless in desperation — knife you, yes, but not shoot you. Their purposes are to get information, to sabotage, to cut lines, even to bring back a prisoner, and to do it undiscovered until safely home. One shot can ruin all that.

We got all lines restored without incident, and returned to our gun position — to learn that someone's nervous observation had led to the rumour that a few enemy parachutists had dropped in the surrounding woods. We relieved the apprehension a bit by pointing out that we were back safely and also that a plane is essential to a parachutist, and no plane had been seen or heard all evening.

The next morning, however, we heard a rumour that turned out to be true. The night before, while we were out working, a 22nd Battery gun sergeant — whom we all knew well and considered a spotlight-hungry neurotic — was found lying in his gun position with a cut on his head. He claimed to have been knocked unconscious by a patrol and that something or other had been stolen after he had put up a valiant fight. Later we learned that his story was quite surely a hoax. An investigation alleged that he had hit himself on the head as a cover-up of some undisclosed act. He was suspected, as well — and this didn't win him points with us – of having been responsible for cutting the phone lines to make his story more believable. Out of it all we knew only that he was briskly shipped out of the regiment, perhaps to a stockade, we guessed, or home to the United States. He was an American, who had apparently signed up in Canada — for a reason that was possibly as strange as he was. The infantry said there really had been a patrol through, however. The American had no doubt formulated his plan from this information.

One day in the army of occupation after the war was over, I was looking through the armed forces newspaper, the Maple Leaf, when there, under the heading, "Wed in Amsterdam," was the former gun-sergeant with his Dutch bride on his arm. But he was not a sergeant anymore. No. He was a company sergeant-major at the "Amsterdam Leave Centre HQ." A promotion and a cushy job! Amazing!

The Ardennes Setback

Thinking about that fellow reminds me of how, in spite of the uniform's tendency to give soldiers a sameness — and certainly they are trained to have a reliable conditioned sameness — their inherent flaws and strengths are not much affected, although they are camouflaged by the uniform. One of the new replacement signallers who came to D-troop gave the general appearance of knowing little beyond the basic requirements of the job. He had a trace of a cold most of the time, and, with the grace of long familiarity, blew his nose one nostril at a time with his thumb. Inside at his command-post signaller's job he, quite noticeably, snuffed it up.

One early morning hour in the post, when no firing was planned or expected, he was alone with the artillery officer. The OP at Groesbeek apparently saw something, possibly a light, and called in the references, with the order for what was more than likely one round of troop fire. The officer was sound asleep. The snuffling signaller did the calculations, sent the figures to the guns and gave the order to fire. The officer, as he himself revealed years later, leaped up at the sound of the guns; and after discovering what had happened, waited in anguish for a report on the possible tragic results. The OP called: "On target! Thank you! That's all!" The officer raged at the signaller, but was so happy that the rounds didn't fall short, or suspiciously off target, that he closed the issue on the spot, for the health of both of them. It turned out that the snuffler was a math whiz. Having taken figures over the phone and watched officers as they plotted on the drafting board, he knew he could do it.

Mistakes in plotting or in some other step in the process were very uncommon in our regiment, a record that would seem to be verified by infantry reports. But I do know of one STOP order that came down from the OP. That single word is unsettling for an artilleryman to hear. The command post relays it to the guns and, presumably, to the next order of command; and it means that all personnel in the chain of events, including the command-post staff, are to freeze right where they are and touch nothing until after the higher command has found the error and who or what is to blame. It was discovered that one gun of our troop had fired on the previous setting. The crew did not

93

Chapter 7

receive the new setting because the loudspeaker at their position was out of order. To substitute until a new speaker could be found, we in signals had put a phone at the gun and run a line to a phone in the command post. The officer in the command post was to be in contact by phone with that gun while he was giving orders to the others by loudspeaker. At the shift change in the command post, the outgoing staff forgot to tell the relief about this arrangement. Hence when the OP called with a reference change, only three guns got the new settings. I have no note of any resultant casualties. One of the two command-post officers was immediately transferred out of the regiment.[20]

Whittington somehow knew and was fond of this officer, possibly from a circumstance before I joined the regiment. When we were told about the fellow's departure — by Shaw, I think — Whittington remarked, half to himself, "I wonder whether it would have been him if he hadn't been Jewish." After the war I thought about Whittington's remark, but never got around to asking him about it.

Along with the signaller who had the nerve to plot and fire the troop's four guns, we had another D-troop signaller whose courage had a more tangled dimension. I never met him until one day in the Salient he arrived back after being AWOL and possibly after serving some stockade time. He was a handsome, sharp and pleasant-natured kid whom everyone seemed to like, except headquarters brass. Perhaps after experiences in France, he had decided that the idea of risking his life was not for him. So, as I understood the story, he just took off after being refused a transfer. He may have found that, in the hands of military police, getting caught AWOL also carries the risk of bodily harm.

At any rate, when he was returned, he decided on another approach: bladder failure. The medical officer diagnosed his condition as faked. They were determined to break him. For what must have been two weeks, he went around with a wet stain almost to his knees. The rest of us in the chicken-house were no ads for a cologne; but when he came in one night and stood by the stove, the stink practically smarted our eyes. The officers wouldn't accept him in the command post. He was assigned every dirty job in the battery. Yet all

The Ardennes Setback

we gunners supported him, probably because we saw something admirable in such determination. He must have suffered dreadfully: cold, legs possibly raw.

Then one day he came in to bid us goodbye. He had his full pack on. They are sending me to a hospital somewhere, he told us, as he gave us a big smile. We never saw him again.

If he had not been long gone by January 17, he would certainly have been one of us on the detail assigned to string barbed wire. It's an awful job. Even in training we didn't practice with it. The stuff seems to grab out at you. Struggling to get a single coil of it to spiral out, let alone trying to stack one on top, makes one look favourably on latrine digging. The job, which ended with the day, created a snagging barrier along the right flank of our D-troop position. It may have been just a nervous twitch of battery headquarters, nervous about patrols.

On January 22 our crew, while snooping around in a section of woods behind the front, found a large roll of German army heavy cable. Its smooth insulation, with no fabric or rubber, was strange to us (and to the rest of the world at the time). Plastic! We had noticed about a month earlier, when we were in the group whose turn it was o go to the 22nd Battery area to see a film on the nastiness of venereal diseases, that their battery headquarters had lights. How fascinating it would be to steal some of that power for a light bulb in our chickenhouse, we thought. The distance would make it hopeless unless we had heavier cable.

And now we did. After wrestling the big reel into the carrier, we made a recognizance run to the power source. We'd never get into the building. The best bet was a tap where the power came in on the side of the wall at the back, a more secluded spot where we might get away with it.

The next day was quiet. We did the deed with the excitement of a jewellery heist, forgetting about the work involved — camouflaging, burying, stringing it in trees, lashing rickety ladders together to go up for the dangerous splice (European domestic power is 220 volts, double ours). That night a glowing light bulb hung above our oak table.

Chapter 7

Keeping it a secret lasted a matter of hours. An incredulous officer came in to look. He ordered us to put a bulb in the battery office. I think one went into the command post as well. Those taps gave us protection, because the officers forbid all other taps. They didn't want the light to be any dimmer. The sockets and bulbs, of course, came out of houses in those abandoned communities. I don't remember switches. We hid our bulb whenever we were all out of residence.

On January 28, the crew of an American Liberator bomber bailed out above us and drifted down in slow motion. The bomber continued on, into Germany, flying in a seemingly normal fashion. A few moments later, while beginning to lose altitude, it made a wide circle and came directly at us from over enemy lines. We looked straight into those four roaring motors as we scrambled for trenches or ran to the side. If it cleared the rise in the land in front of us, it would smear us and our battery position over the next couple of fields. Fortunately it didn't make it. Some of us ran up over the rise to the crash, possibly 400 metres away.

Shortly after the war when Whittington and I were visiting each other, one of the many things we hashed over again was this crash scene. He was surprised that I could not recall the crew member who was sitting there staring blankly and chewing gum ferociously. He was the navigator, as it turned out. As with the crash of the Tempest fighter, the infantry got there first, but we couldn't imagine that they had found anyone alive among those scattered pieces. The navigator may have been the last to jump, or the first, and happened to be the only one to drift down nearby.

Reference to the navigator's gum-chewing reminded both of us how an American serviceman could invariably be recognized by the work he was performing on the cud of gum in his mouth. The 82nd Airborne boys that we met were a good example. The Dutch had commented on the trademark as well.

On January 30, our regiment again moved back into the suburbs of Nijmegen to where it had moved on December 19 for three days. The position was the best that could be found to support the 8th Brigade, which had its regiments out on that flat land again north-east

The Ardennes Setback

of Beek toward the Rhine. I never thought I would feel emotional about saying good-bye to a chicken-house. We all felt it. The luxury was over. What we had carved out and looted for ourselves stood silent and bare down in that hole, especially our lovely table. We made a last check along the shelves — a pencil maybe, or part of a chocolate bar from home. A couple of us had already hooked the signals trailer onto the carrier and snugged up its canvass. Our driver, Ab Harrison, nosed us out into the convoy.

Chickens were in our former house the next time I looked, which was after the war. I stood in the doorway then, peering in for a nostalgic moment, but didn't enter, naturally. The smell of chicken manure can get into one's clothes, I understand. One wouldn't want that.

Our regiment had for some time assumed that the 8th Brigade's assignment and ours for Operation Veritable, the imminent attack into the Rhineland, would be out there on the left flank. In December, well out on that flat land, our regiment surveyed and dug gun-positions and ammunition pits — which was a pretty good hint.

Our carrier crew went out to check on how we would best get phone lines into our D-troop when the time came. But German tactics made it all academic. A short while after the plan was completed, their engineers flooded the area — but just enough to put all that work under water and no more. The regiment now had to set to work on another site, as well as re-plot all planned targets to match the new proposed gun locations. A lot of work! Finally, all seemed ready.

This time the enemy waited until almost the last moment to let in more water and ruin the second site. Obviously the Germans had a fair idea of the Allied schedule. By February 6 the water was rising at about 20 centimetres an hour from the Rhine to the high ground at Beek. The Wyler Meer disappeared — or widened all the way to the Rhine, if you prefer — with farms forming little islands here and there, and water washing once again on that ancient shoreline along which the road from Nijmegen through Beek and on to Wyler ran. The regiment would have to fire from where it now sat. Any closer spot on high land was taken, at least until more was captured.

Chapter 7

We of the line crew were impressed earlier by the quantity of material moving into the Salient. The exodus that had taken place because of the Ardennes setback was now more than reversed. In the first seven days of February, however, the movement reached an incredible pitch. Tanks were rolling in night and day.

Then, from the holding areas in the rear came the British and Canadian troops, 90,000 of them. (To supply these troops required a support staff of some additional 300,000 men.)

The man in charge of Veritable's incredible force was General H.D.G. Crerar, Commander of the Canadian Army. Because of the man and the title of his force, literature on this operation often misleads the reader by giving the impression that this Canadian army was an army of Canadian troops. Actually, it was less than half Canadian at this point, consisting of eight British divisions and just three Canadian divisions: the 2nd, 3rd and 4th (the other two were linked with the Italian campaign). British Lieutenant-General Brian Horrocks was in charge of the British force. Canada's three divisions were under Canadian General Guy Simonds. The U.S. 9th Army which would eventually attack from the south contained 15 divisions.

Under the best of conditions the total front that Operation Veritable could have had was no wider than the distance between the Rhine and the Maas, about 20 kilometres at this point. Because of the flooding, the start line was now narrowed to 10 kilometres. To make matters worse, the weather joined the enemy. On January 28, we were sliding on frozen ponds. Two days later the temperature rose. The snow left us and the mud began. It seemed to be raining continuously. Whether the tragic delay was caused by the Ardennes attack or high-command wrangling indecision, our drive into the Rhineland was now going to be under dreadful conditions, and be much more costly. It is uncomfortable to think that the decision for the timing of such a momentous event hung on the hope that the spring thaw would be later than usual.

Large numbers of amphibious assault boats and various kinds of collapsible boats were arriving. The more common amphibious one was named the Buffalo. It was a tracked vehicle, propelled in the

The Ardennes Setback

water by scoop-like structures on the track links. One end of it dropped down to form a ramp for loading and landing operations. It could accommodate vehicles like a jeep or a Bren carrier, or it could hold 24 men and their equipment. Another, referred to as the Duck (army acronym: DUKW) was shaped like a conventional boat, complete with a propeller out the back, but had six wheels for land travel. Another variety was called the Terrapin, with eight wheels. The smallest was the Weasel, built by the Studebaker company, a tracked vehicle about the size of our Bren carrier which, like the Buffalo, was propelled in the water by the spinning tracks. It was a failure.

Shaw turned down the regiment's offer, made in view of the rising water, to give us a Weasel instead of the carrier — a fortunate decision, we were soon to learn. One of the arrivals was a non-amphibious vehicle, which was nevertheless handy for narrow bits of water. It was a Churchill tank with a long section of vertical Bailey bridge attached to the front. The tank could pull up to a canal or a ditch, drop the bridge and then detach it; but at full span the bridge would not take the Churchill's weight, . It could be useful for infantry and lighter equipment later in crossing anti-tank ditches and narrow canals, but boats were what were called for at the moment.

On the evening of February 7, close to a thousand heavy bombers began their terrible night's business of flattening all communities in front of us, including the city of Kleve, which was only about 15 kilometres away. The earth-shaking ordinance coming down scattered the black sky with bursts of light.

We of M3 would not be laying any line for a few days. Our FOOs, who would float out there on the left flank with the 8th Brigade, would be in contact with the guns by radio only using the standard artillery code to conceal messages and identities as much as possible. We of the line crew were busy picking up as much of our old line as possible that ran to and from our winter position. Shaw thought we might be doing relay work as the infantry advance increased the distance. Anyway, we prepared for it. Normally when charging our radio batteries, two big wet-cells, we had to get the carrier back where the enemy could not hear our Briggs and Stratten charger, which was a

Chapter 7

permanent fixture on the back of the carrier. Now, with constant noise, it didn't matter. We ran the little motor almost continuously, even charging up an extra set of batteries.

8

The Rhineland

Part 1

At 0500 hrs on February 8, along the narrow front facing into the Rhineland, close to 1,500 guns opened up with a crash of sound that drove us to a momentary half- crouch even though we were watching the last few seconds tick off. Except for a brief tactical pause later, it would be unrelenting on pre-planned targets until 1000 hrs.

Several Dutch told me years later that the sound carried into their communities, 30 kilometres to the north. The 25-pounders of six divisions were firing. So was every available 60-pounder and sizes on up to 240 millimetres (9.5-inch diameter). So was every light, medium and heavy ack-ack gun, firing on ground targets. Rockets were firing as well -- surely on targets well back from the front, for their inaccuracy was notorious. All enemy strong-points that had been observed and plotted throughout the winter were now being pounded into oblivion.

At 1030 hrs, when the main attack was to begin, a pre-scheduled concentration of shelling from this artillery force began to fall in front of the attack zone. It advanced 100 metres every four minutes, leaving for the infantry a strip of pounded land with the number of mines reduced and the defences somewhat weakened.

Also at about this time, artillery regiments were, on schedule, breaking off from their role in the big bombardment to come under the direction of their own OPs, with individual infantry regiments.

Chapter 8

Around 1100 hrs, artillery regiments began firing smoke shells to put down a thick smokescreen along the west side of the Rhine, stretching the full length of our miliary operation. It was successful in blocking the enemy's view and reducing his fire from the east bank. I read years later that the length and density of this screen is considered to be an outstanding achievement, and the wind's cooperation for days on end to be remarkable luck.

The general plan was that with two immense forces – Crerar's army striking from the north and the U.S. 9th Army striking from the south — a giant pincer movement would close in on the enemy divisions west of the Rhine, finally putting them into a pocket at Wesel, where the Allies hoped to cut off their escape by capturing the bridges there. The next and final drive would be across the Rhine and into the Ruhr to end the war.

The logistics of an artillery operation of this size are surely impressive. It has been estimated that half a million shells were fired. Our regiment alone had transported and dug in 40,000 rounds for the affair. This enormous quantity of guns, all moved up as close as they dare, had little space between them. And each had to be plotted in with extreme accuracy. A small mistake can be tragic. And again, as in the Schelde, I marvelled at the physical condition and endurance of those gun crews.

In a speech in which he praised the hard work of those who got everything ready, General Crerar cited statistics that help to grasp the size of this operation. He said that preparation required the use of 35,000 vehicles, consuming 1.3 million gallons of fuel, vehicles guided by the installation of 10,000 route signs, with a traffic-control force of a thousand men (most of them, no doubt, on Harley-Davidson bikes). He claimed that the quantity of maps to be used required 30 tonnes of paper, a figure that possibly provoked comments from the commanding officers under him, because he had been noted for irritating them with the volume of his paperwork.

With an unimaginable and unrelenting noise around us since 0500 hrs, my breakfast felt as though it were being pounded down my throat. Earlier, when I may have been still staggering a bit from the

The Rhineland: Part One

noise, and half disoriented from the strange, continuous light caused by muzzle flashes, I walked right into the kitchen's slop-hole — up almost to the knees. I could see that the crew found it funny, but I couldn't hear them. My American bayonet stripped off the more tacky stuff. A drizzle had started. I was going to be wet anyway.

Operation Veritable's main attack which, as mentioned already, went in behind a saturation shelling of 100-metre sections, began west of Wyler and faced the village of Den Heuvel. The time was about 1030 hrs. Because the flooding had narrowed the attack's front to a mere 10 kilometres or so, Crerar could employ only a portion of the huge force under his command. The plan was to spread out after the breakthrough as quickly as possible, bring in more reserves and widen the front on higher ground ahead of the flooding and beyond the Reichwald. Two British divisions poured through and spread out to the right, attacking into the Reichwald and the land up to the flooded area of the Maas River. The 2nd Canadian Division's Maisonneuve Regiment of 6th Brigade took Den Heuvel, and the Calgary Highlanders of the 5th Brigade, swung left and captured Wyler — that dangerous, heavily fortified town we had watched apprehensively all winter. They made their assault from behind, which was surely a good tactical move. Because of the rain and mud and bogged-down armour, the capture was harder and took longer than Veritable's schedule had allowed for, two-and-a-half hours longer. The Highlanders had 15 men killed and 52 wounded. It was just getting dark.

The British 15th Division, with its assignment to take Kleve, was now also behind schedule, for it had to wait until Wyler was cleared. It then moved along the single road between Wyler and Kleve, a road which was deteriorating in the flooding and rain, but was the only one not submerged. This division, like all the invading units, was delayed, too, by the depressing soggy conditions and by mines, including a small variety made from picric acid and called a "schu-mine," which could not be found by the regular detector because they were not made of metal. Their purpose was to blow off the foot that stepped on them. Nevertheless, the division reached the high ground outside Kleve on the evening of February 10.

Chapter 8

The 8th Brigade's role that morning in the attack — along with the entire 3rd Division — was where we thought it would be: on the extreme left flank, water or no water. The enemy strong-points out there were now a scattering of isolated communities, each forming an island, occasionally linked with a piece of soggy dyke. The division was to clear the entire area south of the Rhine all the way to a piece of higher ground on the Rhine across from Emmerich.

The little role of our carrier M3 and its crew in this big event began at 0730 hrs when our signals sergeant gave Shaw his orders. On our carrier's short-wave 19-set we were to serve as a relay between our regiment and its OPs out there on the left with the 8th Brigade. For that, we were to hunt for the best possible site to do the job. The OPs were in touch directly for most of the morning, but from then on they required our service. A fence post came through the bottom of one FOO's Weasel, which promptly sank. No more from that radio! The engine quit in another, and it had to be abandoned. No more from that one! Another, after landing, got stuck in a soggy shell-hole and stayed there. It could at least serve as relay for the FOO's 18-set (a portable radio) until the FOO advanced out of its range. Another, slowly sinking with a puncture, got the crew to a piece of above-water real estate, where they were stranded and out of action for two days. Still another broke down, but the crew waded ashore, carrying an 18-set to safety. This meant five Weasels and four 19-sets lost — not to direct enemy action, but to the water, or perhaps the vehicle's designer. Most who used them, it seemed, classed them as a failure. Back in the Schelde estuary, in the attack from the water by the British on the west side of Walcheren Island, the Weasel let the force down badly.

Fortunately, no one in those five OP crews was drowned or otherwise killed that I know of, but one signaller was wounded. If it were known, he might have blamed the Weasel for that, too; some types of small-arms fire could go right through its sides.

In all fairness, though, it must be said that the machine redeemed itself in one area, in a role for which it was not designed. In the battle for the Reichwald, where carriers and Jeeps unexpectedly bogged down in the muck, it brought out the wounded. Wide tracks and light

The Rhineland: Part One

weight were just what was needed. No one there cared whether it could float or not.

In spite of the problems, the 8th Brigade and its artillery support out there on an unorthodox mission were successful — or at least it fell no further behind than the rest of Operation Veritable did. Zyfflich, just north of Wyler by about seven kilometres, was one of the few, if not the only, strong-points out there in the water that could be reached over a piece of land solid enough to carry heavy armour. The attack was helped with "twilight" brought about by searchlights in the rear, which were shining their beams almost horizontally so that they reflected off low clouds. A big help also came from what were called Scorpions, which were Churchill tanks modified for mine destruction. Each had two booms extending out in front for a distance, between the ends of which was a revolving drum festooned with attached lengths of chain. When the drum was spun by a driveshaft from the tank proper, these chain-lengths pounded the earth and gave a startling display of flying mud and exploding mines.

The town fell by midnight of February 8. Duffelward, a heavily fortified little hamlet considered to be the northern end of the Siegfried Line — the other end was at the Swiss border — was taken on February 11 by the Highland Light Infantry. Also on the 11th, the Stormont, Dundas and Glengary Highlanders reached the Spoy Canal, just north of Kleve. By the 14th a battalion of the North Nova Scotia Highlanders was on the high ground across the Rhine from Emmerich. Those three regiments of the 9th Brigade were now on their objectives.

In the meantime, we were still relaying for the 8th Brigade. Enough 19-sets survived to pick up 18-set signals from various FOOs, and transmit their orders to us. Our frequency never had a silent moment. Fire orders were piled one on the other. We did roughly two-hour shifts in the heavy traffic times. To lift off the padded headset at the end of each shift gave an abrupt contrast — from the strain of trying to hear those fire-orders to the dominating thunder of the artillery and their screaming projectiles going over just above us. The regiment recorded that during that day each of its guns fired 500 rounds. We

Chapter 8

learned later that one of the many fire orders was to deliver a five-minute constant pounding by all 24 guns of our regiment on little Zandpol, after which the infantry entered to find only the dead.

As the brigade advanced beyond Leuth and Zandpol, toward the more distant Dutch towns of Kekerdom and Millingen, Harrison had to keep driving the carrier to various spots for better reception. When the signals became readable, whoever was in the padded earphones would raise his hand, and another of us would slap Harrison on the shoulder to stop. Just after midnight and into February 9, Harrison had to bring the carrier for a fair distance out into the open on the edge of the Beek and Berg en Dal road toward Wyler before a better signal returned. All was going well.

Suddenly, we, the road and the fields were lit up like high noon. A plane had dropped a couple of magnesium parachute flares. Searchlights filled the sky. Except for the person on the radio, we were all out of the carrier to stretch our legs. We scrambled back in. Harrison locked one track, spun around and headed for the trees behind us. Next came the low-level bombing run, dropping three of them on or near the road. The concussion seemed to lift the carrier's back end as we raced to get out of sight. Surely they were not for us. They were probably meant to crater the road, to slow the heavy traffic that they knew it would soon be carrying.

We did ponder the idea that to obliterate us might well have been considered by the enemy to be worth risking a plane. After all, until another vehicle with a radio could be found and set up, there would be no artillery support for the 8th Brigade. But I didn't need to fantasize the job's importance in order to feel comfortable about being away from the battles out in that flooded area. Being shot at while sloshing out of a sunken Weasel filled with numbing February water was not something I hankered for.

Alongside the spot where we ended up on our dash off the road was a low open shelter on four posts, perhaps something under which to pile split wood. Three of us had got out and were standing under it, out of the misty rain. Something for a moment rattled on the corrugated steel like hail; and then came a fragment that almost broke

The Rhineland: Part One

through. The pieces brought to mind that all the metal the ack-ack throws into the air has to come down again somewhere, in deadly fragments. No doubt someone was occasionally injured or killed by a chunk of that stuff falling from the sky at distances perhaps up to 20 kilometres from the gun that fired it.

After daylight on the 9th, the radios on our frequency fell silent, for our regiment was on the move to the now-captured Wyler — just in time, as the guns were getting out of range for supporting the advance on Millingen, the Dutch Millingen; there's one nearby in Germany, too. In the afternoon we got orders, probably from our motorcycle-riding signals sergeant, to come to the gun position. We came out to that dangerous strip of road, the one we were bombed off just after midnight, and headed for Wyler. The road now had traffic on it, moving in with supplies. Our guns probably came by there that morning. Its left shoulder was part of the flooded area's shoreline. In the winter, before the flooding, we had always assumed that the attack on Wyler would take place along this road. If there ever had been such a plan, the water changed it. And the water was still rising, although more slowly.

We were just nicely on our way when a Luftwaffe plane came in from the direction of the Rhine and banked around to line up with the road. His intention to do harm was obvious, so once again Harrison locked the right track and plunged us off into the trees, which must have been close to the same spot as before. The ground was softer this time because a cold drizzle had been coming down off and on since the attack the morning before. As fast as he could with the tracks sinking in, Harrison got us clear — but we came to an abrupt stop that smashed us all to the front of the carrier. We had run over a stump, and it caught somehow underneath. The transmission, an axle or something had broken under the strain. We were bruised, but our bones held together. The steel helmet was a help when my head struck the barrier behind the driver. We put on our DR (dispatch-rider) coats, strapped essentials onto our backs, tied the carrier's canvas down and, at 1505 hours on February 9, walked with a line of infantry over the border into Germany, the first entry for the four of us into the Third

Chapter 8

Reich. I considered the exact time important enough to record in my diary, but recorded nothing about the type of plane that had attacked us or what damage it did along the road. And I can't remember, possibly because of what my memory was to load up with after we entered Wyler.

How that plane, and the previous one after midnight — it could have been the same machine doing both runs — managed to fly in bad weather seemed a bit strange, considering that Operation Veritable was getting no air support because of flying conditions. Apparently the reason was that the Luftwaffe — a part of what was still left of it — was only minutes away in airports just north of us a few kilometres in the yet-occupied part of the Netherlands. Also, the pilots would know the landscape well. A Dutch immigrant once told me that a squadron of Messerschmitt 110s, a twin-engine night-fighter, was stationed near her home city of Enschede. The squadron's duty was to attack incoming bombers on their way to the Ruhr cities at night. But one or two of these planes may have been equipped to carry fair-sized bombs. (It was an ME-110 that Rudolf Hess, Hitler's deputy, used for his mysterious flight to England in May of 1941.)

The Wyler gun-position was in soupy mud. The town and area had been heavily mined and booby-trapped. One of D-troop's gun tractors had hit a mine and wounded two men. At a gun position in C-troop, a mine had killed two in a gun crew, with a fragment cutting the battery sergeant-major. As though the enemy's mines weren't enough, some were being discovered that had been planted by the U.S. 82nd Airborne when it drew back from the Wyler area in September.

I stepped out of the way of a 60 cwt (3-ton) supply truck, crawling along in the mud. When I was at the right rear of the vehicle, its left front wheel ran over a mine. I went to ground automatically but didn't know what happened for a moment. The explosion mangled everything on the left front, and damaged the passenger side of the cab. There had been no passenger, fortunately. The motor, which sat up between the seats in these army trucks, helped save the driver (right-hand drive). But the noise and concussion must have been severe in there. It was bad enough at the rear end. The driver stumbled

The Rhineland: Part One

out a bit unsteady on his feet, but appeared unhurt. A couple of fellows called to him from the door of what remained of a collapsed building. I followed him in. They sat him down and poured him a mess-tin of tea from a pot they were brewing. Staring blankly, he sat with it on his lap for a moment, then leaped up, spilling it all over the place, and shouted several times, "I'm hit." They assured him he was alright and got him sitting down again.

The town had been bombed and shelled into a jagged wasteland. Our dead and wounded had already been picked up, but the enemy's dead were everywhere, blown into distorted shapes for the most part. The more dreadful image was on the Dutch side of the town, the no-man's land, where fresh bodies were among ones that had lain there since last fall or had been blown out of their shallow graves by bombing and shelling, and were now thawed out. A heavy smell seemed to weigh down the air. Pieces of uniforms and other clues indicated that these weathered dead and their parts were of both friend and foe. A particular body that stuck in my mind appeared as though it had been prepared for shipping; both legs were lying neatly along the spine. It was as though someone had just gone for some wrapping and string. This place was different from the Schelde, for it had been a killing-field since the U.S. 82nd Airborne had dropped. My stomach closed up on me. I avoided supper and even the smell of the kitchen. One does get used to it, which in one way is a distressing part of it all.

In and around the town, engineers with trucks and armoured bulldozers were clearing and reinforcing the roads with logs and pieces of destroyed buildings and gravel. We hunted around in the basements of collapsed structures to find a dry and sheltered corner to stretch out our bedrolls — preferably a spot with no dead body nearby in the rubble. The rain was seeping in everywhere. We found something suitable. A few shells came in during the night, but with the help of the rum ration, we got some sleep.

The signals sergeant got us moving early. The day before, Shaw had reported our carrier loss to him and showed him on our 1:2500 map where it was. In this early morning, new orders came at us. A British outfit that had one of its signallers killed or wounded needed

Chapter 8

another in a hurry. Whittington was temporarily assigned to it. Harrison was assigned a driving job in the battery until our carrier was fixed. I remained with Shaw, who was given the radio-equipped 44th Battery half-track and its driver, to continue relay work. He and I and the driver loaded up with spare jerry-cans of gas, a compo pack, a can or two of water, our gear, the regimental frequency for the day, then headed out after an early breakfast — and missed seeing Montgomery, who visited Wyler that day in his staff car and with a trailing entourage, which included an official photographer for whom he posed for a picture. Our regiment eventually received an autographed copy. It is in our regimental history book. Hand-written in several short lines, the inscription reads, "13 Fd. Regt. RCA Wyler, Germany. B.L. Montgomery, Field-Marshal, 10 Feb 45." Headquarter's public relations people — a big crew of them, no doubt — were possibly busy at this sort of thing throughout the war, getting up in the morning from between clean sheets.

In the push east from Wyler to capture the city of Kleve, things had gone wrong. First of all, it became apparent, a little late, that the February 7 high-explosive, 1,400-ton bombing of the city was a mistake. At most, it should have been fire-bombed only. Collapsed buildings and bomb craters blocked all the roads and streets. Armour could not enter or pass through — or bypass, because of the flooding. The city was now easier for the enemy, who were moving into it in force, to defend. British Major-General Hubert Essame called the bombing "oafish stupidity." Second, when the British 15th Division was reported on some high ground just south of the city, it was somehow misinterpreted as meaning that the division was successfully entering the city. As a consequence, General Horrocks ordered into action the British 43rd Division which was to proceed to Kleve, pass through and head on into the Rhineland on higher ground. The result was two tangled, stalled divisions strung out for five kilometres in the mud and rain along a single, slowly collapsing road that was by then 20 centimetres under water in places. If, according to accounts, the rage and frightening level of profanity coming from commanding officers could have been blasted forward with loudspeakers, the Wehrmacht

The Rhineland: Part One

might have voluntarily withdrawn. After hard fighting, a few remarkable manoeuvres and a lot of luck, Kleve was finally cleared on February 12 _ some three days behind schedule. The war was made still more miserable on February 11 by snow mixed with sleet, which changed the colour of the mud for awhile that day.

The Queen's Own stayed in Millingen for a few days after its capture; but the rest of the 8th Brigade, now that Kleve was subdued, moved with the 3rd Division to the advancing front toward Kalcar. Two of our FOOs also stayed in Millingen to direct night-time fire on the far side of the Rhine. No doubt it was for the relaying of these fire-orders that Shaw and I were sent back out with the half-track. At least one other line crew was relaying as well, and Shaw must have been given a schedule which told who was on duty for what hours. I vaguely remember coming on and, by call-letters, asking the radios at the guns and the OP to report my signal strength (from "strength 5," meaning perfect, to "strength 1, meaning hopeless) — at which time the other relay station fell silent and I or Shaw took over the relaying. Some hours later the other relay station would come back on with the same procedure, and we would fall silent.

While two of our regiment's FOOs were in Millingen with the Queen's Own, the best spot for our job was still the high land in and around Berg en Dal. The rest of the 8th Brigade was out of action between Kleve and Moyland Wood on the road to Kalcar, where the Queen's Own would eventually join them. The next action for the brigade was to come after Moyland Wood was clear and the Goch-Kalcar road was secure. This road, in running between those two cities, cut across a major section of the Rhineland, and to cross it was bound to be deadly hazardous.

Overall, things were not going well for Operation Veritable. The Americans, who were to start their attack north on February 10, were stopped cold when the Germans opened the dams on the Roer River just enough to make a crossing impossible, and remain impossible until the reservoirs became too exhausted to maintain the flow. Some of the German force on the Roer was now moved against us in the north, as if the flooding, mines and mud were not bad enough. The

Chapter 8

result of all these conditions was having dreadful consequences. One bright spot was that the sky cleared to let the sun come out (it felt wonderful) for most of the 14th, allowing the air force with its Typhoons to help in finally clearing the Reichwald. But in the open land beyond the forest, the British would still have to contend with strong-points, especially the city of Goch. On the front's northern end, Moyland Wood emphatically stopped the drive from Kleve toward Kalcar. The piece of forest encompassed a ridge of land, ideal for defence. It was manned by first-rate German troops. The approaches to it were over low, flat land, soggy with rain.

Most of the books I have read on this phase of the war are merciful in passing over the Moyland Wood battles rather gently; but there are a couple that take a hard, critical look. Clearing the woods was eventually assigned to our 3rd Division's 7th Brigade, after a brigade of the British 15th Division had tried for three days in fighting so intense that its men could compare it only to their landing in Normandy. On February 19, General Guy Simonds ordered the 7th Brigade to attack. The results were disastrous. Over three more days as one attack failed he ordered another, often with more depleted ranks than the previous effort. The most thorough account of the tragedy that I have read is in the excellent book, *Rhineland,* by Denis and Shelagh Whitaker.[21] Denis Whitaker was an infantry battalion commander in the Rhineland campaign. As examples of the slaughter, the authors mention that three companies of the Canadian Scottish Regiment were reduced to half strength. One company of the Regina Rifles, from a strength of 100, was down to one officer and 20 men. This same regiment at one point, under orders, launched an attack with only one company, a company with only 69 men. They were cut to pieces in an hour. All but five were either killed or wounded.

To read about the force that finally cleared the stronghold emphasizes still more the blundering and tragic pointlessness of those attempts. On February 21, the rain stopped, the sun came out and so did the Typhoons, which made 100 attacks. Artillery fired 100,000 rounds and mortars lobbed in 2,000 bombs. When the Royal Winnipeg Rifles of the 7th Brigade went in, with a dozen Wasp flame-

The Rhineland: Part One

throwers, and tanks of the Sherbrooke Fusiliers, they faced only rearguard action. The main force of the enemy had withdrawn. It was finally over. Moyland Wood fell silent. In the week-long waste of outstanding courage, the 7th Brigade had suffered 485 casualties, and the British almost the same amount.

The British, who had been assigned the area between the Reichwald and the Maas, were now, after 10 days of persistent progress south, in sight of Goch, which was a virtual fortress in the Siegfried Line, and ringed with two anti-tank ditches. It was February 17. Because of intelligence reports that tragically underestimated the German strength in the area, the initial attacks were a catastrophe. One company had two men come back, leaving over 40 captured, 10 dead and the rest wounded. Nevertheless, the city fell to them on February 19, which the Germans acknowledged with an intense and costly bombardment of it for several days. As if the English hadn't suffered enough, the RAF came over on February 21 and bombed them by mistake. That little blunder added four dead and 19 wounded to their casualty list.

No precedent was established by that blunder. On at least four other occasions, Allied bombers dumped on Allied troops. Two of the worst incidents, coming in fairly quick succession shortly after D-Day, caused a total of 700 casualties in Canada's 3rd Division.[22] A foreboding incident had occurred back in Britain in April of 1942, two years before D-Day. The RAF's number 175 Squadron put on a demonstration to show the army what the air force could do. It did just that. A pilot's log records 20 people killed and 60 wounded when spectators were mistaken for the target. Not a good omen![23]

On February 16, when the British were making their first ill-fated attack on Moyland Wood, the 7th Brigade's Royal Winnipeg Rifles, by striking south-east, just below the woods, succeeded in taking Louisendorf and some land below it. Three days later that land became part of the assembly area for another costly attack for Canadians — the crossing of the Goch-Kalkar road about two kilometres south-east of Louisendorf. This time it would be the 2nd Division's 4th Brigade: the Royal Hamilton Light Infantry, the Essex

Chapter 8

Scottish and Royal Regiment of Canada. The attack began on February 19.[24]

Getting on the objectives was one thing. The incredible fight to hold out against repeated counter-attacks for days on end was quite another. For 24 hours contact with the Essex Scottish on the right was lost, and they seemed to have disappeared entirely. The Royal Regiment of Canada was called in from reserve. The Germans attacked all positions at night with tanks, against an infantry with no armour support because Canadian tank units had the policy of withdrawing at night. It would appear that tanks did badly in their support role from the beginning. One 88 gun took out a troop of four Shermans as they crossed the road. A company commander looked back to see all three of his support tanks taken out by another 88, in what he estimated to be 45 seconds. The isolated and battered attacking force of Essex Scottish somehow lost all their three tanks. The real heroes of support for the infantry were the anti-tank guns along with artillery regiments that fired over 5,000 rounds to protect positions against counter-attacks. One account, however, gives the tanks of the Fort Gary Horse Guards, along with a company of the Queen's Own Camerons of Canada, credit for vital assistance in helping those forward positions hang on.

Counter-attacks on the Essex Scottish were made easier because the British did not move up on the right according plan, nor did they bother to inform the Canadians about their change of heart. This act left the right flank unprotected.

In the end the shocking cost to the 4th Brigade of taking and holding its objectives on the other side of a two-kilometre strip of that road stood at some 400 casualties. Its positions, still fighting off counter-attacks, were not relieved until the 8th Brigade formed up in or around their positions, to get ready to move through early the next morning, February 26, as part of the final big, and wildly optimistic, drive of Operation Veritable.

9

The Rhineland

Part ll

On or about February 18, we were called back to the gun position in Wyler. At the entrance to the town a big sign had been erected which read, "You are now entering GERMANY. Be on your GUARD!"

Bulldozers had cleared the main streets. The dead had been buried. The road from Wyler to Kleve had been closed several days earlier — on the day, as it turned out, that the floodwaters were believed to have peaked. Land travel into Kleve was no longer possible. Troops fighting on the left flank, beyond that city, were now being supplied and their wounded removed entirely by boat and amphibious equipment, which was operating between Nijmegen and Kleve in the floodwaters.

We were called back to turn in the half-track and then go to rear echelon to retrieve our repaired carrier. The big half-track had been a luxury for us on this assignment, but hardly the right vehicle for our normal job. It was fast on solid ground, a condition of the ground quite uncommon for us. Although its armour would stop as much small-arms fire and shrapnel as would our carrier, the canvass-roofed vehicle was more than twice as big and with a high profile — too tempting a target for heavier guns if it came into view near the immediate front. And, unlike our carrier which could spin on the spot, it took a ballpark to turn around. It seemed perfect for its job in the bat-

Chapter 9

tery, the vehicle that transported battery headquarters and rescued bogged-down gun tractors. I loved the sound of its heavy Mack engine — something a young mechanic's son would remember.

With the luxury left behind, Shaw and Harrison and I went back with a returning supply truck to the rear shops to pick up M3. The conditions at the rear, we discovered, were startling by contrast to the front. We went through road junctions that were like Toronto's Bloor and Yonge without the lights. Military police in crisply-pressed uniforms, with white belts and gauntlets, were directing a constant string of traffic from all directions. Everywhere seemed to be crowded with soldiers, moving among big marquee-style tents and large enclosed trailers that were hospitals, dental offices, supply stores, sign-painting shops, Provost Corps (police) headquarters and so on. In the huge motor-transport repair area, men with uniforms hidden under overalls were swarming over vehicles.

In contrast, when approaching a dug-in infantry position there were so few men visible that the atmosphere had a twinge of loneliness in it. The men were in holes or spaced in strategic positions. It was certainly never crowded up there. It was so uncrowded that patrols from each side attempted and often succeeded to cross through one another's lines at night, and occasionally brought prisoners back through with them. The enemy's front line, similarly thin — or much thinner at that stage of the war — was up ahead, seldom less than 200 metres, and more often about 500 to 800 metres.

Shaw signed out our repaired Bren carrier after we checked and found that none of its equipment had been switched, filched or stripped — behaviour not uncommon in military circles. At our gun position, we found that Whittington had returned from his assignment. We felt complete again. He had no fond memories of his days with the British, whose officers were in an ugly mood because of the weather, the flooding, the mix-up at Kleve and their upset timetable. At one point, he told us, an officer gave him a message to transmit but did not order him to code it. Whittington sent it straight. The officer informed him, as Whittington uncomfortably remembered it, that "If we come under heavy shelling in the next few minutes, you will be shot." They

The Rhineland: Part II

were a paralysing "next few minutes," he said, but the shelling didn't come.

The next morning we were dispatched out into that chewed-up land from Kleve to the Reichwald, to relay once again. The duty was mostly standby this time. From examining war maps today, I can only assume that whatever firing our regiment did must have been still on targets across the Rhine and perhaps on the occasional by-passed pocket holding out in the Reichwald. All main fronts — Moyland Wood, for instance — were out of range. So we waited and listened to those eerie sounds that come in on short-wave when voices are silent. As well as the odd fire-order, the occasional coded message came through us to the regiment, which I romantically imagined as having great import. In truth, some colonel could have been checking on his dry-cleaning.[25]

The mud, water and wreckage we worked our way through along its north-west edge — part of the Siegfried Line — told us that something terrible had passed this way. We were trespassers in a landscape where disciplined men of each side had stubbornly bled one another. There were also remnants of an earlier invasion, for some open fields had an entanglement of September's gliders of the U.S. 82nd Airborne, which may have landed there deliberately or else overshot the Groesbeek Heights.

The number of Allied tanks, destroyed by mines or hit and burned ("brewed up" was an uncomfortable description commonly used) or bogged down and abandoned, clearly showed the price that Veritable paid because of the cruel weather and the Operation's late start, over ground no longer frozen. The Sherman tank was seriously handicapped — in a number of ways. Only the British Churchill and the German varieties — all with wider tracks — could get anywhere. Because of its strange position we stopped to examine a Churchill resting on its side. It looked precarious. No single "Teller" mine, the standard German mine, could set it up there like that. The crater was huge. The force must have been from a rack of these mines, which held about four, stacked vertically. The tank's bottom held, but was concaved. One thing that came to mind of the many horrors that the

Chapter 9

crew would suffer was the shattered leg-bones of those who were standing on that bottom plate of steel when the terrible force drove it upward.

We picked our way through the Reichwald and through some of the shattered defences in it and along it. From one of the damaged German fixed 88 anti-tank guns, we got loose its attached undamaged binocular and took it with us. It was a beautiful instrument but far too big and unwieldy for us. An attached mounting pipe, which must have been a half-metre long, was part of the frame and could not be removed. The lens arrangement was the type with a right-angle turn. The viewer looked down into the instrument in order to see ahead. Comfortable rubber eye-cups closed out all light. We had few occasions to use it in our work, but it seemed like such a prize that we fondled it a lot.

I have not seen figures on German losses, but have read that in clearing just the Reichwald alone, an area of forest about eight by 12 kilometres, the British 53rd Welsh Division had some 3,000 casualties. Over half of its war's total casualties occurred in the 14 days of Operation Veritable. The 9th Royal Tank Regiment, which represented a portion of the 53rd supporting armour, is a good example of how tanks made out. In clearing the Reichwald it lost 75 percent of its tanks to the enemy and the mud. One report on the Rhineland fighting said that the Germans had only 50 tanks, whereas the three British regiments had about 600 available to them.

The Reichwald victory belongs to the Welsh, but there was a small representation of Canadians with them: the 56th Anti-Tank Battery of the Royal Canadian Artillery, with its self-propelled 17-pounder guns.

In our movements we tried to stay in the tracks of previous vehicles. Some engineers were sweeping for mines and lifting them out, while others with heavy equipment were repairing supply roads with logs and rubble. Also, the British had what was called a "Pioneer Corps." I believe that name was on their shoulder patches. They were used for a lot of the rough labour, and were digging a ditch along a road as we approached. One of them set off a buried schu-mine with his shovel and got hit in the face. Blind, temporarily if he's lucky, he

The Rhineland: Part II

floundered around uttering strange sounds while others climbed wildly out of the ditch. But a couple got hold of him and made his face disappear with leaking bandages. As he was taken to a vehicle, we moved on while the officer in charge was using all his training to get the others back on their shovels.

The smoke screen was keeping this construction and other movement out of view, but guns from across the Rhine were doing some educated guesswork. The sound of their shells' approach would put us to ground. It was big stuff, coming from away back. After all, the distance from the Rhine across to the edge of the Reichwald was only about 10 kilometres. Twice that is possible for a big artillery piece.

Our M3 was called back to the gun position on February 21. The rain had stopped, and it turned a little warmer. We charged batteries, spread our bedrolls out to dry in the sun, re-stocked with everything and managed to write a few letters. I got my scribbled notes caught up from the collection of scraps in my pockets, and tucked them away in my gear in the signals trailer. The mail had come up a couple of days previous, which included the 12th parcel from my mother. Another crew member got one from his mother also. The experience of a parcel from home, with mom's date-filled cookies, cans of fruit, Mars bars — civilization innocently encroaching on savagery — was quite remarkable.

Shaw told us about a rumour he heard at battery headquarters that the Americans were coming from the south. We didn't know it at the time, but in the early morning darkness of the next day, February 23, the Americans, who had been held up until the Roer River floodwaters receded, entered the fight for the Rhineland, with some 15 divisions to start with. Their opening barrage was even greater than ours had been for the opening of Operation Veritable. Also in the early morning of that day, our regiment packed up and left the crushed town of Wyler to proceed to a support position for the beginning of the next half of Operation Veritable's assignment in the conquering of the Rhineland. The move took us through the Reichwald, through Bedburg, past the now-stilled Moyland Wood and on south-east to fields at Louisendorf, the regiment's new gun position.

Chapter 9

The scene of devastation that we of M3 saw along the edge of the Reichwald earlier came at us again as the regiment passed through its middle on the move here today. The forest was laid out in sections separated by roads, what in peacetime would be logging roads. It seemed that around every junction there were one or two crippled tanks or self-propelled guns, very prominently of our persuasion. From the shattered top half of the trees in the forest it was obvious that almost all the rounds that either we or the defenders rained down on one another in the campaign were turned into airbursts, that is, they exploded on hitting the tree-tops and drove shrapnel down onto the troops — an effect harder to hide from than explosions on the ground.

In the 25 or so kilometres of this first half of the British and Canadian assignment in the Rhineland, the total casualties numbered 8,513, of which 1,794 were Canadian. The British had 950 battle exhaustion cases and the Canadians 350. The term once used was "shell-shock" to describe these men who break down under the strain. Many are sent back into action after rest and "treatment," whatever that is. Do they tell them it's just their imagination and its really not all that bad? That after all you can only die once? They probably lean on the bit about letting their comrades down.

Aside perhaps from psychopaths with a death wish, everyone surely would break sooner or later, depending on how many times they repeat the episodes of terror. A Canadian air force historian says that often there were as many as 2,000 airmen at a time in detention for "lack of moral fibre" — that is, for refusing to participate further in the very high risk of dying in the occupation of killing others. The term "broken" was often used. If one just refuses and sits in his cell quietly, is that shell shock? Does he have to be sitting there crying and shaking and soiling himself to qualify? But the topic is just one of those horrible aspects of war that gets little publicity. The greatest absolute number of battle exhaustion cases in the army was, I have read, among infantry riflemen, but the proportion was higher in tank crews. And of all non-lethal casualties on the immediate front line, the ratios of them that were cases of battle exhaustion varied between one in four and one in eight, depending on the severity of the fighting.

The Rhineland: Part II

I was hardly aware of these cases during the war. They would be taken back with the physically wounded and would not necessarily look any different, unless one noticed that there were no bandages. George Myers, our D-Troop OP carrier driver, had mentioned once or twice about fellows curling up in a trench and going mute, but that was about it. Aside from the fellow back in our chicken-house days who was driven to bladder failure, the only other seemingly disturbed behaviour that we of M3 saw was on a stop one day at an infantry battalion headquarters. There was a fellow in full pack, moving around in the farmyard in a darting and random fashion. Each time an officer came out, he would quickly approach and would try to talk into the officer's face while moving along beside him, only to be bellowed at and shooed away. He was still at it when we moved on. We guessed he had been sent back from one of the companies, and perhaps it had been determined here that his derangement was fake.

Montesquieu had it about right. "A rational army would run away."

I wonder whether some of those troubled airmen who were in detention might well have been disturbed by the thought of whom they were killing as well as by the high risk of dying while carrying it out — all under the orders of Air Chief Marshal Sir Arthur Harris, commonly known as "Bomber" Harris. Because pinpoint bombing of factories had proved ineffective, as most of them were hidden well underground, Harris' strategy was to attempt to break the morale of the German troops and workers by killing their families through the blanket-bombing of cities, in raids conducted with as many as a thousand bombers. An RCAF veteran in his book recalls looking into the bomb-bay of his plane which was being loaded for a raid, and seeing the one-ton bombs and the incendiary canisters that were going in, all of which told him that his target would be a German city. One of the ground-crew members said to him: "Strictly women and kids tonight, eh?" [26]

I have never heard about about any mind-altering drugs being distributed in this war to Canadian soldiers, to make the more disturbing parts of their occupation more tolerable. Some forces used these

Chapter 9

chemicals, however. In his book *One Foot in the Ground*, John Ellis writes that 10 percent of U.S. soldiers were issued amphetamines. Their own medical people, he says, issued 100 million tablets and the British medical personnel issued another 80 million.[27] According to a television documentary on the Battle of the Bulge in the Ardennes Forest, U.S. forces were given a blue tablet containing some drug, which soldiers called the "Blue 88." In *A Bridge Too Far*, Cornelius Ryan tells about the exhausted British Airborne troops at Arnhem being issued Benzedrine, but the men were so close to collapse that the drug had unhelpful reactions: hallucinations, euphoria, double vision, irritableness.

The physical pain-killer, morphine, must have been the most significant drug of the front line in this and no doubt in a number of other wars. It miraculously alleviated the suffering and anguish of the wounded, often making it easier for them to die quietly. Medics with the needle were a welcome sight where the injured were being bandaged and loaded onto the open, two-level ambulance Jeeps. One of the more terrible features of war — which, gratefully, I never had to experience — is the suffering of a victim mortally wounded who is trapped in an advanced and cut-off position where there is no morphine. His comrades, emotionally at the breaking point because of his screams, hope for his death soon.

I suppose one has to call the rum ration a mind-altering substance. It always shifted mine somewhat. A soldier would find difficulty in denying its beneficial effect. The effect, however, of another of the military's chemicals, potassium nitrate, was more in question. It is more commonly known as saltpetre, and was persistently alleged to have been added to armed forces food for the purpose of reducing the rutting urge of its members — a presumed effect for which the medical evidence is shaky, I am told. I doubt that its' retarding of our militia's lecherous debauchery deserves any credit for saving Western Europe from wartime moral collapse. Nevertheless, the chemical did broaden the field of jokes. For instance, earlier when we veterans began advancing in age through our 60s, a popular remark of resignation was: "Finally the damned stuff is starting to work."

The Rhineland: Part II

We of M3 were fortunate in having a relatively safe job in those first 16 days of the operation. The second half would be different. What Canadian infantry and armour were about to experience was of tragic proportions. It was called Operation Blockbuster. Before getting to it, though, there is an event or two yet to be mentioned in closing out the first phase.

After our D-troop guns and command post were dug in at the regiment's new position at Louisendorf, we of M3 crew established the usual connecting lines and were then dispatched to lay the fire-control line to the FOO, who had moved with his crew to the North Shore Regiment. As we checked the line back to the gun position the next day, February 24, we drove right into shelling that was coming down on the regiment. The 22nd Battery lost some trucks. It killed one man and wounded two in our 44th Battery.

Also in our Battery, some stored gasolene went up with a searing heat, but no one was close enough to suffer one of the more terrible forms of death. A few men were just starting to unload a big ammunition truck. It caught fire, but one of the men, wounded, stayed with it and got it out, before he passed out himself. He was credited with not only saving the ammunition but with averting an explosion that would have levelled most of the battery, personnel and all. He was awarded the Military Medal.

A British medium regiment not far away took a worse beating, and finally had to change location. When it stopped, we climbed out of some sort of cavity we had jumped into, repaired our cut line to the command post, and headed for what at the moment was safer territory closer to the enemy.

Our tap from the fire-control line we ran into the cellar of a destroyed farmhouse, a good place to hole up. Harrison tucked M3 away close at hand. We were near the Goch-Kalkar road. To get below ground is a tremendous help in a soldier's longevity. But whenever I slept in a dank cellar, I felt as though a jute bag were over my head, a kind that had recently held some old sprouting potatoes. An occasional dominating touch was the smell of wet crushed plaster. The worst

Chapter 9

of these accommodations tended to tighten in on my nostril diameter until by morning I was close to being a total mouth-breather.

Thinking today about what it was like trying to sleep in such a hole reminds me of what strange things soldiers, at least this soldier, would consider noteworthy enough to put in a diary. My entry, in just enough words to bring back the memory, was of a night's rest back in early February in a wooded area of those relatively peaceful hills of Berg en Dal. One evening after Shaw took over the radio from me, I walked up a path through some bushes and came upon a little cottage, perhaps a weekend retreat. It was obvious from the inside that neither Canadian, British nor U.S. troops had found it. It was neat, with no looting scars. At the foot of its only bed was this outsized roll of something, which I took at first to be a thick, turned-back mattress. I picked up a corner of the object. It was — I will daringly say — as light as a feather, and was my first experience, I believe, with one of those big European down-filled comforters, which today in a more flattened form is called a duvet. This European variety puffed to about 20cm thick when unrolled. I told the driver where I'd be and then came back, took off a couple of layers of clothes and rolled that big sack of fluff up over me. It was amazing. It felt as though it were actually generating heat. For a few hours on a wet, cold early February night, I slept an unusual sleep, as war's thunder beckoned in the distance.

We were now far from Berg en Dal, however, and the thunder was not distant. One of us checked the phone occasionally. When the line went out, we knew which direction the break was by the end that could still hear us: the OP or the command post. Mortars were dropping in now and then, as though hunting around for something. They would find it before too long when the 8th Brigade would begin its attack. But at least the next day was quiet, and we got some rest.

10

The Rhineland

Part lll

In North Africa, in Italy and in France, the Allies learned that they had no tanks to match those of the Germans, and apparently never developed a strategy for their use that would help compensate for this inferiority.

The results in battle were not just a matter of a few points; the results were catastrophic. A regiment loses 45 of its 66 tanks in four days. Another outfit loses 16 tanks within minutes. The great German Tiger ace, Michael Wittman, chalks up 141 confirmed victims (before becoming a victim himself under the gun of a Canadian). An outfit comes out of an engagement with only four of its 16 Shermans left. A British armoured unit has to be taken out of action to get reorganized and re-equipped after suffering a loss of 64 percent. A Canadian unit in France loses 19 tanks in 15 minutes. And on it goes, in one history of the war after another.

The Russians quickly realized their disadvantage and built the T-34 tank to even the odds. The Allies in the West relied on overwhelming superiority of airpower — bombers, Typhoons — to reduce German armour. And the superiority was indeed overwhelming; on D-Day in France the Allies made 1,400 flights and the Luftwaffe 319. But planes can't fly in bad weather, and there was the rub in the Rhineland. Mud as a result of bad weather also affected our superiority in numbers of tanks. But dry land in North Africa and France had-

Chapter 10

n't reduced the losses much either. For instance, in the Battle of El Alamein, Montgomery had 1,100 tanks and Rommel had 260. And when the battle was over, Montgomery's tank losses were three times those of Rommel's, even though Montgomery had almost total air superiority, with about 800 planes at his disposal.

To help on our north European front, some Shermans were eventually built with a long-barrelled 17-pounder gun instead of the regular 75 mm. The model was called the "Firefly," and its gun could penetrate a Tiger and Panther. Against these two big machines, however, anti-tank mobile artillery pieces had the best record, with a few credits going to the clumsy weapon called the Piat, which was a poor equivalent to the American bazooka and the German hand-held, one-shot Panzerfaust. We practised on the Piat during training. Its body-slamming recoil was supposed to cock the thing each time. When it didn't, you had to get both feet on it and pull back with both hands while straightening the knees and body, to compress a long heavy coil spring. (Our training camp comedian had fun with that one, too.)

The Tiger II and the Jagdpanther were equipped with the famous 88 mm gun, the most outstanding artillery piece of its kind in the war — and the most feared. The Allies had no equivalent, which seems strange, for it could hardly have been a secret, in that it was designed in 1933, first as an ack-ack gun. It was capable of firing 14 kilometres high, and could put out 20 rounds a minute. As a field piece its horizontal range could knock out a tank at up to 10 kilometres if it managed to hit it. At three kilometres over open sights it was devastating. The gun was also set up as a moveable field unit and as a permanently fixed unit at certain strategic spots. We scrounged our binocular from one of these. The 88's shell often went clean through a Sherman without exploding.

After the war, in a bull session, a tank corps veteran friend of mine who was well aware of the tank's penetrability, attempted to disillusion a Sherman enthusiast by telling him a wild story about how the Germans would wait until two or three of our tanks were in line, and then shoot one round through all of them to save ammunition.

The Rhineland: Part III

As though the score to date were not bad enough, Allied tank losses, and the loss of human life, were fated to begin again, here, below the Goch-Kalkar Road. The early morning of February 26 was miserable. A cold drizzle had been dragging on all night. The OP crew and their Bren carrier, who had been back to the battery for supplies, were forward again with the North Shore Regiment. The phone line we had strung to the OP was still holding. Shaw had been briefed the previous evening. He was told that sometime in the morning the 8th Brigade would launch an attack. The North Shores were going to move down a road and take a town called Keppeln, which intelligence reports claimed was only lightly defended. We were to keep extending the phone line forward and continue it to our OP as soon as possible when the North Shores were on the objective and digging in.

Huddling over our 1:2,500 map, and holding our little British lantern-style "torch," the British term for "flashlight," we could see the road. The Queen's Own would be attacking on our left, Shaw said, and the Chaudière Regiment got some sleep. That was the extent of our knowledge and of our tiny corner in a gigantic event, a corner which narrowed to a soggy cellar once again.

What we were about to be part of was Operation Blockbuster, a name that was given to Operation Veritable's conquest of the final section of the Rhineland that had been allotted to it, which would bring us to the Rhine and meet the Americans somewhere near Wesel, thereby jointly holding the entire left bank of the Rhine. Possibly the new name for the operation came about because the first half of Veritable was so unexpectedly difficult and so far behind schedule that a very different approach was organized.[28]

To begin Blockbuster, the British on our 8th Brigade's right would be attacking on a line extending toward the Maas and then sweeping around with the Americans to close in toward Wesel. On our left were brigades of the 4th Canadian Armoured Division, the 5th and 6th Infantry Brigades of the 2nd Division, and on the end, south-east of Moyland Wood near Kalkar sat poised the British 43rd Division. The drizzle meant there would be no air support.

Chapter 10

The first and very important objective for most units was the ridge of high land extending from Kalkar south to beyond Uedem. Short of this objective was low, wetland, waiting to be churned into debilitating mud. Waiting, too, was an enemy which, although incredibly outnumbered in men and material, was defiant, and consistently outstanding in tactics. There was no reason to believe that its men were going to be any less ready now than they had been since our opening attack on February 8 to match the courage of our infantrymen and outmatch our floundering armour. Yet this attack's formulators expressed an optimism — tanks breaking out and heading for the Rhine, cutting off a confused enemy, perhaps capturing some bridges — which appeared no less outlandish than their optimism at the opening of the first grim half of the campaign. That half ended up some 10 wet, bloody days behind its optimistic schedule.

The barrage to precede this attack was short of the February 8 level, but it was big, with every available artillery regiment firing, along with the dreaded rockets. It began at 0345 hrs. Our sleep was a bit hampered after that. In our section, the Queen's Own Rifles were the first to move. Their principle assignment was to take a cluster of buildings known as Mooshof. Pretty well everything went wrong. The searchlights that reflected off the clouds, in order to create a false twilight for the attack, helped the enemy as well. The regiment suffered losses even before it reached the attack's launching point. The defenders could actually see them moving up, and shelled them relentlessly. At 0430 hrs a company of the regiment attacked and was eventually stopped cold. A second attempt also failed, with losses mounting.

A platoon was infiltrated and its commander killed. A sergeant by the name of Aubrey Cosens took charge. The platoon faced extinction. Only he and four other men were left. At that desperate point Cosens went wild. He ran across open land and climbed onto a 1st Hussar tank, directed its fire at strong-points and then asked its commander to smash into one of the buildings to make a hole, while he rode on top, shouting to his four men to follow in behind it and maintain supporting fire. By entering through the hole, he cleared that building and also the other two, killing a recorded 20 of the enemy and forcing the

The Rhineland: Part III

surrender of as many more. Then, with Mooshof consolidated and after having miraculously stayed alive through a constant focus of bullets meant to bring him down from the time he began his run to the tank — he may have hesitated for a moment in his exhaustion, a moment that the stalking cross-hairs in a scope had been waiting for. He was shot through the head by a distant sniper. Aubrey Cosens was posthumously awarded the Victoria Cross. History books would use terms like "above and beyond the call of duty" and "with complete disregard for his own safety." They would have it right.

On the right flank, the Chaudières (Le Regiment de la Chaudière) began at 0830 hrs to move on the village of Hollen, another village determined not to be taken. They were thrown back several times. The main problem was the shelling, coming mostly from guns in Keppeln, which were not yet silenced. When they were, the Chaudière attacks conquered their assigned area. But it was 1900 hrs, with the daylight gone. They lost 68 men, 17 of them dead. The 22nd Battery's forward line carrier that was bringing line to the OP with the Chaudières struck a mine, wounding two of the crew. The crew's bombardier, under heavy shelling, managed to get forward to the OP with communications. A piece of shrapnel tore a gash in his uniform and never touched his skin. For his exceptional effort he, like Shaw earlier, was awarded the Military Medal.

The silencing of those Keppeln guns and the capture of the town was to be the job of the North Shore Regiment, coming down the middle between its two sister regiments. At 0845 hrs, about 15 minutes after the Chaudières had got under way, the North Shores started toward their objective some 1,300 metres ahead. Eventually they were approaching a farm on the outskirts of Keppeln and suddenly came under a saturation of small-arms fire and heavy guns, driving them to ground and pinning them there. So much for the "lightly defended" theory!

Our signals sergeant, who was accompanying the OP carrier, volunteered to run the gauntlet back and bring up the infantry regiment's Wasp flame-throwers to rush the farm buildings and burn them out. On the way back with them, approaching the buildings again, his

Chapter 10

speedometer between the handlebars exploded in his face from a shot. Then something heavier hit behind his legs and threw him off the bike. As he got up, a Wasp hit a mine as it went by him, which put him down again, this time behind the OP carrier. He managed to climb into it. One Wasp out of the four succeeded in getting through, and burned out the main farm building, which neutralized the self-propelled "88"behind it. This reduced the fire-power enough for the infantry to get into the farm. But Keppeln itself and outlying trenches were a different matter.

It must have been at about this point that Shaw started us moving forward. I know now the name and location of every farm and road we encountered on the way, for I went back to visit 11 years after. I have corresponded with people who lived on these farms after the war, and during the war until bombed out of them or evacuated. They told me that the heavy bombing, which destroyed most of the farms in the area and cratered fields and roads came on the night of February 16-17. Civilians died. They had not been evacuated yet. But on this bleak morning each set of destroyed farm buildings separated by open stretches were just places that offered shelter in their rubble and basements and occasionally trenches, from a shelling that was getting heavier. It was still cloudy but had stopped raining for the moment.

In dragging line across the rubble of a particular farmhouse, something caught my eye in the mangled remains of household objects: a little booklet, which looked official with its stamps containing the German eagle and swastika. I stuffed it in my pocket and went on. Aside from the Canadian mania for souvenirs, I had the mercenary thought since coming into the war that anything containing authentic symbols of the Nazi era might be worth money, if I were lucky enough to make it. I tried to put something in each one of my letters home.

Road intersections — and we were approaching one — were always mean. The enemy kept them that way in order to slow supplies and to catch people like us and the sappers who were sweeping for mines. The fields on either side were soft. There were trees and posts along the approach and at the intersection itself, so our plan was to hook the line up high, over the cross- road. We were preparing for this

The Rhineland: Part III

attempt just a few metres back. I was using our long jointed pole with its forked end to get the line securely hooked up high for the starting point to jump the crossing. Shells were gouging into the road that ran to our left. My strong urge to get down was defeated by seeing that Shaw and Whittington were still on their feet. I remember being concerned that the back of my neck was exposed to the shrapnel — as if there were less chance of a hot fragment tearing into my cloth-covered spine farther down. I shoved my helmet back to reduce the naked exposure.

I now had the line securely up high on the one side. Whittington was drawing slack off the reel. Shaw was tying a piece of it down. It was the procedure to tie the line down on both sides of a crossing so that if a tank or carrier ran over it and snagged it in the track links, it would not pull down the suspended length over the road, a piece that was always dangerous and time-consuming to set up. The sudden louder scream of incoming shells sent the three of us to ground, tight against the far side of the carrier. About two metres in front of the carrier was a three-sided cement fence post, a feature that was common in rural areas. I didn't need a diary note to remember how the sparks were flying off that post, leaving no doubt that ugly pieces of steel were going by. The sight tensed me into one big isometric knot. What was probably less than a two-minute barrage was nudging into an eternity. A dispatch-rider came racing up, obviously intending to speed right through the intersection. Directly in front of us, the pockmarked road and the concussion of a shell slammed him and his bike to the ground, where I expected him to stay, either dead or wounded. Incredibly, he got to his feet, stood up the bike, straddled it and took off with everything that the machine and traction would give him. His desire not to hang around there was understandable.

The barrage suddenly lifted and began again somewhere along the road ahead. Harrison peeked out over the edge of the carrier. Nobody was hurt. Leaving us at our work, he quickly took the carrier through the intersection as its reel payed out cable. Off to the side of the road we noticed an impressive crater, which had to be made by some earlier bombing raid. The cavity contained the body of one of our

Chapter 10

infantry. It appeared as though he had been shot or struck by shrapnel while looking over the rim of it, and then slid down the inside slope, dragging some dirt with him.

We managed to get our line up high across the road. Right where Whittington was tying it down at ground level there was another body. Shaw hollered, "Is that fellow alive?" The body somehow looked as though it might have been. Whittington said, "Yes, his watch is still running." He didn't mean it as black humour. (We talked about the remark years later — about how, in frightening moments, unimportant reasoning shrinks in the mind and leaves only thoughts of how to stay alive and do your job.) In quieter moments later on, we did turn it to black humour, and badgered Whittington about it.

Tanks were going up the road in the distance, well ahead of us. Gunfire of all kinds left no doubt that a battle was taking place. In the yard of a farm somewhere beyond the crossing, I tucked our line away while crouching along through a scattering of our dead. At one point, as I flattened out among them when a couple of mortars or shells came close, I noticed that the shoulder-patch on the body beside me was not North Shore, but Essex Scottish. Because of the uncomfortable moment that it was, I suppose, the words on the badge stuck in my memory. I knew nothing about the regiment, or any regiment beyond those of the 8th Brigade, and did not puzzle long that morning about why these men happened to be there. In my diary that night I was simply to place them "at Keppeln." That was it. The puzzle would be solved for me many years later.

For a short distance we strung our line on foot, staying inside the sappers' yellow tape, which they string out behind them to show how far out they have swept for mines. They were just beyond us, still sweeping. Striking a clear stretch of road, we climbed in, passed the sappers and cranked out line from the back end while on the move, guiding it into the ditch with our forked pole. The carrier gave a slight bump at one point, and a crumpled bundle, stuck in a stain on the road, came out the back end and dropped away from us. We had run over a body. In the tension, identification didn't seem to be important at the time. Harrison just said later that we weren't the first over it, so we

The Rhineland: Part III

didn't feel quite so bad. To swing to the shoulder and ditch would bring the threat of mines or of bogging down. The country road was very narrow.

We had obviously caught up to the immediate front. A cluster of farm buildings were just ahead of us, one of them putting out smoke. The shelling was now behind us, as we were inside the zone of the front, but the sound of small-arms fire was in front of us. Men were moving around on the protected side of the buildings. We did not know the story yet, but this was the farm that the flame-thrower helped take. We knew our location; our map told us that when we plotted our run earlier. We expected, though, to be going to an OP right in Keppeln.

On the approach, we were one more vehicle to run over our signals sergeant's flattened bike. We did not yet know it was his. Harrison rushed us in alongside another carrier which he recognized to be the OP's. Shaw extended the line to the FOO. Our run had been especially valuable, because both the FOO's and the infantry's radios had been knocked out. This radio loss had been the reason that specific artillery fire could not be brought down and that the infantry had been unable to call up their flame-throwers, something that was eventually achieved, as already mentioned, by our volunteering signals sergeant who went back to get them. We did not learn about this loss of communication until the OP carrier driver, Meyers, told us what a welcome sight we were.

Keppeln, about 300 metres ahead, had not fallen yet, we learned. Meyers told us that tanks loaded with infantry had charged into the town and were fighting there. When we swung into the farm, we had seen infantry to the right of the road, coming out of trenches and working their way toward the town. We didn't see him, but Meyers told us later that the regiment's Colonel Rowley, with his long walking staff, had been going along the top of trenches, to encourage his men in the attack.

I eventually learned the story of the tanks in this battle. It had become apparent that Keppeln was not going to fall to infantry alone. Losses were mounting. Two North Shore officers — again, because of

Chapter 10

no communications — had worked their way back to regimental headquarters to report the conditions. A force of 14 tanks of the 1st Hussars and 42 North Shore reserve infantry, riding precariously on the top of them, charged toward Keppeln. Only six tanks out of the 14 made it. Nevertheless, this fragment of the force plus the simultaneous attack by the infantry that we saw struggling forward eventually took the town, while we waited in the farm buildings. And no doubt artillery barrages helped as well, for they could now be called down over our line. The time must have been about 1800 hrs. The light was fading.

The OP carrier — and M3 with Harrison and Shaw, paying out line loosely along the edge of the road — now made a run for Keppeln and got in among the buildings. The enemy was already beginning its standard practice of shelling the positions it had just abandoned, to catch our troops who would be moving in. There were buildings on the outskirts at the far end of the town that were still firing into the streets. That one surviving Wasp was called up to help take out at least one of them, and again did its job. Whittington and I came in on foot, poking our line well off to the side and into protected places. About half-way along I lifted the line to the other side of one of the North Shore dead — a major, I noted. Later, Meyers, our source of all knowledge, said that it was a Major Parker, who had been B-Company commander, one of the two men who had worked his way back to request the tanks and reinforcements. He was killed after he had returned and was directing his company in the attack on Keppeln from the right, while the tanks, with their cargos of men hanging on, were entering on the left.

We had just finished our job when a Sherman tank came down the road and turned right at the edge of the village in order to go around it — and to go right over the top of our line. Another tank was coming farther back. Obviously a troop or maybe a squadron were moving through our position. We learned later that they were part of the 9th Brigade, on their way to attack Uedem. It would be only a matter of time before our line was torn in two. I had a bright idea.

The Rhineland: Part III

Just at the edge of town, a steel power-line pole had survived, the kind that was made out of a coarse latticework of crisscrossed braces. It was right where the tanks were turning. Whittington agreed to run back and tie down the line on something, while I strung it over my arm and climbed the pole. At a height well clear of the turrets, I tied it.

Shells were coming in all through the town. But at that moment, maybe for the benefit of the Shermans or just for variety, a German mortar crew were ordered to put down a few in the area below me. This was a new experience, a new twist on fright. How does one crouch or dive for shelter up in the air? I just grasped the pole in an embrace and squeezed it to make myself smaller. Whenever shrapnel hit the structure, I got a sharp rap, especially on my cheekbone that was flattened against the steel. I could picture my support being gnawed off at the base, to bring me crashing down. The enemy gunners eventually raised or dropped their range, and I scampered down unscathed except for the latticework of steel that may have been imprinted in my chest. Meyers, with one of his uncomfortable observations, suggested that I was a nice still target for a sniper. Although the evening had shrunk visibility, and I had been up no higher than the immediate hamlet buildings, I still didn't need that image.

My count of the disabled Shermans on the battlefield that evening came to five, a figure I noted in my diary. It was not until reading an account of the battle many years later that I learned I had missed three. The total was eight. I learned, too, that out of the 42 men who rode on them, only nine got to the town. The total casualties in taking Keppeln came to eighty-nine.

Sporadic shelling continued all night. We were out repairing breaks off and on until near dawn. The explosions had tapered off by then. A round hitting quite close to the cable would tear it in two and blow the jagged ends away, which required some nervous groping around in the dark to find them. By first light, the enemy seemed to have switched all his harassing fire to Uedem. The original plan was that the 9th Brigade would leapfrog through the 8th after Keppeln was secured, and attack Uedem in the afternoon. But the strength of the

Chapter 10

8th Brigade's opposition at Mooshof, Hollen and Keppeln had been so woefully underestimated that the 9th could not begin the assault until 2100 hrs — a night assault. And it wasn't easy. The city was surrounded by an anti-tank ditch. Those Churchills with a section of bridge attached were brought up. Churchill flails pounded mine-free strips forward. For every section of the city gained, counter-attacks had to be beaten off. Uedem was not secure until late afternoon of the 27th.

Those British and Canadian forces on our left, mentioned earlier, achieved what they set out to do, that is, get onto the Kalkar-Uedem ridge. They, too, with troubling losses, fought viciously for every metre gained. They brought up flame-throwers and used Kangaroos to rush troops forward. With the fall of Uedem, the entire ridge was secure. The powerful American force that was sweeping north with the better footing for tanks on the higher land of its front, in contrast to the terrible terrain on our front, took pressure off the advancing British on our right, to the south. The developing pocket, focussing on Wesel on the Rhine, would soon be closed when the Americans and British met.

After the war, in the several accounts I read of the Rhineland battles, I always paid particular attention to the fighting of the Essex Scottish south of the Goch-Kalkar road. None of their objectives mentioned Keppeln. Also, Hugh McVicar, an Essex Scottish veteran with whom I had correspondence, verified this.

The puzzle of those Essex Scottish bodies was eventually solved for me — solved by strange circumstances. In correspondence in the 1990s with a local historian in North Germany, I happened to mention, in discussing souvenirs, the passport I had picked up. The historian, with considerable effort, tracked down the name of the onetime holder of that passport, Joseph Aymans, and found that he was still alive, a veteran of the Russian Front, and living in Xanten.

When I wrote him — in my best, but poor, German — his niece, Johanna Ambrosius, answered in near-perfect English, a language not familiar to either her father, Felix, also a veteran and living in the Rhineland, or her Uncle Josef. She told me that the destroyed farm

The Rhineland: Part III

where I had found the passport had been the home of the young Aymans brothers before they were called to war. Shortly after this correspondence, another book I read identified two Essex Scottish objectives that other sources did not mention: Göttern and Brunshof. I asked Johanna about them. To my surprise, Brunshof is a farm now — and was the destroyed farm then — located south of that bad road crossing on the way to Keppeln. The puzzle was solved. It was probably the counter-attacked objective of the Essex Scottish where, according to an account I read, its A-Company held on for an unbelievable 36 hours and was practically wiped out. The objective was not "at Keppeln," as I had recorded, but some 500 to 800 metres back. I wrote to tell Hugh McVicar of my discovery, but was sad to learn that he had died since our last exchange of letters.

11

Rhineland

Part IV

To pick up the story of M3's crew again is to go back to the darkened building in Keppeln where, between line-repair runs, we got snatches of sleep on that February 26-27 night.

Earlier, just at dusk that evening, I noticed our signals sergeant in the fading light in a shell-pocked building, sitting on something, with his back against the wall, all alone. The effects of his experiences that afternoon were still with him, experiences that by then I had heard about. I sat down beside him for a couple of minutes. He spoke just a little more than usual, and rather nervously, with a short chuckle between each remark. There was certainly no bravado. He spoke of what the enemy did to his bike. Had it since D-Day, he said. He fell silent before long, so I got up. Soldiers don't praise one another directly, I had found. They say something like, "You went through one hell of an experience." I said something like that when I left him. He, too, was awarded the Military Medal. And he got another Harley-Davidson.

According to my diary, at that fortress of a farm just short of Keppeln a dead woman and baby were lying in a corner of the yard. The incident I remember clearly, but my note, written uneasily in some place in Keppeln that night, could have had the wrong location. We had been through three and possibly four clusters of farm buildings before reaching the one in question. The child was wrapped in

The Rhineland: Part IV

her arms. To see what she was holding, I moved back a bit of cloth. I have used the incident — shamelessly at the beginning, I suppose, and then with shame in later years — as a personal example of how war brutalizes, and how necessary it is to become brutalized in order to remain stable. Brutalizing is part of military training. The military cannot bring in "grief counsellors" or people to treat "post-traumatic stress disorder" after each battle. If you slaughter at a distance, as we did in the artillery, or as the air force mercilessly did near the end, then the images are not as troublesome. I remember mentioning the woman and child to Whittington after the war, and his telling me about an image of his own that haunted him: two dead girls sprawled in the mud in the Schelde Pocket, possibly at Sluis.

In a letter, Johanna Ambrosius said that no one in the area recalls the death of a woman and child, but civilians did die; two in the Aymans family were killed by the preliminary bombing. I do have evidence, though, unearthed some 50 years later, that there were women at that farm. A 1945 Canadian Press item about the Battle of Keppeln says that when the Wasp ignited the farm building, three women and about 30 Germans escaped out the back to Keppeln.

Our M3 crew spent a part of February 27 picking up our cable back to the gun position. Picking up cable was always a job considerably safer, to put it quietly, than stringing it out. But it was hard work — cranking the reel, occasionally digging the line out of debris from a shell explosion, repairing spots that had torn insulation. When passing by a knocked-out carrier, we noticed a compo-pack in it. Ours was almost empty. Catching mess-time at either the North Shores or our own battery was not always easy. So Harrison pulled up alongside, and I lifted it out. If men had been killed in that carrier, they were gone now, as were the other dead. The burial crews had been around, personal belongings bagged, dog-tags removed, names recorded, bodies taken back.

To speak of the compo-pack reminds me of how well our cooks looked after us in the field. They prepared food and ladled it out under the damnedest conditions. In training camps, they were the brunt of grousing and jokes. Not so in action, at least not that I observed. I

Chapter 11

remember one wet early morning somewhere in the Rhineland when Shaw and I had patrolled a line into the OP, a line which ran along in a ditch. Looking back we could see another couple coming in by the same ditch, and dragging something. On the wet grass these North Shore cook's helpers were skidding along a big dixie of steaming hot porridge for their men on duty at that spot. They must have come a fair distance with it.

I glanced back when the place where we had run over the body passed beneath us again — dirty, chewed cloth in a stain of something thinly pancaked out by a multitude of unconcerned vehicles. Will a padre and burial detail scrape around for possible dog-tags if they recognize the spot as remains?

Notices sent home don't go into details. A soldier just somehow dies in the service of his country, or is missing and presumed dead if no identifiable parts are found. If he's lucky, he's a prisoner of war.

Our regiment was preparing to move to a spot somewhere south of Keppeln, where they would stay limbered and draw the wagons into a circle, as they say in Westerns, until the next morning when a space to deploy at Uedem would come available. We moved with the OP carrier and North Shore Regiment through the centre of Uedem. I had seen a lot of dead by this time; but when we rounded a particular corner in that city, I saw my first headless body, with the rest of the body relatively clean and untouched. It was leaning against the curb, giving the appearance of trying to work itself up onto the sidewalk with its elbows. It's another image that has hung around in memory.

On the far outskirts in an open spot, Shaw had us dig in rather than find a good basement in the shattered city. I don't remember why, but can guess that it had to do with radio reception. When there are no lines, we were often on radio standby as a precaution. In a sheltered spot by the carrier, we dug a width to hold two of us — two could get half comfortable in M3 — tore off some cupboard doors in the nearest building to throw in the bottom, staked up our rarely-used pup-tent over it and crawled into our bedrolls. A miserable drizzle was coming down. So was harassing fire, as it was called. Whenever it happened

The Rhineland: Part IV

to drop in our end of the city, it made us shift uneasily in our hole and to speak badly of the bits of dirt that it would jar loose and drop on us.

In the night we heard tanks come up close and stop. The sound of those air-cooled engines as they approached told us they were ours. They were not the newer Shermans, which were built with diesels. When they quieted down, we went back to sleep, feeling more sheltered. Sometime later we were suddenly wide-eyed awake and stiffened with fear at deafening banshee sounds that seemed to be right over us. Flashing lights were showing through our tent's canvas. We were having our first experience of being next to outgoing rockets, actually firing right over our tent and carrier. They were fired from a big rectangle of rocket tubes, 32 of them, which took off in close succession, each with a loud scream. The unit was mounted on a turretless tank. Whittington, too, said that one of the things he thought of when the noise cut loose was that this could really be Hitler's secret weapon coming at us. The troops often used Hitler's threat cynically to describe anything particularly irritating, such as the Sten gun.

At first light, when Whittington and I came out of our hole and packed up, seeping water had just reached our bedrolls. The day turned out to be a rare one of sunshine, however, which brought the rocketing Typhoons out for a few hours but didn't do much to dry out the land. Shaw told us that up ahead the great proposed breakthrough to the Rhine had been stopped cold by rain, mud and the enemy. Our regiment appreciated one or two quiet days after moving into its new position. M3 had a few chores to do; but overall, everyone got a rest.

My diary for those days has just a short reference to an activity quite important to me: that of prowling through scarred buildings, deserted and stilled by war. Uedem was ideal. Looting was a lesser attraction; there was something more. I spent hours cautiously skulking from room to corridor to basement, apprehensive about booby-traps but caught up in the fascination of those structures and in the peculiar sensation of being alone in the silence of an historical event. The slight tremor of a shell coming in a few blocks away would cause a piece of plaster to drop. My scalp would tighten.

Chapter 11

Uedem, which was totally surrounded by an anti-tank ditch, had been German General Alfred Schlemm's headquarters just days earlier. He was the man in charge of the Rhineland defence. I knew nothing of this, or even of the man. In a drawer I found some magazines and newspapers, some old, some recent. I sat for a considerable time, looking through them. Even in my young soldier's coarseness and ignorance, I recall being struck by the similarity of so much in those papers with what was in our own at home, with respect to headline form, layout style and advertisements. And the subject of photographs was similar.

I really don't know what I had expected to find, but I remember just a twinge of embarrassment at the thought of being discovered as naive — as though if someone had been with me, I would have said defensively: "I knew that." Quite certainly I was looking at the equivalent of something like the Family Herald and Weekly Star, and not Julius Streicher's *Die Stürmer*.

From those papers, however, I did loot something: a clipping of a picture of two Luftwaffe pilots. The captions are what caught my eye. My only knowledge of German was from a book picked up on my first visit to London after landing. It was a combination basic grammar and dictionary purchased in Foyle's bookstore ("Booksellers to the World") on Charing Cross Road. But I knew enough to understand from the captions that these fellows hit the press because of their incredible record in air battles. The one identified as Oberleutenant Hartmann had passed the mark of 300 Luftsiege "air victories," or "kills," as our Air Force called them. The other fellow, Hauptmann Batz, had gone beyond the 200 mark.

Years later, I was to learn that in the annals of air war Eric Hartmann is accepted as the greatest ace of all time, ending his career with 352 confirmed kills. He survived the war, was turned over to the Russians by the Americans, refused to train pilots for the Russians and spent 10 years in a Gulag. Finally released in 1955, he became commander of the first wing of the new German Air Force around 1958 as part of NATO, with the rank of lieutenant colonel. I still have that clipping from Uedem in my scrapbook; and again, as I look at it today,

The Rhineland: Part IV

I remember once more a strange feature of the captions. Although they are about 10 lines long each and give age, place of birth, education, reference to parents' occupation, they do not mention the first name of either man. Why would that be? Can anyone imagine a Canadian newspaper's reference to our ace, Buzz Beurling, only as Flying Officer Beurling?

Uedem's anti-tank ditch was impressive. The Siegfried Line had a lot of them along its north end. I remember them as being about six to eight metres across and four metres deep. They were very effective in slowing an attack and making it more costly, but once an objective was taken, and often before it was taken, engineers went to work with Bailey bridges and bulldozers. In one of these ditches, and I think it was here at Uedem, I went down to the bottom to look at a trapped and abandoned Sherman tank.

I had just climbed on top and was peering into the hatch when some mortars came screaming over, so I kept right on going and jumped inside. It was the first and last time I was ever in a Sherman tank, and that brief experience gave me some inkling of what the God-awful stress must be like in there in battle. I didn't know at the time, of course, about that "battle exhaustion" statistic mentioned earlier, but I have no trouble accepting it. When I looked at all those big shells stacked around on the inside, and had already seen what an 88 could do to one of these high-silhouette cauldrons, I wished that I had jumped off and scratched my way underneath it. And I was worried only about a few mortar bombs.

The relatively quiet back streets of Uedem could belie the terrible things happening on our front just ahead of us about a kilometre to the east. Here is a rough geographical sketch of it, made up of what may truly be called the killing fields. Two sections of forest had a gap between them through which ran a rail line to Xanten, the prized city. The gap was about three kilometres long, 200 metres wide where it faced us, but it widened considerably at the other end.

Over a large area in front of the gap and extending back toward Uedem was a low, flat plain, traversed by the raised rail line. The plan was to capture the low plain and the mouth of the gap. And then,

Chapter 11

charge with armour through the gap and race for Xanten and the Rhine. This done, the rail line would become a road to bring supplies up for the Rhine crossing. The plan would appear to have been based on the expectation of an amazing lapse in German tactics. What concerned German General Schlemm, according to an historian who interviewed him after the war, was that the Canadians might do the right thing, that is, go around these forests and avoid this obviously picture-perfect terrain for defence. Such a move would force him back to a less favourable position. He needn't have worried, however, for the Canadians were going to be sent over that rain-soaked plain and into the gap — the trap.

On February 27, while Whittington and I were getting some sleep in that soggy hole, the Algonquin Regiment of the 4th Division's 10th Brigade, backed by four tanks from the South Alberta Regiment, attacked across that plain toward the gap. Those rockets we heard departing over our hole in the ground were part of the barrage to support this action. The tanks either bogged down or were hit, while the whole force was fired on not only from the forests on either side but, quite remarkably, from behind — from the other side of the Rhine, where the river made a dip to the south-west. With brutal losses the attack failed. At dawn another Algonquin attack went in on the right, this time with 12 carriers and more South Alberta tanks. The defenders knocked out the front and rear tanks of the column and then proceeded to destroy everything in between — nine tanks and 11 carriers in all. One carrier was the only armour that survived.

It seems reasonable that a point had been made. Apparently not! The next day, February 28, the 11th Brigade's Argyle and Sutherland Highlanders also tried it, with 16 South Alberta tanks. The tanks, slithering and sinking in the mud, were near useless. The Germans counter-attacked. Of one company's 100 men, 80 were killed and five wounded. The Lincoln and Welland Regiment were sent in to relieve them and received an unmerciful shelling. Every one of their support tanks bogged down. The attack got nowhere.

Nevertheless, on the same day, the Canadian Grenadier Guards of the 4th Division's 4th Armoured Brigade, along with the Division's

The Rhineland: Part IV

Lake Superior Regiment were formed up for still another attack — this time with orders to get on the rail line and rush through the gap on top of it. Having a long column of armour running a gauntlet in single file along a raised rail bed, with 88s in the woods on both sides picking them off, appeared to the regimental commanders as so insane that they refused and formed a different plan of attack. But it all became academic when the enemy laid down such a ferocious barrage that the attack ended before it ever got started. Tank statistics were already bad enough. The First Hussars had lost 82 tanks. I have read no account that mentions their original strength. The Grenadier Guards lost 45 of its 66.

The commanders of these suicidal missions deduced that things would go much better if all those inconsiderate enemy guns such as the 88 would stop firing out of the forests on both sides. So, the 3rd Canadian Infantry Division was assigned to clear the one on the right, known as the Balbergerwald, and the 2nd Division was given the left one, known as the Hochwald. The story of the gap between the forests, which became known as the "Hochwald Gap," was not going to get much better.

The Reichwald experience should have been a warning about what to expect in these two small forests. The Hochwald was the larger of the two, oval-shaped, about two kilometres through and three or four wide. On March 1 at 0730 hrs, behind a heavy barrage, C-Company of the 2nd Division's Essex Scottish Regiment, with more near-useless, mud-bound tank support, moved toward the woods across 400 metres of flat country.

Major Fred Tilston, the commander of this lead company, was wounded first in the head and then in the hip, but it didn't stop him from going forward with grenades to take out a machine-gun position, and to take the first prisoner. The company got pinned down at the edge of the woods. One platoon was reduced to eight out of its 25 or so men.

Ammunition was running out because their ammo-carrier had been hit. The men were picking from the dead in order to keep firing. Tilston himself crossed a treacherous piece of land to bring some back

Chapter 11

from D-Company on his right. Then came the rain, jamming the Bren guns. Tilston put the wounded to work cleaning and drying them. It was now into the afternoon. B-Company, which finally made it up to relieve the desperately struggling group and move through them, had lost a lot of its men just getting there. But it managed to move forward. Tilston, in spite of his two wounds, decided to make still another run to D-Company for ammunition.

A mortar caught him on the way and blew off one leg, leaving the other badly mangled. Eventually it had to come off as well. His citation says that he made six of these trips in all.

Tilston, for that day's work, was awarded the Victoria Cross. Another expression used by the award people is "... total disregard for his own safety...." They got that right, too.

The Essex Scottish suffered over 100 casualties, 31 of them deaths. The Royal Hamilton Light Infantry went through them to clear the rest of the forest on March 2. The enemy had withdrawn.

On the gap's other flank, in the Balbergerwald, the enemy was also determined. The 8th Brigade's Chaudières were sent into the woods on the night of March 1, after a barrage which involved our regiment and probably others. During the attack, however, directing fire on specific targets by the 78th Battery's OPs proved difficult because of the airburst effect caused by the trees, which brought shrapnel down on our advancing troops. All firing had to be deeper into the woods. In other words, it was a repeat of the Reichwald experience, which meant, once again, forward movement would be slow and costly. And once again it was learned that night was not the time to be fighting in the woods. For one thing the searchlight-on-clouds effect was not much help.

The Chaudière attack got nowhere until morning, March 2. Later that day the Queen's own and the North Shores passed through them and did better in the daylight. As the North Shores moved up, we in M3 were back to work. Up ahead we had heard the constant thunder of shelling over the last couple of days, which had been associated with those attempts to go through the Gap. Some suggestion of how badly the attempts had gone came to us as we strung line over the con-

The Rhineland: Part lV

vulsed landscape and through what gave the appearance of being a large graveyard for tanks.

By the time we arrived with phone contact, two of our regiment's FOOs had been wounded. Until artillery could be brought down at one point, an SP gun was firing over open sights at the North Shores. Mortars were coming in relentlessly, cutting our line a couple of times.

Near the front, especially when an attack was going in, some of these mortars were "Moaning Minnies," as they were called. If there was any individual sound that might symbolize the death and destruction that these two armies were bringing to one another, it would have to be the agonizing, soul-freezing screams of the shells from this weapon as they approached. They could scar a soldier's courage. Mine could be scarred with a lot less. Six of them, spaced by a couple of seconds, were fired from a six-barrelled, wheeled arrangement. I don't recall our infantry ever capturing one of the weapons, but Whittington and I had an occasion to get a look at one of the rounds, which had come in with a brace of them but did not explode. It splattered a lot of dirt away and lay in the middle as though on display. They were huge: 150 millimetres (six inches) in diameter. We later toyed with the demented idea of getting well back behind something and shooting it to see if it would explode. But the mental lapse passed.

Virtually all the shelling that our M3 normally got caught in was the enemy's harassing fire, that is, fire brought down on roads, road junctions and other places where there was a good chance of catching something.

Once, however, here in the Balbergerwald, we believe we were specifically targeted and fired on. The driver, who was not Harrison, and I had gone out to repair a break, and we were moving rather quickly along a road through a clearing and parallel to the front. With no warning sound, a shell caught the edge of the raised road and blasted shrapnel and ground into the side of the carrier as well as over it. The concussion seemed to lift the side up for a moment. Only an 88 could come in like that, for its shell was coming faster than sound.

Chapter 11

The driver, too, must have thought 88, for he dove out of the carrier, which must still have been moving. Half-stunned, I followed. We rolled, scampered a short distance, flattened out as low as possible in the wet, opposite ditch, and waited for the next blast, which we assumed would come as soon as another round could be loaded in the gun and sighted. We felt that he wouldn't miss this time — not an 88, even though a carrier is a small target. He only missed that time because his elevation was about 50 or 60 centimetres too low. We waited for M3 to become a twisted mess. And waited! Nothing! Why? Did he want us to get back in first?

The gun was probably a couple of kilometres away, in the German line, where he could see along one of the narrow roads on our side, which cut the forest into a grid. He may have fired at us hurriedly as we passed by at the end of his road. Maybe we had rolled out of his sight, or he had been on the move. We had seen a lot of destroyed tanks in the Reichwald which had been hit at grid intersections.

After several minutes we nervously piled back in. The driver started the motor and we swiftly left while I crouched low in the anticipation of disaster. But the 88 stayed silent. If Harrison had been driving when the shell hit, I think he would have taken off with everything M3 could put out. His machine was precious to him and he could make it do marvellous things, for which the rest of us were continually grateful.

On March 3, our regiment moved to some building remains on the edge of the Hochwald about three kilometres south-east of Uedem. These were busy days, with little time for making notes. In the Balbergerwald, those grid roads were fairly solid, although often cratered. All the line we picked up and laid at the regiment's end, though, was through a mess of disabled vehicles and in earth that oozed up into the idlers, or bogies, of M3's tracks. On foot we plodded through it with weighted-down boots. Salvage crews were reclaiming undamaged tanks from their mud-holes.

I have seen prisoners poked with a rifle to demand that they do certain things, such as start running toward the rear or help carry our wounded, and I once saw a group being taken back in bare feet. I have

The Rhineland: Part IV

heard soldiers laughing about their attempt to stretch a "French safe" over a prisoner's head. Looting prisoners' personal possessions when our officers weren't looking was done, as was looting the enemy's dead. A carrier driver we all knew collected rings. He was alleged to be able to spot one on a dead German at some distance and would defy booby-traps and mines to stop and check. As time was usually of the essence, and a ring is apparently hard to remove under the circumstances, he was said to have solved these problems by cutting off the finger.

Only once, though, did I ever see vicious cruelty. We were grinding forward, passing a column of infantry moving up. A dispatch rider coming toward us, slewing around with his feet out for balance, was repeatedly running into and knocking down a prisoner whom he was herding in front of him in the ditch. By all appearances, he would then attempt to run over him before he could get up. The prisoner — hardly recognizable, soaked in mud — would twist and slither to escape the wheels and then get up to run again. He was limping badly as the scene faded behind us. We and the column of soldiers kept moving, just as our training called for. The prisoner may simply have been the chance victim of a cruel, inflamed mind, or have been a sniper who had been very effectively doing his duty, but had been captured.

Some of our D-Day people told us that in France a French woman sniper was caught after picking off a couple of Canadians — perhaps in memory of her departed soldier boyfriend, or for the glory of Vichy France. When a civilian kills a soldier, murder is what leaps to the military mind, in contrast to authorized killing. No mercy can be expected. Her captors, in a serious rage, beheaded the woman and drove through the streets with her head on the end of a pole. Years after the war, I met by chance a witness to that display.

South of the Balbergerwald, the Chaudières reached a position near the town of Sonsbeck on March 3. Because of the threat of counter-attacks, a FOO of the 78th Battery who was with them called down fire throughout the night that completely circled the position. In the forest on that date the other two regiments of the brigade were under heavy mortar fire and airburst shells. The North Shores had to post-

Chapter 11

pone their attack and did not get on their objective until dusk. We brought in a phone line to the FOO who was with them.

Later that night I was doing a shift on our radio, which was on standby, when midnight rolled up, the hour when the Regiment routinely changed its frequency. I got the coin from my pocket or from some hiding place in the carrier, the coin that fits into the slots of the frequency locks to allow me to twist and loosen them. This done, I started to search for the coded call letters which would be on the new frequency for me to lock onto. But while searching the dial I caught a North American short-wave station on which a fellow was singing "Saturday Night is the Loneliest Night of the Week." Leaving the spot to continue searching was not easy. It may have been a nightclub. I imagined safe, happy people in clean clothes, and couples in the warmth and soft light actually touching one another. I looked at my little calendar. It was indeed Saturday night — still Saturday night, that is, in North America. But I broke away, tightened down onto the new frequency, and returned to the reality of the dark damp night and to the growl of distant killing.

At daybreak, because of the North Shore's position now on the far edge of the forest, the FOO could see targets out on the open land ahead, so the line was used for two or three days. Their consolidation on that evening of March 3 had meant that the right flank of the gap, the Balbergerwald, had finally been cleared.

But not quite soon enough to lessen the effect of more blunders.

On the day before, March 2, Simonds ordered still another of those tragic, bloody attempts to break out at the far end of the gap. Again the enemy was waiting, and still in control of its positions on the attacking Canadian's right flank, a control that Simonds apparently assumed had been crushed, according to plan, by the 8th Brigade. And again, as on the second try on February 28, the lead victims of the blunder were the men of the Lake Superior Regiment, supported by tanks of the Grenadier Guards – a support that turned out to be as useless as before, for the tanks all were either hit or bogged down.

It was now daylight of March 3. The regiment got on its objective but then faced counter-attacks which preceded an unmerciful shelling.

The Rhineland: Part IV

Next came the Algonquin Regiment, which gained a bit more ground, but met the same fate. More of the Algonquins tried and failed to get forward and relieve the carnage. The four tanks that were to support the Algonquins withdrew.

Most of the positions were overrun by 0900 hrs. When the 2nd Division's 5th Brigade arrived on the scene in the early morning of March 4, the German force had withdrawn to be part of the next line of defence, which would be a ring to protect the German army's withdrawal across the Rhine at Wesel. In just this final cannon-fodder effort at the gap — in a series of such efforts which at least one historian likens to the madness of the Charge of the Light Brigade — the result was 268 casualties, 66 men taken prisoner and 14 tanks knocked out.

One account I read of the Algonquin losses in particular makes the ironic observation that in their final battles for the Gap their losses would have been even worse if they had not been short-handed because of the losses they suffered in their earlier battles.[29]

The ring was closing in on Wesel, not so much in accordance with an Allied plan, but with a German plan. There were nine bridges in the vicinity of Wesel, a city on the far side nestled conveniently back in a "U" in the Rhine — the most strategic place for General Schlemm to evacuate his troops from the Rhineland, while at the same time continuing until the last moment, through his talent for tactics, to lure the frustrated Allies into committing seemingly suicidal blunders.

For some time I remained quite ignorant of the war in the sense of examining it in any depth. After all, I was there, and later kept up on what the *Reader's Digest* said about it. What else was there to know? Years later, in my reading for a unit on the war in a Modern History course, I began to look at the more scholarly books, and learned in more detail of events like Moyland Wood, the Hochwald Gap, and Verrières Ridge in France — and of the Dieppe Raid, an especially appalling military blunder, but one which was the responsibility of an earlier and different set of leaders, the key one British. I also learned that some historians were expressing doubt about the

Chapter 11

competence of those who led the Canadians — C.P. Stacey for one, Canada's official military historian.

There is documented evidence that Canadian commanders — in their quarreling, which at times could be called childish — gave Montgomery administrative irritations that he clearly didn't need. It seems fair to wonder how much of this squabbling continued and affected decisions in Operation Veritable's Command Post.[30]

The Americans had now made contact with our front. I have mentioned their thwarted beginning on the Roer. Once loose, however, on February 23, about 14 days behind the original schedule, they had rolled with comparative ease for a time, over hard dry land, perfect tank country. By March 1, their corps on the left reached the Dutch city of Venlo, on the Maas River, and met the British who formed our front on the right. The Americans were now part of the ring.

The British, who took Geldern the next day, had suffered heavily in a recent battle in that sector, losing 14 out of 18 tanks, and having one of their companies of 120 men reduced to 40. The American arrival to take off some of the pressure must have been welcome — a force sweeping up from the south with some 1,400 tanks. Their movement had been slowed abruptly, however, with substantial losses as soon as they ran into the quality of armour and paratroops which Canadians and British had been up against since February 8.

Wissel and Kalkar fell to the British unopposed, but they got stopped about six kilometres from Xanten on March 4. So much for the northern end of the ring for the moment! The British to the south of us on this date were advancing on Sonsbeck, from which the Germans were pulling back to strengthen the ring. Farther south on March 5 and 6, a British force managed in a costly endeavour to seize a strategic ridge near Hamb. On March 4, these troops had had a party of visitors: Commander of the British and Canadian forces General Crerar, British General Horrocks, Prime Minister Churchill, Field Marshal Montgomery and Field Marshal Sir Allen Brooke. At a particular point in their visit, one historian says, they all lined up, under Churchill's request and example, and urinated on what they interpreted to be a segment of the Siegfried Line.

The Rhineland: Part IV

On March 5 those U.S. forces, tank-supported, who were pushing toward the Rhine at the south-east end of the enemy's protective ring were about to learn what it was like to attempt to interfere with the enemy's withdrawal plans. Near the city of Rheinberg, they attacked under the guidance of blinding optimism and misleading military intelligence. One command was reported to have had 50 of its tanks taken out in five minutes. Another lost 41 out of 54.

The catastrophe went on all day and into the evening. One more fantastic dream of a break-through to the Wesel bridges shot! The British and Canadians had had a lot of those dreams, and several were still to come.

On March 6, the men of the 4th Division's 10th Infantry Brigade, those survivors of the Hochwald Gap, were assigned to take Veen, a strongpoint in the enemy's circle of defence. It required four days. The Argyle and Sutherland Highlanders in this effort had a trapped company virtually wiped out. With tank support, the Algonquin and the Lincoln and Welland Regiments attacked next, eventually to succeed and slog on slowly in the direction of Xanten.

After finishing its work in the Balbergerwald in the evening of March 4, the 8th Brigade's fight in the Rhineland was over. The cost was about 100 casualties. The enemy had withdrawn. The Chaudières were out toward Sonsbeck to where they had last advanced. The Queen's Own must have been nearby. The North Shores moved to an abandoned farm just to the east of the forest. Our FOOs did some firing for two or three more days, at targets out toward Xanten, so our lines had to be maintained. We were still receiving harassing fire, and occasionally much more: on March 5 our 78th Battery was heavily shelled, which created a fire that was about to engulf several vehicles. In a daring exploit, a gunner managed to get all the various types of vehicles started and drive them clear of the flames. He was awarded the Military Medal.

On March 7, as we returned to our D-troop gun position, one of our signallers along with the command-post officer and his aid were being evacuated, badly burned. They had attempted, in a mistaken identity of cans, to fill the command-post lamp with gasolene instead

Chapter 11

of oil. All equipment and calculations for the next day's big barrage on Xanten were destroyed. But with a lot of fast scrounging and the work of a new staff, D-troop was ready by morning. We got them a new phone, and set up all their connections again.

This is the first time in the war that I ever felt a twinge of personal loss. I hadn't known the signaller as long as the others of our crew had, but got to know him rather well — through times in the Schelde, in Gent and in the long Nijmegen winter. He had an expression he used when emphasizing caution, especially about booby-traps. "Take 'er cool!" he would say, when we would go to open or shift something we had found in moving into a new position. But on this day caution slipped by all three of them in that little command-post dugout.

With a heavy barrage on March 8 from 0530 to 0700 hrs, using all available artillery, the attack on Xanten began. Our regiment alone that day fired 412 rounds from each of its 24 guns. The infantry of the Canadian 4th Brigade and of a British brigade were assigned to take the city.

In a driving rain they attacked from two directions, with the support of the big Crocodile flame-throwers, and by tanks of the Sherbrooke Fusiliers. Our artillery regiment, and no doubt others, were placed on standby to cross on one of the captured bridges in the event of a break-through. It soon became obvious that there would be no rush to the shoreline. The defenders, under crushing odds that one might think would demoralize them, fought viciously. Just to capture the almost totally destroyed city, the Essex Scottish lost 108 men. The Royal Hamilton Light Infantry, with two company commanders dead and one taken prisoner, lost 134.

The Whitakers mention in Rhineland that a British commander was so impressed by the exceptional resistance of the German force in the city that he saluted the captured defenders as they marched away.

Nevertheless, Simonds kept the break-through dream alive in his mind by considering a point about midway along the closing semi-circle, which faced toward the little village of Alpon. He realized that if the village and its surrounding high land were cleared it would open

The Rhineland: Part lV

a way to the bridges — something which he perhaps thought that the Germans hadn't noticed. As a result of his hastily-conceived orders, an attack, which was considered preposterous by his officers, was begun in the first morning hour of March 9. It resulted in the encirclement and capture of an entire British company by some annoyed Panther tanks and infantry — and no break-through.

As each bridge completed its usefulness in evacuating their troops across the Rhine, the Germans destroyed it. By the morning of March 10 only two of the nine remained. When these two had carried the final Rhineland defenders to the east bank, they too, at dusk that evening, went up in powerful explosions.

The Rhineland campaign was over, a campaign that was to take several days but lasted a month. Earlier that day the North Shores withdrew to an area in the Reichwald, to refit and reorganize for the Rhine crossing. All regiments were assigned some designated spot for the same reason — to lick their wounds and heal, and get ready to cross the Rhine. But it was not to be on those bridges.

During the previous day, we in M3 picked up our line through the now-quiet Balbergerwald and back to the gun-position, stopping occasionally to examine a former enemy position or a knocked-out vehicle that looked promising for loot. Early the next morning, March 10, for the first time since we left our chicken-house on the farm near Nijmegen on January 30, we hooked our packed-up signals trailer onto the carrier. Our regiment's assigned area was a designated section of Kleve. We fell into place in the regimental convoy and headed for that destroyed city, the medieval home of Henry VIII's fourth wife, Anne of Cleves, whom he once referred to in the political incorrectness of the time as the "fat Flanders mare."

Even though the campaign was over, it drizzled that day anyway, through force of habit.

Chapter 11

Photo by Michael M. Dean   National Archives of Canada

The highly-mobile 25-pounder gun, like that of the 5th Field Regiment (above), was the workhorse for the artillery in the campaign to liberate the Netherlands. From farther back, (right) heavy artillery, like this 5.5 in. gun of the 2nd Medium Regiment, took a devastating toll on the dug-in German defenses.

The Rhineland: Part lV

Photo by Colin Campbell   National Archives of Canada

Chapter 11

Photo by Michael M. Dean   National Archives of Canada

The Rhineland: Part lV

Photo by Ken Bell   National Archives of Canada

Throughout the final stages of the war, both troops and civilians had to worry about the ever-present German V-2 rockets like the one (left) that destroyed these buildings in Antwerp. British artillery (above) bombard enemy positions with a 240mm. gun of the 3rd Super Heavy Regiment near Haps, Netherlands.

Chapter 11

Photo by Ken Bell   National Archives of Canada

The Rhineland: Part lV

Photo by Barney J. Gloster   National Archives of Canada

Allied tanks were no match for the better-armour and superior fire-power of the German Panzer (above), which became even more formidable when fitted with an "88" gun. Open terrain made German anti-tank positions difficult to assault, particularly when the Germans' most effective gun, the "88" (left) was part of their defenses.

Chapter 11

Photo by Donald I. Grant   National Archives of Canada

In a land of dykes, canals, flooded lowlands and swollen rivers, improvisation was essential as the Germans retreated. Churchill tanks (above) were fitted with bridges and fagots to cross anti-tank ditches, while larger obstacles, like the Maas River (right), were crossed using floating Bailey Bridges.

The Rhineland: Part lV

Photo by Barney Gloster   National Archives of Canada

Chapter 11

Photo by Donald I. Grant   National Archives of Canada

The Rhineland: Part IV

Photo by Colin Campbell   National Archives of Canada

Members of the North Shore Regiment (above) aboard Alligator tanks wait to go into action near Nijmegan, Netherlands. M-10 self-propelled guns of the 6th Anti-Tank Regiment parade through Knocke, Belgium.

Chapter 11

Photo by Colin Campbell   National Archives of Canada

The Rhineland: Part IV

Photo by Donald I. Grant   National Archives of Canada

Members of the Stormont, Glengarry and Dundas Highlanders (left) cross a Bailey Bridge over the Schip Beek Canal near Bathmen, Netherlands. A raft (above) is made out of a section of bridge and powered by outboard motors to cross land flooded by the German Army to slow the Allied advance.

12

Preparing To Cross

Little was left of the day when our regiment finally growled into Kleve. The distance we covered was a mere 25 kilometres or so. It seemed as though it should have been much more. We covered in a day what had originally taken about 30 days to conquer, instead of the amazing estimates that had been as low as five.

Along the way we saw some of the work that the engineers and service corps of the armed forces were up to — drainage ditches, roads rebuilt, bridges constructed, tanks being salvaged, heavy traffic of supply trucks, freshly-painted signs at all road junctions. The contrast struck me again, as it had that day on the trip back to the shops to pick up our repaired M3. There was a bustle resembling community life and commerce on this land now, a land which, over the previous month, had been subjected day and night to extremely noisy destruction and killing in mud and cold rain.

As they had in the torn countryside, the engineers with their bulldozers had done a fine job on Kleve's main streets. They had filled the craters and cleared the rubble to the side. The house that we got into in the area taken over by 44th Battery was on the edge of the city, and was liveable although damaged. The address was 18 Von Velsenstrasse. After our battery kitchen got set up and ladled out a hot meal, we came back to the house, cleaned some plaster from the floor in one of the rooms and opened our bedrolls. Someone said that the

Preparing To Cross

1st and 5th Canadian Infantry Divisions would be arriving from Italy in a matter of days, which would bring the entire Canadian army on active service together on one front. It would be about three weeks before I would notice any of their shoulder patches; and when I did, I would catch a glimpse of Bud Whitney, a boy from my hometown.

The next day, March 11, orders began to come at us. One of the first was to throw out of all vehicles every bit of equipment that was not army issue and designated for that vehicle. Also, vehicles were to be thoroughly cleaned inside and out over the next three or four days, with every bit of dried mud removed, even from the undercarriage and from the links of tracked vehicles. Some vehicles needed to be repaired, to be painted and have their identification markings touched up. There would be an inspection to ensure compliance. The cleaning-out process was painful, but it did make sense. Every vehicle was loaded with dirt and also with loot of some kind, from souvenirs to various amenities carried to make army life more bearable: pots and pans, sofa cushions, chairs, a small wood-stove and a couple of lengths of pipe in one case, bed-rolls of immense proportions, usually because they contained "liberated" material.

M3 gave up its big post-mounted binocular, which we had taken from an 88 in the Reichwald. I gladly threw out the heavy climbing spurs that Shaw had the rear work-shop make for me back in our winter days in the Nijmegen Salient. From our experience there, I kept saying that we could do a better job of stringing line if one of us was equipped with spurs. In the Salient the number of trees and poles along roads allowed us to string lines, for their better protection, as high as possible, using the jointed pole supplied to us. I volunteered to be the spur-wearer, and actually imagined that I would be able to climb. So Shaw requisitioned them. The whole idea was ridiculous, much to my embarrassment. First of all the shop-manufactured spurs were a heavy, crude affair that were painful to wear. And second, I learned quickly that I couldn't climb even if the spurs had been perfect. A couple of metres from the ground and I was hanging on desperately with both hands, and no way of handling the wire unless with

Chapter 12

my teeth. It was embarrassing, and the crew wrung everything they could from it at my expense.

We shrunk our bedrolls down by removing pillaged mattresses, pillows, afghans and the like. The weather was getting warmer, anyway. Our discard pile apparently impressed the battery officer in his cursory glance at M3. We passed. I eventually put our head of cheese back under the seat on the radio side. We had removed it in case the inspection was detailed. It was shaped like a slightly squashed-down version of a volleyball. I've forgotten, but suspect that it came out of the rubble of some flattened house in the Schelde. When we were pressed for time and hungry, I would lift it onto my lap, peel back the cloth and cut off a slab for each of us with a German jackboot dagger-like knife that was kept beside it. I still have the knife as a souvenir. The cheese is all gone, though. Handling a cheese slab while we were on the run was easier than trying to get into an unlabelled, guess-the-contents can from the compo box. We invariably had some of those circular hardtack biscuits in the carrier as well, but it took an inordinate amount of saliva to subdue them. A prolonged dunking in tea was best to weaken their resistance. I seem to remember the word "McCormick" engraved in them.

Also sometime later we strapped back onto the front of the carrier the German assault rifle, MP-44, which we had found early in the campaign. It and the German Schmeisser, the MP-40, which Whittington carried, were possibly the best of their kind in the war. Certainly our infantry thought so. After the war, some early Russian-front Wehrmacht survivors told me of a Russian gun that they considered to be the best. Years later, I learned that what they were referring to was the Kalashnikov, or AK-47, the most famous automatic rifle in the world yet today. And I also learned that the German MP-44, coming out later in the war, was modelled after it. In the Balbergerwald, some men of the English division on our right came along behind our 8th Brigade lines one night looking for MP-44 ammunition in abandoned enemy dugouts and trenches. Each of them carried a round as a sample, and they were asking us if we had seen any. Obviously these English infantry were using the weapon — a good life-saving choice

Preparing To Cross

when considering their official alternatives, which were no doubt the Sten gun and the awkward bolt-action Lee- Enfield rifle, which should be issued only to trained snipers.

It surprised me to learn sometime later that Major Tilston had carried a Lee-Enfield into the Hochwald battle in which he won the Victoria Cross. In leading and directing his men, most of whom were armed with the rifle, he may have carried it for the psychological effect.

For our own MP-44 we had two or three spare magazines full and a bit extra, and hoped we would never need more. Besides possibly tangling with a patrol, we had the fear that sooner or later we would be caught up in an enemy counterattack, which might successfully break through. Counter-attacks were common shortly after the North Shores or any regiment had successfully advanced and were trying to dig in. Shaw kept us conscious of the threat and was aware of the limitations of our Sten guns and our belt-fed Browning which was prone to jamming on practice shoots. If we survived, we felt, it would possibly be due to our leather bag of hand-grenades and our German weapons. But fortunately our firepower never had to be used.

The discussion of weapons and their killing efficiency is hardly a civilized topic. But when even the most peaceful country is driven to war, it owes its soldiers the best weapons possible — surely equivalent to the enemy's — if it wishes to minimize its casualties. It is not enough to say that war is not our business, so we will just put some stuff together to get it over with. It doesn't work that way.

The Allies would not have had time to copy something like the AK-47 or MP-44. Perhaps our heavy and more awkward Bren gun was the nearest equivalent, which worked well except when it got wet — not a serious handicap in the Sahara, but it was in the Rhineland. There seems to be little excuse, though, for not observing the merits of the Schmeisser, MP-40, inasmuch as it was designed in 1938. It weighed less than five kilograms, used standard 9 mm ammunition, was highly reliable and would fire 500 rounds a minute — a bit wasteful, some said, because it was almost impossible to get just a single shot away, as I found when practising with Whittington's, but there

Chapter 12

was always plenty of that calibre of shell around, and plenty of spare magazines. The weapon, as one officer expressed it, "was a prize."

For something equivalent, the Americans (and, for awhile, Meyers, our OP carrier driver) had their Thompson submachine-gun, with its overkill .45 calibre shell; but the Canadians and British clung to the Sten, the "plumber's nightmare, with its tendency to jam or to fire on its own and kill whenever given a sudden jolt — as in the case mentioned earlier of the soldier who jumped from the back of a truck. It was referred to as "Hitler's secret weapon" (as was the Harley-Davidson motorcycle, because it killed so many Canadians — an outcome, however, that was not the fault of the machine). Early models of the Sten had no safety; but later a sliding pin was incorporated into the cocking handle, which held the block from moving whenever it was pushed in. Mine had one.

War histories are full of evidence against the gun. A lieutenant on patrol sees two Germans. He badly wants them for interrogation but his Sten jams. The noise he makes trying to free it spooks them. One of them fires and barely misses him. In the Balbergerwald the motion of a North Shore man tripping over a root causes his Sten to fire, which leads those up ahead of him to believe they have been cut off. A lieutenant, suddenly having to drop down to fire on advancing Germans, has the weapon jam on him. In the disastrous Arnhem battle, a brigadier's Sten accidentally fires and almost shoots General Robert Urquhart, Commander of the British 1st Airborne Division. In 1942, Britain parachutes in two Czech agents — with a Sten gun, unbelievably, and some hand grenades — to assassinate Heydrich. He almost gets away because the Sten jams, but by luck a hand grenade wounds him, and he died later. And on the stories go.

From literature in 1953, I was more than surprised to find that Canada was still issuing the Sten gun to soldiers who were then in Korea. This was inexcusable. Even the Russians apparently issued the Schmeisser after the war, for I have a picture of a Russian soldier on duty carrying one. I also have a picture of a Norwegian soldier in NATO with one. Yet here were our men in Korea with the Sten — and still complaining about its jamming caused by a poor shell-ejection

Preparing To Cross

mechanism, and about its tendency to fire on its own. A sergeant of the Princes Patricia's Canadian Light Infantry (PPCLI) in that conflict wrote an account about his companion losing his footing in the dark and dropping his Sten. It not only fired one round, but on the ground it chattered itself into a spin from the action of the recoil and fired all the 30 rounds in its magazine as it revolved — and never hit either of them, the sergeant believes, because of the agile dance that the two of them performed during the action. Comedy and tragedy's thin separation again, war's specialty in drama!

The "Humour Hunt" column in the Legion magazine collected accounts of what soldiers found to be better uses for the Sten: the magazine catch made a great opener of beer bottles; the return spring housing cap served as a rum ration measure. The barrel, however, is credited with supplying the most beneficial service. The men of a particular unit in North Africa used it like a straw to suck wine through the small aperture in the top of immense vats of the nectar in some storage facility that they came upon. Possibly as the level dropped, their enthusiasm or inebriation caused them to let a few barrels get away and sink to the bottom. Whatever the reason, it caused a replacement problem for their quartermaster.

After finding the Schmeisser, I don't know what Whittington did with his detested Sten, but it all became academic after he received word on the morning of March 13 that he was going home on compassionate leave. He was to pack up within the hour, for there was a truck he could catch out at that time. His mother was seriously ill, and only his wife, busy enough with their child, was at home to take care of her. We hardly had time to say goodbye, but we made the inevitable promises to write one another. He thought for a moment about taking his Schmeisser home for a souvenir, hidden in various parts throughout his gear. But he worried that he could be jailed for awhile or sent back if he were caught, so he left it with us. He was overjoyed to get out of the war, as we all would have been, I think, except perhaps Shaw. Another signaller would be assigned to the crew eventually.

Our regiment's turn to enjoy the mobile bath came up on that day, too. After the noon meal, trucks took us out to a field at the edge of

Chapter 12

the city where the facility was set up. We must have had a hosing-down, so to speak, since the one in Nijmegen about 40 days ago, but neither Whittington nor I had any recollection of it when we talked after the war of those times. Forty days and 40 nights in the wilderness! Christ's wilderness was at least warmer and drier. It's not that we didn't wash various parts of ourselves on various occasions — and shave, although hardly every day. My feet were wet for a lot of the time. With a pair of dry or nearly-dry socks to alternate, I would peel off the wet ones, slosh them in a water-hole, wring and hang them against the warm motor-cover that formed the left side of my place in the carrier. Rather than try this procedure with my supply of cotton long-johns, I threw the most distressing of them away at intervals, overdue intervals. In our house in Kleve I laundered the rest and strung them up in a room to dry.

In the clear sky of this March 13, we saw our first ME-262, the new German jet fighter, the world's first jet plane in operational flight. Before our uncomprehending eyes was a sample of how warfare and world travel were about to change. Its speed confused us as we gaped skyward, trying to find it by the rushing sound of its engines, which it was well ahead of. When we did spot it, we were then sure that there were two of them: the one we could see and the one making that noise farther back. There were no anti-aircraft guns nearby. Eventually the pilot made a couple of low-level passes over us, across the area — to take pictures of our build-up, we assumed. He throttled back a bit to do this, which gave us a clear but fleeting view of the machine, as we stood with our mouths open in that field after our shower.

At the approach of a number of Spitfires, the jet banked and took off with a speed that had us gasp, a speed that made the plane appear to be arching down — the curvature of the earth — as he quickly disappeared. The Spitfires followed. In what seemed like only a few seconds the jet came back from another direction and continued his picture-taking runs. The Spitfires returned. Again he was gone. This time one Spitfire, high and circling, stayed behind. We waited tensely. Before even the sight or sound of the jet's return came a burst of gunfire high above, then a fleeting view of the machine as it disappeared

Preparing To Cross

again. Who shot at whom? Seconds later there was no question. The Spitfire nosed down, trailing black smoke behind. Several of us were repeating quietly, "Get out! Get out!" There was no parachute. He crashed a short distance away, almost straight in. If the fight continued, it was in some other area. We piled into the trucks and headed back.

I read years later that the ME-262's first appearance in action was indeed in the fight for the Rhineland, but not on our front. A number of them had struck first at the Americans on or about February 23, as they crossed the Roer River and began their advance north toward us.

By coincidence, on the same day, sometime before midnight, we got a brief glimpse of another of the Germans' revolutionary planes. It was a cloudless night, but I don't remember a moon. Shaw and I were out on the street by M3 in front of our house. Perhaps we had the 19-set on, searching the dial for news from the outside world before we bedded down. One of us noticed a pinpoint of light high in the sky and coming toward us. A plane on fire? We couldn't hear anything. It soon became obvious that it was moving far too fast for that. I suggested a shooting star. When almost over us it made a wide turn and started back. Shaw, in one of his rare moments of humour, said that not many shooting stars do that. At the moment of the turn we learned that the fire was flying out of the back end of something. For a couple of seconds it was possible to see a blunt-winged object, and then it was gone at an impressive speed. It was not a V-1; we were well aware of its sound. We must have been given a momentary glance at the ME-163, a product of the Germans' advanced rocket science, the V-1 and V-2 being other manifestations.

At around 0600 hrs the next morning, one of our men committed suicide. He got into a deep trench, lay face down on a hand grenade and pulled the pin. The trench was not all that far from our house, but none of us heard the explosion, or else paid no attention. His body and the earth must have muffled the sound. And it was not as though Kleve was a quiet resort; German heavy guns on the far side of the Rhine were routinely dropping rounds into the city. The fellow was a battery supply-truck driver. The day before, he had hit a dispatch rider

Chapter 12

whom he assumed he had killed. It was apparently troubling him deeply. His friends said he couldn't sleep and had been moving around in the night. He was never to know that the dispatch rider lived.

Sometime in the first several days of our stay, our entire regiment (and probably all units that hadn't recently been taken care of) was issued with fresh uniforms, blankets, socks and, if need be, shoes. Also issued to everyone was a bright new array of shoulder patches which, in accordance with military regulations, were to be sewn in place on our new tunics. For any such work, all soldiers in their first day in the army were issued with what was commonly called a "housewife" — a little tie-string bundle of needles and thread, safety pins, some sort of cutting instrument and pieces of fabric. I was struck with another of my buoyant ideas: I would find a sewing machine and save us all a lot of crude stitching attempts. Maintaining confidence in my ability to run the machine, or even in finding one, was not helped any by one of the signallers who reminded the others of my spurs caper. Nevertheless I went out hunting early one morning.

It was obvious from the day of our arrival that the citizens of Kleve had to leave most of their belongings behind when evacuated. Several blocks away, after finding many damaged ones, I found a machine untouched. Then I found a big wagon and also a bicycle with tires that were still hard. With the sewing machine loaded in the wagon, and the wagon attached to the bicycle, I pedalled and weaved my way back to 18 Von Velsenstrasse. Ah yes! They laughed when I sat down to play. Through keeping my mothers tread-pedal sewing machine working smoothly and watching her sew and wind bobbins and adjust the tension, I had learned enough to get this purloined instrument working perfectly and to sew on patches over a number of days for what seemed to me to be most of the regiment. But the work had its rewards; the demand was so heavy that I got out of mud-scraping and other jobs similarly distasteful.

By the way, this sewing machine and the others I examined had on them the inscription, "Made in Germany" and also the same information in French. They had been made for export, apparently.

Preparing To Cross

I learned in reading long after the war that the detailed plans for D-Day called for special boxes of uniforms and boots, sufficient to equip all the men of the 3rd Division, to be sealed and marked "V issue." These boxes actually landed with the division in Normandy. They were not to be opened until victory was achieved, so that we would be all shiny to impress the vanquished in our parades, I guess. Perhaps the opening of our regiment's allotment of these boxes there in Kleve instead of on the day of victory was what gave us our new uniforms. It may have been decided that we should sparkle for the historic crossing of the Rhine instead. Or maybe our case was similar to what happened to the North Shores. When their boxes were inspected by their colonel at the regiment's refitting break in the Reichwald, he found they had been looted. Considerably enraged, he ordered that whatever remained was to be issued immediately. The boots had all been traded — replaced with oversized ones to the tune of more than 700 pairs. After trying with little success to give them out to every unit within reach, the load ended up dumped in the woods.

That was not the only snafu with supplies. During our fine spring weather on this refitting break, after those 40 days of punishment, the 3rd Division's winter supply of clothing arrived from Britain: mitts, heavy socks, long underwear (no good to me, anyway, with its wool content), heavier shirts, sweaters, even mufflers. Some of this stuff was designated as coming from the Canadian Red Cross. Consequently, among the troops the institution got a bad name because of the delay. The fault was more apt to have been the army's. The Red Cross would not have been responsible for holding up army winter issue along with its own.

Perhaps other infantry regiments as well had needed supplies badly back in those miserable days of late February. The North Shore men certainly did. An officer at one point said that his platoon looked like a band of gypsies. They were wearing looted items. Some had on German jackboots. Cutting some off the top was a common practice. It made them easier to get into, and yet they were still high enough to take a depth of mud. For warmth, many wore a German-issue rabbit-skin jacket. The fur was on the outside. I wanted one, and didn't know

Chapter 12

until long after that I could easily have had any number; a load of them had been captured and were being issued by the brigade quartermaster, who had more than he knew what to do with. Of course, every soldier on signing up was issued a heavy long overcoat, called a "greatcoat" by the military, as a feature of his basic gear. We recruits in Petawawa wore them while training in winter at temperatures down to -30, but I don't recall their being worn in action. They would weigh a tonne if they got wet. Ours remained packed in the signals trailer. The Germans and Russians in the brutal cold on the Russian front fought in theirs.

I always felt a little guilty, unpatriotic, in thinking that the jacket feature of the German uniform appeared to be more practical than our tunic, which had drawbacks, it seemed to me. Its tightened position at the bottom was below the smallest part of the waist, which meant that it would creep up and separate from the equipment-laden belt which was around it; or, if there were no belt on top, the creeping would expose the large belt loops and belt of the very high-waisted pants, which were usually attempting to sag down. The mess around the waist is obvious from any number of pictures in books on World War II. The butt-length, jacket style avoided these problems, as it did for the American and German soldier, and does for most soldiers in modern armies today.

In this war, we and the British soldier created a sort of jacket arrangement for ourselves by wearing the famous leather jerkin with our equipment belt around it, a widespread practice. It formed a much neater set-up. At one point in the war we on the crew were issued a hooded camouflage covering which pulled over your head and dropped down to jacket length. It was made of cotton and was great when the leather jerkin became too warm in the spring. The Russian army had a similar but heavier pullover which formed the upper part of its uniform and came down to cover the buttocks.

The modern Canadian army today has, I think, a much more sensible uniform design, with its jacket style. The high quality of cloth in our old uniforms, however, was incredible. It took me over 20 years with a lot of rugged physical labour before my two pants were worn out. My diary actually records the day. (One of my tunics, duly identified, is in a war museum in Eefde, near Zutphen, Holland.)

I didn't feel as guilty when thinking ill of our footwear. There is no doubt in my mind that our boots were responsible for a significant number of our casualties — and probably the German's boots did the same for the German army, for they, too, used hobnails and steel heels. To what end? The heavy leather might help slightly against a schu-mine, but surely the steel in the footwear would tear up the victim like shrapnel. Perhaps it helped the morale of those on reviewing stands to hear the pounding rhythmic symbol of their power passing in front of them.[31]

I remember my first distressing experience with this footwear. It was on Princess Street in Kingston shortly after enlisting. On attempting to walk down the street's prominent incline, a group of us novices were slipping and sliding, and actually falling in one or two cases, even though almost completely sober. One could not have blamed the citizens should they have pondered our ability, under this handicap, to defend the country. There is an account of three escaped Canadian prisoners who had to make a getaway over a less desirable route because one of the men had hobnailed boots which were sending off a shower of give-away sparks when travelling over gravel.[32]

For much of the time, soldiers were on cobblestones or other hard surfaces in towns and cities, where their boots were a definite disadvantage. In climbing in and out of carriers or Kangaroos, or in trying to cling to the top of tanks, the steel-to-steel was ridiculous. Even when not in a frightened rush, we often looked clumsy in negotiating any vehicle. We of the carrier crew at least got rid of the hobnails.

Harrison, possibly because he was a driver, had been issued with a pair of higher boots, which eliminated the need for those awkward gaiters. To me, his style of boot appeared as though it would be ideal for everyone, eliminating gaiters entirely. Gaiters would occasionally ride up above the shoe-top, become uncomfortable and require resetting. On the front cover of *Battle of the Reichwald* by Peter Elstob, there is a picture of Canadian soldiers, one of whom has a gaiter in just such a chafing mess. The Canadian army today does use a form

Chapter 12

of higher boot, and certainly with a better composition of sole for gripping. All round, the modern Canadian soldier is much more efficiently attired for the job, from helmet to boots. And I like the alternative peaked cap they have, somewhat similar to a variety used in this war by the Americans and the Germans — much more practical than the tam, or the wedge cap that various troops precariously squeezed onto the side of our heads.

An item we were always short of in M3 was leather gloves. We needed two pairs each so that one soggy pair could be drying near the motor. I only made the mistake once of running along a ditch in the dark, looking for a break in a line by letting it pass through my bare hand. I came to such a painful stop that I thought for a moment a bullet had caught me. I was snagged on a number of fine steel wires that had poked through the insulation. It happened to a cable now and then, and was caused by it's being stretched, perhaps by a tank, but released before all its steel strands broke. The relaxing of the stretch would then protrude the broken ends of steel by a few millimetres, to lie in wait.

We had several days with more free time in them after all equipment was repaired, checked and rechecked.

M3 was now cleaned and ready: plenty of spare tubes — valves, the British called them — for the 19-set; oil changed in the Briggs and Stratton motor; jerry-cans filled with gas. The regiment's 24 guns were all calibrated and checked for accuracy. Our ordnance had nothing to compare with the German 88, but what we had was remarkably well-employed, according to historians who know their artillery. Our rate of accidents — rounds falling short, for instance — was low and our complicated barrage patterns were highly successful. Even the enemy had a compliment to make: General Schlemm referred to the shelling he received in the battle for the Rhineland as "a very impressive technical achievement."[33]

I used these quieter days to catch up on my diary and correspondence. The boys who received cigarettes were anxious to thank the senders, in order to keep the supply coming. As a non-smoker I traded the gifts to me for chocolate bars and also for "green envelopes," so-called for their colour. Each soldier was allotted a limited number of these envelopes, which were labelled "Active Service Army Privilege Envelope." It was to be addressed only to "Base Censor," but would be on its way only if the sender signed his name on the outside under the words, "on my honour the contents of this envelope refer to nothing but private and family affairs." In it the soldier was allowed to seal a maximum of three of his letters, all properly addressed, which then, allegedly anyway, went directly to some central military establishment in Canada where its enclosed letters were subject to censorship before being dropped in the post office. I sent all my letters in that fashion. Correspondence otherwise had to be censored by the senders' immediate officers. Call it a neurotic twitch, but I was uncomfortable with the image of officers giggling as they exchanged aloud our clumsy, semi-literate passages with one another.

I also used these days to indulge my penchant, which I mentioned back in Uedem, for exploring through buildings. Hardly a structure in the city was left whole. Staircases, sometimes reaching up several levels, were often all that remained upright in a building's rubble. The bracing nature of their structure, I suppose, made them stronger. Some of the damage to furniture and other household belongings was obviously not the result of bombing but, rather, that stress-induced compulsion of soldiers to destroy. Most of the looting and smashing would have taken place when the city fell a month earlier. Things dumped out of drawers and cupboards bore signs of having known the rains that soaked us over those weeks. As an example of the wanton aspect of it all, a writer in commenting on the topic mentions that soldiers in Kleve had pushed a piano out through a hole in the wall on the third floor of a building just to see it smash in the street.

I read somewhere of a soldier remarking that "You just had to shoot out a chandelier." He was expressing an underlying feeling that lurked in all of us — the urge, one might say, of fulfilling that once-in-a-lifetime opportunity. Picture it! You're standing there with a gun. Above you a sparkling object, festooned with slim glass crystals is hanging from the ceiling. If shells are landing nearby, it may be tinkling.

Chapter 12

In a war's degenerate book of etiquette, pillage is perhaps graded into levels of unseemliness (killing would have a similar breakdown). Placing wanton destruction at the bottom seems proper. Looting to enhance one's fortune may be next, the stashing of gold and works of art being examples. Next may be looting to give a soldier's primitive living more comfort. Found here are bedding and forms of alcoholic beverages and preserved fruit — and cheese. I like to think, for my own conscience, that looting for souvenirs is somewhere toward the upper end. Surely at the top, in an ironic sort of way, is the pillaging of the enemy's superior weapons, in order to get on with the business of killing and protecting oneself. In this category, somewhere in the Balbergerwald, a North Shore fellow pillaged from a German dugout one of the more strange — and practical, he thought — items of the war: a suit of armour, which the Germans must have been experimenting with. In spite of the extra weight, he is said to have worn pieces of it, for awhile, anyway.

Plans for the Rhine crossing were strictly secret. Officers just shrugged. Heavy traffic of supplies was passing through the city to somewhere. I read many years later that the gradual build-up of supplies hidden along the west bank of the Rhine by the combined Canadian, British and U.S. forces came to about 250,000 tonnes. It was concealed in the smoke, behind the stretches of Rhine dykes. The first twitch in our regiment came on the night of March 21, when its 24 guns began a quiet and cautious move to Wissel, a move drawn out over two days. The stealth was warranted.

Wissel, south-east of Kleve, was about a kilometre from the Rhine. It was a small town, relatively untouched by the war. M3 was told to stay put in Kleve; another regimental signals crew would look after D-troop. Why this arrangement we were not yet told. My diary says that the mail, which came up earlier that day, brought me a box of chocolates from an aunt and uncle, the uncle whose parents I visited in Lympstone, Devonshire.

The whole west bank of the river would have been in clear view of the enemy but for those smoke generators that continued to lay down a screen, which extended along the Allied front for some 60

Preparing To Cross

kilometres. A sergeant of the regiment disappeared into the smokescreen on his motorbike during the move, and was reported as missing, until a notice came from a hospital in England where he ended up after he and his machine had smashed into something. In Wissel, the regiment stayed limbered up and hidden in the narrow streets for some 24 hours. It then moved nearby into its previously, and quietly, surveyed firing positions. German guns on the far bank either heard some movement or did some guessing on March 23, for the regiment received a shelling. Three men went out wounded. Hours later in another shelling, our D-troop gun-mechanic was hit, and rushed out with especially dreadful wounds, we were told.

We heard that the men during their brief Wissel stay had come upon basements stocked with preserves and other food. Today, I wonder whether the citizens had been hastily evacuated across the Rhine earlier, or brusquely ignored by our troops. Except for the more seriously flawed, most of us could be uncaring savages only when things had been abandoned and no citizen was around. We of the M3 crew had a jar or two of preserves stored upright in the corner of our compo box, which were from farmhouse basements that we crawled into on those moves through miserable February. The stuff was ambrosia — and saved us, we contended, from some sort of constipational damage. An army meal is hardly a balanced diet, nor were the ones we created from a compo pack. And, of course, there were those binding slabs off that head of cheese. A seasoned infantryman once remarked that if you are terrified often enough, constipation is not a problem.

On that same day that the regiment got into position, March 23, Shaw got orders that dispatched us to the North Shore Regiment, which was still in the Reichwald where it had gone to refit. One, probably two, of our FOOs were also with them, I believe. We now learned what was going on.

For the Rhine crossing, the North Shore Regiment had been transferred to the 9th Brigade, and M3 was to stay close to relay for our artillery regiment's OPs that would land with the North Shores. I didn't like the sound of that landing part, but felt better after Shaw told

Chapter 12

us that we would be relaying from this side and would cross only after the infantry had shoved some distance back from the shoreline.

Why the strategy called for an extra regiment for the 9th Brigade was something I would never consider at the time. For the initial assault, the brigade may have left one of its own regiments behind for some reason. Whatever the strategy, the North Shores, with a good record, had been picked; and, whether the planners had considered it important or not, our artillery had been working well with them. I had noticed from the early Nijmegen days that the "old-timers," so to speak, among the men of the North Shores and among our OP crew seemed to know one another well. The crew was in the North Shore lines far more often than at our gun positions. That's where Meyers the inquisitive got all his information. And since their days in France, Shaw knew and was known by all among them who, like himself, had managed to stay alive.

Experience comes at you fast in a war; and to increase one's odds of living, it is best to pay attention. With Whittington gone, I with all of my six months in action was beginning to be recognized also as an older fixture, someone expected to be seen dragging in line with Shaw. Before we left Kleve, our signals sergeant gave Shaw his replacement for Whittington. The fellow had been with the regiment longer than I, and had worked in M3 occasionally as relief in the Schelde and in the Nijmegen Salient. But his talent was best confined to command-post signals work and to radio operation, whatever required little physical strength and certainly called for no swift physical motion. Our battery had received replacement signallers from the holding unit; but with what we might be heading into, the sergeant and Shaw apparently decided to go with experience rather than take a chance.

We knew the fellow to be a likeable and co-operative person, important features in any small crew. And he would not be liable to panic, if for no other reason than, as a rule, panic entails some form of fast movement. But shifts on the radio and phone he would handle well, and there would be plenty of those.

Preparing To Cross

For their encampment in the Reichwald, the North Shores had taken over former German living quarters, including dugouts and all the amenities that the departing tenants may have left. Perhaps it had been a unit headquarters. Parts of the area now looked like a furniture sale under a marquis of military tarpaulins. The men had made themselves comfortable with tables, chairs and sofas looted from somewhere. They had apparently been eating well also, for the remnants of a deer were still hanging from a tree. The underground quarters they inherited were well appointed. "Dugout" is a misleading term for the structures that the Germans built in the earth. They were an impressive combination of living quarters and fortifications. The walls as a rule were made of masterfully cribbed, dove-tailed logs. The ceilings were metal sheeting on logs, topped off with a tapered mound of earth more than a metre thick. The quality of their fortifications in general was surely one reason why they could take our horrendous bombardments and come back fighting. Inside one dugout that the North Shores used, the smell of decaying flesh drove them to dig into the roof. They found a body buried in it.

This day, March 23, on which we were sent to the North Shores, would also be the historic day of the Rhine crossing, but not until well into its dark hours.

I imagine that the companies of the regiment moved out of the Reichwald and up to their start line in the evening. My diary mentions only that M3 moved with the regiment's battalion headquarters to an area across from Rees, at which point we crew were on standby with our carrier's 19-set, ready to help with communications — and to be taken across when the bridgehead became reasonably secure.

13

The Rhine Is Crossed

The incredible force set for the attack consisted of eight British, four Canadian and 12 U.S. divisions, along with a British commando brigade and two airborne divisions: one British and one U.S. The initial assault onto the far shore at certain strategic points would be carried out by two of the British and two of the U.S. divisions, with the Canadian 9th Brigade and North Shore Regiment attached to the lead British division, and by the commando brigade whose eventual target was to be the city of Wesel.

Into the bridgeheads established by these men, the rest of the force over a 12-hour period would move, leapfrog through one another and expand onto a wider front. Early in the landings, too, would be an armoured unit with its floating Sherman tanks known as DDs (duplex drive), buoyed by a system of inflated canvass contraptions. More tanks would be floated over on rafts. Then, out of the sky some 12 hours after the initial landing, the two airborne divisions would drop.

The weight poised for this effort was distributed for about 40 kilometres along the river's west bank, with Wesel on the far side being about mid-way. Forming the left half of the line, beginning just north of Rees, were the British and Canadians. The U.S. divisions formed the right half. Distributed on airfields across England and the Allied-occupied portion of the continent were bombers and paratroopers,

The Rhine Is Crossed

loaded and waiting to drop into, and glide into, an area of enemy territory ahead of our advancing ground troops.

In reading today the details of what it took to ready these million-plus men for the attack strains the imagination. The total men in the force from the shoreline back through all the services came to about three million. An enormous force of engineers laboured with such duties as bringing up and having ready all forms of boats for the crossing and all the heavy equipment for constructing bridges as quickly as possible. The Herculean task of planning and getting ready the biggest airborne force ever to fly, including the force amassed for Operation Market-Garden, is a story in itself. In some respects this D-day would not be unlike the one on June 6 the year before. Also, compared to our February 8 launch into the Rhineland a month previous, this invasion launch would be twice the size, because of the American army's presence. And it was about to begin.

Harassing fire came in occasionally, but otherwise this March 23 evening was relatively quiet. The weather was calm and, blessedly, without rain. Then, at 2200 hrs, men and equipment, which had been camouflaged under nets and behind earth embankments in a mist of smoke over that 40-kilometre distance, came alive. Loaded DUKWs growled into life and slithered their way into the water. With their revolving tracks, Buffalos dragged themselves in. Engineers wrestled storm boats to the shore, and helped pushed them off when they were full.

At the moment of launch along the various assault points of the front, a barrage of 5,000 guns opened up with a crash that must have rattled dishes in Berlin. The war, at least on the Western Front, had never known a barrage of this size. And it was all coming down on the far shore where the boats were headed, and on inland strong points. After that horrendous opening explosion, the noise blended into a solid roar. Every gun was firing just as fast as the gunners could reload. The barrage had three times the number of guns that supported the attack on February 8, but this one had a more widely distributed front to obliterate. How anything could possibly survive on that far shore is something of a phenomenon. One might expect that under

Chapter 13

such a pounding and cratering a long section might well break off and move downstream, dissolving into a thick slurry. Survive, however, is what some of the defenders did, although weakened and stunned. And they came back fighting.

With split-second timing, the barrage moved back to let the men come ashore, and then continued to pound just ahead of them as they advanced inland. It is in this sort of close co-operative action on a massive scale that good communications can be seen as vital if there is to be no tragic inadvertent reversals in the artillery's role to support life on one side and bring death and destruction to the other. Messages going through, which M3 would occasionally have to relay, would no doubt concern commands and calculations to avoid such tragedy. I have no diary notes on that night, but my memory tells me that we were not in the midst of those barrage guns as we were on the morning of February 8. We were ahead, near the shoreline, when they opened up.

I have read that because they were with the first group of British to land, the men of the 9th Brigade's Highland Light Infantry of Canada claim to have been the first Canadians to cross the Rhine. The landing was the one near Rees. Another British force crossed near Xanten.

One serious glitch in the crossing was caused by the Evinrude outboard motors used on the storm boats. They offered good evidence of being flawed. Military authorities had been shown beforehand that something was wrong with them. First of all they were hard to start. Then, in mid-stream, they had a tendency to stall, and no amount of cursing would bring them to life again. Like the defective Ross rifles in World War I that were issued to some Canadian soldiers, their purchase had probably been defended for political or economic reasons by some lobbyist or government official. According to the accounts of problems that night, these motors surely must accept no small measure of blame for deaths during the crossing. Boats that drifted off course, while men paddled with whatever was available, made them an easier target.

The Rhine Is Crossed

The 1,600-man commando brigade, crossing near Wesel, was one of the many units that had its enraging and delaying moments with this motor, but it managed nevertheless to land and beat its way to a planned position along the left side, almost behind the city. There, its men waited less than a kilometre back and watched for the city to be destroyed before their eyes. Unlike the planners of Moyland Wood and the Hochwald gap, the generals in charge of this operation accepted that a frontal attack by troops alone on Wesel would be suicidal. So another approach, in keeping with the savagery of war, was devised.

On schedule, the RAF arrived with 250 Lancaster bombers and, with 1,100 tonnes of bombs, turned most of the city into burning, jagged remains. The commandos were fighting in the ruined city by midnight, and by dawn had it mostly secured.

At 0950 hrs that morning, March 24, the all-absorbing barrage, which had been unrelenting, suddenly stopped. It created an eerie effect. I remember it happening in our February 8 barrage — a moment's pause to listen for clues on enemy movement, we were told. This one was lasting much longer. Shaw either knew or deduced the reason: paratroops were coming. Because of the traditional uncertainty in the landing accuracy of either parachutists or glider troops, all shelling had to stop until they were down, consolidated and their exact positions were known (again the vital role of communications).

Their objective was a large area north-west of Wesel, which had numerous enemy heavy- gun emplacements active in shelling the invading ground troops. Also, over water courses, there were a couple of valuable bridges to be taken and held. In general, the area had a number of strong-points that were deemed best taken from the air, which would be swifter, and help bring about a breakthrough into the interior sooner. To protect these divisions in their air approach, the barrage had been shelling all known machine-gun and anti-aircraft sites, and the RAF had been bombing and rocketing them up to the last minute. The lessons learned at Arnhem were said to have been heeded in the plans for this air operation.

But again, the enemy was underestimated. The moment the German commanders saw that the attacks were focussed on their anti-

Chapter 13

aircraft positions, they knew immediately what was coming and proceeded to bring in ack-ack guns from everywhere possible, eventually ending up with many more than they had at the beginning of the attacks.

We in M3 were not to see this air armada. They were coming in low some 20 kilometres away. We could hear the roar and occasionally see fighter planes to our south, as they would circle and disappear again. They would no doubt be elements of the protective cover, watching for enemy aircraft. A cluster of dignitaries had arrived to watch the show, and were set up for this purpose on a high spot near Xanten. They included Churchill, Montgomery, Eisenhower, Field Marshal Sir Alan Brooke, Generals William Simpson, Lewis Brereton and Matthew Ridgway. Those last two generals were the men responsible for building the air armada that was approaching. Apparently "Bomber" Harris did not come; but, of course the Wesel civilians had been evacuated.

At a little before 1000 hrs the incredible spectacle arrived. It was nine planes wide for five kilometres back -- 14,000 troops up in the sky, in over 4,000 planes and towed gliders, and escorted by a swarm of fighter planes high above. First over their drop zones were the 8,000 British and American paratroopers, including the 1st (and only) Canadian Parachute Battalion, which formed one of the battalions in the British paratroop division. Next came the release and run-in of the gliders.

That the enemy was waiting became quickly and tragically apparent. In the enemy's favour to begin with was the poor visibility over the drop zones and landing zones. Although the day was sunny and calm, the smoke and dust still lingered from earlier bombings and from the smoke screen that had helped the ground troops. Some zones were missed. Gliders came down on one another. But the force of the catastrophe was brought about by the defender's machine-guns and anti-aircraft guns, with their numbers increased and waiting. The slow, lumbering targets were easy to hit and could not shoot back. Gliders, raked with machine-gun fire, landed with cargoes of dead and wounded. One parachutist battalion reported having over a quarter of

The Rhine Is Crossed

its transports shot down. The paratroops that did manage to land in one piece invariably faced fire from a dug-in enemy covering their zone.

Even three hours later, when the paratroops were generally consolidated on their objectives and many of the anti-aircraft guns were put out of action, the enemy could still make air travel dangerous. To deliver supplies, 240 Liberator bombers came in low to make the drop. Flak managed to bring down 15 of them and damage over 100.[34]

Overall, the great air armada that day had almost 3,000 casualties, 1,100 of them dead, many of them shot while they were still in the sky. Ground and air troops linked up several hours later, which meant that the front was consolidated possibly 10 kilometres farther on to the north east, and it had all happened in less than seven hours. The barrage that had stopped at 0950 hrs resumed at 1330 hrs — very much to the relief of ground troops, who were suffering severe counter-attacks, which the Germans were able to launch while they were not being pounded by shells.

There were military leaders at the time and military historians later who questioned whether the value of the airborne venture was worth the price paid in blood.

Supporters of it contend that the cost would have been as terrible had the area been conquered by ground troops, and it certainly would have taken very much longer. The drop is given credit for silencing 90 guns, some as big as 155 millimetres.

Sometime before the midnight of that especially unmerciful March 24 day, Shaw got word that we were to be taken across from a point on the shoreline just north of Rees. Fewer rounds were coming back at that moment, no doubt because of the paratroop success. The silencing of the guns! It was not to last, though. They found more somewhere.

The big door that formed the whole end of a waiting Buffalo dropped down to form a gangplank, and Harrison drove M3 up into the amphibious machine's dark alley of an interior. The crew drew up the door and fastened it. I have no recollection of our getting a "Mae West," or life-preserver, for the crossing, but I do remember undoing

191

Chapter 13

the laces of my shoes so they could be kicked off quickly. I was peering apprehensively over the side, as we nosed into the water. How high would the water come up? As it kept rising, I pictured my pessimism being confirmed: surely a lot of the Rhine is getting in somewhere unnoticed, and this thing is not going to float. But the water stopped rising short of the top. Archimedes Principle on flotation was still holding.

The boat vibrated as the motor revved up so that the buckets on its spinning tracks would scoop us forward. In mid-stream a plane came over quite low, an FW-190 from what we could make out. Whether from lingering smoke or from clouds, the night was quite dark, but we couldn't imagine his not seeing us. We huddled down in that dark steel-sided alley and waited, but he did not come back.

From reading historical accounts today, I assume he was looking for bridge construction, on which he would immediately call down artillery or some other unpleasantness. We needed bridges badly to get heavier armour across and artillery: and, of course, the enemy knew it. Engineers were hard at constructing them, but not here.

The Buffalo crawled up onto land and released us. I am guessing that battalion headquarters of the North Shores had crossed at the same time. In the darkness, our Buffalo loaded something to go back. It may have been a double-decker ambulance Jeep with strapped-down wounded. We moved inland in the dark, following their regiment's carriers, bypassing Rees, which had not yet fallen, judging from the gunfire. We stopped in a field near some abandoned German trenches on the approaches to a place called Speldrop, where the 9th Brigade's Highland Light Infantry were having a tough fight to relieve a unit of the British Black Watch which had gotten itself surrounded. Because mortars were coming down too often for comfort, and because we thought we might be here for awhile, we got into the trenches. They were rough in the bottom, so, during a lull in the shelling, another crew member and I each grabbed a big armful of hay from the remains of a pile -- and exposed a German soldier, who stood up, smiling sheepishly, and turned his palms forward in that shrugging

The Rhine Is Crossed

gesture which in any language means something like: "What can I say?"

One of the infantry boys quickly began to frisk him and took him away, probably to the battalion office for questioning. Others scuffled the hay around, hoping to find a pistol or a Schmeisser. Nothing!

After a startled stare for a couple of seconds over our armsful of hay, we finished conditioning our trench.

Our stop turned out to be short. The North Shores were directed to move on to the approaches of a fortress village named Bienen. The advance to this point had been across a number of farms and through damaged farm buildings. The suffering and death of domestic animals is another unpleasantness of war. We came upon horses standing in a field, while nearby a couple lay dead, ripped open by shrapnel.

As a boy with some knowledge of farm life, I found this strange; for when my grandfather killed a beef or hog, he always had us move the horses to another barn. They became upset at the scent of blood, he claimed.

In a stable, I found a farmer standing behind a bloody gutter. Crumpled in front of him were at least two cows, torn apart and distorted, their heads still locked in stanchions. He looked at me for a moment and then turned away. Their suffering had ceased, so I didn't need to shoot them. A round of artillery had obviously come through the barn.

The civilians in the towns and cities had apparently been evacuated, as in the area of the Rhineland that we had just left. But in that area, livestock must have been removed as well. At least I never saw any in that previous month — nor farmers, either. Inland on this east side of the Rhine, livestock stayed and so did a number of farmers, probably remaining below ground while the war passed over them. But the farmer's families would appear to have been taken to a safer place.

A battle was raging in Bienen. The North Nova Scotia Highlanders of the 9th Brigade were fighting it out with remnants of the 15th Panzer Grenadiers, some of the best soldiers in the business, who were not given to backing up, even though they had next to no

Chapter 13

tanks. The fight came to a stalemate that evening at the far end of the town. Assuming all was secure, Shaw brought us in a street or two.

We knew that in the morning we were to move with the OP carrier and the North Shores, who were scheduled to pass through Bienen, push on toward the town of Millingen and take it. Off duty until then, we got into a cellar of what was left of a house on the street, tucked the carrier against the lea side, so to speak, of the ruins, and tried to get some rest through what turned out to be a night that couldn't be less suited for such a purpose. We would have found a place farther back had we known that the Germans were still in the other end of the town and were quite naturally pounding our half at close range with mortars.

Sometime in the early morning, the North Nova's sister regiment, the Highland Light Infantry, attacked the German-held part of Bienen and, after a prolonged struggle, took it. It was one tough town. I have never seen the total cost of taking Bienen, but did read that the North Novas alone had 114 casualties. It was an objective that was to have fallen in a matter of hours the day before. The 15th Panzer Grenadiers didn't agree.

In the meantime in that cellar, it was for me perhaps the longest night of sustained fright of the war. The floor above was scattered with rubble. In our experience with destroyed buildings, we had noticed that their strongest part was invariably the stairwell, so we always tried at least to get our bedrolls underneath it.

It seemed as though everything except the Berchtesgaden bathroom fixtures was coming down on the town that night — including the occasional Moaning Minnie, which can make a person seriously consider never coming up to the surface of the earth again until after the war. On the enemy side our cellar had a small window, which we had banked up with debris before submerging. Some heavy calibre of ordinance at one point hit close on that side and knocked part of our building's wall onto the floor above. The concussion and shrapnel blew out the little window and smashed pieces of stuff against the far wall in a shower of sparks. I was already cowering. It was difficult to cower further.

The Rhine Is Crossed

That was the closest of the night, but other rounds frequently shook the building and propelled more stuff onto the floor above us. Most of the fright was in knowing that if a shell of a reasonable size makes a direct hit on the floor above, none of us may ever pay taxes again. Shelling was a standard routine, of course, in these situations. Each side tries to destroy as much of the supplies and communications as possible and to kill or maim or scare into emotionally crippled uselessness as many people as possible on the other side.

Shaw suspected that because of the intensity, we were closer to the enemy than we realized. In a left-handed sort of way, he saw a bright side to the shelling. "We won't be counter-attacked while it's going on," he said. If it should suddenly stop, he told us that we had better get out and take up positions, with the MP 44 and our other weapons, because a couple of potato-mashers, German stick grenades, dropped in here would have something of the direct hit's effect.

In digging around in a remote section where civilians had piled belongings they apparently had to leave behind, I uncovered a box of preserves and a couple of bottles of some sort of libation, probably a homemade wine. We quickly recognized its ability to take the edge off the shelling. A North Shore infantryman, having no doubt spotted our carrier from his own trench or cellar, slid down in with us. He had visited us in other basements back in the Rhineland.

I remembered the measured and unusually couth way he used to ask the question. It went something like: "Have you fellows found anything that I might like to experience?" I remember, too, that he was a North American Indian — and of few words, like the other Indians I met in the army.

We took the beverage in intermittent swigs. On the preserved fruit, however, we gorged ourselves as usual. The taste of those half-peaches, half-pears, whole plums, fished out of the liquid with our big army-issue spoon — or speared out, as Harrison did with his stiletto — was a revitalizing experience. Our meagre supply in the carrier had been exhausted for a time.

We were bone tired — so tired that we did manage a kind of collapsed sleep in short stretches. As for bowel and bladder movements,

Chapter 13

Harrison spoke for all of us when he said something like: "I'm sure as hell not going outside." We agreed on the corner with the drain hole. With the threatening distractions from above, the deterioration of the small cellar's air quality was of no great concern.

With the morning's light, after the HLI's success and the German withdrawal toward Millingen, there was a decided drop in the ordinance coming in, at least until the enemy could get his guns set up again. So, with Bienen subdued, there was time to look around.

My main looting quest through stores was for long cotton underwear. No luck! But while indulging my penchant for simply prowling through abandoned buildings, I found another unbroken jar or two of preserves and also a long sword, beautifully engraved on both sides in that entangled German script. I picked it off the living-room wall of a house, made a few silly Errol Flynn gestures and eventually put it on the floor of the carrier on my side. At the end of the war, in order to get it into a package to ship it home, I broke it in two, discarding the broken-off part — an act of wanton looting and destruction not easily understood in more rational times.

It was now noon of March 26. The North Shores moved through the badly scarred town to the far edge, to begin the push toward Millingen and capture it. M3 and the OP carrier moved up with them. Shaw had Harrison pull into a protected spot about a block back from the OP carrier. Shaw said we should keep apart to help the odds on at least one radio — and crew — staying alive. The carrier had rubble in it that morning but had survived. We had piled up stuff to protect the radio.

With their men now clear the German OPs were at work, looking for good targets. One such target was a troop of tanks, which had come up the street past us at mid-day and stopped at the town's edge, right in the midst of the infantry. About as long as it would take a German FOO to send back the reference, a couple of ranging rounds came in. The colonel of the North Shores, John Rowley, ran out to the lead tank to tell them to get out of his regiment's position because they were drawing fire. A mortar round landed quite close and killed him. Someone in our OP crew saw it happen, and I have a recollection of

The Rhine Is Crossed

his saying that the colonel had climbed up on the tank. Tanks, at least some of them, had a phone on the outside to talk to the commander. Maybe this one didn't work. The colonel was well-liked by his men. They were a subdued bunch when food arrived from the kitchen a bit later. We ate with them. Some said that, for the rank he held, he took too many chances. He was the one at Keppeln who went along the top of the trenches with his walking staff to encourage his men to move forward.

Under their new leader, a Major J.N. Gordon, the North Shores advanced toward Millingen, which was possibly two kilometres away. They came in behind a heavy advancing barrage, which was coming from our Regiment and others. Smoke was put down on both flanks of the attack for some strategic reason. The closer the men can follow a barrage, the safer they are from the enemy, but they can overdo it. Four of them got in too close and went out with shrapnel wounds.

As the attack advanced, we too moved along, trying to stay in less exposed areas while listening on the radio. From it we learned that on the left a Tiger tank had been spotted in a barnyard. That gave us pause. If he eventually sees us, we're dead. He had been firing. Two Shermans were hit. But he was in some sort of trouble. A number of its crew were out and feeding things underneath the tracks. He seemed to be bogged down.

As the infantry got closer the crew took off to their own lines, and our infantry moved on. The tank was out of action, our radio told us. In a pitch of curiosity we advanced quickly with the carrier, passing the two Shermans that he had hit. Near the farm I leaped out excitedly with my pistol drawn like a B-Western cowboy, ran into the barnyard, climbed up onto the tipped, bogged monster and got down inside. I couldn't imagine that they had had time to set booby-traps. The motor was off, but the radio was still on. I snuggled into the earphones and raved insanely out over the German airways. The response was never more than "Roger," but the pronunciation was always with an "o" as in bolt.

Harrison tried to start the motor but there was some catch. We got out and left smartly with our own little machine after realizing that a

Chapter 13

Typhoon might have been told about the tank, but had received no cancel order. To us there seemed to be nothing wrong with the beast. The tank commander had obviously been no farmer. It appeared that he lost his machine by running over the remains of a manure pile which, with the heavy spring rains, had become a deep soggy pit underneath. He ran out of time — and possibly killing ability if the pitch of the tank made it so he couldn't lower that big gun far enough. The humiliation!

Millingen was secure by late afternoon, certainly more quickly than Bienen was; but besides artillery, the attack had the support of Typhoons with their rockets and also a number of tanks from a British unit. Sporadic street-fighting went on for awhile, because of holdouts in some of the buildings. I heard a Millingen anecdote sometime later about the North Shore officer who came around a corner and saw a couple of Germans up the street. He thought they were stragglers from a number who had surrendered earlier, so he hollered at them to get moving.

He apparently didn't notice the bazooka, the Panzerfaust, at their feet. He just had time to leap into a doorway after he saw one of them drop to one knee and grab the bazooka. The shell hit and brought down pieces of the wall where the officer had disappeared.

My notes say that about 300 prisoners surrendered to the North Shores on this advance. I got a surprise when I asked a group of them if anyone spoke English. Several did to some extent, but one of them was fluent.

He had lived in Montreal until a couple of years before the war. While in the army of occupation after the war, I was to meet several more from the German armed forces who, in the mid 1930s in the Depression, had returned to Germany from Canada or the United States. Jobs and better working conditions had lured them back.

The British 43rd Division passed through Millingen and headed north. We had a peaceful night, as return shelling was sporadic; but the North Shores sent out patrols into the dark and also into the morning light, trying to determine what the situation was toward Emmerich, their next advance.

The Rhine Is Crossed

Otherwise, March 27 was a day of rest. The infantry fed us and gave us our rum rations. For a touch of bourgeois living, we dragged mattresses into a basement for those two nights and opened our bedrolls on them. If our fruit-loosened bowels should happen to get us up, we would go outside with a shovel, as better classes of people tend to do.

On the morning of March 28, we and the OP crew moved with the infantry quite close to the city of Emmerich, to a little town called Dornick. It was another catastrophe of war. As usual, I prowled through buildings, one of which was a church, badly smashed. Lying along the book ledges of the pews and scattered on the floor in the rubble underneath were little single-fold squares of paper. I put a few of them in my tunic pocket. They were death notices of those from the church's parish who had died in serving their country. Inside, each had a picture of a serviceman, about our age, in uniform, his brief history, name of parents, brothers, sisters, occasionally a wife, date of death.

On the front of each was the biblical quotation: "Der Tod ist das Tor zum Leben": Death is the Door to Life. That's one way of looking at it — a comforting way. Inside the fold, a different biblical selection for each of the fallen had been chosen. I eventually sent home the few in my pocket by way of letter enclosures. One complete notice and half of two more have survived. They are in my WW II scrapbook.

In prowling through a church earlier in the campaign — it may have been in Uedem — I climbed up into the mangled organ loft, with the weird idea that if the organ got its air pressure from a manual pump, maybe one pipe would still be connected and I could put out a single shrieking note, to represent the agony of the wounded city. But nothing worked. We or the enemy had put a shell through the once-disciplined soldier-like columns of organ pipes. They were mangled. No more music! Even with my calloused-over feelings, a bit of symbolism in those dead pipes got through to me. Years later I considered that perhaps the insight of theologians might benefit if they could spend the night among dead bodies in the darkness of such a church torn asunder — not so much in communication with their God as in

Chapter 13

contemplating why humankind sets up its God to give to both sides comforting and insulting explanations for the stopping of so much music.

Church structures certainly had their place in the military of both sides.

When M3 and the OP crew crossed the Rhine, our battery had already established an OP on the west side of the river in a small place across from Emmerich called Warbeyen. Our regiment's history doesn't say what they were observing from, but I would wager it was a church steeple. The history does, however, mention a most unusual condition that this OP observed.

It happened to be positioned so that the FOO was, in effect, observing from behind the German lines, and could see our own troops who were fighting their way forward, toward him. What the FOO had seen was no doubt the troops who took Dornick the day before we moved in. The main duty of that OP was to bring down continual harassing fire on the enemy in the Emmerich area in preparation for an attack on that city.

On this day of our move to Dornick, the Queen's Own and the Chaudières were ferried across the Rhine near Rees and moved left toward Emmerich. The North Shores were transferred back to the 8th Brigade. The three regiments were together again. M3 and the OP crew stayed with the North Shores.

The 7th Brigade had been assigned Emmerich. From attacks on the city yesterday and again today, it was obvious that the enemy had been ordered to hold. The 8th Brigade was to pass through when the city fell; so with the North Shores we moved up close at dusk. We were not going to get in, but were to have ringside seats to a flaming destruction of the city. Every 20 minutes — I timed a few intervals and noted it in my diary — a wave of twin-engine bombers, hour after hour into the night, dumped their load on the city. How many in each formation I don't know, but based on my plane-spotter courses in training, I identified them and jotted them down as B-25s or B-26s. These two makes looked identical except that the B-25 had a double

The Rhine Is Crossed

tail structure. Many of the bombs must have been incendiary; the fires were horrendous.

Through the next day, units of the 7th Brigade struck in force. In support, three artillery regiments (72 guns) pounded the enemy's rear area. It took most of three days to subdue the city. There were parts still holding out when we moved in with the North Shores during the afternoon of March 30. The Queen's Own and the Chaudières moved on to the north-west along the Rhine's east bank, to occupy the town of Hüthum.

Emmerich, wherever we looked, was scarred and charred. Ugly smoke oozed out of building skeletons. Here and there a muffled explosion told of another can of something flammable that the heat had reached. M3 was cautiously snooping through the city. At one point Harrison eased by the parked OP crew and nosed the carrier cautiously through the rubble to the end of the street. It looked out into an open area. I had just jumped out of the carrier for some reason. In the middle of the area, possibly 40 or 50 metres ahead, was a huge storage tank, the kind that appears to be suspended part-way in a pit, and no doubt held a form of gas. Something was burning beside it.

Understandably, no one was in sight. While Harrison was slamming into reverse, and the danger was dawning on me as well, the tank exploded before my eyes, with a flash and a rush of searing heat which drove me down or knocked me down to the cobblestones. I remember those swirling steel plates high in the air, as I tumbled myself into the shelter of a doorway. Any one of them could make a messy attempt at slicing a person in two.

Other debris thrown up by the explosion was coming down first. I could hear someone shout a couple of times, "I'm hit!" The other signaller in our crew was in the carrier, crouched down, with a piece of red clay tile from a roof lying in the centre of his back. Shaw picked it off gently. His tunic was not torn. Other than having a badly-bruised sore spot, he was alright.

I felt strange for awhile, but was soon back prowling around. I was so taken by the clean, attractive shower and washroom area underground in a synthetic-oil plant that I brought in my bedroll and slept

Chapter 13

there that night. It was well within the twisted but unburned plant, so it was not damaged. From what I saw in this factory and in the one in Kleve, I was impressed by how much better the conditions had been here in Germany for factory workers. I have already outlined the deplorable factory conditions under which I had worked before signing up.

Of course, we soldiers knew nothing yet about a different set of conditions and about another body of workers, who were rented out by the SS — tattoo-numbered slave labourers, whose conditions were as a general rule well below those of the domestic animal.

We left Emmerich the next morning, March 31, and headed with the North Shores toward what had been known to be a strongly defended ridge in a wooded area called Hoch Elten, north of the town of Elten. But it no longer was. It had been receiving a concerted artillery beating over the last three or four days that may possibly hold the war's record for the artillery saturation of one small area. All day on March 29 alone, the 72 guns of three artillery regiments fired a simultaneous salvo into the hill every 10 minutes. It was also pounded by those frightening rockets. It has been recorded that the hill received a total of four million rounds. When I read after the war the tragic details of Moyland Wood and Verrières Ridge, I thought of Hoch Elten and wondered if perhaps the Canadian high command did not want another scar on its judgment by again sending men up a hill into machine-guns. So they chose first to level the hill into oblivion. However it was decided, that was about what happened.

We stayed with the North Shores, who with the Queen's Own advanced on the ridge from the east while the Chaudières advanced from the south. The only resistance was from a couple of snipers who had apparently moved back in on the fringes, but they were taken care of by artillery directed by the FOOs. The place was a wasteland, the proverbial moonscape. Some giant animal had gnawed the trees off and spit the pieces around.

It appeared that whatever force had been here had withdrawn into the Netherlands. I don't remember any German surrendering in our area, and can't imagine how he would have survived.

The Rhine Is Crossed

We nestled into some farm buildings that night and, because return fire was sporadic, actually slept above ground for the first time in a fair while, but between protective hay bales just in case. For my taste, dusty loose hay under a bedroll in a barn is infinitely superior to a civilized mattress in a cellar. The smell of dry hay soothed me to sleep in sweet comfort — and with two clear nostrils. Tomorrow we would enter another country.

14

From Emmerich To Zutphen

The Russians would have large and terrible battles yet, but the assault on the Rhine was the last massive effort of the Allies on the Western Front. There was some suffering and dying yet to do ahead of us, but the battles would be smaller and dispersed across various units. The Americans and British, both heading for the Elbe to meet up with the Russians, were each rolling into Germany on their own fronts, the Americans to the south, surrounding the Ruhr, and moving on a front extending from Hannover down to Nuremberg. The British were moving toward Bremen, Hamburg and Laurenburg. Their advances were rapid, without serious losses.

One exception was a startlingly arrogant, self-serving military manoeuvre by General George Patton. He dispatched some 300 men with over 50 vehicles, which included 15 tanks and three SP guns, to travel 100 kilometres into enemy territory, which was off the line of his advance, to make a dramatic rescue of his son-in-law who was in a POW camp. It was a disaster.

The force was essentially wiped out. Only about eight or nine men straggled back days later. The rest were lost — prisoners of war, wounded, dead. Patton's son-in-law and the raid's assigned commander were among the wounded prisoners. What can one expect from a General who once blurted out: "Compared to war, all other

From Emmerich To Zutphen

forms of human endeavour shrink to insignificance. God, how I love it!"?

Patton also put a unit silently across the Rhine on the night of March 22, but like the Remagen Bridge crossing on March 7, the terrain, which military leaders on both sides knew, was not suitable to launch a major invasion force. Patton would know that, too. It would appear that he did it to be able to say that he got across before Montgomery's force 24 hours later.

The Canadian Army was now operating on its own, with its five divisions together for the first time. Its strength also included the 1st Polish Armoured Division and the 49th British Infantry Division. Our job was to clear the remainder of the Netherlands and a section in the peninsula in north Germany that contains the principal cities of Oldenburg, Emden and Wilhelmshaven.

So, to begin this mission, we struck north on the morning of April Fool's Day — which was also Easter, but I never thought of it at the time. We crossed the Dutch-German border somewhere west of a Dutch town with the strange name of 's-Heerenberg, already cleared by the 9th Brigade, and reached a point just north of Beek before stopping. The day was closing down, so we stayed there for the night. It had been a pleasant, leisurely run of under 10 kilometres, with the Dutch enthusiastically waving the recognizance parties in and informing them of the time and direction of the opposition's departure.

The guns of our 13th Field Regiment on this day moved up to the Rhine across from Emmerich, where the British were just finishing the construction of a floating bridge. At dark they started across — nervously, because two planes of what was left of the Luftwaffe showed up but failed to cause any delay.

The recce (reconnaissance) party, which had been taken over at Rees earlier, led the guns through Emmerich and on north, crossing the border close to where we had, finally stopping late in the night in a wooded area near Zeddam, less than five kilometres from where we were, near Beek. There was no harassing fire — and the Germans had laid no mines, the Dutch assured us — so installing a line back to the guns was a leisurely saunter.

205

Chapter 14

The Netherlands has at least four places called Beek; but this one, in Gelderland province, was here beside us on that first day of April, 1945. Unlike the other Beek, south of Nijmegen, I had no notes on it other than that we stopped there overnight, a quiet night. Whether the FOO tried any observing before dark or in the morning, I have no idea. If he did, and followed the standard pattern, he would have used the steeple of that Roman Catholic church in Beek, and Shaw and I might have dragged in a phone line, possibly through the headstones of the church graveyard, generally a place safe from vehicle movement. (Even tanks seem to avoid crashing through tombstones.)

I certainly would have scribbled a lot of notes had I known that a boy, George Miller, from my home town was buried in that cemetery, with seven other crew members of a bomber shot down in 1943. His grave possibly had a marker with his name on it. I wouldn't be paying any attention to graves. Staying out of one was more my concern.[35]

On my 1995 visit to the Netherlands for the 50th anniversary of the war's end, a Dutch couple took me to Beek cemetery. The first in a neat row of eight official military headstones, beautifully attended by the Dutch, marked George's grave. The callous on my feelings about the war was not as secure as I thought. Imagination's twist on war stories, romantic interpretation of accounts — all that was one thing. But this was real, and it got to me. In our late elementary school years he was in the gang of us who used to play hockey on frozen ponds at the north end of the town's cow pasture. Unlike some older kids on the ice, he was not rough with us younger ones. His speech and vocabulary had an edge on his peers, and he did not swear. When we fished for perch in the spring along the elevator breakwater, he was frequently there, catching more than us younger set. He would put up with our hopeful casting of our line close to his. The time would be the mid 1930s. Germany under the Nazi Party was getting stronger, with Western help.[36]

George's bomber, one of 457 on the mission, was shot down on the return from a raid on Essen and crashed onto a road in Beek. Whatever number of people died in Essen that night, 11 more died in Beek: the eight crew members, a Dutch father and his two sons. The

From Emmerich To Zutphen

three Netherlanders are buried near the airmen. George was the only crew member who could be identified; his identification tag managed to stay with him. The bodies were burned beyond recognition. Each was placed in a wooden box by order of the German authorities, who buried them with military honours.[37]

When we continued north on April 2, following the infantry, Kilder was the first hamlet we were waved into by the citizens. Our 13th Field guns deployed and fired from here, the first shots since crossing the border. Our infantry brigade moved forward until within sight of Wehl. The North Shores, the OP carrier and M3 were having it easy, because the next attack, at some point beyond Wehl, would be carried out by the Queen's Own. The Regina Rifles of the 7th Brigade had been assigned Wehl. They attacked on April 1 but were stopped.

They then planned a night attack assisted by tanks to begin at 0400 hrs; but the tanks, it was said, wouldn't participate until daylight. At some point the infantry did advance — and with armoured help, as my diary seems to indicate. Sherman tanks came through our position and stopped ahead of us to confer with an infantry officer before moving on into the town. We then heard a sharp crack of tank or anti-tank fire, and, as we learned later, one of the Shermans got hit. But the town was secured around 0900 hrs on April 2, and the 8th Brigade passed through, except at least for some of the North Shores, who stayed for the night. M3 and the OP carrier stayed with them. On the main street the Sherman was still burning. I eventually learned that three of the crew were cooked in it, but the other two managed to get out.

Some distance north of Wehl, resistance stiffened for the Queen's Own. Our regiment's two OPs with them called down fire on strongpoints. One of these FOOs on his 18-set radio called his carrier to move up. A little sloppy on their map reading, the crew brought the carrier through the infantry lines and into the view of a distant German SP (self-propelled) gun, which got a shot at them while they were moving forward, and another after they wheeled off the road and headed, highly motivated, for the shelter of a nearby building.

Chapter 14

They were lucky that the gun was an SP. Unlike a tank it has a limited traverse, and must turn its whole tank-like structure when a target moves beyond its traverse range. A carrier, highly manoeuvrable, is very small compared to a tank and can do better than 60 kilometres an hour.

The enemy was shelling of the Queen's Own as they advanced and dug in near a destroyed bridge on the Oude IJssel River south of Laag-Keppel, about three or four kilometres north of us. The occasional round was coming back into Wehl as well. It was just getting dark. I must have been assigned to be near the radio, for I started to dig a trench near the carrier. As I was finishing it off at a satisfactory depth, the enemy suddenly got serious with its artillery or mortars. I started to scoop sideways at near panic level, for I had just noticed my stupid location: under the limb of a tree.

A shell can explode if it hits a limb, turning into an airburst and driving shrapnel down, as happened continually in the Reichwald and in other forests. By the time the barrage stopped, my terror-driven effort had torn a big enough hole into the side of the trench to put me back almost out of sight. Although the barrage didn't last long, the occasion was the most scared I had been since Bienen — and it was the only time in the war that I can remember praying because of immediate terror. I didn't deliberately stop to pray, but, while gouging dirt frantically, I beseeched the Lord to get me out of this blunder alive. Being all alone in the trench made a difference, I think. And the fact that I had made a tactical mistake was important, too.

In exchange for my life I didn't promise anything, an omission which no doubt saved me serious anguish later — an anguish, as I once read, that became an emotional problem with the occasional soldier who had pledged reforms in his life that he couldn't possibly keep.[38]

The rest of the night was quiet. In the early morning of April 3, I prowled around but did not look inside the now-cooled shattered tank, subconsciously avoiding it perhaps. Later in the day the Chaudières on their front found a still-intact bridge over the Oude Ijssel River, crossed it and took Laag-Keppel. The North Shores advanced to a

From Emmerich To Zutphen

point near Doesburg, where our OP had a good view of the city. We strung a fire-control line back to our gun position which was now at Achterwehl, about three kilometres west of Wehl. While we were laying the line, a farmer with a container of milk came to the carrier and poured us all a big dipperful. For a moment I was home. It was nectar from heaven. My previous drink of milk may have been at the last training camp in Canada. Then, as though to help in this imaginative transport, parcel number 14 for from my mother was waiting at the gun position.

Eventually the other two infantry regiments followed the North Shores and took up positions overlooking Doesburg. A prepared attack, with artillery targets set, was called off at the last minute, as not being worth the cost, because the town was virtually surrounded, and the force inside was not formidable, according to the Dutch, and would probably surrender. The Chaudières stayed in position, while on April 4 the other two regiments moved beyond the hamlet of Baak toward Zutphen.

Our guns followed north and deployed in a field beside a church in Baak. The regiment did a lot of heavy firing from here on the enemy across the Ijssel River north of Doesburg and also on targets in support of the 9th Brigade which was pushing forward near us. An enemy OP found the location of these guns, and brought down a barrage that broke up some equipment and evacuated three men. It tore the arm off one of them, Sergeant Ike Thompson, and badly crippled a leg. Harassing fire dropped along roads as well. We did a lot of line repair that day.[39]

On April 5, M3 and the OP carrier moved with the North Shores to Almen, about seven kilometres east of Zutphen. They and the Chaudières were to attack Zutphen at two points on the east side, the North Shores to advance into the north part of the city and the Chaudières into the south. The Queen's Own were assigned to take care of some resistance in the area. M3 got stuck with the forward exchange this time as an additional job. With our map we planned out our best routes. A railroad ditch was going to be a help, so we went back to the guns and started forward in it.

Chapter 14

At one point I crossed a garden and was surprised to find many items already up. Back home the frost would be still in the ground. The lettuce was well along. I ate some and then stuffed my mouth full before moving on. Maybe because of our regressed military existence, I was urged to eat it by some instinctive need, which allegedly brings dogs to browse on grass.

We set up the forward exchange in what seemed to be an ideal spot: in an isolated house alongside a railway crossing, which could be easily pinpointed for other line crews. The residents had probably been evacuated but some furniture was still there. We left the new crew member to operate the exchange, which we installed in the living room among comfortable surroundings, with part of a compo pack, a supply of water, a lantern and some gasoline for cooking. We continued to lay line into the early morning, including one for the infantry from the exchange to battalion headquarters, a job for which we got special mention in the history of our regiment. It wasn't for bravery — the night was relatively quiet — but for the sheer bull-work endurance involved.

In this performance Shaw and I eventually had to leave the carrier because of barriers, and proceed on foot. We lifted off a fresh reel, put a stick through it, each grabbed an end and started up the ditch. Shaw told Harrison to go around by the various roads (possibly three times as far), meet us at various crossings and finally at the infantry and the OP location, where we should eventually arrive.

Shaw, throughout our time together in the war, went out on all line installations and line repair sorties that were on foot without the carrier, and alternated between Whittington and me for a partner. After Whittington left, he always picked me to go with him. Even though the odds of a shortened lifespan increased on such occasions, I still felt proud of being picked. I knew what he was up against in choices. Shaw moved fast, with long strides, and did things fast.

The other signals crew member was, to put it euphemistically, more measured in his movements. To me, repair runs out into the thundering darkness were not done as service to king and country but as service to Shaw.

From Emmerich To Zutphen

Those big reels were heavy. It would grind into my glove for a moment and then into Shaw's. The light had now left us. Whoever dropped into a hole or stumbled had the full weight come down on him. We alternated sides to distribute the pain and shred up both gloves equally. When we stopped to get our wind, I would flop down, but Shaw with his 30-calibre carbine would just crouch at the edge of the embankment, listen and try to see what he could in the darkness. Patrols were always a worry. A flash in the distance disturbed the blackness in front now and then, but a fire-like glow in the sky behind us was a puzzle. There had been no shelling or bombing.

With a grin, Shaw mentioned on one stop how I should notice that the reel was getting lighter as the wire ran off. I wasn't noticing much difference, but was determined to stay with him. Someone who had known him in pre-army days in the 44th Battery's home area told me that he was noted for the distance he could cover in the northern Saskatchewan forests with a quarter of poached moose on his back.

It had not been long since this rail line had been used, nor too long since a passenger train or German troop train was stopped along it for a length of time. At a spot where we had to cross the tracks, my free arm was out in front, helping me to carry my share of the weight and crawl up the embankment. At the top, while trying to get to my feet, I ran my gloved hand into a pile of human excrement. Such a substantial pile could only have been from a train toilet. The disturbance of it brought the stench up to standard. The glove was precious to me, but we parted. Its rips and worn holes had reduced its sanitation factor, but there was no shortage of dewy grass for wiping — and wiping. Shaw's amusement with it all completely masked any trace of sympathy.

As I said, it was into the early morning before we completely finished. According to the map, our run along the railway had been about five kilometres. Voraciously we stuffed ourselves with cold food from M3 supplies, including slabs from our head of cheese — all washed down with water.

We then strung our private line tap into a barn to get some sleep before we were off again to follow the attack in at first light. While

211

Chapter 14

we were bedding down, Shaw, listening on the phone, heard a complaint about getting a call through, so he asked our exchange operator why the problem. The fellow answered that he was having trouble making connections onto the exchange in the ditch, but he was alright now. "Why are you and the exchange out in a ditch," Shaw asked. "Because I burned the house down," came the reply. There was our answer to the glow in the sky. Shaw, disgusted, told him he'd better live with it; we were not coming back tonight.

A day or so later, we learned the story. He told it as though some cruel hand of fate was responsible for it all instead of his own suffocating stupidity. He thought it would be nice to have a fire in the fireplace. To hurry things along (after all, there's a war on) he used gasoline.

At 0400 hrs that morning of April 6, the 3rd Division's artillery began a fire-plan that progressed forward in three steps to the edge of Zutphen. The two infantry regiments followed in tight, and attacked into the outskirts the moment the shelling stopped. That was about 0600 hrs. The artillery could give no more heavy barrage support, for most of the city's population of 20,000 was still there. The FOOs, directing one or two guns, worked on pockets of resistance around the perimeter.

Heavy supporting fire for strong points encountered within the city was to be handled by tanks. Dutch intelligence reported that the defending Germans inside had no tanks or anti-tank guns except, perhaps, Panzerfausts — one-shot bazookas. But as it turned out, our tanks could not enter until engineers got them past at least one of the destroyed bridges.

The North Shores attacked into the city at the point where a rail line enters, the rail line that Shaw and I had laboured along the night before. While we were waiting with phone cable some distance back, the leading platoon passed under a road and into a ravine by the tracks, where they were infiltrated by the enemy who rose suddenly out of trenches in their midst and from all sides. Even our FOO got involved.

From Emmerich To Zutphen

With his pistol he shot a German who was wrestling with one of the North Shores. With considerable effort, which involved a North Shore officer who picked up a Bren gun and began firing – "from the hip," as one of the OP crew described it — the ravine was held. We brought in phone contact. Many of the Germans in Zutphen, it was discovered, were from the Hitler Youth, who had been quickly trained and brought into service. By reckless fanaticism they made up a bit of what they lacked in experience.

The first of our dead that Shaw and I came upon when bringing in phone contact was right on the rails just before the road overpass. The I-beam of the bridge above had a scarred concave which must have been caused by one of our barrage rounds that didn't make it over. The fellow may have been caught by the shrapnel that came back from it, but more than likely he was dropped by a shot from the ravine area ahead.

The North Shores decided that to enter the city along this rail line would be too costly. So, the next morning they proceeded south-west along the road that passed over the tracks, a road called Deventerweg, which would lead into the city. Our FOO moved with them while M3 followed behind, stringing out cable. On the 1956 visit I learned the name of that road and of a street or two involved in the fight that day.

The road eventually came to a destroyed bridge, with its pieces lying in the water. The carriers, and tanks that were to give support, could go no farther. The water was actually a preserved part of the moat from the city's medieval times.

A few hours later cameramen must have taken several different shots of this collapsed structure, for I have seen them in three or four different places in books on the war. This was actually the Chaudières entry point. They had crossed earlier and turned left, or south, into their assigned part of the city. The North Shores had now crossed and turned right into theirs. We lifted the reel off M3. Shaw told Harrison to go back and check on the house-burner, pick up another signaller for a crew, look after the line from there to the guns and then come back here to the bridge and wait for us.

Chapter 14

We started across. In the thigh-deep cold water, stuff began to shift under my feet on my side of the reel, and I had a thrashing few moments of frightened scramble to stay upright. I thought that disturbed chunks of cement and I were about to go down a hidden slope. What a touch of irony that would be: a modern soldier in a mechanized army, attacking a medieval city, drowns in the city's moat!

But we wrestled the reel up the other side, turned right along a street called Coehoorn Singel to where it turned left. Some of the infantry at this point were crouched at the corners of houses, which told us that no one was going to make that turn to the left and stay in good health. Another indication were the intermittent bursts down the street from a Schmeisser. The next street over from Coehoorn Singel was held, on this side only, by the North Shores, we learned, and our OP was in one of its houses. We worked our way through shrubs, hedges and fences in the back yards of these houses and entered one of them through a rear door. Under all the windows facing the front on both floors were crouching infantry. On the other side were the Hitler Youth, crouched below windows in buildings along a street that ran off at an angle — their first building at the corner being no more than the width of the street away. In the triangle formed by these streets was a small park, which contained a pond. There may have been trenches in the park.

With the phone line established, we had time to stop, empty our boots, wring out our socks, dry our feet with drapes, curtains or whatever was handy. That's about all you can do unless you are in a place where you can build a fire. You will always dry eventually — and hardly think about the misery of it when faced with more disturbing matters.

Our FOO couldn't call down artillery. We and the enemy were nose-to-nose. And besides, there were to be no barrages within the city. We could only wait until the engineers got armour over the moat. In the meantime, snipers on both sides were taking shots at foreheads that appeared, or were imagined to appear, above windowsills or around corners. The Lee-Enfield's crack when fired in an enclosed room sets one's ears to ringing. One bit of savage excitement was the

From Emmerich To Zutphen

discovery that a German was in a trench along the edge of the road at the intersection at the end of the street. It was assumed empty until someone looking down into it from high up in the end house saw movement. Sniper fire gnawing the edge of his trench — and possibly his image of a hand-grenade coming next — drove the youth to make a run for it. The FOO's aid could see the episode from his position. A few metres into his dash the fellow grabbed a power-line pole and seemed to slump behind it. While the sniper was shouting, "I got him, I got him," his target took off again and made it to a building on his side of the street. The aid, who got a good look at him, said he didn't appear more than 16 or 17 years old.

Just before dusk, engineers managed to get three North Shore flame-throwers, Wasps, over the moat. As Shaw and I had, they came along Coehoorn Singel and stopped before coming under fire at that left turn. By the infantry radio or by our phone, the crews must have been given the layout. Shaw and I got into the house at the end of the block and had a perfect view down into the street, and also a perfect view of their target: the house across the intersection. The lead Wasp nosed out into the open, slewed himself straight and came up the street gathering speed, with the other two following behind. Their machine guns were blazing, and the enemy's fire was sending sparks off the carriers' steel. The first Wasp, and then the other two, let go their stream of flame.

When the fire went through the windows, I actually turned my head for fear of witnessing what I had heard often happens: men coming out in flames and screaming to death in agony. I had been gripped by that nightmarish kind of terror before - as a child when I saw my grandfather and uncle hold down a screeching pig to cut its throat and then watch it stand a few seconds in its draining blood.

But it didn't happen this time, and I had the treasonous feeling of relief. Those defenders must have dashed to the back of the house at the last second — or died instantly. In any case, the Wasps as they withdrew were being fired on from other locations. In the attack, a crew member in the lead carrier caught a bullet and died. Another got creased across the bridge of his nose. The infantry near the intersec-

Chapter 14

tion managed to gain a couple of better positions out of it all; but except for the front of that one flaming building, Hitler's boys were still over there, putting a burst through one of our open windows now and then to make that clear.

Comedy is not something war is noted for. When it happens it is usually in the sense of choosing to laugh rather than to cry — or of trying to keep some measure of sanity. But there are moments.

After night settled in, Smitty the OP signaller, tired of sleeping in dank holes and basements, curled up in a small front room of one of the houses on the street, a room with no infantry in it on watch. It may not have had a window. He was the kind who could remain calm, with a humour that steadied his crew's nerves. I think that's why the FOO chose him. Shaw and I had a room picked at the back, with our tapline and our German phone set up in it.

We were out for awhile because the OP line got cut. Just as we returned, crouching into the hall through the back door, something crashed into the front of the house. We dropped. It was probably a Panzerfaust, the German bazooka, that one of those teenagers, after half a bottle of Schnapps, decided to let go. It apparently struck the wall of the signaller's room, or maybe a window, and scattered debris around. As we straightened up, his door creaked open and he came out, dragging his bedroll with bits and pieces on it.

We threw questions at him: "Are you hurt? Are you OK?" … He ignored us as he shook off his bed, spread it out and began to get back in. Only then did he speak. He looked at us, pointed back to the room and said, "God, it's noisy in there."

By daybreak, April 8, the engineers had a Bailey bridge over the moat and tanks rolled up Coehoorn Singel, through the now quiet intersection, over the adjacent railway crossing and on to the north. The enemy had withdrawn and had set up very effective sniping positions along the edge of the city to the west and north-west. We followed the North Shores west to the rail yards and railway station. Some of the railway buildings here were burning, maybe started by the young retreaters, who were now up ahead, sniping.

From Emmerich To Zutphen

The infantry took a number of casualties. One of their officers was picked off as he crossed the freight yards. I went into the big empty station. Sounds seemed magnified in it. My boots scrunched loudly in the debris on the floor. In a moment of silliness, I went behind the counter and shouted out an announcement through a wicket: "Chicago, Milwaukee and St. Paul! Change for Minneapolis!" It is something remembered from childhood, but I have no idea how or why I had picked it up. It sounded great to me in that station, though.

The infantry's advance into the north corner was plagued with snipers, who would withdraw and then set up again farther back. Shaw and I ducked into the back of a particular building and found the infantry eating apples in a juicy flourish of delight. They pointed down to the basement. It had a big storage room. We followed suit, filling our pockets and keeping our mouths jammed full. Even more so than the preserved stuff, this fruit was ambrosia in a starch-filled world of army fare.

Looking out the basement window, a couple of infantrymen were saying things like: "Look, look! Ten to one this one doesn't make it!" They were talking about civilians, down the street behind us, making a dash across to a building on the other side. One who didn't quite make it was helped through a door. Hitler's boys were shooting from a good distance up the street, but could they not see that they were firing on civilians? And what about our attitude as we watched out that basement window?

A sad number of civilians were killed in Zutphen. Many seemed to be moving about on that day, April 8, taking a chance. I eventually came to realize that April 8 was a Sunday. Church! Mass! That may have been the answer.

The infantry got our OP into a good spot, high up in a warehouse on the north-west edge of the city. It looked out across the Ijssel River flowing by below, and could bring down fire on targets beyond. In the few minutes it took Shaw and I to bring up the extended phone line and approach the warehouse, the enemy had set up again in his new sniping positions out in the dock area of a harbour at the river. Our tanks were in some other part of the city. When the first "swit" of a

Chapter 14

bullet ripped by, we were almost there, probably about three doors back.

We ran off a bunch of slack and left the reel. After watching those civilians, we had been moving quickly whenever in the open, but managed some extra speed now to get us into a doorway. After a quick survey of what path would help our odds, we began running and crouching between obstacles and doorways, each moving separately in uncoordinated patterns.

In attempting to catch us in our dashes, those devoted youth up ahead could not be faulted for lack of effort. Every ricochet and display of sparks increased that fright of having something sear home. After we got there, I hoped that the phone kept working and I would not hear Shaw say: "Let's go!" I have no idea what happened to my pocketsful of apples. I must have dumped them out to be able to move faster. One's priorities and focus can be shifted quickly on such occasions.

Years later, those few short moments were among the experiences that came to mind when reading what John Keegan — an exceptional military historian, it seems to me — had to say about what soldiers feel.

Their main sensation, he thought, was fear. Their main desire was to escape, and their main objective was survival. That's not a bad sketch of those at the sharp end, and occasionally for the likes of Shaw and me back a bit on the taper.

But the line didn't go out. The evening and night were quiet for us, although the FOO hammered away at targets for awhile to the west. The fellows who had been firing at us from the dock area escaped across the Ijssel under darkness.

In the morning, April 9, Zutphen belonged to the Dutch again. We found M3, Harrison and the forward exchange's careless signaller at the bridge. Harrison said that he began to wonder whether we had made it, and was about to report us as missing if we had been any longer in showing up. He and the careless one had packed up the exchange, did some work back at our battery and then, that morning, reeled in line up to the bridge. Our regiment was now firing in sup-

From Emmerich To Zutphen

port of the Queen's Own, who were having trouble with counter-attacks. Two of the crew in a 44th Battery OP who were with them were wounded, we learned later. As we were about to leave the bridge, we saw Prince Bernhardt, surrounded by a swarm of cameras and citizens — for a newspaper spread, no doubt, on the capture of Zutphen.

Chapter 14

Photo by Donald I. Grant   National Archives of Canada

Soldiers of the Third Canadian Infantry Division (above) escort prisoners through Emmerich, Germany. Members of C Company, North Shore Regiment (right), cross the canal near Zutphen, Netherlands.

From Emmerich To Zutphen

Photo by Donald I. Grant   National Archives of Canada

Chapter 14

Photo by Donald I. Grant   National Archives of Canada

View of Emmerich (above) under mortar and Typhoon fire of German positions before Allies enteredthe city March 30, 1945. Members of the Algonquin Regiment (right)heading into battle hitch a ride aboard a Sherman tank of the South Alberta Regiment near Louisendorf, Germany.

From Emmerich To Zutphen

Photo by Harold Aikman National Archives of Canada

Chapter 14

Photo by Barney J. Gloster   National Archives of Canada

From Emmerich To Zutphen

Photo by Colin Campbell   National Archives of Canada

Wet and cold mixed with mud were a constant in the final push into Germany. The Queen's Own Rifles (left) patrol in winter gear near Nijmegan in January (left); members of the Chaudière Regiment (above) slog through the mud along a canal bank near Nijmegan during the push toward Kleve.

Chapter 14

Photo by Donald I. Grant   National Archives of Canada

From Emmerich To Zutphen

Photo by Donald I. Grant   National Archives of Canada

"Crocodile" flame-throwing tanks (above) in Emmerich proved an effective and terrifying weapon in dislodging dug-in troops in street-by-street fighting. Members of the Stormont, Dundas and Glengarry Highlanders aboard a Universal Carrier get a warm welcome passing through Bathmen, Netherlands in April.

Chapter 14

Photo by Daniel Guravich Natioanl Archives of Canada

From Emmerich To Zutphen

Photo by Michael Dean   Natioanl Archives of Canada

Members of the 15th Scottish Regiment (Canada) stand ready to go into battle (above) near Nijmegan. Infantry of the South Saskatchewan Regiment take advantage of some welcome cover at a farmhouse to fire on the enemy near the Oranje Canal, Netherlands, in April.

Chapter 14

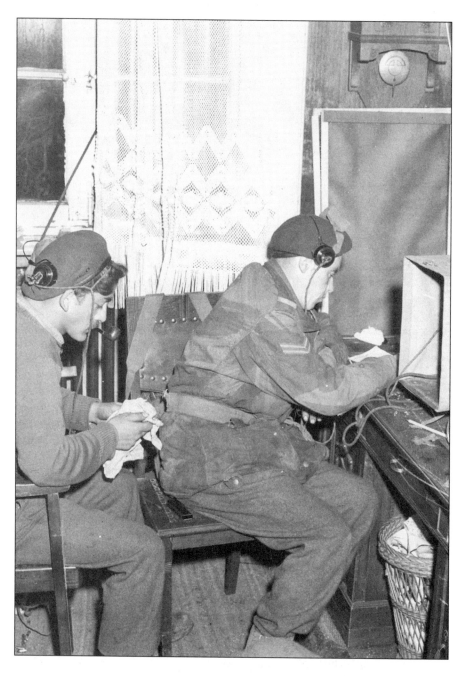

Photo by Charles H. Richer   National Archives of Canada

From Emmerich To Zutphen

Photo by Daniel Guravich   National Archives of Canada

A Universal Carrier (above) makes its way through the streets of Holten, Netherlands amidst a welcoming crowd in April, 1945. Members of a parachute battalion signals platoon (left) find some rare comfort when they set up shop in a German house in Lembeck, Germany, in March, 1945.

15

From Zutphen To Gorredijk

The steel of M3 felt good again. We reeled in the rest of our cable within the city and took up residence in a school. Harrison had brought up our mail. My share of it was the delectable 15th parcel from my mother plus a carton of cigarettes from my Great-Aunt Nellie, through a Cardinal service club. The cigarettes, as I've said, were currency, barter, for me. I went for a walk around the city. Earlier, I had seen a statue of some Englishman. There it was, and still is: to commemorate Sir Philip Sidney. I noted it in my diary, but can't remember what I thought about it at the time.

I checked him out in an encyclopaedia eventually — this commander of English troops who helped the Dutch to free Zutphen from the Spaniards in 1578. Swift runners no doubt looked after communications for that one. A glance at the history of the time shows that the Dutch surely repaid the British. They gave valuable help to Britain in destroying subsequent Armadas — there were at least two more — which came after the first big one in 1588. The Dutch fleet eventually took over the entire sea war with Spain, and was victorious.

Our victory in Zutphen on these three days of April in this much-later war was not without losses. I have never seen the official figures, but the padre, Major Hickey, is quoted in the history of the North Shores as saying that he buried more than 20 men there. The estimated total casualty list jotted in my notes was 80. And the Chaudières may have suffered something equivalent.

From Zutphen To Gorredijk

On April 10, we left Zutphen and joined our regiment about five kilometres to the north, near the little town of Joppe, where it had moved from Baak on April 7. Its guns the next day were firing in support of the 1st Division, which had crossed the Ijssel River and was fighting westward below the Ijssel Meer, as was our 5th Division.

This is the first that we had spent any relaxed time with the men at the guns since we parted in Kleve on March 21. The enemy was retreating north, so all of us were soon on the move again. Deventer had been cleared by another 3rd Division brigade. We moved beyond it to a position below Wezepe on the 12th and on to Heino and then Wijthmen on the 13th. The people of one hamlet after another were joyfully waving us through. However, on the outskirts of Zwolle on the morning of the 14th, citizens were not waving. No one was in sight — a bad sign. Two men of the Chaudières went forward to check. One was killed. The other managed to contact the underground and learn that the Germans were packing up to leave. Before long the Chaudières moved in, receiving a grateful reception from the populace.

We reached a point south-east of Meppel on April 14. It was getting dark. Our guns deployed, ready to fire. Perhaps it was not known yet that Meppel had already been cleared the day before by a couple of platoons of men from the Toronto Scottish Regiment of the 2nd Division, whom the division had sent over to make a check on the security of the left flank of its advance north through central Holland. But citizen contact eventually brought us up to date, which included word that the enemy had withdrawn well to the north. With this known, we all slept above ground through a peaceful night, except for a brief disturbance that I brought upon myself.

Our crew had crawled into a hay mow and bedded down in relative luxury after our rum ration. I was closest to the eave and had squirmed my way into soft comfort and on into oblivion. My next sensation was of being folded up and thrown into some sort of cage with hay. When the dust cleared I could make out long vertical poles arranged like bars. Then it finally got through to me. I had rolled over in the night, dropped through a feeding hole and into a manger below

Chapter 15

(a hole that had been covered with a forkful of hay — a procedure I well knew — to help keep the stable warm). In the Netherlands, mangers were often constructed with spaced poles, tapering into the wall at the bottom to form a V, which held the hay — or whatever happened to come through the hole. Cows would feed through the spaces.

Whenever I told the story in later years, I said that I could see only pairs of eyes all focussed on me on the other side of the bars, which I knew was not an enemy patrol because I had never seen Germans with eyes that wide-set. Later still, I added that three very bright-looking fellows came into the stable with gifts while I was wedged in the manger. Will R. Bird, in his history of the North Shore Regiment, mentions an incident in the Meppel area which seems to show confidence that the enemy was truly well to the north. One of the infantry boys, who got stuck with a shift of guard duty in the night at a small bridge, was approached by an officer and his driver in a Jeep. It was a raw, greatcoat kind of night. The password was "Cold - Hot." The guard, probably feeling miserable, just seemed to stand there in the road, so the driver volunteered, "Cold!" The guard, who simply had to be a Newfoundlander, stepped out of the way and replied, "Yeah, she's a son of a bitch, ain't she, boy?"

One of the notes in my diary at this point is an indication of what I could consider important in the midst of war: "Liberated 3 eggs this morning for breakfast. A feast!" Regardless of how the acquisition is described, the eggs of course were stolen. I had optimistically checked henhouses at every opportunity, through the Rhineland and beyond. The competition was severe. A healthy proportion of those men in the North Shore Regiment were farmers' sons. They knew where eggs came from. I could never suck an egg, but quite a number of them could. The technique had an advantage: one left the henhouse empty-handed, looking innocent.

Battle-scarred Arnhem, which we had bypassed off to our left nearly two weeks earlier, was finally taken on April 14. It contained the "bridge too far" in Operation Market-Garden the previous September. Even this time it took three days of hard fighting.

From Zutphen To Gorredijk

Canadian engineers with their boats and bridges managed to get units of the British 14th Division across the Neder Rhine to the city's south and over the Ijssel River to its east. In house-to-house fighting they were supported by tanks of the 5th Division.

April 15, from the first greying of morning until evening dusk, was a day of a long run to the north, with many stops, better than 50 kilometres, over dry, uncratered roads, across a pleasant landscape that had for the most part escaped the physical destruction of war.

We passed through Steenwijk, Wolvega and Heerenveen, at which point we turned west to Joure, where our regiment's guns took up positions. The 8th Brigade had no contact with the enemy in our movement north this day, but plenty of contact with Dutch citizens.

They cheered in the streets and waved the Dutch flag. Members of the older and more formal generation dressed up in their finest traditional garb and, with flowers in their hands, stood by the side of the road in a silent and beautiful vigil. The day was bright. Colours flashed and swayed as we ran the happy gauntlet from town to town.

There's no denying that the reception had a strong emotional effect on us, which led us to respond in slightly different ways. Some of us waved, some of us just smiled, some of us put on a warrior's demeanor, which held to the serious business we were about. But there is little question that we all felt very important and noble.

We were, it seems, a powerful force in the fearless pursuit of righteousness. Regardless of how strained the idea may have been in reality, it felt good. The conditions and high spirits of these citizens stood in shocking contrast to what their fellow citizens were suffering in the cities in the west Netherlands at that moment — and had been suffering all winter and would continue to suffer for nearly a month yet. They were starving, many literally starving to death. The story of this outrage comes up later.

The 8th Brigade, and most, if not all, the 3rd Division, were now in the province of Friesland. We had crossed into it about eight kilometres north of Steenwijk on the way up. It is the home of prosperous farms and of the famous Holstein breed of cattle — and, according to many of their more southerly countrymen, the home of an "independ-

Chapter 15

ent and stubborn" people known as Frisians. The fact that they have kept to their own dialect over centuries perhaps feeds the reputation.[40]

The Dutch generally seemed tall to us, and the stretch was more noticeable in Friesland. The difference between the average height of Canadian soldiers in World War II and the average Dutch citizen was pronounced, more pronounced, surely, than it would be today. Perhaps the Canadian racial and cultural immigrant mix was an influence. The men of the Chaudière Regiment, for instance, were noticeably shorter. And the Depression diet in the 1930s was not too enlightened about a balance in food groups, especially for those fellows riding the rails in search of work. I have heard the Dutch mention the difference indirectly on more than one occasion, in ways such as: "We were so happy when the Germans left; but we didn't know at first who these little people were who were coming into our village." If these troops happened to be British, the difference would much more pronounced than with Canadians. Because of poor diet and health standards in the lower levels of its citizenry, the British class system in pre-war years had a visible physical aspect. The writer Hans Koning has pointed out that in World War II the difference was so pronounced in the British army that even if all soldiers were standing only in their nightshirts, one could easily separate the officers from the bottom ranks — not only by the enlisted men's shorter stature but by their bad teeth and skin and by their older appearance.

At six feet two inches (187 cm), I was considered unusually tall in the battery, yet I met in that province one or two Frisian girls whom I could look almost straight in the eye — and a good many who were not much shorter. We may be over the silly notion today, but in that era the woman in a match-up was not to be taller than a man. Our movies made sure that she never was — unless it was to be a joke. I commented to a crew member at one point that, in a group of Frisian youth by our carrier, a particular pretty young girl would be quite a beauty when she grew up. "Yeah," he said, in a disapproving tone, "all six feet of her."

It had been an exciting day — in a much more civilized sense; that is, not the excitement of trying to stay alive. We stretched out our

From Zutphen To Gorredijk

bedrolls on the classroom floor of a school in Heerenveen and slept more enjoyably than we had for some time. The war had shut down, it seemed. It was so quiet as to be eerie. The next morning our artillery regiment and the infantry regiments were ordered to operate in a way rarely seen, I was told, outside the text-book and training exercises. Each of our batteries, along with its FOOs and forward line crews for each troop, attached itself to its infantry regiment and broke away with them. Three small fighting units being directed here and there independently!

The Chaudière unit moved on the city of Sneek, but found it already under the control of the Dutch Underground. We with the North Shores and our battery passed through to attack Bolsward, and found the same situation. M3 served as a relay station in Bolsward that night. The next morning, April 17, our unit struck south through Workum to Koudum, where our eight guns deployed to support the North Shore attack on Staveren.

Not a shot was fired. The Germans had gone, by boat, apparently. On the way down a Dutch girl jumped into an infantry carrier and served as a guide, advising on where to be cautious. One of the OP carriers had the same charming fortune. On the way back the North Shores stopped at Eksmorra, to keep a watch on Makkum, which was about four kilometres to the west, on the shore of the Ijssel Meer, and believed to be the last German stronghold in our area.

M3 returned with the 44th Battery to a small place called Schettens on the road from Bolsward to the famous 30-kilometre dyke, the Auflsuitdijke, across the north end of the IJssel Meer. To the army, it was "the Causeway." The day was beautiful — glistening under a bright sky. Our unprotected faces exposed to the sun and damp wind off the water, for several hours over some 40 kilometres down and back, gave a few of us susceptible ones a bad burn. We didn't realize it could happen. A sunburn in April!

The other two fighting units had more success than we did in finding the enemy on that day. Late the day before and on this day, the Chaudières and the 78th Battery, moving south from Sneek, cleared the area down to De Lemmer. The enemy left by boat, but suffered

Chapter 15

casualties from shelling in the meantime. At a blown bridge during this advance, the 78th Battery OP carrier was raked by machine-gun fire from the other side.

The Queen's Own and the 22nd Battery attacked toward the east end of the Causeway. They were soon faced with a roadblock by the enemy that knocked out two of their Bren carriers and killed five men. A sniper picked off another of their men later at Pingjum, on their right flank. The 22nd Battery OP called down fire on the roadblock, but the infantry advanced only a short distance farther. Our three artillery batteries moved up to Schettens and came back under control of regimental headquarters.

On April 18, the 8th Brigade launched an attack on Makkum and the east end of the causeway, following in behind a severe barrage by our regiment, assisted by a battery from the 3rd Canadian Medium Regiment, a troop of tanks from the Sherbrooke Fusiliers, a troop of 17-pounder guns, and two platoons of Cameron Highlanders with 4.2-inch (10.7 cm) mortars.

The enemy was believed to be 200-strong, with very little artillery and no tanks. Our shelling was so heavy that the infantry got unusually close to enemy positions before being seen. Some moved forward by wading in the canals between fields. By dark, both objectives had been taken. A tiny place called Wons near the end of the Causeway was part of the battle scene for the Queen's Own.

Years later, the survivors of the regiment constructed a monument in Wons, which contains the names of every member of the regiment who died in this war — almost 400. They are engraved in bronze. Its wounded numbered 873. Barney Danson was one of them. Years after the war, he became a federal cabinet minister and secretary to Prime Minister Pierre Trudeau. His wound came in France. A piece of shrapnel hit the rim of his helmet, entered his skull, went down behind his eye, the left one I think, blinding it for life, and finally protruded through the roof of his mouth.

Our regiment put down harassing fire on positions farther out on the Causeway after dark; but by midnight it was all over. The few Germans who were out there probably continued on west to leave

From Zutphen To Gorredijk

eventually by boat. The 8th Brigade with its supporting 13th Field Regiment had just fought its last battle on Dutch soil.

North of us to the sea was cleared by the 9th Brigade. Its Highland Light Infantry Regiment experienced some opposition in the city of Harlingen on the coast north of the Causeway, but might have experienced a lot more if so many of the garrison's troops had not been drunk. It depends, I guess, on whether they were ugly or happy drunks. At any rate, 400 surrendered. That's a lot of men. I'd vote for happy. Schettens was our regiment's last deployed position in the Netherlands. The situation there had been unique. Curious citizens moved among the guns. Children inundated the place. When the guns were standing down, they climbed all over them, and were given rides in Jeeps and on motorcycles.

Although war's ironies and contortions offer opportunities for profound thought, it is not a common diversion. But I couldn't avoid a twitch of abstract considerations when I watched a couple of the more daring children, in all their innocence, be allowed to pull the firing lever and send a screaming shell on its mission of death.

For a period of clean-up, maintenance and rest, the 8th Brigade moved to Sneek, and the 13th Field went to a beautiful little town called Gorredijk, about 10 kilometres north-east of Heerenveen. It was April 19. A mobile bath unit and a change of clothes were waiting for us. We were flushed with the rumour that the war might be over for the 3rd Division. The townspeople in a delightful show of warmth billeted us in their homes. Some of the long-term fellows like Shaw or Harrison may have been given a 72-hour pass. Passes were being issued. (Gent is where Shaw would be heading, to see that girl with the beautiful handwriting.) Whatever the reason, my billet partner was not from the crew but was another D-troop driver named Nattrass. He and I lived with a barber and his wife. Their living quarters were at the back and above the shop, which was complete with the candy-cane pole outside.

The tallness of the Dutch did not reflect on their stairs and door clearances, something that had early become obvious to the troops. Stooping to go through a Dutch doorway was not uncommon. The

Chapter 15

stairs leading to our bedroom were steep and narrow. The depth of the step would accommodate possibly half an army boot. After the first clumsy assent, we became more couth and left our boots at the house door, with the shoes of the rest of the household.

Although our bedroom was small, the bed had been built for lankiness. And as in Gent, sleeping between sheets, with no interruptions, was a beautiful experience. I can't remember what they used for lighting, but like most items it must have been tightly rationed, for in the evenings we sat in the half darkness in their living room and talked. Army generators and wire put a light in some of the houses where the officers were billeted, as well as in places where soldiers and civilians were gathering.

I have a vague memory of a dance; but dances were not something I would generally make a note of, because I was always one of the goofs standing along the walls, as afraid of the dance floor in some neurotic way as I was of a mortar in the physical sense. I made up excuses. Never having learned to dance was one of them. Disliking the music was another. Anything but cowardice, which some sweetly call shyness. But girls were invariably along those walls as well, for their own reasons, and I got a charge out of sitting close with the excuse of helping them to improve their English.

The English of our hostess was quite good. Although in thinking about some of her strange phrases years later, I decided that her Dutch-English dictionary had been developed in her own country, without the assistance of English lexicographers. When she was orienting Nattrass and me on the day of our arrival, one of the features she pointed out was the place to "piss." In true Canadian fashion, we two soldiers, although living with a military vernacular so foul-mouthed and degrading that even Caligula would be taking notes, were startled by her using that word — a word that mothers back home might expunge by washing out young mouths with soap and water. But it was no doubt the word, or one of the words, in her dictionary that she innocently found to match the Dutch equivalent.

Their household had a third member, whom the barber introduced as Henk Lippens, their boarder. His English was that of someone who

From Zutphen To Gorredijk

had had a lot of opportunity to speak it. He seemed mysterious to us. I noticed that one leg was slightly crippled, but we could not see his face from where he sat in a corner in the darkness each evening. His questions required a little more thought from us than those usually asked of soldiers of our rank. As we left the house each morning, he was not about.

Like our billets, the community was neat and spotless. On one of those days I borrowed a boat and went rowing on the canal that runs through the town and the countryside. Once clear of the houses and the sound of the excitement that the army's presence had stirred in the children, it became country-quiet. A cow or two giving voice somewhere and a waft of manure now and then gave me thoughts of my grandfather's farm. But there were differences: a wide expanse of fields with no fences, but yet fence gates were visible, standing alone here and there. The canals and connecting ditches that separated fields served as fences. The isolated gates stood at the bridges between fields.

Somewhere in Friesland, possibly on a walk outside, I stood in amazement and watched a boat in the distance coming across farmland. It seemed to be plowing slowly, effortlessly through the earth, coming right up to the edge of the field I was in and then making a turn to strike off in a new direction. The field was enough below dyke-level that I could not see the canal network, but only this boat riding high in the meadows.

At our battery kitchen on the evening of April 20, we were told, to an undercurrent of groans and curses, to be out and ready to roll first thing in the morning. A unit of the 1st Polish Armoured Division had found that tanks were unsuited for their assignment in a section of rain-soaked German soil (familiar-sounding conditions), this time north Germany, and the 8th Brigade was being sent in to relieve it. So much for the dream! We at least had two elysian nights in billets. Grateful Nattras and I left with our host and hostess what remained of our tucked-away store of goodies from home.

Nattrass had gone to the compound for the carrier and parked it in front of the house. Just as I was climbing in, the man who sat in the

Chapter 15

shadows came out and walked the few steps to the carrier. He was short for a Dutchman and older than the barber and his wife, who were already in the street. He handed me a letter and said he would be most pleased if I would deliver it to his sister in Amsterdam after the war. I expressed surprise. We were a long way from Amsterdam and would soon be farther still. I was sure to be there after the war, he said, and much sooner than he. Apparently all postal service had virtually stopped, and there was also a ban on civilian movement because of the fear of an epidemic from the starvation in the west part of the country. I cautioned him that both the letter and I might very well remain in the soil of North Germany. He looked at me hard and said: "I don't think so."

With the war just about over, I was grabbing at anything that might help get me through this last part; so I fantasized that his remark and the letter were a kind of protective shield of some mystical force. I tucked it away in my inner tunic pocket as we bid them good-bye and moved out toward our forming-up area.

I was carrying in my pocket another communication as well. Three days earlier as we were rolling slowly into the town through welcoming lines of people on both sides, a young girl ran alongside the carrier and handed me a little photo of an area in the town, which I still have. It shows the street with the canal. The inscription at the bottom reads "Lange en Brouwerswal," which is the street's name or the name of the area, I presume. She had written on the back:

"Souvenir van [from]
Tina Naula
19-4-45
Gorredijk"

16

Into North Germany

Both our regiment and the weather were sullen. Germany was about 100 kilometres to the east, but the route we were taking would cover about 140km. We came back to Heerenveen, struck north about 30 kilometres to Leeuwarden and then turned east.

Later on in passing through Groningen, it was obvious that the city didn't fall without a fight. Our convoy moved along a street of rubble, with injured buildings and a knocked-out Sherman at an intersection. The city had been taken by units of the 2nd Division on April 16, and suffered 200 casualties in doing so. Whether the troops knew it or not at the time, some of the defenders they were fighting here were Dutch SS. I learned after the war that a hometown friend, Jack Biccum, was in this fight. Jack was either a fast worker on that day, or else at war's end he was stationed or spent leaves there, for he married a girl from Groningen.

Farther on we turned south at the city of Winschoten, which had been cleared earlier by units of the Polish Division. It began to rain. We pulled the tarpaulin over us and fastened it down. I wanted to be aware of crossing the border; so at each hesitation in the convoy I leaned out into the drizzle, looking for clues. It was getting dark. During one of our stops a citizen was walking along the edge of the road. With mostly gestures, I asked him where we were. From a map later, I discovered that the place he was pronouncing and pointing to

Chapter 16

back behind us was a little village called Nieuwe-Pekela. Some 10 kilometres to go, we estimated.

Without being aware of the moment, with no customs stop or ceremony, cold and huddled under a tarpaulin in the drizzle, we crossed the border somewhere near Rhede and took up positions in fields about eight kilometres south of Weener.

It was now dark as well as cold and wet. Sergeant Buswell, dripping in the rain, astride his motorcycle, with his big gauntlets and his DR coat and helmet, gave Shaw new orders. My diary note for that night mentions only how miserable the setting was — not because of enemy shelling; there wasn't any. Shaw and the other crew member must have been assigned to lay a fire-control line, and I was to remain at the gun position. They no doubt found a dry corner in a barn at the OP.

At the gun position there were no basements to get into, no buildings of any kind, no former German dugouts. I remember standing there in that soggy field for a moment in my own DR coat, surrounded in blackness, and wondering where I was going to lie down. The gun crews propped up tarpaulins over the gun breaches and slept in their gun tractors. The command post was probably in the half-track.

I crawled under the tarpaulin of the signals trailer and squirmed into some measure of comfort on top of its cargo. Later, a heavy squall came up and pounded down on the tarpaulin. To experience the hypnotic massage of those thousands of exploding beads of water salvaged at least a bit of a wretched night. For a moment it was startling, and then it put me to sleep. Nevertheless, in pure misery and loneliness, although with no enemy action, that night holds some sort of a record in my memory of war experiences.

Later, I learned about the experience of the North Shores who arrived before us that night and took over from the Poles. Coming in, they passed several farm buildings burning. The only farmhouse in the vicinity not on fire was the one where they met a Polish commander. The Poles had torched them all except this one; he asked the North Shore officers if they, too, would refrain from burning it, because the inhabitants had been good to him, and he had promised to

Into North Germany

leave it standing. Our fumbling forward exchange signaller's house-burning outside Zutphen notwithstanding, the wanton torching of buildings was not a characteristic that Canadians shared with the Poles.

But then, our country had not been savagely overrun, either.

Glad to be relieved, they gave the advance party of the North Shores a quick run-down on conditions and then promptly pulled out before all the relief troops had arrived.

To make matters worse, some of their tanks went forward a short distance, fired off a lot of their ammunition and then took off, waving good-bye. The Polish army had a number of impetuous characteristics that set them apart. The North Shore party went through some moments of anxiety, anticipating a retaliation from an irritated enemy, on a regiment not yet complete. But it didn't happen.

The enemy's main defence line in our section was farther back at a town called Weener, where it was preparing for the morrow.

First light of April 22 revealed the landscape. Several of us in the battery were given the unusual job of escorting a number of farmers to do their chores on the farms that we could now see in the distance around us. Cattle had not been evacuated. There must have been the suspicion that the farmers might be taking messages to a patrol holed up in one of the buildings. Our infantry line, we were told, was only three or four kilometres beyond.

A woman had come into the gun position and asked for permission to return to her farmhouse for some reason. An officer picked me to escort her under guard, and warned me to watch her every move, and also to report back to him — with her, he emphasized. He didn't need to tell me to watch her. I couldn't take my eyes off her, simply because she was female. She looked the officer in the eye, but not me. I felt slighted.

My memory of her is that she was slim, had a kerchief on her head and wore a coat, with some skirt showing below it. She was possibly three or four years older than I, a distance that dissolved as I walked near her, a half-step back so that I could stare. I forgot about my first vision when given the assignment: she shouts something in the house

Chapter 16

and I am suddenly looking down the barrels of a couple of Schmeissers.

The house had been severely ransacked by somebody, possibly a different Polish unit on its way forward, whose men settled for looting like the rest of us instead of burning. After she stood for a moment among scattered and smashed belongings, I saw her begin to sag, and grabbed her before she dropped. I sat her and myself down on a high box-like bench against the wall. She was out cold for a few seconds and her head dropped over on my shoulder. I held onto her and never wanted to let go again for the rest of my life.

Living in crudeness and cruelty suppresses the flip-side of more tender emotions, as it's supposed to. When a sudden flip like this occurs, the effect is strong. At least it was for me.

I could feel her stiffen for a moment when she came to. She straightened up and looked me in the eye briefly as I released my hold. It felt good to be acknowledged as existing. She moved slowly through the house, set a couple of objects upright as a token gesture and then moved out the door, with her head up and no tears.

When we returned to the officer, she looked me in the eye for the second time and quietly said thank you in German. The officer asked me whether she had put anything in her pockets. She hadn't. That was it. Back to killing and destruction!

Later that morning, more of Sergeant Buswell's orders became apparent. I was assigned to D-troop OP as a wireless operator. The OP carrier had made a trip back to the guns at daylight, so I returned with it to the North Shore's position. The calm and cool Smitty may have been sent on leave, which he deserved, for I think he had been on the crew since back in France. I was uneasy about the new job, to put it calmly, but I wasn't going to start wetting myself to get out of it. I know only that I was now up there and scared.

Years later, I learned that the first assignment of the 8th Brigade, supported by all three of the 3rd Divisions' Field Regiments whenever necessary, was to clear the area within the inverted "U" of the Ems River, which stretched out to the north of our present position. It was an area of about 25 by 20 kilometres. The water that would be on our

Into North Germany

left during our advance is actually a big lake-like southerly bulge in the Ems, known as the Dollart, as the river swings westerly to widen into the North Sea.

The 7th Brigade, moving north along the Dutch side of the border on our left, was to advance up to the bottom of the Dollart.

From the number of officers I had come to know in some way, the FOO with whom I was placed was the very one I would have chosen to work under at the OP or anywhere else. Captain Campbell was a bit different — less militarily formal and rank-conscious, and with a straight-faced sense of humour that could include dramatic action, such as reverting occasionally to what would later be called an Art Carney-like sketch when picking up the phone at the OP in more quiet times.

My first OP experience with him as his signaller, on the other hand, was dead serious. The 8th Brigade's three regiments began their attack toward Weener, the target, on that early afternoon of April 23. Fortunately I did not know until later that an OP carrier with the Chaudières on our left was hit shortly after the advance started, killing two of the crew. That would have been all I needed to become incoherent on the radio. The objective of the Queen's Own brought them to within sight of Weener, and the North Shores moved through them to strike at Weener itself. From our OP we could see the edge of town and the regiment's company that was going forward. The area had received artillery barrages in supporting the Queen's Own.

But the defenders were ready again. In a moment the company went to ground, depressing themselves into recesses and ditches. There was a barricade set up where the road went in. From it, machine-gun, MP-44 and Schmeisser fire was practically mowing the grass. The company withdrew, and the FOO called down fire on the barricade and area for 10 minutes.

The intensity and volume was extensive. The whole area seemed to percolate and shake for those minutes, in one staccato of explosions. I must confess that it's a savage, fascinating experience in power, efficiency and accuracy — and death — to be part of those fire

Chapter 16

orders, and then to hear those ordered rounds come over your head and explode on the target right in front of you.

On the next try, the North Shores entered Weener without much trouble. We followed in quite closely with the carrier. After the town was consolidated, more than 100 prisoners marched away to the rear. But the enemy had a lot of dead and wounded that remained. Our infantry took several casualties, who were lying here and there, but were being quickly loaded and strapped down on those ambulance Jeeps by the fast-moving medics with their morphine shots. Quite a number of the enemy's troops in this area were former sailors in the German navy who had been retrained for the Wehrmacht. All their warships and submarines in these harbours in their northern ports were surely never going to sea again.

Their wounded here in Weener were being attended by German female nurses, five or six of them. Where the nurses came from I don't know. The town's citizens had been evacuated. Perhaps they were in a basement shelter. There may have been a hospital nearby. Prisoners brought the wounded to a specified area, and the nurses were moving from one to the other with bandages and needles.

I watched them with the same feelings I had when I escorted the German housewife to her farmhouse, feelings of wanting to draw back to some innocent world, quite remote from violence and destruction. The infantry officers had made the immediate area out of bounds to the troops, but our carrier was parked quite close, and I had an excuse to be with it. Their tender gestures toward their care, and their body movements in those sufficiently form-fitted uniforms, held me fascinated. I hungered for just a glance from one of them, but they ignored me entirely as they swished about.

Some of the infantry boys went a little wild in the town. They may have found a cache of liquor somewhere. Smashing out some storefront windows, they dragged the clothes dummies into the street and danced with them. A part of a dummy dropped off occasionally in the aggressiveness of the dance, but it didn't seem to matter. Some dance partners started out simply as a fragment. That out-of-bounds order for the sake of the nurses was a sound move.

Into North Germany

I didn't dance with it, but I looted my last supply of long cotton underwear from a clothing store in Weener. I still have a section of the waistband of one pair, containing the manufacturer's name and the word "zweifädig," which I interpret as "double-knit." Later, in the army of occupation, I stopped throwing my dirty underwear away and started to use a civilian laundry. It was remarkable how much longer the supply lasted. I brought much of it home with me and wore it for years whenever I put on my army pants for rough undertakings, such as working on my stone wall project.

The advance in this area came up against a couple of new defensive twists. The Germans had blown enormous craters in all strategic spots to deter vehicle movement — holes the like of which we hadn't seen since antitank ditches back in the Rhineland. Prisoners told us that they were made by burying large aeroplane bombs deep down and exploding them electrically with a detonator charge. Some had to be conquered by a section of Bailey bridge. Engineers were busy developing roads around many of them. Filling them in was a slow process.

The other unanticipated feature was the enemy's use of Panzerfausts — the anti-tank, hand-held, one-shot rocket — against our infantry. They would fire them in the air in a very tight arc so that they would land and explode among advancing troops, to scatter splinters of steel for some distance. We first experienced them coming down as we entered Weener, but assumed at the time that they were a mortar with a quieter approach. Some of the infantry casualties were from splinters from them. The enemy was probably low on mortars, but had a lot of these things.

The next day, April 24, the Chaudières on our left captured Bunde, but met their strongest opposition north of the town later. One of their officers, Major C.R. Lamoureux, displayed some outstanding bravery in this operation, and was badly shot up. He was awarded the Distinguished Service Order. Years later he served as Gentleman Usher of the Black Rod in the Senate in Ottawa.

Our regiment's OP with them may have been spotted by its German artillery equivalent, for a well-placed round came in and took

Chapter 16

apart a good measure of the FOO's house, fortunately with no casualties. This reminds me of an incident that Meyers told us about back in the Rhineland.

The FOO and his crew were in the attic of a building and were trying to shut down a machine-gun nest in the low land out front. A wide chimney going up through the house divided the attic. The crew were on one side of it. The FOO's ranging round fell beyond the target. When he dropped 50 yards, the whine of the next round going over was uncomfortably loud, and seemed to be over the house. He made a tighter adjustment and ordered another. This one didn't make it. It caught the ridge on the far side of the chimney, shook up the crew and deafened them for a minute — and let in a lot of sky at that end of the house when the dust settled. An infantryman from down below stuck his head up above the ladder and glowered. The FOO told him it was an enemy round coming back. He wasn't believed, Meyers said.

At the time of the Chaudière's movements, the North Shores were advancing toward Kirchborgum, north of Weener along the Ems. We of D-troop OP were moving with one of their units. The unit that C-troop OP was with suddenly came under fire from what were later determined to be two permanently-mounted 88s, among other things. The men went to ground.

The unit we were serving moved up in a parallel position but apparently could not be seen clearly by those enemy strong points. We worked our way closer with the carrier, protected by a dyke. With his 18-set radio, Campbell and an infantry officer worked forward a few more metres. Because he could see the enemy positions, he asked our D-troop guns to fire red smoke shells on them so that they were clearly marked, and then ask the proper authorities to call the Typhoons.

I must have passed those calculations and orders over the carrier radio, but as always would have no idea what they meant. My concern would be my accuracy and the accuracy of the repeat-back. That the orders weren't for Chinese food is about all I would know.

But the successful and frightening result of the order is still in my memory. The stronghold out in front was in or alongside a building that turned out to be a brick factory. The Typhoons arrived, circled

Into North Germany

overhead and then came in from behind us in a low dive, drawing machine-gun fire from in front. Even my padded earphones came far from closing out the scream of those rockets, which seemed only a couple of metres above our heads, and then the explosions that followed them. How many passes they made, I don't know, but the process seemed endless, and I was frozen in the terror that our end would come quickly if a pilot got sneezing on the way in.

The reputation of Typhoons was that they were devastating and demoralizing for the enemy — but with a troubling inaccuracy on occasion, a feature that made their friends nervous. It was accepted, I have read, that they were too dangerous to be used less than 250 metres ahead. Each plane carried eight rockets, four under each wing. Each rocket contained nearly 28 kg of explosives. As an additional nasty feature, the planes were equipped with 20-mm cannons, which they used coming in, to disturb anti-aircraft fire.

If Campbell factored in that 250-metre guideline, there couldn't have been much slack left. When the last banshee screech and explosion ended, we were dusted over with debris. At least one of those rockets came close to taking us out. I passed a radio message to Campbell: "They want to know whether you would like another round."

His hearing was no doubt just returning. The message didn't seem to register. Then suddenly it did. "No! No!" he shouted. "Definitely not! A fine job!" After I relayed his reply and he was looking ahead with his binoculars, he was still emphasizing the point with comments like: "Turn in your planes! Go on leave! See your girlfriends! Just don't come back!" Certainly they had done their job. The guns had been silenced. The brick factory was a mess. Our infantry moved up and found Kirchborgum no problem.

Somewhere on our advance toward Bingum which was about two kilometres farther north from this "Typhooned" area, Campbell, with his aide and the 18-set portable, went ahead with the advance party of the North Shores, while the driver and I and our conspicuous carrier lagged behind. When all seemed quiet ahead, we moved in a little closer, but were soon raked with machine-gun fire. Fortunately we

Chapter 16

had our heads down. That was my first experience with direct machine-gun stutter gnawing into the steel of the carrier. It is not at all calming. A carrier can take a Spandau calibre of shell but not the bigger stuff that might be next, like 20- or 37-millimetre — or even an 88, which considers carrier-sized vehicles to be similar to fly-swatting. And even if a small calibre gets in and ricochets around inside, the result can be ugly.

There was a barn a short distance to our right, which the infantry had checked on the way forward. Meyers spun us around and took off toward it with all the speed he could get geared up to, which would have been about 38 miles (60 km) an hour if he had time to reach it. The barn was open, so instead of going alongside he went straight in. He slammed on the brakes at the approach, and we went through the opening with the carrier practically standing on its nose. The locked tracks plowed up a lot of barn floor before bringing us to a halt at the far doors. There was a mow with baled hay in it on the enemy side of us. We felt good about that. Tightly packed, it's fine protection when there's enough of it. The machine-gun was somehow silenced, and we were soon moving again.

Our North Shore unit's next attack was on Bingum itself, which fell with little resistance beyond some covering machine-gun fire from a distance as the enemy withdrew. Once consolidated, we had ideal protection behind a dyke — with one little catch: it had an opening in it possibly four metres wide, with steel gains on either side for dropping in logs in times of flooding, no doubt. But it had no logs now. A German machine-gunner out there somewhere was having fun taking a shot at anything that passed by the opening. A North Shore sergeant-major and his driver raced by it instead of leaving the vehicle on the other side of the opening and crouch by in the wet ditch along the road.

The odds on making it were quite high; but, then, odds are all about the distances from certainty. On the way back the Sergeant-major took a round right through his web belt. We heard the shots, saw the driver stop, and then move on to where the medics were. Later, the driver walked back along the safer route — wearing the officer's belt

Into North Germany

with its 9-mm Browning. That's why he had stopped: to get if off before he got to the medics. He showed us the hole in the belt. He would hold the Browning for him, but he felt sure the officer was dead or soon would die. It all seemed rather cold-blooded, which shouldn't be a surprise in a war.

I rode a motorcycle here for the first time, and the only time, in my life. The Germans had to abandon it, apparently without even enough time to throw the distributor cap away. After a booby-trap check, I fooled around to find neutral, tramped down on the starter and had the surprise of its coming alive. After some experimenting, I enjoyed several solos back and forth between the dyke opening and a point where the road came up into the enemy's view — about 150 metres in all.

Just where the road tapered up was a big church with a good steeple from where Campbell had a great view, which included the small city of Leer across the Ems. I believe this was the first time I had seen Shaw and the crew since leaving for the attack on Weener three days ago. He and the crew brought in a line.

On our left, continuing on from the success of the Chaudières north of Bunde, the Queen's Own moved quietly farther north in the night to a vantage point near Ditzumer Verlaat and waited till morning, at which time they could see a good number of the enemy working at something in a field. They had obviously been unaware of our infantry's approach. A-troop OP called down 22nd Battery artillery fire on them. It was a highly productive shoot, as the military would call it, which translates as a high body count. The field was littered with 38 dead and 26 wounded. Later that day, April 25, as the Queen's Own shoved forward, German artillery came back on them with a heavy shelling. A-troop's OP crew managed to get to ground. They were sprayed with rubble; the barn where they had their OP was hit and burned, and their carrier was destroyed. An airburst wounded two of the crew. The FOO and one other member survived unhurt. That particular A-troop OP unit had called down its last target.

As it worked its way north, the 8th Brigade took a persistent shelling all along its front, mostly from the other side of the Ems.

Chapter 16

Some of it was big stuff with a long reach, which included some 88s, believed to be set up near Emden. A lot of it was focussed on our Regiment's guns, which were moving frequently as they followed tight behind the infantry regiments in their sweep up into the curve of the Ems. They took a few rounds every day, and lost a gun or two and some equipment, but miraculously had only one serious injury in the crews that I know of: a gunner was evacuated from 22nd Battery on April 24.

Around this time, the driver and I made a run back to the gun position for something, and witnessed a bit of the shelling's results. D-troop command post had just been demolished, and its shook-up staff were in a wet basement underneath. The staff had set up the post above ground to get away from the wet they were now standing in while trying to get organized again.

Our trip down that day took a little longer than expected. The carrier threw a track, which twisted us around so that we snagged a tree that kicked us back onto the cobble-stone road and set us spinning for two or three turns. I felt sure some part of my skeletal structure was broken. Abrasions brought out a few drops of blood — probably enough, as the driver unfairly suggested, to get a Purple Heart if I had been in the American army. Both of us had mean aches and pains in a number of spots for awhile, but we got over it, thankful that the carrier didn't flip. The soreness wasn't helpful in the bull-work of getting the track back on.

But we made it. The joint between each link of a track works on a long pin, making a hinge. One of these had ground off its cotter-key and come out. The pins are inserted with their heads to the inside; so if one begins to work out, it hits the frame, to make a ticking or scraping sound with each revolution. Normally we would then stop, tap it into place and insert a new key. But neither of us heard it this time. It was on the left side, away from both of us.

The day before the Bingum area was secure, a number of 9th Brigade's top brass came up to our position because they had heard about our OP's view of Leer, which the 9th would soon be attacking. I was on the 19-set in the carrier. They asked me to check with

Into North Germany

Campbell to see if it would be convenient for them to come up. Back came the answer on his 18-set, which they couldn't help hearing: "Yes, tell them to come ahead if they're not afraid."

They gave no indication of amusement. As they started for the top of the slope, I pointed out that from there to the church they would be exposed. Suddenly they dropped in unison as a Spandau or two chewed at the path along the crest of the dyke, which these belt-fed machine-guns did occasionally to keep us awake. They raked some pieces off Campbell's steeple as well, which gave a chorus of ricochets whining about. The would-be observers walked briskly back by the carrier and left.

By the next morning, the Spandaus and their operators had retreated across the Ems. The 8th Brigade's assignment to clear out the inverted "U" of the Ems was now completed.

The next task of the 3rd Division would be a bridgehead across this river at Leer, in order to enter and help the advance up the Emden-Wilhelmshaven peninsula, which lies between these two cities or, generally, between the Ems and the Weser Rivers. We came out with the North Shores to Weener for a break. Our guns were close by. It was April 26.

The North Shores' A-company should especially have appreciated the break; for a day or two earlier it had been dispatched to take a non-existent bridge across the Ems into Leer. One of the FOOs of our battery was with them. He and his crew ordered no rounds but simply kept their heads down and tried to stay alive, because the fighting was considered too close, or confused, for our artillery — and also turned out to be pointless and costly.

A disgusted A-company lieutenant was said to have pointed out that, if the planners had asked, aerial observations people could have told them two days previous that the bridge was not there. The enemy had blown it up. The company, pinned down for several hours, had 10 men killed and two wounded. It also lost a lot of equipment from 88 fire. The only success in the blunder was that an antitank gun with the company actually knocked out one of the 88 gun emplacements.

Chapter 16

Sometime — and it had to be after April 12, as that is the date on the forward — we soldiers were issued a small 26-page booklet from "HQ 21 Army Group," called *Your Future Occupation*. At the top of the cover in capital letters and underlined is the word "restricted." At the bottom is the command, "This document must not fall into enemy hands."

I can understand why, but I doubt that my reason is the same as HQ's. In military thought, propaganda is necessary to entice sufficient people to hate and kill and risk their lives in doing it. Fortunately, there are just not enough people who are inclined this way, so something must be done to create the image of an appealing cause and awaken primitive instincts to fight for it. Distortions and outright lying is a way to do it.

In this war, the enemy's obvious aggression made heavy propaganda less necessary; and recruiting in a depression clearly had its advantages. In World War I, because of the terrible losses, propaganda was more vicious to entice recruits and encourage fighting. One might wonder what the propaganda was to entice British and Canadian troops to kill in the Boer War, for they were definitely on the unjust side, and did terrible things, according to Boer historical accounts. One of those was to originate concentration camps, where it is alleged that 30,000 Boer women and children died, mostly of starvation. They had been rounded up in order to force the Boer men to stop fighting. It worked.

Now, with our war closing out, along comes this propaganda booklet telling us what to expect when entering Germany. It is an unbelievable screed, the type of attitude-structuring and brainwashing that would have been necessary had we sent soldiers to Vietnam. The opening sentence says: "Don't believe there are any 'good' Germans in Germany," and then goes on to quote a Belgian major who tells us that: "A German is, by nature, a liar."

Under the heading, "Women," comes the presumptuous statement: "Your attitude toward women in Germany is all wrong." This is followed by the question: "Do you know that German women have been trained to seduce you?" They "conceal knives in the hems of

Into North Germany

their coats," a Dutchman testifies. Among other places, women may carry messages "in their underwear." (There's some deeper truth to that.)

We must not give candy to children in Germany as we have been giving it to children in other countries. We are advised to "Watch when the dead are placed in the coffins, and forbid civilians to follow the corpses from the house to the cemetery."

On it goes for 26 pages! When I first saw the title, I thought it was a book of suggestions for post-war careers, such as the cooperage trade. It is dreadfully written, incoherent in places, and paranoid throughout. We are to suspect that a German underground resistance movement will be set up to fight the army of occupation. Ironically, an underground did develop — not to carry on Nazism in Germany, but to smuggle its most wanted members out of the country. And it did its job pretty well, while we were being warned that brass knuckles might be hidden in the clothes of a baby in a carriage.

Surely it's reasonable to feel uneasy about a leadership that would produce this sort of thing. It sounded like something from the mind of Field Marshal Douglas Haig of World War I, whose incompetent leadership in that conflict slaughtered thousands of his own troops. He is reported to have said that the next war — that is, World War II, the one now concluding — would be brought to an end by a great cavalry charge. Horses? Well, he had that covered, too. Bullets, he said, have "little stopping power against a horse.[41]

Yes, that booklet was his kind of stuff.

17

The Last Days

As mentioned in the last chapter, the 1st Canadian Division struck into the west Netherlands under the IJsselmeer (the old Zuider Zee), captured Apeldoorn on April 17 and fanned out some 15 kilometres beyond.

Nothing was handed to it; the cost was 506 casualties. The main German defence line, that was to stop any farther advance west, ran roughly along the Grebbe and Eem Rivers, about 30 kilometres west of Apeldoorn. By April 22 the fighting part of the war was over for the 1st Canadian and the 49th British Divisions, as they sat facing what became known as the Grebbe Line; but they had a mission of mercy yet to perform.

An agreement was reached with the Reichskommissar of the Netherlands, Arthur Seyss-Inquart, who said that if our forces did not attack across the Grebbe Line, the defenders would not consider it militarily necessary to flood still more Dutch land, a flooding that would increase the suffering of the Dutch.

The three and a half million people in German-occupied west Netherlands, especially in the densely populated areas, were starving. The German authorities received pleas from Sweden, Switzerland and the Allies, the weight of which led to this agreement — with an official, the Reichkommisar, whom Canada's official historian, Colonel C.P. Stacey, refers to as an "obnoxious person."[42]

The Last Days

He would not surrender until Germany itself surrendered; but, under a ceasefire, he would allow food to be brought through the lines by truck and also to be dropped from the air at marked locations. The arrangement was accepted.

The Allied air forces in 5,500 flights dropped 12,000 tons of rations from April 29 to May 8. Trucks moving through the front lines hauled about 1,000 tons a day from May 2 to 10.

The suffering of the Dutch during that winter should not be underestimated. It all started because of a wave of joyous optimism that swept over the country in the previous September, 1944. The Allies were moving up from the south. Airborne troops were dropping into Groesbeek and Arnhem. Surely the country would be free in a matter of weeks, maybe days, the citizens thought. From Britain, Queen Wilhelmina with the Dutch government-in-exile called for a general rail strike throughout her country.

She was badly advised. The order was a mistake. It succeeded in little more than enraging the enemy. For what was essential to them, the Germans simply brought in German railroad operators. For what was essential to the Dutch — food shipments from the breadbasket areas in the north and east — the Germans simply cut off, and diverted for their own use. Eventually, citizens were forbidden to bring in food by any means. Food rationing was drastically tightened.

False optimism about the war's end also emboldened the Dutch underground, who in one incident attacked the car of the SS police chief in Holland, General Hans Rauter, killing some of the passengers and wounding Rauter. For this the SS took 117 Dutch hostages to the site of the attack and shot them. I wonder whether the underground ever committed an assassination or an attempted assasination which had one iota of benefit to its country that was worth the inevitable vicious, ten-for-one or so retaliation that followed. Throughout Holland are numerous monuments to people, who usually had nothing to do with the event, who died in reprisals.

On the other hand the underground's outstanding achievements in gathering and passing on information, of smuggling out downed air-

Chapter 17

men, of hiding and feeding large numbers of citizens who were Jews, must be given high praise for the saving of lives.

Gas and electricity were shut off in October, and soup kitchens were organized, for which citizens had to surrender ration coupons. As winter moved in and fuel was scarce, bombed-out or abandoned houses were stripped of whatever would burn. People began to dismantle their own places and break up their furniture. The cold and hunger often drove people to stay in bed, fully clothed for 14 hours or more a night. In November, about 60,000 able-bodied workers were rounded up to work in Germany and at locations elsewhere in Holland, which left families with no one to scrounge extra food. The food ration itself, which in the spring reached as low as 400 calories a day, was starvation level. In January sugar beets were shipped in to help.

The health of about 100,000 people was severely affected by starvation, and some 10,000 died as a result. They walked or bicycled — usually on rims, as there were no tires — into the countryside, loaded with their personal belongings to trade with the farmers for food. Parents sacrificed for their children. Among the more haunting images recorded is that of a starving and exhausted parent, out searching for food, lying — or dying — by the roadside, while a child is sitting alongside her, waiting for her to get up.

John Vanderzyde, a Dutch immigrant and good friend, who as a teenager survived that winter with his family in Voorburg just outside The Hague, has an effective way of relating the kinds of incidents that do more than just tell the story. He mentions the frustrations in attempting to catch his first seagull, which he eventually did with a fishhook baited with a small amount of precious food. With the head, guts and feet of this first catch, he now had very tempting bait for an ingenious trap made from a large square of chicken wire, which caught several at a time. Volume was necessary, for the meat on a gull is painfully little. When the trap dropped, he waited until they all had their heads poked through the screen so that they could be snapped off conveniently.

The Last Days

The weather that winter was one of Holland's meanest on record. Food grew ever more scarce — including tulip bulbs, which eventually had to be rationed. The Vanderzydes ate their family cat. Pets in general disappeared. It made more sense to eat them than to let them starve to death. At one point, John got a job in a slaughterhouse, where employees were allowed to gather the blood in a container for themselves. When no one was looking, he would drop in slivers of meat, which would be hidden within the dark redness. He carried the pail of blood home, a distance of some three kilometres.

Going well beyond a German checkpoint, he managed to get some potatoes once during a food hunt. To get by this checkpoint on the way back he took a route off to the side, along dykes and through farms, for a distance which he thought was beyond danger. He had miscalculated, which brought him back to the main road too soon. The German on guard took the potatoes away from him — a contemptible act, he said, that still brings hate to mind.

He speaks of standing in line for some rationed item, and watching fleas scoot about on the neck of the person in front of him — knowing that the fleas on his own neck are being studied by the fellow behind him.

When you are weak from hunger, with no soap and hardly enough water to drink, let alone for laundry and bathing, fleas will find you sooner or later.

Having an idea of these conditions, which Canadians knew about only marginally at the time, makes the ecstatic welcome received by the British 49th and the Canadian 1st Division at the war's end more understandable.

On May 7, our 1st Division was transported on waves of citizens' joy into Amersfoort, Utrecht and Rotterdam.

Before telling of the 3rd Division's closing assignments, it seems fair to relate, very briefly, the actions of the other three Canadian Divisions and the 1st Polish Division up to their final accomplishments and positions at war's end. With the major flush of the conflict over, the Canadian's final month or so tends to be neglected. I have gleaned these synopses from reading their histories.

Chapter 17

After their successful effort at Arnhem on April 14, the 5th Canadian and the 49th British Divisions advanced west and secured most of the territory approaching the bottom half of the Grebbe Line. Units of the 5th Division turned north to capture Barneveld, and eventually reached Harderwijk on the Ijsselmeer, an advance that cost them 14 tanks in an encounter south of Putten.

Tank problems were not new to the division: 169 were lost between the end of March and its fight at Arnhem. And it had some killing and dying yet to do. It headed for the north-east Netherlands on April 19, to take over the 2nd Division's front. After securing the surrounding area, it faced the port of Delfzijl on the Ems estuary. To attack it would be wrong-headed, some of the Division's officers thought, for the port was not needed and could be sealed off until the end of the War, which was then a matter of days. The port was protected by flat low land, mines, barbed wire and bunkers, and by guns firing from Emden across the estuary. But capture it, the division was ordered to do — and did, on May 1. The division's war was now over. It had suffered 236 casualties in subduing Delfzijl and surrounding strong points.[43]

On April 20, the 2nd Canadian Division, now relieved by the 5th, arrived from the Groningen area, and entered the Front south of Oldenburg, below the Küsten Kanal, which is 30 metres wide and runs from the Ems to the Weser. The division's heaviest fighting in the area was in the advance on Oldenburg. The city fell easily on May 3, but it was getting there that caused the trouble. Rain added to the misery on April 28. In four days up to April 29 one of its Brigades suffered 130 casualties. After Oldenburg, the division continued its advance north of the city to a point east of Bad Zwischenahn in the direction of Rastede on May 4. Its war, too, was over.

The 4th Canadian Armoured Division, which had been advancing up the east side of the Netherlands, turned right into Germany on April 8, got over the Ems about 60 kilometres to the south at Meppen, to be followed by a part of the 1st Polish Armoured Division. (The other part advanced north between the river and the Dutch border on

The Last Days

its left, to where the 8th Brigade and we of the 13th Field Regiment relieved it on that miserable night of April 21.)

This flat, low country, the mud and the enemy made the going rough for armour, and took their toll of men and tanks. All bridges over every canal and river were out. The biggest obstacle was the Küsten Kanal, reached on April 10.

On April 17, after the failure of armour to cross, the 10th Infantry Brigade succeeded north of Friesoythe, led by the Algonquin Regiment. The brigade held on tenaciously for two days until the engineers got a bridge across. The division then struck north, and by April 26 was approaching Bad Zwischenahn. The enemy moved out and the town was spared. The force moved on to Westerstede and, by May 4, to Grabstede south-west of Wilhelmshaven by about 17 kilometres, where it met the 2nd Division. Those were the 4th Division's final advances.[44]

One unit of the Poles reached the Küsten Canal on April 19, and crossed it even though half their boats were destroyed before they were ever launched. Amazingly, they also built a bridge on the same day and had tanks crossing over. They took Papenburg, and reached a point farther north by April 21, where they waited for the bridgehead that was about to be established by the 3rd Division.

Another Polish unit farther east fought their way over two small rivers, losing five tanks in one engagement, and eventually got as far as Astederfeld on May 4, also about 17 kilometres south-west of Wilhelmshaven. For that unit of the Poles the war was over with respect to advancing, but it still shelled.

That leaves the 3rd Canadian Infantry Division.

When I left its story and my part in it, we were having a break with the North Shores in Weener. It was April 26. We were with them for about a day and then returned to our 13th Field gun position — at Inkrum, my diary says, which I cannot find now even on a very detailed map. I had simply noted that it was across the river from Leer. The men were finding German equipment that had been left behind, and were gathering up souvenirs, as they realized that the opportunities were just about over. And we were allowed to send parcels home.

Chapter 17

My first one went out on April 27, full of every object for which I had a duplicate, just in case it would never arrive. It contained German badges, medals, insignia, Nazi Party armbands, numerous swastika-stamped articles and air-dropped propaganda pamphlets of both sides.

For wrapping parcels, I had found in a factory, and hid away, a roll of amazing material that none of us had ever seen before — no doubt one of the multitude of products the German chemical industry developed when its research broke through into the wonderful world of plastics. The roll was about 15 centimetres in diameter by 3 or maybe 4 centimetres wide. Much later after the war we would eventually know it at home in domestic form under various brand names such as Scotch tape.

The division's rest lasted two days. On the afternoon of April 28 — the day, by the way, that Italian partisans murdered Mussolini and his mistress — the 9th Brigade attempted to cross the 300-metre-wide Ems behind a 30-minute barrage of our artillery plus 2-inch mortars and the dreaded Typhoons.

The Highland Light Infantry lost two boats and 15 of the men who were in them. In spite of the bombardment, the resistance was still too strong, so the attempt was put off until the next morning. With a better plan of attack, and after a further artillery hammering during the night, the brigade established a bridgehead in the morning and captured about half the city, suffering a total of 70 casualties. The 7th Brigade moved through them, took the other half late on the evening of April 29 and moved on to a little place called Loga about two kilometres east.

Our 13th Field Regiment had to deal with a discipline problem around this time.

Civilians, at least those operating farms, had not been evacuated from this area. Some of the regiment's men billeted themselves in nearby houses. Two women in one of these houses attempted to hang themselves, and were cut down just in time. They claimed that they were about to be raped. But the men who were accused swore that they had only ordered them to wash the dishes, and that the language

The Last Days

barrier had caused the confusion. Headquarters accepted the story, and a Court Martial was averted.

Also after we had left, a German patrol was reported to have crossed back over the Ems just north of the gun position. This sent the regiment into an alert, which got all the gunners checking their small-arms. Bren-gun and belt-fed Browning posts were set up on the perimeter. The party was arranged, but fortunately nobody came.

Our OP crew with the North Shores on April 29 crossed over the bridge that had been repaired by the engineers, and moved through Leer. The place had taken a heavy beating. On the outskirts we took over from the 9th Brigade, which swung north in the direction of Emden and Aurich. As we pulled up and stopped at one spot, a German who had been hiding in a dugout beside us came out with his hands up. We were pleased he wasn't a suicidal fanatic, who could have cut a fair number of us down with a Schmeisser. We were getting pretty careless by this time, for an order had just come to us to cease all firing unless fired upon as we moved forward from here on.

The Germans were obviously aware of the order and were probably given a similar one; for at our OP we watched them occasionally come into view in their lines during the day — something you would stare at for hours to get just a glimpse of in an earlier time. On this day, too, Kesselring surrendered his German forces in Italy.

And on the next day, April 30, Hitler shot himself — with a PK-2 Walther, incidentally, the same pistol model that Shaw carried. The Führer's troops on another section of our front, however, had other plans for their ammunition.

They were strongly objecting to the 9th Brigade's movement north along the east side of the Ems toward Emden and Aurich. Our 13th Field Regiment, normally firing only for our 8th Brigade, was asked to help retaliate, which it did, with 165 rounds per gun, a rather heavy response — perhaps just to get rid of ammunition and lighten their load.

On May 1, our crew and the North Shores moved ahead into Hesel, which the western section of the 1st Polish Division had cleared just an hour or so before. As planned, these Poles had come

Chapter 17

into the Leer bridgehead shortly before we did, and had now veered off to the north-east in the direction of Wiesmoor. They were the group that we had relieved on that rain-soaked night of our re-entry into Germany.[45]

From Hesel on May 2 we moved north with the infantry toward Bagband, about five kilometres away. The retreating force is alleged to have fired a few rounds.

My diary makes no mention of it, but does mention that the North Shores, at least the company we were with, never fired a shot that day. Nor did they have any casualties that I know of. Nevertheless, one of the FOOs with another of the infantry's companies called down artillery. Our guns had crossed the Ems on May 1 and deployed at Brinkum about eight kilometres north-east of Leer.

Early that morning they moved up behind us to Hesel, from which position they did the firing. The North Shores continued the advance on Bagband, and we entered the small hamlet with no sound but the clanking of carrier tracks. The steeple of the big church that dominated the little hamlet was an excellent OP. From a window high up we exchanged waves with Germans to the north, who were taking less than minimal caution as they packed up and retreated farther on.

Those few artillery rounds that our regiment fired on the way up took their human toll. The victims were to be the last dead bodies, friend or foe, that we would see in action in this war. Almost to the day, 50 years later, in early May of 1995, I discovered that there had been at least three. During that commemorative visit, I had been reading the names and dates from headstones in Canadian war cemeteries and in those churchyards in the villages of Kilder and Beek.

There in the cemetery of that Bagband church I found three military headstones of a different design. The date of death on all three was "2 . 5 . 1945." As I had stood before George Miller's grave, with my memories and considerations attempting to form a pattern of sense, someone with similar thoughts has surely stood before these graves at various times through the years — before the marker, for instance, of Ernst-Wilhelm Gessner, born in September of 1926, a boy 18 years old on that day in May when he was killed.

The Last Days

I was 16 when Germany went into Poland. Gessner was 13. His grade seven teacher would tell him of how the Poles started it, and how it would all be over long before he and his classmates finished their school year.

We took up residence in the hamlet's hotel, or Gasthof; and although there was no one around to give room service or any other service, it was perhaps the only time in my span of the War in which we slept and ate in a place where normal travellers do. I don't remember crawling under any duvets, so I imagine that the bedding had been evacuated also. I have a recollection of dishes, though, and our semblance of guest-like behaviour in eating our meals from the crowded hotel tables, meals carried from the North Shore kitchen.

The next day, May 3, the guns of our regiment also moved up to Bagband. The Chaudières struck north on the left flank, where they were reported to have approached German defensive positions ,but did not attack.

We stayed put. The Queen's Own moved up to some point on the road toward Aurich. They may have been fired upon. But whatever the reason, the FOO with them ordered some rounds in their support. They would be the last rounds ever fired in action by our regiment — its final attempt to destroy things and kill people, part of the business of war. We heard that earlier a German had come through the Chaudière lines with a proposal that a meeting between the military leaders be held to negotiate a surrender of the German forces in this area. The meeting was rumoured to be now in progress.

Possibly because there had been no casualties in the North Shores — at least none that I know of — since we crossed the Ems, the men were subdued in their possession of this little hamlet. Finding no liquor possibly helped. There was no shattering of windows nor smashing of furniture. Nor did I have the usual urge to snoop around for something to ship home. The rumours and firing restrictions were having their effect. Civilization, it would seem, was creeping back into us.

After our second night at the hotel, we loaded up our OP carrier and checked out with the North Shores. It was now their turn to push

Chapter 17

forward. The date was May 4. The ground was not shaking from a barrage, and I was not tensed up and crouched in front of the radio. I probably had one ear out of the headset or maybe both, with the set straddling my neck. Whenever the noise level was down, I could easily hear a call, and put them back on. Often when an attack began, Campbell would be out conferring with an infantry officer, but I think this time he stayed in our carrier.

Quietly, without a shot fired in either direction, we moved onto our objective, a little place called Ostersander, about six kilometres south of Aurich. The Germans had left. This advance turned out to be the North Shores' last, and our last, military action of the war — or any other war, forever. What I remember most about the little place was sitting in the street in the carrier, listening on the radio for news of what was happening. Eventually it came: German troops had surrendered in North-West Europe. I jotted a time in my diary: 2020 hrs. I must have loosened the frequency locking screws on the radio dial, for I was listening to news broadcasts probably from all over the world.

In those days, especially in Europe, even news of striking import was not delivered in any high emotional fashion. I can recall no excited tones of rejoicing coming from any station that night. The emotions, be they of grief or hysterical joy, were left to those who were listening. News was information then, a public service, delivered with a sense of dignity. In the 1930s, the British Broadcasting Corporation required its announcers to read the news in a dinner jacket. Perhaps the practice continued into the war years. Today the news is entertainment, drama, and, too often, created by the media themselves. It is not primarily a service to the public, but to a sponsor who has rented its delivery. On that 1945 night, however, the BBC would be calm and correct as usual, quite separated from the emotions that were, doubtless, released in British streets.

18

The War Is Over

Another part of my memory of that evening of listening on the radio was about how sleepy I got while searching out further broadcasts. No doubt I wanted to hear it said in different ways over and over, but while listening, I would actually fall asleep and slump over until my head hit the top of the radio. After a couple of these, I gave up, shut down, carried my bedqroll into the building beside me, and collapsed into a sound sleep on the floor in the darkness, among others of our crew and the infantry who were already stretched out.

The excitement all that day, and over the last couple of days, in anticipating the end was perhaps more exhausting than we realized. We were not digging trenches; and the fear of oblivion or of having body parts torn off was considerably reduced. Yet, to me the good news seemed to bring physical exhaustion as well as a collapse of tension, and had me half asleep before I hit the floor.

I think most of us were affected the same way, for I remember no clusters of men sitting up and talking into the night as was common later on. Generally speaking, the news to us, the troops, was -- using the term that so many have used — an anti-climax. "Phlegmatic" was a word that the Dutch brought up to describe our reaction. That it would appear so to them is understandable, for there was a very sharp contrast between our two reactions. Theirs verged on the ecstatic.

Chapter 18

More than a little of our reaction was from the awareness that the high pitch of excitement was all over. Most of us would not want it back and have to take what goes with it — certainly not front-line infantry — but it did leave us subdued for awhile.

The next morning, May 5, we parted company with the North Shores and came back to our own 13th Field Regiment in Bagband. It felt good to be back in Shaw's and Harrison's company again. Where any signaller specifically belonged now was not important. The carriers remained at the gun position, and the two crews were together most of the time. It was difficult to grasp that we would never again roll into action in these machines — unless those prisoners-of-war were right, those who had been telling us that we would all soon be fighting the Russians, something none of us wanted to think about. Campbell and the other FOOs had disappeared into the ranks of their own kind. We had eaten together for the last time. The structure of hierarchy had moved sharply back in.[46]

The official end of the war for Canadians and Germans in northwest Europe, we were told, was at 0800 hrs on this day, May 5. Nevertheless, one of our men was shortly to die.

We were ordered to form up on parade to receive a quick thank-you message from, I think, our regiment's commanding officer. While lining up, the Sten of someone accidentally fired into the back of the man ahead of him, who staggered out and fell to the ground in front of the ranks. He was quickly removed in time for us to be thanked for our job well done.

We heard he was dead where he dropped. Were we ordered to have our issued weapons with us? Possibly! I would have my P-38 as always, but don't remember carrying my Sten gun. I recorded only the bare details of the event. At the time, my position was possibly some 10 metres farther along in the ranks. Our regimental history book makes no reference to the incident.

A man dies several hours after the war's official end in our sector and, without further thought of it beyond feeling thankful that we were not the one, we all move slowly into an awareness of this new phase of our lives. We heat water, wash, shave, read our mail, write

The War Is Over

letters, and realize that the civilians who will now be returning to their homes are no longer the enemy but, rather, citizens of a conquered country. And their soldiers, who have also ceased to be enemy, are now officially "capitulated troops," under the authority of their own commanders, who in turn are under the authority of the commanders of the occupying force.

We are made aware, too, of the ban on fraternizing with German civilian and military personnel, which many of us label as just a mean-spirited rule to keep us away from German women — and not a rule, as the authorities profess, to protect us from the actions of a so-called "Werewolf" organization that has vowed to carry on the fight underground.

The North Shores later on when they went back into the Netherlands found that a corollary of the rule applied there as well. They were given the names and addresses of 50 Dutch women in the area who had collaborated with the Germans and with whom the men as a result were not to associate.

The next day, May 6, a Sunday, our regiment held a service in the Bagband church and, as well, heard an address from the pulpit by our regimental commander, Colonel Ostrander.

Besides the routine of thanking us and giving a sketch of our accomplishments, he outlined that the priority of getting us home would be as fair as possible and that some of us would be part of an occupation force, which would be staying behind for awhile.

The parish of that church, which sat at what was little more than a crossroads in a farming district, could not have been very large. And there would be the church of at least one more denomination somewhere nearby. Yet lining the walls around us that day as our commanding officer spoke were 24 wreaths, one for each member of this church's parish who died for the fatherland.

I remember screwing my neck around to count them for my diary. Of course, back home in the churches of my town there had been commemorative ceremonies over the past four years. The universal nature of loved-one's tears! In spite of my narrow perspective at that age, the irony of it all did not elude me.

Chapter 18

In simple terms, I thought of how just days ago, even one day ago, the purpose of each of these armies was to destroy members of the other. A standard method was to tear holes in the bodies of one another so that our blood would run out and we would die. Records show that 12 Canadians, and quite probably as many Germans, died on the last day of the war in North-West Europe.

The 13th Field Regiment numbered over 700 men. It suffered 166 casualties in the war, 45 of whom were killed and 121 wounded. Three men were captured. Those were the three in the forward line crew (the fourth was killed) who went through the front line by mistake. Out of those 166 casualties, 61 of them belonged to that very small percentage of the regiment's strength who were in our forward line crews and OP crews.

The North Shore Regiment's casualties totalled 1,230. Of these, 380 were killed and 850 wounded. Only four of their men were captured, which some thought may have been a record for an infantry regiment.

Altogether the Canadian force in north-west Europe, which included a few women in clerical and nursing roles, came to 237,000.

Of these, 11,000 died there, a number which exceeded the Canadian deaths in France and Belgium. Over 2,200 were taken prisoner. Some statistics are arranged in strange ways. For instance, Canada is calculated to have had nine 100-fatality days in north-west Europe. The last one was on March 10 at Xanten and Veen in the Rhineland. Seven of April's days had 50 Canadian deaths each. In the war's last five days, May 1 through May 5, 115 Canadians died. Packaging the figures in different ways must not diminish the image of terror and suffering that went with each of these deaths.

In the 1950s, when I was in Carleton University, a fellow student happened to be a German army veteran. At that time "Armistice Day," as it was called, was commemorated with more ritual at universities than simply the minute of silence. Students moved into the auditorium and remained standing for a brief eleventh month, eleventh day, eleventh hour memorial service.

The War Is Over

We two veterans happened to be standing together. When the dean, clergyman, or whoever, referred to "the enemy," my friend whispered: "He's talking about you, you know." I whispered back, "No he's not. You were the enemy."

In mock sincerity we had a couple more quiet "is-isn't" exchanges, but left the matter unresolved. I imagine that he had given some thought, as I had, to the consideration of who the real enemy might be. One of my simple descriptions is that the enemy is in the greed and power-hunger of those who set us at the throats of one another, who spark the disturbed and psychopathic into monstrous cruelty — and the rest of us into cumulative compromises.

Our colonel's name, Ostrander, and the name of the area of Germany we were in, Ostfriesland, reminds me that our regiment was heavy with names of German origin: Steinauer, Schultz, Holtzman, Manning, Schulmeister, Morgan, to name a few. And many of them spoke the language, which showed up occasionally when we asked questions of civilians. I learned eventually, however, that at least two of these occasional interpreters were Jewish. Because of the nature of our pre-war immigration, the Canadian army could have been in most any country on the Continent and found someone in its ranks who spoke the language. In our duties later on in dealing with displaced people from Russia, the couple of Ukrainians in our regiment were valuable.

In the First World War, whatever the variety of languages that might have been found in the Canadian army, 50 percent of our soldiers, even as late as 1917, were not born in Canada.

The next day, May 7, the fighting stopped on the Russian front, except in the city of Prague, we were told.

Our regiment left Bagband, passed through Aurich and on to an area near Westerloog, about 10 kilometres north-east on the highway toward Wittmund. We commandeered sufficient houses for living quarters, kitchens and offices. The polite word now was "requisitioned," and it was done through the area's Burgomeister, who made the arrangements with the occupants.

Chapter 18

The army worked only through him. Requisition forms were properly filled out and signed. Should some civilian possession turn up missing, the word "stolen" took the place of "looted,' and military law was quite nasty on the matter.

Gone were the days of smashing things, booting people out, taking a chicken for supper and breaking into stores of wine and preserves. An army in today's terms would probably bring in truckloads of counsellors of some variety, under the assumption that without help to make the transition we would be in danger of psychic damage. In the transition later to civilian life, the danger did have significance.

Not necessarily dangerous, but certainly a transitional unpleasantness for most soldiers was the return to parades. And over the next week we had a slew of them: battery, regimental divisional and corps parades.

May 8 was made the official Armistice Day in Europe. We gathered to hear Winston Churchill speak at 1500 hrs, and then King George VI at 2100 hrs. Headquarters left us alone that day, but the next morning the process of getting ready for these shows of force began. Even though our vehicles and guns would quite surely never see another war, they were to be brought back up to fighting standard and be impressively clean.

On May 14 we who lived with these machines got clean also, when it became our battery's turn at the mobile bath unit and fresh clothes. The unit had set up during the week. It was the first of these complete ablutions since Gorredijk in the Netherlands on April 19.

Our infantry were attending to the enemy disarmament procedure. The Germans, parading through a designated compound, were placing their weapons in piles according to type: rifles in one pile, grenades in another, and so on.

The procedure was surprisingly casual, with their troop movements carried out under the direction of their own officers. Who eventually hauled the ordinance away, where it went or what happened to it, I have forgotten — if I ever knew. Someone took a photograph of German soldiers dropping their weapons onto the piles. Our regi-

The War Is Over

ment's newspaper, which began publication at the war's end, printed the picture in an issue later on. It's in my scrapbook.

Although we were told of an order issued to the German troops and civilians that all depictions of the swastika must be destroyed at once, no attention was paid to the Wehrmacht's belt buckle, on which a small replica rested below the traditional eagle. It was a great belt, of quality leather, and many of us used one to hold up our pants. I had also sent a couple of belts home in those early packages.

One of our jobs between parades was hunting for weapons that might have been hidden before the surrender. Citizens were questioned. Barns searched. Engineers moved around with mine detectors in attempts to find buried caches. We found nothing that I can remember.

All the while, clusters of displaced persons — or DPs, as they would come to be called — were moving westward along the highway, heading home from places like Wilhelmshaven, where they had been brought to work by the Germans during the war. Many were from the Netherlands. These, relatively speaking, were the lucky ones, who had a home to go to. The DPs who were brought from Eastern Europe or who fled west ahead of the advancing Russian army were a different story, as we would eventually discover.

Moving on the highway as well, led by their officers, were sections of marching German soldiers coming from somewhere, perhaps north Holland, and now going to designated areas to the north of us, where their process to civilian life would begin.

The German military machine was an incredible fighting force. Within the Nazi government a madman directed an unparalleled evil, of which the populace on both sides remained ignorant or, for various reasons, indifferent; and the same madman directed its military to disaster (which in the end made our victory possible). But what was there about those German soldiers — General Schlemm's men in the Rhineland, for instance — that could bring a British Brigadier, following the fierce battle for Xanten, to salute the surviving defenders as they marched away as prisoners? In his book, *The Bombing of Germany,* Hans Rumpf states it well, I think: "It is Germany's tragedy

Chapter 18

that this tremendous example of bravery, self-sacrifice, determination and faith was wasted on something that was not worthy of it. Nevertheless, its grandeur cannot be disputed."[47]

It is not unfair, it seems to me, to consider that remark, too, in the light of the Canadians and Australians, for example, who marched, for an undefined cause, in large numbers to their death in World War I on the orders of a general staff whose incompetence bore signs of mental derangement. And we have in this war the undisputed grandeur of those victims of tactical madness who died on the beaches of Dieppe and, on a smaller scale but with no less individual agony, in the Hochwald Gap and on the slopes of Verrières Ridge and Moyland Wood.

But our war was behind us now. We had our final parade on May 14. Lieutenant-General Simonds inspected the 3rd Division's artillery units and then took the salute of the march-past. Our regiment packed up the next morning and began a long back-tracking journey through Leer, Weener, over the Dutch border at Nieuwe-Schans, on through Winschoten, Groningen, and then a long run south to Deventer, Apeldoorn and on south-west to a little village called Lunteren, which is about five kilometres north-west of the city of Ede.

In the fields along our journey the plowshares had returned and the swords had gone. We stayed overnight somewhere on the way down, a run close to 300 kilometres.

As the little village was already billeting the British 49th Infantry Division, our arrival jammed the place to capacity. For several days, with the help of officers and a distributed pamphlet called "After Victory in Europe," we were enlightened about a reallocation questionnaire and the point system that decided the priority for returning home. Bearing in mind our points, we were asked on the questionnaire to decide on one of three choices: volunteer to fight the Japanese in the Pacific, join the Canadian Army of Occupation Forces (CAOF), or return home for discharge.

Those who signed up for the Far East had the highest priority for ships. Next came those with sufficient points to get out. The points were based mostly on length of service, with weight given to awards

The War Is Over

for bravery and to infantry service. My accumulation fell short of home and discharge. So, with no particular fondness for steamy swamps and malaria, I signed up for the CAOF.

In spite of his high points, Shaw signed up for the Pacific war. So did some low-pointers in our outfit, on the gamble, as they acknowledged, that the Japanese would be defeated before they got there — a successful gamble, for that's what happened. Many of them who had no more than arrived in Europe were home again.

About 10,000 of us chose the CAOF, which eventually grew to 22,000. In this expansion would surely be most of the nearly 13,000 National Reserve men, the so-called Zombies, who had been conscripted for overseas service.

Given their stand, I doubt that any of them would have volunteered for the Pacific campaign. Before the end of the war, fewer than 10,000 got onto the continent. Of these, only 2,463 were in action. They had 313 casualties, 69 of whom were killed. It was to the army's credit that once these men landed overseas, they were simply mixed with other replacements, unidentified. Whenever a new man came to our regiment, no one cared or even thought about the topic. The obscure little "GS" on the sleeve of us volunteers had lost all meaning. I doubt that many of us transferred it if we had to have our tunic replaced.

On May 20, our regiment moved from crowded Lunteren to Zeist, about 35 kilometres west, near Utrecht. The batteries were spread out, with plenty of room, in private homes that were previously occupied by German troops who had been stationed there.

The town was very attractive, with tree-lined streets and beautiful homes, some of which suggested a community of wealth in quieter times. To me, communities in general in the Netherlands — and this was after they had endured four years of occupation — seemed to be much more advanced than ours at home. Of course the communities I was familiar with in Canada were not exactly the country's more affluent. Nevertheless, the interior designs of Dutch homes in cities and larger towns, especially the designs of their kitchens, were not common in Canada for another decade, and were then called modern.

Chapter 18

German troops in the west Netherlands were forming up to go home, over a long 500-kilometre trek that would take them up the west side of the IJsselmeer, over the Causeway, across the north Netherlands and over the border to that area in the Ostfriesland peninsula previously mentioned. On May 22, a 250-man force of us was sent to Haarlem to serve in escort duties. I was with those assigned to patrol the columns with our carriers, Jeeps and scout cars. When they eventually began the journey, every 180 men were accompanied by five horse-drawn vehicles to carry the necessary supplies, and were expected to cover about 25 kilometres a day. Nurses along with the sick, wounded and crippled left by boat. Their troops in the west Netherlands numbered over 100,000.

At the end of our shift the next day, another gunner and I went with a truckload of us Canadians to Amsterdam, about 15 kilometres away. He came with me as I delivered Henk Lippens' letter to his sister Carla, almost one month to the day from the time he gave it to me when leaving Gorredijk.

The street name sticks in my mind even yet, without the need of my notes: Rombout Hogerbeetstraat. The number was 91.1. She seemed genuinely delighted to get the letter, not having heard from her brother for a long time. We accepted her offer of tea and a couple of hardtack biscuits, for which she apologized and explained that it was part of the food that had been dropped by plane during the winter and spring of starvation. Strict rationing was still in effect, she said. But while sitting there eating her precious hardtack, I and bottom-rank soldiers in general did not really comprehend what had taken place there.

How ignorant we were of the reality of things beyond our military life! And how indifferent to it! Several years after the war, at an age when my mind would tolerate the disturbance of contemplation, I thought about how ridiculous we were to accept her rationed tea and hardtack — and what she must have thought of us for accepting it, when she knew that we could have brought our packs bulging with food for her.

The War Is Over

Over several days the German columns began their journey. Again, their marching and attitude was something many of us had to comment on. They probably got a pep-talk from their officers. At any rate, they had no trace of a defeated, hang-dog look. Quite possibly the striking of their jackboots on the cobblestones was more brisk on the day they entered the Netherlands five years earlier to the month, but they still had the bearing of a well-disciplined army. There was, however, to be no music. Their officers were told to order their men not to sing on the march.

Our patrol of the staging areas and of the moving columns extended for about 40 kilometres and lasted over four days. We ended up south of Beverwijk on the way toward Alkmaar, from which point the 1st Canadian Division was responsible for escort to the far end of the Causeway. Here, our 5th Division took over to accompany them to the German border. The last of the long column would not be clear of Dutch soil until June 15.

An officer in charge of us explained the purpose of our escort duties. We knew that at war's end in north Germany we carried out no patrols of this nature. Under their own officers and after the surrendering of arms, their columns moved off to their army camps. Here, the circumstances were different, he pointed out.

It seems that when an army capitulates in a hostile country and lays down it weapons, the victorious army is responsible, under the rules of the Geneva Convention, to protect these soldiers who are now defenceless. This was the purpose of our escort duties. By now, late in May, the serious problems of vengeful attacks from segments of the population were over; so our tour, and possibly the others, was quiet.

At the time of the German army's surrender here in the west of Holland, however, the situation was tense. Military rules of conduct came into play which frustrated and angered the Dutch underground and the newly formed militia known as the Interior Forces, whose men had suffered, and had witnessed suffering, throughout the war. The code that exists between military forces is not commonly known, and when it exhibits itself, it can be a shock.

Chapter 18

The first minor shock came at the historic signing of the document of unconditional surrender by German General Johannes Blaskowitz and Canadian General Charles Foulkes in Wageningen on May 5. By order of Foulkes, the only people present were himself, General George Kitching, Prince Bernhard and General Blaskowitz, along with aides and interpreters. The press and spectators were shut out entirely. One of the points in the decision was that Blaskowitz "had been a pretty fair enemy," as Kitching was said to have put it, and might be spared the humiliation of flashbulbs and the entire media circus.

The command by Foulkes that truly stunned the Dutch was that no civilians, including the Dutch underground and the Interior Forces, were to bring weapons into the streets, and that the German forces would remain armed and be responsible for maintaining order.

But he also commanded Blaskowitz to round up and disarm all those that the Dutch considered traitors — the Dutch SS, the Landwacht (militia of the Dutch equivalent of the Nazi Party), and Dutch police members who willingly did a lot of the dirty work for the Reichkommissar — and bring them to a central location. These were the people that the Interior Forces and underground groups were principally after.

But for Foulkes' order, there might well have been an orgy of revengeful killing rather than proper arrests and indictments. There were killings as it was, because a few disobeyed the no-arms order and pursued vigilante justice, often savagely.

Blaskowitz asked for and was given by Foulkes an extension of 24 hours to accomplish everything he had to do. This required delaying the arrival of the attached 49th British Division, which had been given the job of collecting and securing the German army's weapons.

Foulkes must have considered the extension necessary, but it was an added irritation for the Dutch, because it meant that the disarming of German forces did not begin until May 8. In the meantime, ironic situations developed.

Hen Bollen and Paul Vroemen in their very informative book, *The End of Five Years of Terror in Holland*, mention a couple of these. As

The War Is Over

the Canadian 1st Division, being given a tumultuous welcome, moved along in west Holland cities, armed Wehrmacht were keeping some of the intersections clear for them to pass through. At least as late as May 9, armed German and Canadian soldiers were jointly guarding the transport of food through the streets of hungry Rotterdam. Pictures exist which show them at work.[48]

Armies, even opposing armies, recognize that, along with the general life-destroying nature of their vocation, they have in common an order and a discipline — and of course the essential power that goes with these features. In this respect, they are often partners against a common enemy who happens to be disturbing their order.

So it was with Foulkes and Blaskowitz for a week or so in some cities after their war ended. Rarely, however, is such cooperation for a humane and decent cause, as it was in this case.

More often both of the cooperating military forces are in the contemptible business of imperialism. After the Japanese surrendered throughout the Far East, the British forces in Vietnam allowed the Japanese forces to stay armed and active for a period of time to continue to control the Vietnamese, who had the silly idea that foreign nations should not be occupying their country.

Britain, in an imperialist agreement, had promised France that she would keep the Vietnamese crushed down until the French army could get back in and take over. In imperialism's heyday, Britain, Portugal, France and later the U.S., to name a few of the worst ones, supplied money and arms to maintain some of the Third World's most vicious and often psychopathic military regimes — all so that those regimes might enforce order and discipline in their countries, for the political and economic advantage of those First World nations.

The protocol of rank that once existed and perhaps still exists between armies, even while at war, is a study in itself. Much of it, I suppose, is in the rules of the Geneva Convention. A Canadian pilot-officer who was shot down over Holland tells in his autobiography about how a German corporal was ordered to take him to a prison camp.

Chapter 18

The corporal, in tune with his own rank, took his prisoner into a second-class compartment on the train. Later, a German officer passing by did a double-take on seeing where the Canadian officer was sitting. He bawled out the corporal and ordered him to take his prisoner into first class at once.

Convention rules were inevitably be broken by both sides here and there. The Germans were reported to have shackled a number of Canadians who were captured in the Dieppe raid (for which Canada responded in kind with German POWs, until assured that the Canadians were released). On the other hand, "dumdum" bullets were issued to at least some of the Canadians who took part in this tragic raid. There is no doubt about what the Convention thinks of shackles and dumdum bullets, a type of bullet that flies apart in the body to do gruesome things, and is invariably fatal. Veteran Brian McCool, one of the few survivors of Dieppe, who had gone ashore as a major with the Royal Regiment of Canada, has told about how he cleaned his pockets of these bullets and surreptitiously dumped them in the drain hole of the font in the church where Canadian officers were first held when captured. When he came back in 1967 to vist Dieppe and the area of the slaughter, he checked the church's font but found the drain clear. The water from the first post-raid baptism, with its image of new life, was perhaps blocked or trickled through these dumdums, which held quite another image.[49]

Perhaps within its interpretation of the Geneva Convention, the Canadian military establishment went a breathtaking distance in one case to respect the common bond of discipline and protocol that it shared with the capitulated German force.

On May 13, 1945, the war had been over eight days Our regiment in North Germany was still three days away from being pulled out and sent here, into West Holland. The German forces, now disarmed and in camps, getting organized for their trek home, had a matter of discipline to take care of: carrying out the execution of two of their men, Bruno Dorfer and Rainer Beck, who had been sentenced to death for desertion.

The War Is Over

To get a good grasp on the colossal madness that is about to take place here, one has to see — regardless of what motive these men had for deserting — they are in effect to be executed because they would not help kill Canadians.

The Canadian military apparently had no trouble understanding the German army's dilemma. At the Germans' request, the Canadians supplied rifles and ammunition for the firing squad, and trucks to transport Dorfer and Beck and the party to the execution site, where the killings took place. It is alleged that a Canadian officer then complimented the German officer in charge of the firing squad. It had all been properly and efficiently carried out.

Some of our boys in the 1st Canadian Division must have had some knowledge of the affair, for the division supplied the ordinance. The German weekly magazine, *Der Spiegel*, broke the story in September, 1966. The Canadian Press then went to work on it in October, checking with witnesses, and found one who said that after the affair was opened up in *Der Spiegel* he had given the whole story to the Canadian Defence Department. Yet several days later Canadian, Defense Minister Paul Hellyer said in parliament, in answer to the queries by John Diefenbaker, that any statement about Canadian officers being involved is "completely without foundation." When witnesses, German and Canadian, eventually made denial ridiculous, the Canadian Ambassador to West Germany called the controversy "a tempest in a teapot." Hellyer and his crowd took a beating over the affair, but they moved on. The students' journal of McGill University found "our Army's behaviour immoral and callous and their legal exoneration just astounding."

On the broader topic of crime and punishment in the post-war era, a couple of Heidelberg professors spoke of the difficulties caused by "the degeneration of the sense of what is unjust." As will be mentioned later, we Canadians helped the German military round up many of its deserters who would not risk their own lives trying to kill us for the Fatherland.

I have not read of how many Canadians, if any, were executed by their own command in World War II. The United States put 142 of its

Chapter 18

men before the firing squad. In the First World War, 23 Canadians were executed by the British, because Canadians were under British command. (They executed 327 of their own.) The French army in WW I got the name of being particularly vicious in killing its own men for refusing to go over the top. An alleged remark by a French general: "If the little sweethearts won't face German guns, then they'll face French guns."

The colossal barbarity of war and the laws of civilized society overlapped for a moment in the injustice to Bruno Dorfer and Rainer Beck. Months earlier they could have been just two more rain-soaked corpses lying somewhere in the Hochwald forest among those of the Essex Scottish or the Algonquins.

I recognize the preposterousness of speaking of these two deaths as a tempest in a teapot, and recognize that the most tedious of legal debates must be carried out. But attitudes are seriously askew when military establishments can go on producing those other corpses in battles and continue to provoke no great outrage over the injustice of it all. Eli Wiesel once said in an interview that in a conversation he had with a friend, a Christian clergy member, the topic of the Holocaust and of human suffering came up. His friend mentioned the suffering of Christ on the cross. Wiesel remarked — and said he apologized for doing so, because his clergy friend wept — that he knew any number of children who had suffered far more than Christ had.

Our tour of duty finished on May 26, and we returned to Zeist. Another group relieved us. A parcel from my mother arrived the next day, severely battered as usual but hanging together. She always wrapped them well and tied them with so much "Eaton's cord," as we called it, that the parcel was secured within a coarse net of string. Families, at least in our financial bracket, saved the cord that came around all packages from Eaton's — and from Simpson's, too, but somehow this company was not given the free publicity.[50]

We were all kept busy, by first giving every vehicle and gun another cleaning and then, with many gallons of khaki paint, bringing them back with a complete coat to what must have been close to their original lustre. Vehicle identification figures came alive again. All

The War Is Over

tires were blackened. On days off and in evenings without guard duty, we were free to join truckloads going to any city where we could be back before morning — and where some of us could sell our buildup of cigarettes. The sin that a lot of military personnel had in common was Black Market dabbling.

Only a few were into it in a seriously criminal way. Most of us just wanted to live a tad above our military means. Cigarette sales were enough to do this comfortably for me, a non-smoker. Shipments of cigarettes as a gift from home by Service Clubs meant total profit, of course. But even when bought at the serviceman's price of $3.25 for 900 — three cartons with 300 each — the profit was enormous. For 100 of those 900 cigarettes, the going price was one English pound, which was fixed at $4.47. The policy of us small-time racketeers was to accept only the English pound. It was stable. Then, to get the currency of another country, it was simply a matter of going to a bank in that country. Conscience in the military is not a big topic. In my defense, however, I can say, and it is true, that I never sold food. Had I been a hooked smoker, I probably would have. Stuff like chocolate bars went for good money — and almost as good as cigarettes as barter in a bordello, I was told.

On returning from one of our evening trips in the usual canvas-back 60-cwt truck, we struck a woman who was walking along the road. The locked brakes slammed us all to the front. When the people in the cab hollered that we had run over someone, I remember the dread I felt, and how hard it was to jump out the back, anticipating still another broken body.

She had indeed been run over but she missed the wheels and had ended up with one leg, probably broken, wedged up above the back axle. She was cut and gouged in numerous places, but alive and conscious. Fortunately speeds in those days of lumbering army trucks and narrow roads, were not fast, possibly not over 50 kilometres an hour.

We lined up along the side of the truck and lifted what we could to increase the clearance, while a couple of fellows got her out and into a near-empty truck which had stopped behind us and which now rushed her off to a hospital. I don't remember hearing of how she

Chapter 18

made out, or how she got under there. She may have fallen down in front somehow. No bicycle comes to mind.

I went to The Hague on June 1, about 70 kilometres away, mostly to see the V-2 launch-site there. As with going through stilled factories and buildings, empty of people, I got an emotional charge out of examining places like these.

The debris and scarred earth offered evidence that all take-offs were not a roaring success. An attempt to end these launchings — at least that was the excuse given — led to the tragic Allied blunder on March 3 of bombing the city instead of the site — a blunder that destroyed over 3,000 houses and killed 511 people. That sounds like an awfully big raid for one launching site.

The Dutch suffered a number of these wretched errors by the Allies — surely very difficult to understand. The little town of Zeelst near Eindhoven was flattened without warning, leaving its families mutilated, dead and dying — a town incomprehensibly mistaken for an airfield a considerable distance away.

To cite another example, a Dutch immigrant and friend, John te Grootenhuis, was a boy of 13 years as he looked up and, as boys would, counted the Allied planes, 15 of them, that were approaching, on their way into Germany as usual, he assumed. Instead, they dumped their load on the farming community of Dale, near Aalten. He escaped with just a piece of shrapnel in his leg, but his two younger brothers were among the nine people killed.

Later that evening of June 1, while I stopped for a moment to watch some sort of street fair in the city, a well-dressed man and his wife, whom I designated as "old" in my diary — they were probably not over 60 — approached me, began a conversation and eventually invited me to their home.

It was reasonably sumptuous, it seemed to me at the time, somewhere that I in my hobnailed uncouthness would never be invited in normal circumstances. I remember how curious they were about why we came so far to fight in the war; but, my diary entry on the visit was not much more than the name and address: G.J. Jacobs, Eikstraat 26, 's-Gravenhage (The Hague).

The War Is Over

Utrecht we visited quite often while in Zeist, as it was only 10 kilometres away and a beautiful university town. I went to Hilversum once also, about 15 kilometres farther north from Utrecht, for I had heard that the country's big short-wave broadcasting station was there. I don't know what I expected to see. A sight right in Zeist that surprised me was the number of children in this affluent-appearing town that showed up after each meal at our kitchen's big slop-drum where the men emptied their mess-tins on the way out. They hovered their own containers over the top of the drum and asked us to dump into them instead. Most men did so; others would bellow to scatter them away. A particularly mean one of us on occasion dumped in his mixture of tea-soaked powdered potatoes and cigarette butts, a charity that broke him up with humour. I always cleaned up my plate, so to speak, except for the shattered fragments of mutton bone; but after my first encounter with those hovering pots and pans, I grabbed extra bread to have something left over. It was an easy way to feel good and forget the scene.

June 6, the anniversary of D-Day and the landing of the 3rd Canadian Infantry Division on the coast of France! All the vehicle painting and tire blackening was for this day. A parade of the entire division was held in Utrecht, where General Crerar took its salute as it moved through the city's market square.

It was the last parade in which our guns ever rolled. Only our regiment's men with long service took part, for which I was thankful. Spit and polish was not my thing. Glistening M3 was there, almost unrecognizable, with every scar painted over. The German MP-44 was no longer strapped on the front. My head of cheese under the seat was long gone. The gleaming signals trailer behind M3 had its scrubbed canvass pulled flat across and secured, no longer bulging with all our equipment and loot — and among which no soldier is ever again likely to squirm, trying to get some sleep out of the rain.

For the parade, I believe that two of the longer-service command post signallers made up Shaw's crew, along with Harrison. Shaw would not have his American 30-calibre carbine, and no one would be carrying Whittington's Schmeisser; for an order had come out a few

Chapter 18

days after the cease fire that all German and other unauthorized weapons were to be turned in and only issued weapons were to be carried from then on. No one surrendered pistols, however. Shaw's little PK-2 Walther and Meyers' big American .45 calibre no doubt rode the parade, resting in tunic pockets. And Harrison would have his stiletto.

For the next couple of days after the parade my diary mentions no specific duties laid on. We exchanged home addresses with those we got to know better than others. Some had to think for a moment about where a letter might reach them.

Meyers told me just to write "Emo, Ontario" under his name. He said he would probably go back there for awhile. I asked about a box or street number. He had neither. If the post office in Emo doesn't know you, he said, you don't live there.

Some of those who volunteered for the Far East were already gone. A few high-pointers were on leave in Britain. Shaw, as a Far East volunteer, left early. I made no note of when I bid him good-bye, or whether I actually did at the moment he left; but I do know we exchanged addresses at one point, for I was surprised that the best he could do was tell me just to use "Prince Albert, Saskatchewan" and say that it's to be picked up. "I'll be coming in there once in a while," he said.

Norm Hunter, a fellow who had to be dug out of a collapsed trench when the air force bombed the regiment by mistake — and he carried the shovel scars to prove it — gave me instructions similar to those of Meyers: just put down "Wadena, Saskatchewan." Ab Harrison gave me an additional address: that of his aunt and his grandparents in Northern Ireland. I had told him of my plans to go to Ireland as soon as I got my first long leave.

On June 10, we saw the last of all our guns and vehicles, except Jeeps and trucks, which were to be signed over to the army of occupation. The drivers were ordered to deliver them to an ordinance depot somewhere. M3 was just a memory now. A few old-timers shed no tears over the departure of the 25-pounder. These men landed in Normandy not with this gun but with the American-built self-propelled 105 millimetre unit. The exchange had taken place at the begin-

The War Is Over

ning of August, almost two months after D-Day. If there were any tears, that's when they were shed. The high command had decided that the lighter gun would be better from then on.

I was given a three-day pass to Paris on June 12 — three clear days there, with travelling time extra. After a stop-over in Brussels, I continued on to Paris by train on the 14th and got a room at the Hotel Paris Denard. The details have left me, but somehow I knew, perhaps from a supplied list, that this hotel was one of those that had some sort of agreement to accommodate soldiers on leave.

Whatever the cost, it would not be a problem. My pockets were crammed full of Belgian, Dutch and German currency of all kinds, money possibly picked up from the Schelde campaign on. Some bills would be worthless, but I didn't know which.

A fellow who had been on leave to Paris told me about a branch of the British Lloyds Bank there, and how they asked no questions. I felt uneasy, stuffing those wads through the wicket. But the teller just smoothed them out, put them in appropriate piles, shoved the useless ones back at me, and poked out some sort of document to me, which I signed. He then counted out crisp, new, colourful French francs. The ease of it all surprised me. What did I put my signature to? I never gave it a second thought at the time, but have imagined later that I most likely lied my head off about the legal origin of the money.

Nor did I give a second thought to being armed in a Lloyd's Paris bank. Inside my left tunic pocket rested the P-38. Even in the aftermath of a war, and for a couple of decades or so later, the outlook and attitude toward firearms was strikingly different from what it is today. Therein rests a sociology study.

I walked out into a sunny street of Paris in the summer, an ignorant kid, who knew nothing more about the city than what his grade 10 French textbooks and French teacher had imparted. She had been to Paris — not a common experience in the 1930s — and told us how she had saved up to help make the trip by putting away all fifty-cent pieces that came to her in change. Somewhere, perhaps at a leave centre, I had been given a booklet published for the military, which

Chapter 18

showed all the available tours of the city and district. On these I spent most of my time, and enjoyed them all.

The groups were small, a busload, and consisted of a motley variety of uniforms, mostly American.

The guides seemed genuinely concerned that we be somewhat enlightened. Again, the interior of buildings, even though they had no holes blown in them and were not ghostly vacant, fascinated me. Something learned in one of the great structures stayed in my memory outside my diary. In the Palais des Invalides, which holds Napoleon's tomb, the guide spoke of some newly acquired artifacts relating to Napoleon and his conquests. The guide said that Hitler ordered they be brought back from museums and other places across the Europe that had then been conquered by the Germans.

More than I in the group were surprised by that. Perhaps it was one conqueror's respect for another — acknowledging the pedigree, so to speak.

Hitler's little so-called dance — he lifted his right leg up and down again, once — outside the railcar, at the time of France's humiliating surrender ceremony that he orchestrated, is well known. Lesser known is the whirlwind tour he made of Paris, apparently to indulge his obsession with architecture and his fascination for grandiose structures. He made no triumphal speeches. No ceremony was laid on. He came quite early in the morning apparently, before the city had entirely awakened. One writer proposes that he wanted to get a sense of what gave the city its grandeur, for he planned to build a Berlin that would outdo it. I have seen one picture of what he considered for an area of his capital's centre. The "Great Hall" as shown in the plans is so humongous that the old Reichtag becomes a tiny structure off to the side. Even his architect, Albert Speer, must have winced at being a part of such grotesque proposals.

My last tour was to the Palace of Versailles and its grounds, a few kilometres south-west of Paris. One of my more clear memories is of our guide's ill-concealed disgust for the pre-revolution French monarchy. We were shown the extravagant splendour of the Bourbon dynasty by way of its corruption and irresponsibility.

The War Is Over

In Louis XVI's bedroom, he explained the King's ritual of getting up in the morning — of a line of obedient servants waiting by his bed for his eyes to open. Marie Antoinette held a special place in his bile. In the palace's resplendent Hall of Mirrors he showed us where Woodrow Wilson, George Clemenceau and the others had sat for the signing of the Treaty of Versailles. In terms that emphasized the decadence, he also told of the lavish banquets held there, pointing out that the immense chandeliers of candles had little to catch the dripping wax, which he assumed must have spattered occasionally into food and onto ladies' gowns.

Even though ignorant beyond the pamphlets with their historical outlines, I was truly stirred by just being there. The stories I could write to the family, and could tell them when I got home! That was important to me. Wherever possible, I bought post cards of the places I had seen — not to mail in Paris but to put in letters in place of photographs when I got back to the regiment. Outgoing mail in the military was free. The cards were wartime productions. Wherever a picture included people in the street, there was occasionally a German soldier — my equivalent, I suppose, sightseeing among them. Judging from the tepid manner of any transactions I had in restaurants and taverns, I could imagine that the average Parisian had no particular preference or affection for any military personnel, be they Allied or German, beyond what they might spend.

Over a half-century after the war, I watched a TV documentary on the role of military cameramen. One of these cameramen acknowledged — and had the film clip to show the results — that he paid or otherwise rewarded a group of young French women to grab and kiss U.S. soldiers marching in Paris after its liberation in World War II. Because of a lack of excitement among the citizens along the street, he had to do something to get a good shot for the press. I could understand that he would not get the performance free.

After a stop-over again in Brussels, with a visit to the city's medieval main square, along with a purchase of more postcards, I caught a train to Nijmegen on June 17 and hitchhiked from there to Lunteren, to where the regiment had moved back. The cool OP sig-

Chapter 18

naller — Smith, L.K., the regiment's nominal roll called him, but known to us only as Smitty — had looked after my gear, and grabbed a room for the two of us in billets at 67 Ackerslaan, an attractive house on a beautiful cobblestone street. He had also picked up my mail, which included Mother's 18th parcel. We ate a good bit of it that evening after bringing back mess-tins of tea from the kitchen. Later we lay in our bedrolls and talked well into the night's darkness. Over the next three days we were given literature on rehabilitation and other aspects of returning to civilian life, which only reminded me that I wasn't going home for awhile.

Some sports equipment showed up, and ball games got organized. I wrote letters about my Paris and Brussels adventure and enclosed those postcards. In my letters I spoke of visiting the capitals of three countries in three weeks, which I thought they would find as impressive as I did. My June 1 trip to The Hague was the first of the three.

On June 21, Smitty and I parted. With the other high-point men he remained in Lunteren to be shipped out in a draft very soon, while we who had signed up for the Canadian Army of Occupation Forces (CAOF) were sent to a holding area just north of Lunteren. We were issued a small tent for each two men, which my partner and I pitched in one of the designated spots that had been precisely staked out in a pattern of rows in a big field. The luxury of billets would not be back for a couple of weeks. The need, though, to dig below ground was gone. There was some comfort in that.

19

The Canadian Army of Occupation

Part 1

In Lunteren, civilians had told us that just north of their town during the war, the Dutch Nazi Party under Anton Mussert had constructed a building, perhaps a headquarters, along with a form of outdoor amphitheatre, where they held mass rallies and listened to speeches of Party officials. It was in the fields adjacent to this complex that we were now camped.

I got into the complex as soon as we were settled — my penchant for those silenced, empty structures again. To form the amphitheatre the area had been landscaped into a large concave half-saucer that curved gradually up to a high ridge running along the back edge. There were no seats. The mass of faithful apparently sat on the grass of the gentle slope. They would be facing a building, perhaps three stories high, although there were no windows to indicate floors, except for the top floor. The building was nestled into the face of a sharply rising hill that closed off the end of the half-saucer. This long structure — ugly, as I see it in my photographs taken years later — appeared to be imitating the side of a ship, with its top-floor round windows like over-sized portholes, and with a deck, complete with railing, running along the structure's length.

Midway on the building's face, high up, was a protruding bit of railed balcony from where speakers no doubt harangued the followers. On a visit to the building one evening at dusk, I came out onto that

Chapter 19

balcony. Our camp beyond the ridge was quiet. Baseball and volleyball games would be closing down. Truckloads of us after the day's last meal had gone into Lunteren and beyond. The hushed amphitheatre sloped toward me. If this were Canada, a dog would bark somewhere in the distance. Dogs were uncommon in the Netherlands in these times, which is not very puzzling.

Standing there, I felt as though I were trespassing in history. As well as the routine of Mussert, some top visiting Nazis had no doubt stood there and held forth, with their kid-gloved hands on the railing. I thought that Hitler might have visited at one time; but that would be highly unlikely. The gathering would not be massive enough. I read that at a Nuremberg rally he once stood for three minutes after the crowd hushed before he uttered his first word. Now that's charisma, or maybe hypnotism.

The light was fading. This ghostly stillness just had to have a fracture. Because my knowledge of Dutch was near nil, I strung together some memorized fragments from my German text from Foyle's, gripped the railing and blasted out a five or six second senseless harangue that reverberated off the ridge at the back.

Silence quickly came back in, and I was more aware of it than before. How irreverent and simple-minded this fracture would seem to the people who created this edifice and once stood here with tremendous power, and who had made so many suffer for interfering. Years later, when reading George Orwell and his remark that the desire for power is the main driving force in humankind, I thought about this place. Had this balcony, a metaphor of power, meant as least as much to Mussert as the Nazi cause?

I had the power now, in all my political innocence, to stand there and mock what once was his. I had no clear understanding of the evil that had been in his power, nor the good that was in the one that allowed me to stand there. I was a soldier. So were Shaw and Harrison. So were those Wehrmacht men whom we saw begin their long march home.

The military slackness that had been so pleasant since the ceasefire was now tightening up. The Canadian force chosen for the army

The Canadian Army of Occupation: 1

of occupation was the 3rd Division, but it bore little resemblance to the original, because most of its men would have enough points to go home. To designate that we were CAOF, we had to sew a blue strip, about a centimetre wide, just below our regular blue divisional patch. For stitching these on, I could not this time go out and loot a sewing machine, as in Kleve. A few men went into town, though, with a chocolate bar as payment to get them installed. All units of the 3rd Division CAOF were to be identified on records through a slight change in their number identification. For instance, I was now with 2/44th Battery of 2/13th Field Regiment RCA.

A couple of civilians were coming into our encampment now in the evenings to take photographs of us, at a cost of so many cigarettes. My tent-mate and I had one taken together. It turned out well. I sent my copy home to my mother. The civilian who brought cherries to sell was my favourite vendor. I ate great quantities of them, and paid his high price with British-brand cigarettes, which we got because we were on British rations — and which brought only half the price of American brands on the black market. The British brand-name was "Capstan."

On July 7, ours and four other artillery regiments of the 3rd Division CAOF left for our assigned area in north Germany, in the province of Ostfriesland, the area where we fought our last battles of the war. We rolled north through Apeldoorn, Zwolle and on to Assen, where we pitched our tents for the night. In the morning, July 8, we moved on. Crossing into Germany this time, in daylight and with no rain, was much less depressing than on that night of April 21. The convoy moved through Leer, where the various regiments broke off to go to their assigned locations throughout the peninsula.

We of the 2/13th Regiment continued on to an open field adjacent to a little town called Zetel. We pitched tents there for the first night, but moved into billets in commandeered houses in the town the next day. Zetel was not badly located for some place to go in the evening — 16 kilometres south-west of Wilhelmshaven and about 35km north of Oldenburg.

Chapter 19

The group I was with took over a house at 319 Urwaldstrasse, which allowed two of us to a room. I believe we were each given an army-issue cot and mattress, although my diary doesn't mention it. Our privy — outhouse or backhouse, as we would call it — was in the backyard, appropriately enough, and was of the rural European style, which catches everything in a large tank where it is treated with lime, diluted with water and then pumped out at intervals to be distributed as fertilizer on fields. This process startled us a bit, and gave us some emotional conflict during our first purchase of items like delicious ripe tomatoes. But we got over it. Even when tamed with lime, the odour on spreading days was powerful.

Our kitchen and dining hall — our mess, that is — was in what we referred to as a bowling alley. Actually it was a skittle-alley, or Kegelbahn in German, in which the lanes are narrow and concave. Skittles was a common game in Europe and may be still. Out at the rear, around the slop-drum, hungry children collected just as they had at our mess back in Zeist in the Netherlands — and they were treated in the same variety of fashions. I did my same conscious-easing bit as at Zeist. One day as I came out as a straggler near the end, a man was standing there, dressed in a suit and tie, with a hat on. I thought he might be a German official from some aid society. When the children had moved away, the man stepped forward to the drum as I was leaving, opened up a newspaper he was carrying, ran his cupped hand around a morsel-laden grease-ring inside the drum, placed his big scoop in the newspaper, folded it up and walked away. He, or a friend or a pet, had to be awfully hungry.

Some CAOF men had to complete a military training program — those who had had no experience in action, maybe. I was assigned to a group who were put on police and check-point duty. The Ostfriesland peninsula was traversed by what was called the Ems-Jade Canal.

There were 200,000 German troops north of the canal, we were told, who were under their own commanders and were gradually being processed for discharge by their military authorities. One of our duties was to see that no German military personnel crossed the canal

The Canadian Army of Occupation: 1

without certain papers. A citizen who could not produce an "Ausweis" or "Kennkarte,' which were identity cards, was to be arrested.

On one occasion I was on shift with a sergeant at a main highway bridge over the canal. He took one lane and gave me the other. We had a vehicle with a 19-set radio. The length of the canal itself was patrolled by another unit of us. All was going well, with nothing out of the ordinary, until I flagged down this particular German vehicle. A German officer briskly stepped out, clicked his heels and gave me the Nazi salute, which he quickly and sheepishly pulled down into a regular salute and handed me his papers. They were in order.

I was certain that he had acted on reflex, the result of having snapped up that stiff-arm dozens of times a day for possibly four or five years. I acted as though I hadn't noticed — as if one could possibly miss it — and sent him on. Over in the other lane, the sergeant had a group of people stopped. I was afraid to look across, and was hoping he hadn't been paying any attention. He had.

"Why didn't you shoot him," he yelled. "You had the right. Remember what they told us?"

The sergeant was correct. He grudgingly accepted my explanation, but told me not to let it happen again. I planned that from then on I would get up against the door of any flagged-down German vehicle that appeared to hold an officer, and take his papers through the window. But I had no more on any of my shifts. Most of the traffic was on foot and on bicycles.

What the sergeant was referring to was an instruction, verbally given by one of our commanders at the time of the ceasefire, that we were to shoot at once any hardcore, arrogant fanatic who defiantly gave us the Nazi salute in our face. If I had ever had to do such a thing, regardless of the provocation, and of the military reasoning (authority must be brusquely and immediately established), it probably would have haunted me for the rest of my life.

At a later time, either I or the sergeant stopped a vehicle driven by a young civilian and his friend. Neither of them had the vehicle's ownership, which meant that we had to arrest them and seize the car. The car is what has me remember the incident.

Chapter 19

My father had been a garage mechanic. I was looking it over with great interest as the sergeant was on the radio getting instructions. It was a DKW, Deutche Krupp Werke, with a motor that had only three cylinders and appeared to be not much bigger than our Briggs and Stratton battery charger. In the light of motors as we knew them in those days, this thing was phenomenal. Some of the canal guard had gathered around. The sergeant asked something like, "Who thinks he can drive this thing?" Already wedged in the tight space behind the wheel, I quickly announced my ability, based on two or three minutes of experimental fooling with gadgets.

With the two boys in the back and a guard sitting beside me, we were dispatched to a headquarters a fair distance away, probably Aurich. The first bucking and gear-grinding half-kilometre was pure trial and error. The gear-shift was just a straight plunger that came out of the dash. Gears were selected by pushing in or pulling out the shaft to different locations and by twisting the handle. But we got there, and I enjoyed the whole education.

Not long after our arrival in Zetel, I had my first swim in Europe, in a quarry that some of the boys had found just outside the town. It was a hot day. By mid-afternoon, the water was crowded with naked bodies. I thought of the quarries and ponds at home — and most of all, of the St. Lawrence River, which on those hot summer days cooled us river rats who lived along its banks. Soldiers like myself who came from communities associated with this big lumbering watercourse sneered at what the Europeans called a river.

My first mail in the occupations force came in on July 13. It was my mother's 19th parcel, packed with toothsome food and the usual letter. She called it my birthday parcel, and reminded me that as of the 5th of that month I was 22 years old. If the war hadn't been over, I doubt that she would have reminded me. She held to most of the regular superstitions and had a few of her own making.

She told me also that according to our local paper a relative of mine from the area, Merton Burchell, had won the Croix de Guerre for some action in France, and that a hometown boy, Allen Pettem was in Amsterdam. Merton I knew, of course, but I didn't know Allen per-

The Canadian Army of Occupation: 1

sonally in civilian life. He was a number of years older than I (so was Merton), and had attended the Royal Military Academy in Kingston. My age group in town were more amused than awed by the stunning array of uniforms that Allen came home in, and by the way he walked in a starched, robotic manner with his swagger stick, trapping it in his armpit whenever he required the use of both hands. In church he would come to a halt in the aisle and make a crisp right-angle turn in order to proceed into the family pew. He probably served well as a commissioned officer. It's just that his image to us ignorant younger set seemed to have no connection with fighting a war.

If anything was left of my birthday parcel, I may well have stuffed my pockets with it two days later, when I was among 18 who were picked from our unit for guard duty at a medieval castle called Schloss Godens, about 15 kilometres north of Zetel. Something to nibble on helped to absorb the time in the more lonely hours of such a job. The castle had been commandeered for the headquarters of the CAOF 3rd Division's Royal Canadian Artillery. Having no field guns, we were artillery in name only, of course — five regiments of men armed with the standard .303 Lee-Enfield rifle (which had been issued to us in place of the Sten). The army mercifully assigned a new guard every 24 hours, picked from various places in these regiments.

It so happened that on our castle-guarding day, according to my diary, the fraternization ban was lifted. It had been pretty well ignored, anyway, by about the third week after the ceasefire, at least as far as talking to the male citizenry. The ban's main emphasis concerned fraternizing with women. We heard that the Americans kept their ban in force longer, and even executed several of their men for disobeying. Dating in the traditional sense did not seem to be an option for us, ban or no ban, for there were no prospects of our age who would yet dare come out into the open in the area. Parents kept their daughters well chaperoned. As a result of these circumstances, the guard detail was bursting with optimism of a more carnal texture when it was given the evening in Oldenburg the next day, after 24 hours of defending the castle. The city, about 35 kilometres to the south, has a present-day population of about 137,000. With the sex

Chapter 19

trade's history of free enterprise linked firmly over several millennia with the history of military forces, there was no reason to be worried that the Oldenburg market might have been missed, or that the city's new military service centre, known as the Beaver Club, would not have its boxes of condoms.

And the Club had lots of beer at a heavily subsidized price, which it served outside as well, in a "Konzertgarten." With tables set among trees, and a trio or so of musicians playing, it was quite pleasant. On this or a later Oldenburg visit, I met another Prescott boy, Jim Whitney. We talked and drank together for a couple of hours. Because of European influence, Canadians in the armed forces overseas were quick to become accustomed to drinking where everyone could see them — even women and children, for heaven's sake.

Back in Canada soldiers on leave in their home towns, who wanted to have a drink with the boys, were sitting in dingy "beer parlours," with high or stained-glass windows or windows near the ceiling so that the innocent could not look in. The wafting movement of the swinging doors into the usually filthy washrooms would be blending the smells of urine and beer. For years after the war, I could not legally drink an alcoholic beverage in my own yard if the beverage could be recognized as such from the street.

For the last half of July and the first half of August, I was with a force assigned to round up Russians who, during the war, had volunteered or had been forced by the Nazi government to come into this section of Germany to work. Some must have come from prisoner-of-war camps, for they were wearing Russian uniforms, or parts of them — even the women. The CAOF learned quite early that its problems in maintaining law and order were not to be with the demobilizing German forces nor with the citizens, all of whom invariably co-operated. Problems came from the understandable desperation of these Russian workers, who were DPs, a term mentioned earlier. Europe had a large number of DPs after the war, whom the Allies held in camps, awaiting resettlement. They had nothing — their homes destroyed and their home countries in chaos. Some eventually became Canadian citizens.

The Canadian Army of Occupation: 1

These Russian DPs, however, were a special case. Whether they were forced or volunteered to come to Germany made no difference to Stalin. Either way they were considered traitors, for which the penalty was usually death. These workers suspected that they might be so classified, and, quite reasonably, did not want to go home. As well, they were reported to have found conditions here much better than in Russia. But Stalin demanded their return. To keep peace in the Allied family, Britain and Canada complied.

It was a cruel business. We helped in the roundup, but I believe that British troops had the task of forcing them onto ships bound for Russian ports. They hid on us in haystacks and wooded areas and came out to steal food at night. Citizens, by way of military orders passed through local German government, were told that they must not give shelter to these people, many of whom had worked as farm hands on these farms during the war.

A July 22 note in my diary reminds me of our coming upon a distraught woman whose farmer husband had just been stabbed to death because, as we interpreted it, he wouldn't hide his assailant. It was the only killing that our particular patrol came upon in the course of these roundups, and we never found it necessary to fire a shot.

Whenever we levelled a rifle at the poor souls, they stopped and gave up. Hunger usually brought them out. At the compound where we took them they were well fed. For much of the time I was in an armoured scout-car — not that we needed the armour, but with the large wheels and four-wheel drive, we could go over practically any terrain in pursuit. Our companion vehicle in the unit was a small truck. Theft of a variety of goods, even cattle, became common with these fugitives — items no doubt for a black market. Patrol units in another area had a couple of alleged rapists to track down.

My July 27 diary entry would give the image of the casualness, even the callousness, of it all. It says that we caught seven Russians, presumably a good day, and that I got a letter from my mother, in which she told me about the disappearance of our family dog. The entry adds also that two days earlier I received 600 cigarettes from the Cardinal Service Club.

Chapter 19

The Russian women among these displaced persons — and there were quite a number — gave us no problem. They stayed within the designated compound, where they put up forms of decorations around the barracks to make the place less bleak. They sang and did folk dancing to the renditions of a group of musicians among them. We stopped on our patrols to watch and listen whenever nearby. In a sort of desperation, it would seem, some competent artists among them, men or women, had painted busts of Stalin on enormous posters that were erected about the camp.

Some 30 years after the war when I was a high school teacher-librarian, a woman came in to do volunteer work in the library, in accordance to a standard invitation to parents.

She had a boy attending the school. As we talked for a moment one day, she mentioned that she was a post-war immigrant, which brought up a reference to war's dreadful disruption of people. I spoke of my experience with rounding up displaced Russians in north Germany, to be sent back to appease Stalin. I know, she said. I was one of them. It startled me. She verified the terrible business, and explained how her life was probably saved. As the train she was on pulled slowly into a station in Russia, she noticed by pure chance some of her relatives and friends standing among a group on the tracks on the opposite side of the train, a distance short of the platform.

She jumped down and blended into the group, apparently unnoticed, and went home with them. She had been shielded by the train for a moment as it pulled on ahead to the platform on the far side. Either a Gulag or the firing squad might have awaited her otherwise.

In those years after the war, when soul-searching literature began to appear — searching someone else's soul, as a rule — with respect to the responsibility for and the acceptance of Nazism, I thought about my part in this rounding-up of displaced persons. What would be my argument if somehow the tables were turned and I stood in the dock to face questions?

"Are you telling the court that you participated in the hunting-down of innocent human beings who were to be shipped from the

The Canadian Army of Occupation: 1

country and possibly murdered, because it was your duty to obey orders? Did you not question such an order? Were you possibly one of the soldiers who helped force your escaping sacrificial fellow soldiers back onto the ship for Hong Kong to . . ." "Objection! The defendant is not on trial for . . .." Eventually, within the same reversal of tables, someone writes a book of drivel telling how such behaviour can be traced to a national trait inherent in the Canadian psyche, as revealed for example in the Boer War's civilian slaughter, the annihilation of the Beotuk Indian, the eagerness to get into the killing in World Wars I and II, the export of Indian children, the torturing to death of a Somali citizen — a book to help ward off enlightened perception.

But the tables were not going to move, and we got on with the round-up. At least on one occasion, though, our patrols performed a better type of service. Two groups of us were on the night shift covering a designated area, one group with a scout car and the other with a truck. The truck, some distance ahead in the early morning darkness, told us on the radio that a horse and wagon in considerable haste had just come out of a farm lane ahead of them and that they were going to stop them. By the time we pulled up, a worried farmer was explaining that he was taking his pregnant wife in labour to the hospital. The boys convinced him they could get her there faster. They got the stretcher from the truck, loaded her on, slid her in the back, climbed in and, with the farmer giving directions up front, headed for the nearest hospital, which was at Neuenburg some 18 kilometres away. We tied the horse to a tree and went back to work. The other fellows would return in an hour. They called us later on the radio to say all was well.

The next day, in true soldier fashion, they enjoyed telling us how, at about 0300 hrs, with the woman on the stretcher, they barged into the sleeping little hospital while boisterously calling out for a doctor and nurses and waking up all the wards. We all talked about going back to see the child and the family later, but none of us did that I can recall. Our job was more the threatening of life than a concern for nourishing it.

Chapter 19

The CAOF Command in our area did try to establish a good relationship with the citizens, and it chose possibly the best way: through the children. It set us to work organizing a children's party, with jeep rides, extra food including candy, and a projector with cartoons. About 700 children attended. It was a great day for both the children and the parents. The event loosened us up, which resulted in a warmer relationship from then on. A community dance that evening helped as well.

An element that we had been cautioned to watch for among German veterans and civilians made only one symbolic appearance quite early, in the image of a werewolf — or Werwolf, in German — painted in black on the side of a building. I mentioned this alleged clandestine German underground organization earlier. The painted image, which had indications of being put on by way of a coarse brush and a large stencil, showed, in silhouette, a character in a slightly stooped Groucho Marx stance, wearing a cloak and a hat with a wide turned-down brim. German veterans we talked to considered the scheme a joke. Certainly no other image ever appeared in our area, nor did anything occur that could be interpreted as resistance, beyond a few black-marketeers who were accused of receiving stolen goods from the Russian DPs.

On one of our policing patrols, we stopped at what must have previously been a small auxiliary Luftwaffe airport. Some damaged planes were still parked there. I got a peculiar thrill out of nestling into their cockpits, to "[pull] back the stick and hurtle into the sun," as the poet Roland Flint puts it. From the onomatopoeia coming from other planes, I think that we all got a kick out of it. There were three different kinds to play with. I could still identify today the FW-190. The other two numbers in my diary mean nothing to me now: JU-188 and JU-352.

We four of our crew, on a day off, went to Wilhelmshaven for the first time. Unlike Oldenburg with hardly a scratch, the city had taken a terrible beating. Large areas were flattened except for those remarkable columns of stairs, which often survived, reaching up through what were once several floors. It would be possible to climb them,

The Canadian Army of Occupation: 1

flight after flight, if one felt silly enough. I saw my first electric busses here, running from overhead cables like a streetcar. On pneumatic tires, they seemed to move in ghostly silence, through streets of half-buildings, piles of rubble, and scaffolding. The date must have been August 14, for we heard that Japan had surrendered.

With a leave-pass to Ireland in my pocket, I was up early on August 17 and on my way to Nijmegen in a returning army supply truck now loaded with leave-takers on their way to hundreds of different places. There was nothing out until the next morning for me, so I went to a movie, *The Suspect*, then had a good night's sleep in an army hostel and took a train the next day to Calais, passing through Brussels about midnight. After a boat to Dover, I set my watch back an hour and caught a train into Euston Station in London. While wandering around London with a few hours to spare, I came out onto the street from a tube station just in time to join a line along the curb to catch a look at a royal procession that was approaching. I saw Clement Attlee and the King and Queen go by, on their way to Westminster Abbey, I was told.

It was a Sunday, August 19. This accidental viewing was quite a thrill to me and would certainly be in my next letters home. From London's St. Pancras Station I had another overnight train ride to Stranraer on the west coast of Scotland, arriving at 0500 hrs the next morning. The boat trip from there is about 50 kilometres across the North Channel to Larne, on the Irish coast north of Belfast, to where I took a train and found a room at a Service Club.

On a bicycle from the Hotel Kensington's rental business, I toured about during the week trying to see everything the Service Club recommended in its brochures. Cycling forays clear of the city had a special appeal to me. The countryside in any of the European countries that I came to know had a settled atmosphere, allowing a beauty to be formed, in contrast to our frontier attitude.

My only memories from our school geography lessons on the Emerald Isle were of the teacher telling us that it is saucer-shaped, with most of its rugged higher land hugging the shoreline, and that it

Chapter 19

really is exceptionally green, the result of the soil and of prevailing winds off the warm and moist Gulf Stream.

I knew nothing of Ireland's political and religious conflict; and if Ab Harrison had told me that his relatives in Belfast, whose address he had given me, were Roman Catholic, it would have had no significance for me politically.

But within a short time of entering the house of his grandparents and aunt, I was made disturbingly aware of how significant it was.

When the IRA went into action many years later, I was surprised that it had taken that long for severe violence to erupt. Ab's grandfather sat me down at the kitchen table and brought out a pile of documents, maps and clippings. In anger, he laid out the second-class existence of Catholics in Northern Ireland: 35 percent of the population yet not a single representative in any level of government; electoral boundaries erratically carved out to ensure that condition; virtually no Catholics on police forces or in any other civil service job; housing discrimination. His clippings were of anti-Catholic riots, beatings and murders. He had British posters and proclamations going back to the Easter Rebellion of 1916, which outlined the offences such as curfew violation for which one would be shot on sight. It was an enlightening afternoon for me.

His daughter got him calmed down long enough for us to have a cup of tea before I left. You must take "the word" back to Canada, he told me. He never asked about my religion. Actually "the word" did come back with me. This experience, and the one to come in a few days time farther south, helped me in teaching the "Irish Question" in the grade 10 modern history course.

Accidentally once again, I stumbled within the aura of notable personage. I just happened to be in the street in a good location when General Eisenhower began the review of his honour guard in front of Belfast's Queen's University, where he had gotten or was about to get an honorary doctorate, I was told. Somewhere through the day he picked up also the Freedom of the City. I felt as though I had one of those myself.

The Canadian Army of Occupation: 1

On August 27, I rented a civilian suit for 10 shillings so that I could get across the border into the Republic of Ireland, officially known as Eire. It was the only way the customs would let me in. Even the few Irish from Eire who had enlisted in the British forces could not come home in uniform. One of them crossed when I did, both of us commenting on how strange we felt out of army clothes, and how weird the whole thing was. In contrast to the uniform with its heavy wool, my suit let every little breeze go right through to the skin.

My train took me across the border, stopped for customs at Dunkalk and then went on to Dublin. The economic and political contrast between Ireland and the United Kingdom was striking. I was hardly there two days, and only in Dublin, but just in that time surprises came at me from every direction. The Irish soldier's uniform was a different shade of khaki than either the British or ours, and an entirely different cut — closer to the German style, actually — and his footwear was clearly similar to the German jackboot, except that it was brown.

The stores were full of goods, and at a cheaper price than in the UK. The restaurants seemed to lack nothing, not even steaks. In the pubs a mug of beer was four pence, hardly believable. In the UK a mug was one shilling and four pence, or four times the cost. Of course, one would have to know about wages and taxes there to make a true comparison. A Dubliner in the British army told me of the first contrast that struck him when he came back on a leave in the middle of the war: the shops, homes and streets were all lit up. He had grown used to the continuous blackout in the UK, whereas Dublin glowed against the night sky.

I went to a movie in the evening. It was called The *49th Parallel*, and was about German saboteurs coming ashore somewhere in the Canadian north. They are passing themselves off as something or other that made movie sense. As they talk in a shack with some French Canadians, the topic of the war comes up and how it got started. A German asks the question: "Who started this war, anyway?" A French-Canadian replies: "The Germans did, of course." At that,

Chapter 19

shouts and boos erupted throughout the theatre. A few people actually stood up for a moment to express their anger at the answer.[51]

With the cheaper price of goods in the Republic, smuggling was bound to be a problem. At the stop for Northern Ireland customs after crossing the border, every passenger had to get out onto the platform. Officers searched the train and all luggage — and the passengers, if anything looked suspicious. They confiscated a pair of wooden-soled sandals off the feet of a woman who had been sitting near me.

Arriving back in Belfast in the evening, I got into uniform again. My Irish leave was up if I were to have a day or so in London and still get back on time. So, by retracing my steps back to Scotland and catching a night train out of Stranraer, I reached London in the afternoon of August 29, got a room off Sloan Square and then headed out into the big city's evening. Out of the hundreds of thousands of military men spread over Europe, I walk into one of the city's Canadian armed forces drinking holes and find Sergeant Roy Buswell, sitting alone at a table, nursing on a pint of beer. This type of moment is strange, even disorienting. I'm back in the war for a moment, and then suddenly I'm not. A man is waving with a gesture of friendship that does not belong to him — flagging me over to his table while he orders more beer for us.

He was considerably less reticent now, and seemed very pleased to find someone he knew. He acknowledged he had been watching the door for a familiar face in spite of the slim odds. We talked about our close calls in the war, and some of the funny parts. He wanted to hear about my home life, but he could not be lured into talking about his own. We spent the evening together, which included a lot of drinking, a good meal and then a show on Piccadilly, called *Blood on the Sun*. He was waiting in a camp in south England, he said, and was soon to be on a ship home. He did not really seem pleased at the prospect. Later that night he took the tube to Waterloo Station to catch a train. I would never see him again. We possibly shook hands. I don't remember. Or maybe we just said, "So long." That was common.

Although blind tired, I found my way back to Sloan Square. Among the great joys of a military leave is being able to ignore a

The Canadian Army of Occupation: 1

morning and actually get slept right out, in a room all your own. It was wonderful to come out of the Square at about noon the next day and have a big "breakfast." The afternoon is neither in my diary nor memory, but that evening I went back to the Regent theatre on Piccadilly and saw the movie, *A Bell for Adano* — possibly from the best seats, by using one of the expensive ticket stubs, a sneaky trick earlier mentioned.

A train out of Victoria Station just before midnight began my return trip to duty: Dover, a boat to Calais, an overnight train to Nijmegen, with a stop for tea at midnight in Brussels. The new day was September 1. In Nijmegen I found a supply truck heading for Oldenburg, and from there another one to Zetel, a town returned to its civilians; the 2/44th Battery had moved.

20

The Canadian Army of Occupation

Part ll

While I was on leave, the 2/13th Field Regiment, along with the 2/12th, had moved into one place: the accommodations of the large, former Luftwaffe airfield at Jever, about 17 kilometres north-west of Wilhelmshaven.

I hitch-hiked from Zetel to Jever on that September 1 evening, and was so taken up with exploring through the big hangars there that I didn't bother checking in until the next morning. I had picked up my gear from somewhere, probably the guardhouse. I was in the office of one of the hangars when I decided finally to quit for the night. Scattered in the office drawers was an unusual kind of paper clip. I put a handful in my big pack; and a few of them are still here in my den, 55 years later. As it was getting somewhat late to find a barrack bunk, I removed the pins from a door and placed it on the cold concrete-based floor and opened my bedroll on it.

In the morning I reported back from leave, picked up a parcel from my mother, which she had numbered as "20," and was directed to the quarters of the 2/44th Battery. The barracks were large, attractive three-storey red brick buildings, which formed four sides of a huge parade square. The men of the Luftwaffe were certainly well looked after. The floors in our building were in wood parquet pattern, quite handsome, a type of floor that few of us had ever seen. Nor had many of us seen such attractive toilet and shower areas. The sleeping

The Canadian Army of Occupation: ll

quarters were in pleasant rooms of various sizes, with tables, chairs, closets and shelves, and were entered off either side of a corridor which ran the length of the building.

In constructing these buildings, the "Thousand-Year Reich" would appear to have been in mind. It all seemed solid and permanent. The mess hall, even the "other ranks" one, was a pleasant place to eat. The interior of the officers' mess was impressively finished in wood -- impressive to me, anyway, as a wood-lover. I was somewhat startled, though, to see a gleaming wooden casket suspended on chains from the ceiling above the tables. Attractively inscribed messages were written all over it.

I managed to get one line written down before having to move on: "Es ist so schön im Puff zu sterben." "It is so beautiful to die in a brothel." Other lines may have been standard warnings to pilots, like, "Don't let them get between you and the sun!" But I assumed that one to be some strange warning against the same venereal diseases that our armed forces had to fear.

Freshly-cut evergreen trees placed upright in holders and changed at appropriate intervals had helped to camouflage the airfield. They were still standing on duty, dry and brittle. No one had told them it was all over.

It appeared as though the place had never been bombed. I once asked my RCAF veteran friend why this target was missed or neglected — a large airfield closer to England than Lübeck or Hamburg and only half the distance to Berlin. The records, he said, indicated that it was once raided, but they showed no damage assessment. Other small airfields that we eventually saw in Ostfriesland had bombing scars all over them.

It may not be phenomenal that I would, in the course of my time in Europe as one of some 280,000 soldiers, come upon 10 soldiers from my hometown of 3,000 people. If in the statistical analysis of chance factors that figure is what might be expected, then it seems to me that I should have come upon 10 soldiers of every comparable town of 3,000 in Canada. And I may very well have, as far as I know.

Chapter 20

However, be that as it may, on this second day of September I met another hometown boy, Merwin Place. He was curious also about the planes that were sitting in front of some of the hangars. The Stuka was easily recognized, and just had to be sat in. All the planes had been robbed for parts. The British had taken over the airfield at the end of the war and had shipped home everything of interest to its military.

The most interesting aircraft carcasses there were of the ME-163, the rocket plane, which the Germans nicknamed Die Komet. It could fly at something close to 900 km/hr. Unquestionably the British had packed up all the good specimens of those, for they were revolutionary. This was the craft that Shaw and I saw briefly one night the previous March over Kleve. Those left behind had broken wings and obviously had things removed, including the little nose cone, which may have contained an instrument. All canopies were gone. Each looked like a short, fat cigar with blunt wings and a vertical but no horizontal tail-piece, and no wheels other than a little pup-wheel at the back. A heavy skid formed part of the fuselage along the bottom.

The plane did its take-off run on temporary wheels but left them behind on the runway. Its skid landing was done on grass runways, the only kind Jever had, I think. I got into one that was upright. It barely had room for a seat between the two big rocket-fuel tanks, which were covered with a soft rubber-like material at least a centimetre thick. I peeled off a slab of it and, along with a switch of some kind, mailed them home in the next parcel.

One of the craft's remarkable features was its bullet-proof front windscreen, which was about eight or nine centimetres thick. Earlier I had read an article on this development. The first Allied discovery of the glass was from a shot-down FW-190, it said. The initial response to the report of the discovery, understandably enough, was disbelief, because with the incredible deflection in glass at that thickness, a pilot couldn't hit a dirigible, let alone another plane. But there was no mistake — and no deflection, either. I held up a loose one and looked through it at all angles. And then, to confirm what the article said about the structure of the glass, I pounded it with a heavy piece of steel until a slight dent revealed that it was indeed made up of alter-

The Canadian Army of Occupation: ll

nate layers of thin glass and a mysterious soft substance, one layer somehow cancelling out the deflection of the other, with a final zero deflection result.

In 1992, I received a Christmas card from a friend in north Germany. The picture on it was an artist's conception of the ME-163 in flight, in its full WW II markings — on its way to engage the enemy, it would seem, judging from the vapour trails of a formation of bombers above. Ironically, the card was an import into Germany. It was made in the United States in Macon, Georgia. The caption, in German, below the picture ends with the phrase, "a first step toward the space travel of today."

To keep us busy when off duty, regimental headquarters emphasized competitive sports and supplied equipment for them. On September 3, all who were not on duty were transported to the army's big divisional sports meet in a Wilhelmshaven stadium. It was pleasant to have this on my second day back from leave, rather than having been stuck with road-block checks or rounding up displaced persons. From our regiment, an officer by the name of Waugh — a broad-shouldered, athletic type, who years later became the commander of the Gagetown New Brunswick army camp, had just been determined as the winner in the shot-put. We gave him a round of applause.

Among the spectators were German soldiers in bandages or in casts of various sorts, probably from a nearby rehabilitation camp. While the officials reeled in their tape and spectators began moving away, a big German on crutches with a cast on his foot slowly scooped his way forward and into the shot-put circle. His friend with him picked up a shot, gave it to him and then held his crutches. The men in the marker area looked up and moved to the side. With only limited assistance from his bad leg, and without a spin, he arched back and dropped the shot just beyond Waugh's stake. He took back his crutches and moved on to another event.

I don't know whether Waugh saw the throw or not. My group, which had watched him closely, fantasized about how he was a shot-put medal winner for Germany at the 1936 Olympics in Berlin. He may have been. After all, that event had been only nine years ago.

Chapter 20

Inevitably we talked about Jesse Owens with his four gold medals and how he "showed" the Germans at that Olympics. But we didn't talk about how at that time Owens, in German society, would have been more free than he had ever been in his life. He could drink from the same fountain, for instance, and enter a building by the same door as everyone else. In his own country in particular circumstances, he could still be lynched or burned to death because of the colour of his skin. No, those things never came up, because we were indifferent and ignorant. For the same reasons we were unaware that certain German athletes, because they were Jews, were not allowed to compete in those 1936 Olympics.

Canada never had its own food supply system. Our rations were British rations throughout the war, and here in the occupations force continued to be. There was no direct shipment of food from Canada to the Canadian armed forces. We knew that while on our leaves in Britain we could order pork chops or steaks if we had the money. Not only were we getting none of this here in camp, but we were getting less of the standard fare.

Our staple protein came from canned Argentinean corned beef and from a canned mixture called "M & V," meat and vegetables in heavy gravy, a concoction we had known from our compo pack in action. Other features of the British rations were powdered eggs, powdered potatoes — and "sawdust sausages," as they were called because of their deficiency in any form of meat.

To make the issue more irritating, our kitchen was buying fresh vegetables from local farmers with the profits created by a successful canteen that had been set up, profits that would normally be fed back to lower the canteen prices. German citizens at the time were hard up for money and food. Consider that scene around the slop drum in Zetel! The farmer sold to the highest bidder: the army. Some of us, including myself, bought the occasional egg or two on the black market and fried them up in our rooms, on a hot-plate bought on the black market. Electricity, by the way, in our area of Germany, and perhaps elsewhere, too, was shut off for most of the daylight hour.

The Canadian Army of Occupation: ll

Complaints had gone on for about a month, with no effect beyond a statement that rations had naturally been reduced from war standard, but they had been checked and found to conform in all ways to the military standard for peacetime. One of the more literate among us wrote a letter to a newspaper in Canada and sent it to his parents to mail, while also asking his parents to call their MP. I have forgotten how all that turned out; but both my memory and diary record the outcome of a protest scheme devised by the troops.

The regiment was allotted a day for something called "tabloid sports," a fixed pattern of events for a day's sports meet. It was set up on a sports ground in the area, and we were all ordered to be there and to fill every event with our participation. We told our NCOs that of course we would obey, for disobedience was a serious charge; but the military brass ought to be informed that because of the poor quality of our rations we would not be able to perform well. As was the plan, our efforts portrayed malnutrition. The 100-metre dash, for example, was run at not much more than a fast trot. My name went on a clipboard for some event, but I can't remember what it was, or whether my turn came up before the whole thing ended.

And end it did, abruptly, when it became quite obvious to the brass what was going on. Our regiment's colonel, who was watching the charade, issued an order to an underling and walked away with his entourage. Commands were barked. The meet was cancelled. We were formed up and marched back to our parade square where we were drilled for the rest of the day, and then confined to barracks.

What punishment awaited the rest I have long forgotten; but for a group that included me, it started early the next morning, September 7. An officer picked out 18 of us, seemingly at random, for the precarious job of working with a German army-engineering unit assigned to bomb-disposal, or the disposal of any of the war's unexploded devices left around the countryside.

We were sent to Vielstadt outside Bremen, and joined the Germans there. Their crews were made up of about six men each, I think, and each crew was required to have two armed Canadians with it at all times — armed with the big clumsy .303 Lee-Enfield rifle. In

Chapter 20

threatening terms, our duty was laid out to us. We were to observe all operations and see that every item collected was accounted for and turned in at a depot each day.

The German crew dropped us off at our camp at night and picked us up in the morning. Once the explosives were turned in, neither of us were under any strict schedule. Their headquarters and compound were not far from where we were staying. Apparently our Command feared that the Germans would hide explosive devices and eventually use them in some nefarious scheme. After a couple of days together, we came to realize that hiding away mines and shells was the last thing on these fellows' minds — minds that we found loaded with thoughts similar to ours: of girls, alcohol, home, staying alive, keeping a low profile to avoid authority.

The German unit's headquarters had a large map on the wall. People, mostly farmers, would call in to report an unexploded bomb or shell or other device on their property or in one of their buildings. The location would then be marked on the map by a pin and recorded. Each morning the German sergeant from each of our crews would go in and be given several of these locations to investigate and solve.

We guards didn't have to go in, but I always did because I found it so fascinating. Perhaps in there I was an "everyman" in the sense that I remember the term's use in a literature class on drama many years later. It was as though I were invisible in one of those war movies which is depicting the activity in a German command post. I moved around with no one paying any attention, while heels clicked, jackboots glistened, salutes snapped up, and officers bent over tables of papers. Naturally things were not the same without the black leather Luger and P-38 holsters. I was now standing there with one of those P-38s in my left inside tunic pocket, where it had been since the war ended. When my crew's sergeant had received his list of potential catastrophes to attend to, he checked around to catch my eye and we left together. I wasn't invisible after all.

Each crew had a couple of German army vehicles. The one of ours that I remember was a long, canvas-topped car with a V-6 air-cooled engine called a Daimler "Speil," a word that my dictionary

The Canadian Army of Occupation: ll

defines as "skewer." It apparently loses, or gains, something in translation. But then, North America once had a car called the Dodge "Dart." With the English fragments of several crew members, they managed to tell us about a little air-cooled engine in a car called the Volkswagen, an oddity that we had heard about, but few of us had yet seen. Back home, twelve years later, 1957, the VW would become our family car, and would continue to be for 24 unbroken years thereafter.

The ordinance we were gathering consisted mostly of mines, along with artillery and mortar shells and bombs that had failed to explode. To disarm and gather up this stuff was risky business. When something was determined to be too critical, the men used a detonating charge called a "Springkörper," a block of an explosive about the size of a half brick, and with a small hole in which to insert an ignition cap. A control wire was attached to this cap and reeled out to a safe distance, where it was attached to a little plunger-generator similar to the big one seen near the end of the movie, *The Bridge on the River Kwai*.

I was always pleased to see them choose this option; but if a shell, for instance, was in a hay mow, the option wasn't always viable.

One explosion turned out to be more than expected. A particular item on our list was determined by the engineers to be a phosphorus bomb, a firebomb. It was well out in a large bare field and buried almost out of sight. For some reason, maybe just to see the effect, they decided to blow it, but were concerned about whether the Springkörper was strong enough to start the chain reaction. They had already disarmed some mines, "Teller-minen," that day, so they snugged a couple of these up against the little detonating block to help out.

And they probably re-armed them. They reeled out a lot of cable, and we got ourselves into the depression of a ditch a good distance away. The explosion was quite pronounced, but the unexpected part was the column of black smoke about the diameter of the field, which climbed straight up ever higher into a clear calm sky. Our fellows mentioned something about how maybe the phosphorous ignited peat

Chapter 20

in the soil. Eventually a plane came over and circled the column — probably a Mustang from the Americans in Bremen.

We had drawn attention. We waved in a casual manner in an attempt to indicate that everything was alright. The field cooled down after awhile and we moved on. We had created one more crater wound in the landscape for some military detail with the proper equipment to come along and heal. Our crew sergeant said that he faced some questions over the matter, but stressed to his officers that it was too critical to leave and too dangerous to be dealt with any other way.

I was glad that he wasn't removed and assigned to disarming kitchen pots; for we taught one another our language all day long.

To mention Bremen reminds me that the Americans occupied that city for some reason, even though it was deep in the Canadian and British zones.

One of our decommissioning assignments, a bomb, happened to be inside the American zone's boundary. On the way there we had picked up a hitchhiking British soldier. Eventually, we were stopped by an American sentry, who logged our purpose and assorted nationalities. When we moved on, our crew sergeant smiled and remarked in his budding English that: "An American sentry has just checked a German army vehicle containing one English soldier, six German soldiers and two Canadian soldiers." That little anecdote I found in one of my letters written home.

I do remember, and have it recorded, that our crew de-fused two large bombs in our time together, 500-pounders I would guess. One man did the work, as I recall; but before each move, the others would move up to give their agreement and move back to a safe distance. I assume that a big crane came along later and took the neutered monsters out to sea, or whatever.

The war, I suppose, had more or less conditioned, or numbed, all of us to the risks. Simply driving around with mines, shells and the extracted detonating charges piled in the trunk or under our feet was a considerable risk in itself.

Our crew came through unscathed, but one of the Germans in another crew either made a slip or fell victim of a pure accident in dis-

The Canadian Army of Occupation: ll

arming a mine. He was killed instantly and his partner near him was wounded, but the Canadian guards were untouched. Two days later, September 14, his crew, including the two Canadians, attended his funeral.

The guarding business became ever more ludicrous, except when brass was in the vicinity. When getting into the vehicle I eventually found myself first passing my rifle in to one of the engineers.

Once, two of our crews heard that a dance was to take place at a Gasthaus on a country road that evening, so we made plans to attend. Beer was either there or the Wehrmacht boys found some. The dance went on till near midnight before we all reported back. A crazier part of that evening was that the so-called guards were dancing as well, with rifles stacked in the corner. We tried to make sure that someone was watching the road at all times for an approaching military vehicle, the only vehicles that had gas.

We just had one nervous moment. Shortly after dark a German noticed headlights in the distance that had turned onto our country road. He came in hollering at us while he ran to the corner and grabbed rifles to bring to us to speed things up. Although a bit dishevelled, we were out when the vehicle got there — and kept right on going. "On with the dance! Let joy be unconfined!"

The Germans knew that if our brass ever discovered the charade, the happy times of all of us were over, which was an understatement for us Canadians — abandonment of guard duty over explosives, and voluntary surrendering of weapons! That's prison talk in peacetime — possible firing squad in war.

One day at noon on a farm where the men had disarmed and removed some piece of ordinance from a barn, the farmer invited the German sergeant and I to stay for noon dinner. I'm guessing how it happened.

Possibly the ration trucks were down the road a short distance at our next assignment, and our crew had gone ahead, leaving me with the sergeant who had possibly been in a conversation with the farmer. In the centre of the table was a large pot containing a delicious mixture of assorted vegetables and meat. I think that the woman of the

Chapter 20

house handled the big ladle as we held out our plates, which were like large soup dishes. A glass in front of me was full of what looked to me like milk, so I took a hefty draft and almost gagged.

The others seemed startled for a second and then amused. It was buttermilk — not the toned-down variety that we get from grocery stores, but the real tonsil-shrinking stuff drained from the butter churn. I had drunk lots of strong buttermilk at home and at my grandparents. But you have to see it coming.

The woman and a girl who looked to be just out of her teens — the woman's daughter, I assumed — had been preparing the table when we came in. The girl was now sitting across from me. At one point when she reached for something, I noticed a tattooed number on her arm. (It would be her left arm.) I knew next to nothing of what this was all about. Years later when I had learned more of the mechanics of the colossal evil — how, for instance, these number-identified Jewish victims, time-tabled eventually to be murdered, were SS slave-rentals — I thought about that girl. She may have come from this part of Germany, returning after the war to find that she was the only member of her family who survived, and was taken in by the farmer and his wife.

Or perhaps she had been in a work party somewhere here in north Germany when the war ended and had become suddenly free when the guards ran off. That happened with a numbered Auschwitz survivor I came to know after the war. She was a slave labourer in Silesia when it all ended.

Information that was coming at us over the last couple of months began to expose the unbelievable.

Newspapers showed pictures of what the British and American troops had found in the concentration camps they had overrun. The Russians, although they would release little information, had come upon the destroyed or nearly-destroyed extermination camps in Poland. At the camps in Germany, citizens who lived in the area had been compelled by Allied authorities to come in, with their children, and file by the piles of corpses. We found that the citizens in general, however, and the Wehrmacht men we worked with, considered the

The Canadian Army of Occupation: ll

stories of an extermination policy to be vicious propaganda and wouldn't even talk about it. There was simply a resettlement policy which tragically collapsed in the chaos at the war's end. In the excitement of our own military lives at this point, we soldiers rarely talked about it either. It was not until I began to read the better literature on the subject years later that the full truth reached me.

Back in May at the time of his surrendering of his troops in the Netherlands, German General Blaskowitz was told about what had been found. He and his officers considered the stories preposterous propaganda. So the British sent a Jeep, a photographer, and one of the general's officers to Bergen-Belsen, where the photographer took pictures of the bodies, while being sure to have the German officer in each. When Blaskowitz saw them, he put his head in his arms and wept. Yet what he saw was nowhere near the ultimate dimension of the Holocaust. Bergen-Belsen was not an extermination camp — they were in Poland — but one of the concentration camps which had, like many others in the last days of the war, become ridiculously overloaded with emaciated prisoners forced-marched and shipped west ahead of the Russian advance. Then, with the guards and camp administrators having run off because the Allies were drawing near from the west, thousands of inmates were left to starve to death or die of typhus.

Whatever the explanation for that young lady's whereabouts, she was the first of three people with the tattoo whom I have met. Another was David Shentow, who has the scars of a hole that had been shot through his hand by a guard who compelled him to hold it up for target practice. The third person will come up later.

To our Wehrmacht companions whom we had been with for 15 days, we bid goodbye on September 22. Our unit called us back to the airfield — disappointed, as one of the crew cynically suggested, that none of us had been blown to pieces. Four days later a unit of us, complete with a kitchen, was sent for guard duty at an ammunition dump in a forest just outside the village of Tannenhausen, near Aurich.

The dump was a fascinating place. A small-gauge rail track snaked among the trees, disappearing down into widely dispersed bunkers

Chapter 20

and emerging again on the other side. A couple of little gasoline engines pulled flatcars along these rails. Down in the deep bunkers were racks of shells on either side of the tracks. The camouflage seemed ideal — an innocent-looking forest. There was no indication that it had ever been bombed. Our job was to patrol the entire perimeter.

A crew of German soldiers with this toy railroad network was gradually moving the shells out to a grown-up rail line, where we imagined they were transported to the coast, which was only 20 kilometres to the north, and then taken to sea. Off duty we reverted to children at times, pushing a little flatcar as fast as we could and then flopping on, to plunge down into a dark bunker and come out the other side.

As soon as it got dark, we stopped walking the perimeter, with the agreement of our NCOs, and spaced ourselves out at hollering distance, then got comfortable, probably for a two-hour shift. A girl used to come around after dark. I think she spent more time with me on her rounds, because all I wanted — or, rather, all I asked for — was that she would snuggle up and give me German lessons. And my items of food, including chocolate, were as good as what the others offered

Another among the amenities of this guard assignment was that seven of us at a time when off duty were given transportation into the northern Dutch city of Groningen for a day and an evening — for wine, women and song, to put it in less museum-visiting terms. Groningen was one of the more tolerant cities. Possibly because of its northern position, it was late in experiencing Canadians. Certainly, none of us would be going to Utrecht. In September, because Canadians had behaved so badly there, the city was placed out of bounds to us, owing to Dutch complaints.

On October 2, we had another break, my diary says, during which we came to Jever theatre to see something called Lifebuoy Follies. I have no memory of it now, but suspect it was a live show from Canada.

The concept of actually guarding anything was as farcical here as on the previous tour of duty. One of us, though, did fire his rifle — to

The Canadian Army of Occupation: ll

drop a deer on a nearby reserve. We got the animal back without incident, skinned and cleaned it for the cook, and ate remarkably well for several days. We were there until October 14.

Many of us were back on police duties by the end of that month, to make sweeps of the area with house-searching parties of four or five, one of whom was to have some knowledge of German. I brazenly professed to have it because I thought it would get me out of carrying a rifle.

It didn't. It required only the ability to ask some standard questions, to order locked doors opened and to check the identification papers of all occupants. Black-market military canned goods were to be seized and the owner reported. Something about the numbers (there were no labels) on the cans supposedly gave a clue.

When cans were found in cupboards, I squinted at them and assured my fellow searchers that they were a German make, a groundless decision, but much to the relief of the occupants. To me it seemed cruel to be leaning on these people at the bottom end of the chain of law-breaking. Stuff was being sold and traded into the black market by those searching and ordering the search.

Our compound even had a water truck disappear. The story in the ranks about where it went was probably accurate: into Rotterdam, where stolen vehicles became non-existent within hours, motors in one direction, tires in another, and so on. There was an investigation, but the driver had witnesses that he never left the area all that weekend. Money for big transactions was deposited, by arrangement, to accounts in British banks.

The black market business became enormous in the months after the war. We, with our cigarettes from home, were small-time dealers compared to the larger picture.

Members of the Allied forces were the biggest suppliers and also significant buyers. Allied authorities possibly found it easy to ignore any German government protest about the effects of this enterprise on the deplorable straits of its citizens — our buying up scarce fresh produce, for instance, by offering big money.

Chapter 20

But it was no doubt harder to ignore the Dutch government's protest. Dutch writers years later tell about how the their Queen herself complained officially to the Canadian government about our activities, particularly the black market buying of stolen items such as art treasures. Canadians stood out more in the Netherlands than did the other Allied forces because they stayed so much longer in large numbers. Our criminal activities were said to have reached "frightful proportions." In all politeness, the Dutch press eventually suggested that Canadians should now go home.

In Germany, however, we were not going home just yet. The black market participation of the Allies would continue. One particularly vicious aspect of it, dealing in pharmaceuticals, was portrayed in the movie, *The Third Man*, made in 1950.[52]

A key reason for a check of identification papers on our current house-searching sweep was, we were told, to find deserters from the German military forces, who were to be turned over to the German Command. We who gave it some thought found this situation puzzling. Why would a German desert when the war was over and he would soon be discharged? As mentioned earlier, we knew nothing of the Dorfer and Beck insanity, and had no idea that these men, whom we were now to watch for, had deserted while the war was still on — which at the time was surely what we had hoped they would do. The numbers of them were apparently not small.

Several months earlier, according to one regimental history, the regiment was ordered to make a sweep at 0500 hrs of the city of Varel, and netted around 170 German soldiers, most of them deserters. Twenty-two of these men were officers. They were turned over to the German military "to be disciplined by their own commanders."[53]

One might reasonably suppose that the German Military Command had asked the Canadian CAOF to help in rounding up these people who were a disgrace to the Nazi cause. What happened to these men who, by design or not, helped the Allies? Could it be that the Dorfer and Beck case was not the only one of that type that the Canadians participated in? The Allies, of course, were not without

The Canadian Army of Occupation: ll

their share of deserters as well, filling jails and detention compounds, as mentioned earlier.

The sweeps conducted by our units went on for at least a couple of weeks, but my part in them lasted only one day.

Sometime earlier I had asked to be paraded, as it was called, before the colonel of the regiment to make my pitch for setting up and operating a craft shop here at Jever airfield. The morning after my day with the police action, my request came through. Standing before the colonel, I made my case — healthy recreational activity to keep troops busy in the evening, and so on. I was apparently convincing enough for him to take me off all other duties at once, to begin work on it immediately, with the warning that he would make an inspection in about two weeks. If he were satisfied, I would be left with it. If not, I was in trouble.

I was given the open top floor of one of the buildings, as requested, and worked at feverish pitch for those two weeks. My enthusiastic friends in the regiment were very valuable, chiefly through their remarkable scrounging ability, and their purchases, with barter, of tools on the black market. To sweeten the bartering a bit, I dipped into the parcel from my mother, which had just arrived. The airfield hangars had workbenches with vices. Two electric motors showed up which, as was admitted later, were taken off air-exchange blowers in the basement of one of the airfield's administration buildings. I spent a couple of days in the 8th Brigade workshops, building a simple, small wood lathe. Leather was hard to come by. One of us had discovered that the fuel tanks in the wings of a particular make of German plane at the airfield were leather-covered. A couple of the boys went out at night, cut the wings open and carefully extracted the leather. I still have a picture that was taken of the gutted plane, with slices of its wings hanging down. It was never going to fly again anyway.

I opened the craft shop on November 5. It was an immediate success. When the colonel inspected it a couple of evenings later, the place was packed. He must have given the nod. I was quickly transferred to the group that had to do with recreation and education. My

Chapter 20

living quarters, which were now changed to the ground floor in the same building as the craft shop, was a pleasant room that was shared by just one other fellow of the group.

For the first time in my army career, I was enjoying my duty. My little home-made lathe was seldom still. Chests were built, wallets made, blowtorches gave heat to solder and to form glass and steel. Luftwaffe dining hall table knives, each complete with its flying eagle and swastika, were shaped into souvenir letter-openers. One is on my desk here today.

We all brought in strange pieces of machinery to disassemble for their bolts and nuts and for whatever else they would yield. I removed the hand-cranked centrifugal starter out of one of the planes and set it up in the shop as a toy. It became an immediate success. Men would work themselves into a sweat to bring the flywheel up to an incredible speed, and then do things like spin little wheels on it until their bearings caught fire. I set up a German tailor in a little anteroom off the shop where, for money or cigarettes or items of food, a uniform could be tailored to fit properly. He got plenty of work, a fair amount of it from the officers.

The army hired a number of local citizens for various jobs at the airfield and, as was the tailor, they were often paid in barter — which, they shortly discovered, was frequently taken away from them at the main gate when they left — by either too-serious guards or crooked ones. When the tailor told me about it, I asked him to leave his pay with me and meet me down the road from the camp. Soldiers in or out were not checked. Because the word spread that I could be trusted, a couple of others brought their barter to me. My roommate and several others helped as well.

The citizens were badly off — a consideration, as I've already suggested, that provoked no great concern in the military. They were short of food (except for the farmers) and many other things such as soap, clothing and fuel for heating. The general feeling, when anyone thought of it at all, was that their suffering was minuscule compared to what was felt in the lands their forces conquered. Taking advantage of the losers was all part of a rough justice, it seemed, as though free will were responsible for what side we were on. Choosing to be born in Saskatchewan or Quebec instead of Ostfriesland kept us from being frozen to death on the Russian front, and kept our young ones from scooping out of the victors' mess-hall slop drum. The aftermath of war has no place for the simplest of philosophical concepts. We were not going to accept that the pitiful fellow behind us in the streets of Wilhelmshaven, who is picking up our cigarette butts, could ever possibly be the uncle or father of any one of us in a reversal of circumstances.

This thought somehow brings to mind an event in a paint shop, possibly in the town of Jever.

I had brought in a big globe from the light over the stairway that led up to the craft shop, and was scuffling in my best German to explain that I wanted the term, "craft shop" in block letters painted on it. Another fellow from the back came up, wiping paint from his hands, and said something like: "Yes, we can fix that up for you, soldier," — with an American accent right out of New York. And that's exactly where he had lived for 10 or so years. He told me that when the depression hit the U.S. in the 1930s a good number of young German immigrants who had come over earlier returned home to get jobs. We talked for awhile about the dirty 1930s. He remarked that what he found on returning was prosperity — a job first of all, a shorter work week, holidays with pay, cleaner factories. A war was not in the political rhetoric at the time.

The tailor found a woman to do my laundry, a woman who really needed the business. She had children under foot, and a couple that were school age. But she had my mother's years, which would mean that she was more likely the grandmother. The mother could have been killed in one of the bomb-flattened cities, and the father, her son perhaps, could be buried at Tobruk. I saved for them what food I could from the mess hall and bought more, along with soap and other items, at an army canteen which had now been set up — perhaps all done selfishly for cheap laundry. One way or the other, it was certainly with no great sacrifice. As with most civilians, she did not want money, but goods.

Chapter 20

In the middle of October, the artillery regiments of the 3rd Division finally put together enough commandeered German printing equipment to produce a newspaper, which they called *The Gunner*, appropriately enough, and they published it in a building in Jever. A couple of fellows with some printing experience from civilian life had gotten permission to attempt it — much as I had with the craft shop. It was a big success, a weekly with a reporter from each unit and with coverage of the week's relevant events in Canada. Pat Clay, one of its cartoonists — an exceptionally good one, at least for my sense of what was funny — was an officer from our D-troop of the original 44th Battery, until that command-post fire in the Rhineland, which had put him and a signaller out of action.[54]

The craft shop was so successful that I asked for an assistant and got one. He in turn was given some help when on November 25 I received a two-week leave in Scotland — just in time on that day to miss General Montgomery's visit to our Jever airfield, with attending parades, inspections, speeches, the whole bit. He actually came on a special train.

I was happy, though, to jump in the back of a truck heading for Osnabrück, about 150 kilometres to the due south. The city had taken terrible bombings. It was strange to see the street-cars operating in the midst of this devastation. You could actually get a glimpse of one now and then moving along on the next street over, because there were so many flattened buildings through the block. I stayed in a German army barracks that night and a westbound train in the morning for a slow 370-kilometre trip across the border into the Netherlands and on to Hoek van Holland on the coast west of Rotterdam. Train rides, as I've said, were always a pleasure for me.

As for long boat rides on open seas – that's a different matter! And this 10-hour overnight ride on the *Vienna* from Hoek to Harwich, England, across a piece of the North Sea, was no exception. It was my roughest ride ever on water. It placed me continually on the verge of throwing up, without ever succeeding. I met another Prescott boy, Alex Bantford, on that boat, but felt too rotten to talk very long.

The Canadian Army of Occupation: ll

At Harwich I took a train to Edinburgh and got a room on Rutland Square.

Edinburgh, I wrote my mother, is a city that has only one side to its main street. The other slopes gently away as a park and flower garden, beyond which the land eventually climbs sharply to a castle, high above, overlooking the city.

I filled pages in a letter to her in the first week and another in the second week, and included packs of post cards with their pictures of what I had seen. She loved flowers, so I described the big flower clock in the park and how its hands, laden with colourful plants, really did tell the time. I repeated the history lessons of a lady guide who conducted parties of us military tourists of assorted nationalities through Scottish history by way of historic sites.

I also took a coal-mine tour, 488 metres (1600 feet) below the surface. If nothing else, it gave me an appreciation of claustrophobia. The shaft walls didn't bother me. But those men, on their sides, squirming back into deep seams that were no more than 50 centimetres high, with 488 metres of the world pressing down, gave me a twitch of the condition. The posts that they were cutting and driving into position to support the ceiling of the seams looked ridiculously puny.

Every visitor, a citizen told me, must view the famous Firth of Forth bridge, which required a short bus ride to the town of Queensferry. My diary mentions also how strange it was at that time of the year to see a farmer with horse and wagon bringing in loose hay from a field. It was December 1. And it was on this day as well that I met Lloyd Kirkby, another soldier from Prescott.

Perhaps my greatest pleasure of this leave was skating in nearby Dunfermline, on artificial ice. I went there many times. A dance floor of equivalent area was adjacent to the ice, a very pleasant arrangement. I stayed in skates, however — rented ones, which were hardly up to Canadian standards of sharpness, but good enough for another on-leave Canadian renter and me to show off our skills, like a pair of demented clowns.

Chapter 20

Down a side street in Edinburgh, an enterprising Scotsman had set up a press-while-you-wait shop for army uniforms. He was fast and he was good. The slack of the cord hung from above on a spring. On a solid table he would pound with the oversized iron as well as glide it, while the customer stood there in his shirt and underwear — long underwear in my case. On my visit, the bench of waiting clientele in the steamy little room was crowded. I imagine the section of the Polish army stationed nearby helped his business. There were more Polish soldiers than other nationalities on the city's streets. They were easy to spot even at a distance, for either they all had the broad upper body of Victor Mature or else their uniforms had padded shoulders. I believed the latter.

I headed back on December 8, reversing the same route. The boat this time was the *Duke of York,* and the sea was calmer. After stopovers and some time spent in Hoek, Osnabruck and Oldenburg, I was back in Jever three days later. Two parcels from home were waiting.

In the nearby city of Aurich, the trial of famous SS General Kurt Meyer took place during this month. He was commander of a Panzer (armoured) regiment in Normandy, who was accused of being responsible for the murder of at least 41 captured Canadians by troops under his command. He was acquitted of 23 of these deaths; but, he was held responsible for the remaining 18, he was found guilty and sentenced to death. General Chris Vokes, one of the judges on the military court panel, eventually commuted the sentence to life imprisonment. He served something like five years of it in Nova Scotia's Dorchester penitentiary, giving enough time for the war's vengeful spirit to subside, and then was released.

PanzerMeyer, as he was called, was a high-profile, highly-decorated figure — at 32, the war's youngest general, considered a military genius for his brilliant tactical use of armour, while greatly outnumbered, that in turn embarrassed the Russians on their front and then the Canadians in France. But rather than hate him and seek vengeance, the Canadian officer staff admired him. Vokes obviously passed the death sentence to appease the inevitable cry for blood in the land of the victors. While in prison in Aurich, he was said to have been escorted from his cell one night to attend his birthday party that Canadian officers threw for him in their officers' mess.

Both sides on the Western Front shot prisoners, of course, and probably in proportional numbers. It's one more ugly outcome in an ugly business. (The Eastern Front is a more hideous story.) A part of the testimony introduced in Meyer's defence concerned German prisoners who were allegedly shot by troops under the command of Brigadier Foster, who was, now as a major-general, one of the panel of officers sitting in judgment of the accused. An effective point but, of course, it was not Foster who was on trial. Veterans interviewed on TV during the 50th anniversary of the war's end acknowledged POW killings by Canadians. Most of it was done in the high-pitched fervour of the week or so in Normandy following D-Day. And on the Dieppe raid earlier, in 1942, veteran survivor Brian McCool, previously mentioned, has suggested that the enemy surrendering during that raid were to be shot rather than taken prisoner.

Prisoner shootings were occasionally acknowledged, both by subtle suggestion and with some bravado. A regimental history speaks of a soldier being told to take a POW back to a compound, which were always well to the rear, and then says: "It seems he was away only 15 minutes." A war history book tells about a tank which knocked out an artillery gun emplacement, after which the tank sergeant says he went up "and shot all the crew of 14 cowering in the trench."

An RCAF officer among prisoners who were being flown to Italy, probably from North Africa, was advised by an Italian Red Cross worker to take off his Canadian badges. When he asked why, the Red Cross worker told him of the hatred generated because "the Canadians in Sicily did not take prisoners."[55]

An American veteran, Paul Fussell, in his memoir *Doing Battle*, tells of 15 to 20 Germans caught in a crater who were trying to surrender, but were shot to death by men in his company who were laughing and howling with delight. "The Great Turkey Shoot," they called it. The Americans at the Battle of the Bulge found 71 of their men, while prisoners of war, had been shot to death near Malmedy, in Belgium.

Chapter 20

As well as the trial of Meyer, Christmas Day fell in that month of December, too, maintaining a regularity. It was quite warm, and the grass was green.

For our regiment at Jever airfield, New Year's and not Christmas would be our big blast, we were assured. So no special meal had been planned for that day, although somehow I obtained an orange — "illegitimately," is the word my diary used, which probably meant that one of us got into a supply truck or depot, broke into a crate, and sold them off one at a time. (It also meant that my dictionary scuffling was picking words more by their size than by their appropriateness.) I went to Tannenhausen with the padre to give him a hand with a party that the Canadians were giving for the area's children. I brought with me most of my chocolate hoard, not as bars, but appropriately broken into their scored, small segments. With a delightful number of children showing up, the party was even more successful than the previous one at Zetel. The civilians were settling in to accepting us now.

I later got a ride back to Wittmund, because I had heard that a few of our boys had found some liquor and were having a party there of a different sort, in one of the old German barracks. It was all true and it was a good one if you like drinking to oblivion — Canadian and German soldiers together, slowly going incoherent in two languages.

First, I had supper at a local mess hall and then joined them just long enough to get feeling good. The stuff was real hard liquor, but the kinds and brands have left me, if I ever knew. Possibly the Germans had rounded it up after being bankrolled with the wealthy Canadians' money. It was a common business arrangement, for Canadians weren't always trusted in certain echelons of the black market.

Another fellow and I hitched rides that eventually got us to Sande, about five kilometres south-west of Wilhelmshaven. We wanted to visit one of the boys from our unit who was in the German hospital there. The hospital appeared to be operated jointly. It seemed a modern and pleasant place, with a central radio and earphones at each bed, and with some sort of intercom system. Those things spelled modern to us at that time.

The Canadian Army of Occupation: ll

A children's choir was singing carols through the halls. Stille Nacht, heilige Nacht! Silent night, holy night! The sweet sound of innocence from the children and the sweet young woman's image of purity as she shepherded their orderly movements contrasted strangely with our coarse military image and with our friend's bad case of gonorrhea. I had stepped to the ward's doorway when I heard them approaching in our hall. The shepherdess smiled at me as her little ones passed in full voice. A smile! Our pariah status with young women of our own age — ones not in the sex trade, that is — had been fading for some months. The change was valuable emotionally. It had a calming, a civilizing, effect.

The outside world, so to speak, would on this occasion be all smiles and could well be listening sometime in the day to a broadcast of the famous Oberkirchen Children's Choir.

But we, first-hand that evening, in Sande Hospital corridors, had the music of these few children. And I had the delight of that soft smile from their shepherdess. It would be enough for this Christmas.

21

The Countdown To Home

My roommate and I and a couple of our friends in adjoining rooms — all of us a part of the recreation and education group, like everyone on that floor — never bothered on this New Year's 1946 morning to get up for the mess-hall breakfast. We made our own from our pooled parcels from home.

About a week earlier, I had received two parcels two days apart from a dear aunt — and then just the day before, number 25 from my mother, my Christmas parcel she called it, which had a remarkable inventory of her traditional Christmas delights.

From those tightly sealed packages of coffee that were in many of our parcels, we brewed a good strong pot this morning, for we had done a fair amount of drinking the night before to bring in the New Year. The army film-people had supplied us with a recent movie. And somehow we had managed to get German-manufactured firecrackers for midnight. I remember thinking it strange that the Germans, during the war, would have been spending resources to make fire-works.

In any event, we set them off when the New Year dawned and threw them around like a bunch of kids. I thought about the display the previous New Year that the Germans had put on when they were facing us on their front line at Wyler.

Our regimental command was true to its word about a New Year's bash. Both dinner and supper were served in the attractive Luftwaffe

The Countdown To Home

airfield hall, while a German band played. There was an orange at each place setting, my third orange overseas. Every traditional food preparation of the Season and the New Year was there, in unlimited quantities. The command had apparently hired a German catering service. The waiters saw to it that no platter or dish on the tables ever became empty. And, more important to many of us, they moved swiftly about with large pitchers of beer and kept pouring until we either turned down our glass or fell away from the table.

In terms of pleasant setting and of eating and drinking gratification, this had to be the military's finest hour — the most incredible gesture that any of us in the bottom ranks had ever experienced in our army careers.

Three days later I received a letter from my brother Glenn, which first brought me the news of our grandmother's death, on December 22 — my mother's mother, a woman who was very important to her children and grandchildren. She was strong-willed, and worked the farm with my grandfather as an equal partner. They bought a car in 1934 or 1935, in her name. For a woman in those years to be driving a car was extremely rare. My grandfather never learned how, although he was as strong-willed as she was. Their attitude toward a marital partnership was a way ahead of their time. I had written them now and then. There was always something from them in my mother's parcels — such as that Christmas 1944 turkey leg.

Some time in the early part of this month I was notified of being picked for the NCO's course. One of the last things I wanted to be was a non-commissioned officer. So once again I asked to be paraded before the colonel, and was obliged.

He listened to my plea — an outline of the success of the craft shop, my satisfaction in operating it, my unsuitability and complete lack of desire to attain any higher rank. I feared that he might assign me to guard duty somewhere just for spite. But he didn't. He let me be.

Those of us on that floor, with our special recreational and educational duties, were relatively content. Most of the CAOF personnel may have been by this time; guard and police duties were strung away

Chapter 21

out. The equipment, facilities and organization for a surprising variety of sports were available, even hockey on artificial ice in a nearby city. The school offered courses on a good number of subjects, and was well attended. I took German classes from a teacher who had been an officer in the Wehrmacht.

Apparently, though, the RCAF boys in Britain had a grievance of some kind. A note in my diary, with no explanation, says that they went on strike on January 10. I assume that their grievance had something to do with the slow rate of their repatriation. There were no Canadian Air Force fellows with us in north Germany that I know of; but almost every day one of them flew a Spitfire into Jever airfield from somewhere in Britain, to deliver and pick up the CAOF mail.

In late January it stayed cold enough for several days to freeze the ponds and canals. My roommate and I went to Oldenburg several times to skate in the park. My skates had been in an earlier parcel from home. I met a striking young woman skater there from Mannheim, whose grace on the blades would have been enough in itself to provoke my fraternizing. But there was more.

She had an elegance that made me struggle for all of her company I could. Except for skating dates, she was out of my chocolate-bar class, however. Yet I believe she may have been the fräulein I took — surely through her suggestion — to an opera in the beautiful Oldenburg theatre. It was Beethoven's *Fidelio*. My level of couthness at that time was such that I could laugh at the old joke about how in opera people sing when they get stabbed rather than bleed. Many years would pass before some understanding of operatic form reached me. The army's cinema, borrowing the name "Kraft Music Hall," had a different show every two to four days. Movies almost always played to a full house.

For the lower ranks, an amenity cutely called the "COF Drop Inn" opened on January 29 in Jever. Its dance hall opened a week or so later. The Inn was operated by something called the Canadian Army Welfare Service, which could well be proud of its achievement.

The place was attractive and very successful, serving full-course meals on Saturday and Sunday evenings, on tables surrounding the

The Countdown To Home

dance floor — tables with real tablecloths — while a dance band performed on stage. There was an adjoining games room, a lounge, a library and a snack bar. Lounges and writing rooms of any military recreational facility always had a supply of writing paper, ink and straight pens. I wonder if there was ever a shipment of ink in a supply truck along with bombs and bullets! The letterheads on stationery indicated that the the writing materials were donated by service clubs and organizations such as the Salvation Army and the Knights of Columbus.

With these forms of amenities, the military command seemed determined to bring home as many of us as possible with no serious cultural regression. Also, it seemed to have become established with families in the area's communities that the Inn was a place in which the reputation of their daughters would not be compromised by attending with their Canadian soldier friends. The dance floor seldom thinned out. What a difference in attitude three or four months made! A letter to my mother, which I read again after the war, speaks of the German bandleader announcing that the next piece was for a particular group of fräuleins and their Canadian escorts.

Our Jever airfield also had a library with a reading and writing area, and a few Canadian newspapers and magazines, usually somewhat out of date. Always on time, however, was a one-folio Russian newspaper in English, giving the news of the world, from the Russian point of view of course. If copies were placed in all reading rooms across the armies of occupation, the Russians would appear to have had sturdy delivery service across Western Europe.

On the airfield's library shelves was a book that contrasted almost treasonously with HQ 21 Army Group's booklet, *Your Future Occupation*, mentioned earlier. It is called *Spreading Germs of Hate*, by G.S. Viereck, published in 1931, and is an examination, complete with illustrations, of the outlandish propaganda put out by both the German and Allied sides in the First World War to make the troops more willing to kill one another. Allied material was considerably more vicious — a baby on the end of a German bayonet, for example — perhaps because the then-neutral American public had to be

Chapter 21

enticed into the conflict. According to a stamp on the flyleaf, the book came from the Salvation Army, bless its discerning heart!

An omission in the propaganda thrown at us in World War II reveals the anti-Semitism of that era. Nowhere in the encouragement of us troops to hate the Germans was there any reference to the Nazi's treatment of her own and, later, conquered Europe's Jewish population — not a single trace of it, for instance, throughout the 26 pages of that God-awful booklet. We did not know at the time about the "final solution," but we certainly knew of what German Jews had been undergoing since the mid-1930s. Our propaganda formulators may have suspected that incorporating this treatment would not be worth the chance of its having the opposite effect. Canada was no less anti-Semitic than the rest of the Christian world. The refusal of the Canadian government (along with other Western governments) to accept a shipload of close to 1,000 Jews, who were fleeing Germany in 1939 and were pleading for asylum, showed this rather clearly. The United States, refusing even to answer their request, sent out a gunboat to keep them away from the shoreline. They were compelled to return to Europe, where some eventually died in Auschwitz.

Our anti-Semitism was everywhere — in sports clubs, sororities, the Knights of Columbus, the Loyal Orange Lodge, and in Canada's director of immigration in the 1930s, who apparently spoke for the country's majority. Although a small quota did enter during those years because of pressure from certain concerned groups, a government official, when asked about how many Jewish refugees should be allowed in, is said to have remarked, "One is too many."

Prime Minister Mackenzie King's diary reportedly shows that he wanted to help, but had to accept a closed-door policy because of the country's anti-Semitism, especially in Quebec, where it was strongest, and where the Liberals wanted to maintain political strength.

As literature that I have read on the issue mentions, and as my Holocaust survivor friends have verified, the Jews for a considerable time after the war kept quiet about their suffering, for they felt from long experience the unfavourable mood around them, and they knew that much more than a Nazi government in Germany was involved.

The Countdown To Home

Many were rounded up and slaughtered and buried without ever seeing a German. They saw Hungarians, Romanians, Ukrainians, Latvians and Lithuanians, to name a few. When the Romanians invaded Russia with Germany, they carried out exterminations all on their own, in Odessa, for one place. Without the willing participation of the volunteer locals, who formed as much as three-quarters of the killing forces, massacres of such horrendous proportions could not have been achieved. French Vichy government officials and sympathizers assisted enthusiastically in the round-up and shipment of French Jews.

Survivor Alexander Donat in his book, *The Holocaust Kingdom*, portrays a common post-war attitude by mentioning a remark he heard in a hostel in Poland, uttered by a Pole who had been a prisoner himself, still wearing a prison uniform. "I thought we were finally rid of them," the fellow said, as he watched the occasional Jewish survivor straggling in, "but there seem to be quite a few coming back."

Also they felt, quite correctly, that they themselves were being blamed, because they submitted too passively in the beginning and because eventually Jews turned on Jews in a competition to stay alive. The SS administrators saw to it that the camps were run by the prisoners themselves. The incentive was basic: You live only if you help destroy others. Years would pass before good writers and thinkers began to explain the Holocaust and what can happen to humans under torture and the threat of death, when all dignity is stripped away.

But an understanding was slow to develop. Sometime in the 1960s a friend of mine who worked for Canadian Press, who interviewed a group of battle-experienced Israeli soldiers, was surprised at the reaction to his suggestion that their fighting spirit was related to their previous generation's struggle. They brusquely denied a relationship, and said there had been no struggle. That generation, they said, had passively surrendered. As young well-trained soldiers, well-supplied, they had a confidence that skewed their perception.

In this period of the survivors' silence and the West's foot-dragging, evidence was overlooked, documents disappeared, witnesses died, murderers escaped, years of crops grew over the burial pits. And when the next generation began finally to cry for a recognition of the

Chapter 21

evil and for murderers to be brought to justice, they were dealing with old men — and with Holocaust-deniers and neo-Nazis, all of whom had gained strength through those years of delay. The reason for a significant part of the foot-dragging, especially by the United States, was that those who had participated in the Holocaust in the East-European countries, now controlled by the Soviet Union, were also anti-communist, with an underground network deemed valuable to the U.S. in the Cold War.

Germany's Nazi Party, however, under a demented and obsessed anti-Semite, must bear the responsibility for taking advantage of Europe's general anti-Semitic sentiment and deliberately setting in motion the Holocaust, by using German efficiency, industry and technical ability, to make it function as an industrial and commercial enterprise, with the drive of a giant corporation — its industrial centre, so to speak, being Poland.

The stockholders were of many countries. Looted art treasures were sold far and wide. Gold from fillings arrived in Switzerland in boxes clearly stamped "Auschwitz." The complicity of Pope Pius XII and of leaders of other denominations is well documented. So is that of many of the western world's industrial giants of the time.

We in the army of occupation were not really aware of this unprecedented genocide, which began in December of 1941, and would become known as the Holocaust.

In our narrow world, we were more aware that the black market was quite intense in the New Year. After the middle of February, when we were told officially that we were going home sometime in April, the underhanded business increased.

Armed with cigarettes, Black and I and another fellow went to Wittmund and Wilhelmshaven, trying to track down a fellow dealing in cameras. The top line of camera in those days was German. The dealer had sold out and gone. Another fellow and I made a rather daring run down into the dockyards at Wilhelmshaven, looking for a Luger pistol dealer whom a couple of the boys had found. Perhaps we weren't trusted or there had been a scare. All we found was shrugging shoulders. We settled for an exploration of the bombed and burnt-out

The Countdown To Home

German light cruiser *Köln,* resting in dry dock there. My friend had a camera. We took pictures of one another on board.

In accordance with our high command's orders that swastikas had to be removed from everything or the object destroyed, souvenirs with the symbol were hard to come by — items such as flags, for instance. I had already sent home my battlefield items, but was now attempting to round out my collection of other objects. When the word spread that I was hunting and had money to get rid of, things began to come my way: a two-volume set of large-format books on the 1936 Berlin Olympics, with excellent action photographs; a single volume of the same style on the 1932 Olympics in Los Angeles (no swastikas there); a book called *Deutschland Erwacht* (Germany Awakes), a history in word and pictures of the growth of the Nazi Party; and an array of other items.

These all went home in parcels, along with things one might not expect to survive but did, such as a four-piece porcelain set of dinnerware, along with knife, fork and spoon, purloined from the Luftwaffe dining hall supplies at the Jever airfield — every item having on it somewhere the Luftwaffe flying eagle with a swastika in its claws. I thought in my 22-year-old mind about what fine conversation pieces these things will be, and how valuable they will become as souvenirs of an extinct Nazi structure. But festering neo-Nazi cults have kept the corruption and its symbols alive.

The books, however, have value as historical documents of the time. When the Canadian runner, Ben Johnson, had his achievements expunged because of his steroid use, I went back to the volume of the 1936 Olympics which contained the running events, to look again at the pictures of Jesse Owens in action — and then to bore my friends, I suspect, by stressing what a sleek and truly superb athlete looks like, in contrast to a bulging, chemically altered product of business and commerce who, quite possibly, will be treated as a throw-away health problem in later years.

Another fragile item to make it home safely was my porcelain tea cup that I stole from the London, Midland and Scottish Railway, possibly during the return run from Edinburgh to Harwich. The fact that

Chapter 21

it could be identified by the letters LMS on the side of it obviously, in my range of thought, qualified it as a souvenir of Great Britain and its railways.

Somewhere in Wilhelmshaven during black-market hunts and evenings of carousing, I met another Prescott soldier and high school friend, Art Smith, who was a bank manager's son, as I remember. We were together there on a later evening — on February 7, my diary says — for some serious drinking and less serious thoughts on our hometown.

Late on February 23, we got our first snow that amounted to more than a few ephemeral flakes. About two centimetres came down. On Sunday morning, usually a quiet time in the airfield barracks, a voice coming from the parade square outside drew me out of bed and to the window. The time was about 0600 hrs. What I saw was one of our fellows, in his underwear and bare feet, running in the snow in a large circle that took in most of the square, while his "trainer" stood in the middle, shouting encouragement.

In the army you get used to ridiculous sights, but this one had a certain distorted imitation of sanity to it. Bleary-eyed, the runner pitter-patted by our window with his head back and elbows swinging, possibly starting his second round. Fortunately, two or three fellows, possibly from the guardhouse at the gate, came out and grabbed them to get them out of sight before some irritated authority was awakened. They were both drunk out of their minds. The alcohol possibly kept the runner's feet from freezing.

They may have gotten into what we called "V-2 juice," a potion alleged to be made from the methyl alcohol in rocket fuel once used in the V-1, V-2 and ME-163, and sold on the street. It seemed to have a more crazing effect.

We had a fellow go blind for awhile from the stuff, which scared him half to death, but didn't deter others. One of the items on the front page of the first edition of our newspaper, The Gunner, was a warning against "V-2 in Bottles," pointing out that the concoction is not just bad liquor, but is poison. The medical corps was getting annoyed over the number of cases on sick parade. There were mixtures of regular

The Countdown To Home

ethyl alcohol on the street as well, but most of it was terrible — "ape sweat," we called it.

In the last week of March, in preparation for going home, we had quartermaster parades to bring us up to full equipment level and to turn in worn items for new ones. It surprised me that the army did not compel us to keep all our loot down to what could be concealed in our regulation packs, which included one brown kit bag. Instead, we each were issued two large white kit bags with our name, rank and number stencilled on them, along with our military district number — in my case MD-3, in Kingston. We didn't have to carry these, if I remember correctly; for the army shipped them on ahead. This unexpected military kindness saved us from frantically wrapping and mailing parcels to reduce our inventory.

One touch of the frantic did remain, though. It was the effort to get rid of all our varieties of European money, which the army would certainly not redeem, nor would it at this late date issue any more leaves that would help us spend it. From our canteens we bought everything we could possibly use or trade on the black market. But the canteens, too, at the end would accept only the special temporary currency issued to the Allied occupations forces. I bought up all the possible items that I thought my laundress could use. Among my more desperate purchases were great quantities of razor blades, most of which came back with me.

The next day, April 6, we were starting our journey home. I had been saying goodbye to the people I had come to know over the last nine months. There was no girlfriend among them, however, who might be on the train platform with protestations of love. For most of us, relationships were seldom beyond brief encounters. The girl from Mannheim was my only beautiful interlude; but one day she was gone, back to her flattened city perhaps, to pick up the pieces with her parents, should they have survived.

I visited my laundress to bid farewell and retrieve my last bundle. The kids were out somewhere, but I left my final supply of treats for them. I shook hands with her — shook hands, for God's sake, when I ached to hug her but was too much of a bashful coward. Maybe she

Chapter 21

would have drawn back, but I don't think so. Hugging, though, was not big in those years unless you had made some financial or bartering arrangement for it. Killing was big, but not hugging. Today people hug when their hockey team scores a goal; and so do the players.

It would seem as though the military chose to have us leave as quietly as possible. Roll call was at 0400 hrs. We left behind Jever airfield and the most comfortable barracks that any of us surely had ever known. Some men readily admitted that they would like to stay longer. I was not one of them, even though, as I have said, it was the least unpleasant period of my military life. According to historian C.P. Stacey, the British did want us to stay two years, but the Canadian government held to just one.

The train took us to the German marine camp at Delmenhorst, about 100 kilometres south-east, near Bremen on the Weser River. We stayed at the camp three days. I wrote and mailed my last letter home from there. We wandered around Delmenhorst, but with no money nor barter now — well, none that we were going to use. Most of us had English pounds, but they were for Great Britain beginning tomorrow, or to be exchanged once home.

As for barter, my brown kit bag was solid cigarettes, still in their cartons of 300 each, for the streets of London where they were still going for one pound per hundred. It's doubtful that our black market activities in the CAOF was what Major-General Vokes had in mind when he came to visit us there on April 8 and, in an address on the camp square, lavished us with high praise for a job well done, and wished us all the best in our civilian lives soon to begin.

Roll call was just after midnight to begin Saturday of April 6, which was to be our last day on the continent. We left Delmonhorst station at 0300 hrs and headed north accompanied by the Weser River, stopping for breakfast at Bremerhaven, where the river meets the sea, and then on to Cuxhaven, for a total of about 100 kilometres. There, we boarded a ship called the *Clan Lamont* for a 28-hour trip on the North Sea to Tilbury docks in London — every waking hour of the trip a miserable one for me.

The Countdown To Home

Those of us carrying concealed weapons went through a tense moment on the docks. Members of the ship's crew had told us that a search in customs fashion is carried out on the arriving troops occasionally. (Our issued weapons and ammunition were turned in earlier.) They said that if we see tables being set up on the docks as we are getting off, that would be the signal. Some of us had disassembled parts of pistols distributed over our bodies and throughout our uniforms in various ways. I had shipped my P-38 holster home, packed the P-38 in grease, bound it up tightly in a piece of gas cape with some of that magic German tape and was carrying it in my inside tunic pocket. My plan was to drop my gear beside a friend, get straight to a bathroom in a building on the docks, place the package in a toilet water-tank which were high up on the wall in European toilets, and then retrieve it after inspection.

Fortunately, no tables appeared. We were simply formed up, counted and marched to a train. My naive plan would have failed, of course. During inspection times, they would surely post guards around the perimeter. From what I learned years later, weapons may not have been the concern at all but, rather, bigger game such as some stolen priceless artifact or a gold bar, about which the authorities had received a tip.

We arrived at a camp at Whitley, near Farnborough, at 0300 hrs on April 11; and there, in the hut that I entered out of the early morning darkness, were Bud Scott and Junior Peterson, two more soldiers from Prescott. We three frequented possibly all the pubs in the towns of the area over the next three days and took in all the shows we could find. Busses ran frequently between all places. The three of us being in the same hut indicated that we were already sorted in accordance to our military districts.

On April 15, I got a two-week pass, spent a day in London and then took a train out of St. Pancras Station for Inverness, Scotland. With train changes and stopovers, it was a 16-hour trip of some 800 kilometres, and I enjoyed them all — the incredible scenery, the meals and beer in the various towns and cities, and the lunches for the train, which the waitresses in restaurants would pack for me.

Chapter 21

Inverness is, or was then, a quiet and beautiful place. Except for the Scottish troops, on their own home turf, I can remember only one other outsider there on leave: a Belgian sailor by the name of Peter D'Assargues, whose French accent was heavily British. We paired up for several days, rented bicycles and toured the countryside. Brochures and the citizens gave us directions and history lessons. Loch Ness, of course, had to be seen, and also Culloden on the nearby Culloden moors, where in 1745 the Scottish Highlanders with their Bonnie Prince Charles were viciously defeated by British troops under Lord Cumberland, who picked up the nickname "Butcher" because of his vengeful conduct in the battle's aftermath. There was no excuse for his cruelty, but it was understandable that he would be more than slightly irritated after the Bonnie Prince and his Highlanders had invaded England almost to London, and the British had to recall their troops from France in order to drive them out. Be that as it may, we gazed on the battlefield and the "Cumberland Stone" from which Cumberland is alleged to have directed his troops.

Because Inverness in its remoteness had not been trampled by Canadian and American soldiers, the Belgian and I were invited to several homes for afternoon tea, for meals and once as guests at a gathering of citizens — all from meeting our hosts, and occasionally hostesses, in the city's pubs. D'Assargues' leave was up before mine. We exchanged addresses, but I don't think either of us ever wrote.

Through these pub contacts I met a man introduced as Mr. Hyman, who either managed or owned a hotel. He took me with him one day in his rather luxurious car to Lord Lovat's estate, of some several thousand acres, near Inverness, where he had to do business with respect to food supplies for the kitchen of his establishment. Lord Lovat who, by the way, led a British commando group in the numbingly tragic Dieppe Raid, would not be in the manor, and very rarely ever was, Mr. Hyman told me.

Business was carried on by a Mr. Fraser, who was in charge of some aspect of the property. While we were having tea with him and his wife in their cottage on the estate, he asked the inevitable question: "Where are you from in Canada, soldier?" To mention in Europe in

The Countdown To Home

the 1940s a small town in the vastness of our country seemed almost pointless. Nevertheless I always did, each of the many times I was asked the question — but not without including the province and a couple of nearby large cities. This time, in a small thatched-roof cottage in rural northern Scotland, was no exception. Mr. Fraser repeated the name pensively to himself a couple of times and then interrupted his wife, who was talking to Mr. Hyman.

"Did you hear that?" he asked her. "Prescott! Is that not where young Jack Ross and Bill Elliot settled when they went to Canada?"

My brush cut turned to tingling bristles for a moment. I knew both these men. One was the janitor of the Prescott high school. The coincidence was as astounding to those three people that day as to me. They drove me a short distance to a cottage down a country road to visit Bill Elliot's mother. Although she must have been in her 80s, she was wiry and alert and full of questions.

Before leaving Lord Lovat's spread, I had another experience of a different nature. The two men and I were standing in the yard. Mr. Fraser had called to one of the estate hands. The man approached with that subservient half trot that one sees the serfs do in movies set in medieval times. On the way he removed his cap, clutched it to his chest and then stopped a couple of metres away. Serfdom was still alive and well. I noted it in my diary, and remember feeling uncomfortable at the time, as I had felt in seeing those kids around the slop drums. But, again, that was it. I sat in a lot of British pubs after that, but never brought up the topic with locals — never even thought about it. All those experiences came back in a different light once I entered teaching and had a slight edge taken off my ignorance of sociology. Did the fellows in those Scottish and English and Welsh regiments, who served alongside us Canadians, fight and die for a society that still nourished serfdom? What would that fellow who was clutching his cap have been taught in school? Had he been given subtle encouragement to know his place and to radiate subservience?

I had planned to leave Inverness and Scotland a little early in order to visit Wales on the way back. The hotel man, Mr. Hyman, told me he was going on a business trip to Glasgow, and I could go that far

Chapter 21

with him. The route was strikingly scenic, and he explained it all to me like a tourist guide — along Loch Ness, Loch Lochy and on to Fort William. There I learned that my host was also a hotel association official of some kind. We were warmly greeted by the manageress of Fort William's Palace Hotel. She had bicycles ready, and the three of us cycled through the landscape of Glen Nevis at the foot of Scotland's famous mountain, Ben Nevis, which rises 1,343 metres, the highest peak in Great Britain. We and a female friend of hers had dinner that evening at her table. They were all middle-aged people, and I think they got a charge out of me as a kind of oddity from the colonies. At any rate they made me feel comfortable. I sent the manageress a box of chocolates when I got home but never heard from her. Imagine what the chocolates would be like in a flimsy box thrown around for a week or more in the summer heat!

We headed out after breakfast into a dewy and head-turning landscape along Loch Lomond, and on to Helensburgh on the Clyde River. I could see Greenock on the far side, where we of the *Niew Amsterdam* disembarked almost two years earlier. The *Queen Elizabeth* was anchored offshore and getting her civilian coat of paint. I found myself staring at her impressive size, and thinking for a moment, too, how hard she would have been to miss if she had ever been spotted. I went on to Glasgow with Mr. Hyman. We said goodby and exchanged addresses but, again, I don't believe we ever wrote.

After a day in Glasgow, and a memory now only of Souchihall Street, I took a train to Manchester and then across to Bangor, Wales, for three days. I was determined to visit all the countries of the British Isles before going home.

What does a naive soldier perceive in a country in three days? Three days of atmosphere, I suppose, and whatever can be seen in that time of the suggestions in the service club brochures! And then there is Dr. Johnson's reply when his biographer James Boswell remarked that not a penny's worth of knowledge was to be gained by visiting some famous place or other: Yes, but there's a penny's worth of superiority over those who have not been there. That's the spirit of what he said, anyway.

The Countdown To Home

As on other leaves, I bought post cards whenever possible of things I saw. A memory I still have of Wales is of going into pubs and hearing no English spoken — all Gaelic. I had never experienced this total emersion elsewhere in the Isles. The language of those Welsh drinkers switched only when talking to me.

I arrived back in camp from Wales on April 29 — into my hut and into a more familiar language emersion, a Canadian-accented English. That leave was my final long one in Europe. I had visited my last — number nine — European country.

On May 2, Junior Peterson and I went to London for the day. I took my kit bag of cigarettes. Instead of selling them a box at a time, 300 for three pounds, a safer way of doing it, I wanted to get rid of them all at once and get it over with. Some of our boys who were into the business on a larger scale, building their accounts in British banks, told me that the big dealers were on Shaftsbury Avenue, one of the streets off Piccadilly Circus. When we came out of the tube at the Circus and I told Junior of this plan, he said something the equivalent of, "Are you out of your mind?" and pointed out the scheme's lack of wisdom. But, with the confidence of the ignorant, I went up the Avenue anyway.

In broad daylight, and with people in the street, the threat of our military police (MPs) is slightly enhanced, but the odds of being attacked by a gang and robbed were reduced. Those bigger handlers must have told me also to watch for a group of crap-shooters in the street and tell them you have something to sell; for that is what I did.

One of them scurried off, came back and directed me to a fellow standing just inside an alleyway. Cigarettes came in 300 to a carton. If my memory is correct, a kit bag comfortably held 12 cartons, three cubes formed from four cartons each, which amounted to 3,600 cigarettes. I named the rate and the total cost of 36 British pounds. He agreed. I can remember being scared. My tunic was open, with the P-38 resting in the left inside pocket. I was confident that I would draw it if those crap-players started to move into the alley.

With my back to the wall, I hunkered down with him and shook the cartons out on the ground between us. He checked the seals on

349

Chapter 21

them all, opened one, and then counted out 36 pounds. I left, overjoyed to get out into the street movement again. That amount of money today looks so trivial, the equivalent at the time of $160.92. That amount, however, as late as 1956, a decade after returning home, was more than 10 percent of the cost of a new Volkswagen.

Would my threat with the pistol have been enough if they tried for everything? More than likely! But in the atmosphere I lived in during those years, I considered that shooting a leg out from under one of them was preferable to being beaten up and left with nothing. To consider it all years later with a more mature mind was to conclude that I would probably have been caught and the course of my life altered — a civil indictment and/or a court martial and a long time before seeing home. Considerations like that never seemed to come up. The false confidence of youth, with values set awry by war!

Military prison would bring me a new set of associates. One of them in the exercise yard would perhaps tell me about how he was there unjustly, for all he did was beat up and rob a "fruit" when the fellow came on to him in a dark street. I mention this imaginary case to bring up the war years' barbarous treatment of civilian homosexuals by a few soldiers, who actually bragged about their deeds. I suggest that a large segment of our society in general, let alone the military, had no serious problem with Hitler's concentration-camp solution for these citizens. But it was common knowledge, and passed over with a forbearing chuckle, that there was a breed of soldiers who, in London's blacked-out years would go up in a group to Marble Arch, which was the known meeting place for gays, and "roll fruits," as it was termed, that is, beat them up and steal their money.

After my cigarette caper, Peterson, the brighter of the two of us, and I met up again, possibly in some pub in Soho by pre-arrangement. I have no notes on the rest of the day other than our getting back to camp quite late. No doubt we took in the movie at the Regent theatre on Piccadilly. It usually had the newest releases.

May 7 was to be the last day in Europe for the Canadian contingent in Whitley. A troop train took us to Southampton. We boarded the *Isle de France* and sailed out into the English Channel at 1600 hrs,

The Countdown To Home

following that initial quiet movement when the tugs were working somewhere, to make England appear to drift slowly away to the east.

Although my stomach could still feel the soft ocean swell, the crossing was beautifully calm, under mostly clear skies and with striking sunsets and sunrises. Porpoises put on a continuous show for the 7,000 of us on board, a number announced on the loudspeaker. Each of us got a free issue of 100 cigarettes early in the voyage. These I would give away. The black market days were over. Nobody on the ship was picking up butts, and there were no children scooping from the kitchen slop drum.

At some point, possibly in Whitley camp, we must have had a pay parade for Canadian money. At a canteen on board, I bought a box of chocolates for my mother. At intervals between playing cards with three Prescott boys, I walked the deck while memorizing the words to "Lili Marleen." That seemed important to me. They were on a crumpled page perhaps torn from some German publication picked up in the Rhineland rubble. The song was surely the war's most memorable.

On our first visit after the war, Whittington spoke of his voyage home over a year ago. Because he was a gunner, he was assigned to do shifts on the Bofors gun that the ship carried, even though he had never fired one. That part he worked out, but he considered that with no experience he probably couldn't have hit a German zeppelin at close range. Fortunately he never had to pull the trigger.

He told me also that shortly after he was home he was talking to a newspaper reporter whom he knew and who had been over on a war story assignment. The reporter happened to mention that he was lucky to get a ride out of Nijmegen all the way to Kleve in a returning 3rd Division artillery supply truck that had just brought a soldier out who was on his way home. "I was that soldier," Whittington told him. The reporter then related how on the way back to Kleve they hit and killed a dispatch rider who came across in front of the truck, and that the truck driver was very upset over it. I then filled him in on driver Weynert's suicide and about how the dispatch rider lived after all.[56]

In the early morning of Monday, May 13, the engine pulse of the *Isle de France* fell quiet. Our hammocks were still. We were stopped.

351

Chapter 21

We came out onto the deck and into an early morning fog that allowed only a few metres of visibility. With the mournful, deep baritone of a foghorn in the distance we sat in this shrouded calm for seven hours. It must have been near noon before the fog lifted to verify that we were indeed waiting at the mouth of Halifax harbour as the loudspeaker had told us. I remember marvelling at the navigation skills that could bring a ship that close under those blind conditions. She was finally docked with tugs at 1515 hrs. The crossing had taken six days, the same time as that of the *Niew Amsterdam*, on which a load of us sailed out of this harbour two months short of two years ago.

We soldiers would have little interest in the ship that now brought us back to this harbour, other than in its sufficient buoyancy to get us there. Nevertheless she had a proud past. I learned that when launched in 1927 she was the largest liner that had been built since World War I. A luxury liner! Just to sail on her, it was said, was a destiny in itself.[57]

I remember coming down the gangplank onto the dock — Canadian soil, as it were, which gave a strange feeling of relief, as though a more certain security was now in place, even though the war had been over for a year. In the early morning hours of the 14th a loaded troop-train of us left Halifax. We made remarks about how it was comforting to hear a real train whistle again. Having grown up beside railway yards, and with the Toronto-Montreal main line nearby, I had then, and still have today when I hear them in period movies, a strange affection for those drawn-out lonesome, musical notes of the steam whistle. But on that morning it was not the whistle that drew the louder comment. When the engine rammed back to gather slack and then yanked forward again to get rolling, a great yell went up throughout the coach in a mixture of expressions such as: "Now I know we're back" and "We're home. Watch for falling luggage!" We had all become accustomed to the smooth operation of lighter European trains.

The anticipation, as I recall, was intense. No actual locations were going to be familiar yet for another day, but I still stared out the window to catch the names of the small stations as they went by, and to

The Countdown To Home

look at vehicles on the roads and waiting at crossings. My diary has no notes on how the troops were fed on the train. We may have moved a coach full at a time to a mess car. I got some sleep, but was wide awake at first light, because the conductor had said that I could be home for breakfast.

Letters and the hometown paper had kept me up on who was back from the wars, and who would never be. One of the boys safely back much earlier was Cecil Brown, from the air force, a couple of years my senior. He comes to mind because of the unplanned comedy of his homecoming, something I learned about long after.

In the military everybody's hometown got mocked, even if it was a big city. Toronto, for instance, became Hogtown, where they rolled up the sidewalks at 8 o'clock. And so on. When Brown on his troop train mentioned Prescott, the derision began — and got worse the more he tried to defend his beautiful little town, telling them they would change their mind once they saw it. Suddenly they were there, but the train was not stopping. The conductor grabbed the cord, the brakes came on, and the long procession shuddered to a halt across the Merwin Lane almost a kilometre beyond the station. The narrow dirt road had a couple of houses at the south end, and then there was nothing but an orchard, some cattle, open fields, and stretches of woods off to the north. The road was famous as a quiet location for parking and necking.

Brown demanded that the train back up. Because it was on a downgrade, it couldn't. Disgusted he got out and decided to walk down to the highway. Men now hanging out of the coach windows, were having a field day at Brown's expense, with shouts about Prescott's beauty — its cows and its little dirt road. Their derision was drowned out by another bit of comedy.

When the train blew to signal its start, the whistle stuck. Attempts to fix it failed. So, with it still blowing, the train continued on to the railway shops in Brockville. People along the way thought the whistle was announcing the Japanese surrender. My comedy of overshooting our hometown station back in my basic training days wasn't in the same league as Brown's drama.

Chapter 21

On this morning, the train was not going to stop at Prescott either — but deliberately not. There were to be no scheduled stops between Cornwall and Brockville. After Iroquois station I remember watching for the place that had been very important to my childhood, my grandfather's farm, and thinking about how my grandmother was no longer there. The rail-line embankment formed the south border of his 200 acres.

Neither my memory nor diary tells of other Prescott boys on the train. To move 7,000 troops would take several trains out of Halifax, so we may have been split up. I got off in Brockville at 0745, walked down to the main street on this pleasant May 15 morning and out to the east end, on "Highway 2," as it was then called, rated as the most heavily travelled highway in Canada. Hitchhiking was never a problem for soldiers. A ride to Prescott dropped me off by the rail yards at the east end, by the white-washed cattle pens at the foot of my street, Russell Street. Our family, like most, had no phone. They knew little about when I would be home beyond my last letter from Germany and beyond some guesswork perhaps, following the news of a troop ship's arrival at Halifax.

On approaching our house in my tense walk up the street, I could see on the front porch door a sign in big letters in fancy script, formed diagonally through a decorative pattern. It said: "WELCOME HOME, JOHN." With my penchant for noting times and dates still intact, I checked my watch. It was 15 minutes after 9 o'clock, on this morning of May 15. I would not normally use the front door, but would this time. It seemed right. On the way up the street, I had passed Mr. and Mrs. Rooke's place.

22

Epilogue

After several days of uncomfortable elation as the focus of attention, I became quite joyously aware of freedom. It had no relation to the military's hedonistic periods of relief, born of the Faustian bargain, which help to keep soldiers driving the degradation of war. I was still in the army, of course, but expected to receive only one more military order: report for discharge.

The lighter fabric of my work clothes gave an intimacy to anything I picked up or brushed against. The anticipation of accomplishing something clearly of my own values was powerful. Maybe I was Goethe's Faust, so to speak, working toward redemption with my hands in the soil, as I spaded and cultivated and planted the garden that spring.

By bicycle for the most part, I eventually got around to visiting and thanking everyone who had sent me cigarettes and other parcels. I pedalled down to my grandfather's farm frequently, and picked up a hayfork to help him out. He was 77 years old and still doing many of the chores. We talked while we worked.

And with a most comforting satisfaction, I went back to the cooper shop, timing it so that I would catch the end of the day's run before shut-down and hear the pounding of the machinery, belted off the lineshaft. Stan Collison, the fellow who had taken my job as foreman, was still there. He thanked me for the German insignia and badges I had

Chapter 22

sent him. My only pleasant twinge of nostalgia came from the smell released from the shavings: ash, elm, birch, beach, striped and birds-eye maple. It was not going to draw me back to the adz and the bench, though. I had helped destroy factories which had toilets and running water and sinks and tiled showers and equipped kitchens. I had seen the elephant.

On my rounds of visits, a man of the previous generation asked me a question that affected me strangely. I must have been more emotionally askew than I realized. He asked me whether I had killed anyone. My mind at once went into some sort of wig-wagging conflict. I began to stutter and to develop the symptoms of a panic attack — sweating, increased rate of heartbeat.

And I just wouldn't shut up. I kept right on stuttering until the fellow's wife broke the spell with some exclamation like, "What a stupid question to ask!" followed by other berating comments and a complete change of subject. It bothered me enough that I was troubled with a stutter for a few days.

There was an answer I should have given. I should have said: "Of course! We all killed, one way or another. Some dropped bombs; some fired cannons; some a pulled a trigger; some cooked food or trucked ammunition for the fellows who dropped bombs, fired cannons and pulled triggers. Some burned people to death with flamethrowers."

It took me a good while to face up to why I didn't say something like that, and point out that an extremely small percentage of soldiers are ever faced with directly killing an enemy soldier. Like most people, he saw the bulk of both armies coming together in battle, face to face in most cases. Because I was involved in that image of kill or be killed, I did not want to damage it. I think I wanted to say yes, which would be a lie in the sense of what he meant. But to say no was to damage the glory I was basking in. Therein was the stutter. I probably at that moment became a bigger fraud by creating the image of a soldier whose duties to shoot and bayonet the enemy were so disturbing that he couldn't speak of them. Most soldiers are wise enough to maintain the image simply by saying nothing. Nevertheless, there are

Epilogue

those survivors of that very small percentage from the sharp end who have memories and burdens that make them choose to remain silent. Some are in institutions.

All my letters from overseas, as I have said, were enclosed in those "Base Censor" green envelopes. This unknown censor, my correspondents have told me, opened only four of them, scribbled his initials on them, but removed nothing. Of my mother's numbered parcels to me, four never made it.

My 14 parcels sent home apparently all arrived, for nothing seemed missing. I had a great time showing off these souvenirs — exaggerating and sucking in a glory shamelessly at odds with scrupulous accuracy.

On June 18, I caught the train to Kingston and reported, as ordered, to Fort Frontenac, MD3. The next day at noon, as a civilian, I walked out through the stone archway of the fort where I had become a soldier in 1943 on October 12, three months short of three years ago. Junior Peterson had apparently been discharged the same day, for we hitchhiked home together. It was only a little over a month earlier that he and I had spent a day and an evening in London.

I went to Ottawa later in June to visit the Department of Veterans' Affairs for career counselling and for guidance on how best to use my education grant. Because they talked me into a trades course, I signed up for one in Electrical Construction in September, at a DVA school which happened to be here in Prescott, in the federal building known as the Dominion Lighthouse Depot (DLD) at that time — a location no doubt influencing my choice. I was finished in March the next year and labelled an electrician, a profession at which I worked for awhile, along with an assortment of other jobs until called by the Hydro Electric Power Commission of Ontario (eventually named Ontario Hydro), where I had earlier applied. With my education grant gone and my clothing allowance of $50 spent, I had only a free dental check-up left, which had to be taken within a year of discharge, I think. And those English pound notes? After watching their value drop week after week, I finally exchanged them at the bank.

Chapter 22

On Saturday night, November 23, 1946, Prescott threw a banquet in the town hall for all us local veterans, for which we dressed in our clothing-allowance finest. The place was packed, and we put away a lot of turkey. Before arriving, an understandable number of us had also put away a substantial amount of alcohol in some form or other. This was Canada; so, if you weren't drunk when you arrived at the banquet, you were not going to get drunk there.

Well, that's not quite true, for nestled in inside pockets there were a lot of mickies being surreptitiously nursed on. No waiters here were running around filling our glasses from pitchers of sinful beer. The town, as it should, obeyed the law. Completely and boringly sober I ate and enjoyed my turkey amidst the stimulated gaiety of those less intimidated by our home country's stultifying statutes. The banquet was a fine gesture on the part of the citizens.

Some of us veterans, perhaps in the shock of abruptly leaving the military with its structured and dictated direction, took to drinking rather heavily. A few eventually drank themselves into an early grave. Others appeared to be trying, but eventually straightened out and moved on.

I remember what a start it gave me on my first occasion of being greeted on the street by a fellow veteran and former school friend who, after a moment of conversation, asked me whether I had a dime to make up what he needed for a bottle. Cheap wine at that time cost about 80 cents for a size we called a "26er" (750 ml).

It is ironic that there were those in the military and — as there are those in society in general — who see themselves as free only when they are under a disciplined structure that consistently and reliably sets out a course of action for them.

Leila Kelly, a local lady with exquisite handwriting and script-pen ability, inscribed our names on a large scroll, as those "members of Prescott High School' who were in the armed forces. Some of us had never reached high school, but we were all included. The names of those who died were etched in the town's War Memorial, under those of World War I.

Epilogue

Most veterans became members of the Canadian Legion's local branch, enjoying the camaraderie and the licensed bar. I didn't join, mainly because of my dislike of joining anything. I love freedom, as lonely as it is. Also, I was not fond of the Legion's attitude in the beginning. It hung onto and fed the propaganda and distortions of truth that the military finds necessary in wartime — long after much of that sort of thing was becoming an embarrassment to those who did any thinking. As examples, during the war it considered NRMA soldiers (soldiers who would not volunteer for overseas service) to be traitors, and demanded that the government label them so. In 1946, it wanted all Japanese in Canada deported, with the exception of those who were veterans. To its credit, however, it did lobby government strongly for active service veterans' benefits; and its local halls and activities afforded for many a more tolerable transition into civilian life than would otherwise have happened. Today, the social activities of each branch are a valuable feature in its community.

Just as my diary had led me gradually toward the war with its entries beginning in September of 1939, it now in 1946 blends gently back into civilian notations.

It records those times Whittington and I eventually got together. He took over a small dairy business from his wife's family immediately after the war, and helped deliver the milk from door to door himself.

Once when I stayed overnight, I drove the truck for him on his morning route. We joked about our war days, especially the crudeness of them. His milk delivery time could be reduced, I suggested at one point, if I just cut across all the front yards with the truck, smashing through the hedges and fences and stopping at each door — similar to our short-cuts made in the Netherlands and Germany.

In 1993 he had a stroke, which took away his ability to write and to speak above a whisper, but left his mind clear. His wife died a year later. I visited him in 1995 to tell him all about my trip back over some of our Bren carrier's route in the war. A nurse, who had been reading my letters to him, said that they lifted his spirits considerably, so I began to write once a month for his last years.

Chapter 22

He died in September of 2000. As far as I know, I'm the last surviving crew member. Harrison was on the Regiment's Last Post listing in 1998.

In the late 1950s, I got a letter from Shaw. He reminisced about some of our events together in M3, and told me that he was a Conservation Officer — a game warden, that is — for the Saskatchewan government, with a patrol area (speed-boat, snowmobile and plane) that extended to the Northwest Territories. It was the perfect job for him for a number of reasons. I answered his letter but never heard from him again. The Regiment's reunion organizer told me that he moved to British Columbia when he retired, and died there sometime before 1995.

About 10 years after the war I decided to write to the government for my medals, which the government's Department of Veterans' Affairs had been requesting that veterans do. I had certainly been awarded no medal for service "above and beyond the call of duty." Just "the call" was strain enough for me. There were four, the military told me, including the Canadian Voluntary Service Medal (CVSM) and clasp. The others were the 1939-1945 Star, the France and Germany Star and the War Medal 1939-1945. I have never known the specific qualifications attached to each, other than they have to do with length of time of active service in various countries, or on various waters and in various campaigns. Each of mine is still in its little box along with its appropriate ribbon.

Baron de Montesquieu, I venture, might suggest that they are awards for being irrational, in keeping with his proposal that a rational army would run away.

Because of heavy European emigration to Canada, along with the political and economic effects of the Cold War, the mixing of nationalities, friends and recent enemies alike, took place more quickly than what one might expect after such a bitter war.

A member of the German military attended university with me. Another, and several Dutch, were fellow high school teachers later on. In my early teaching days, perhaps a quarter of some of my classes were teenage offspring of Dutch and German immigrants. The moth-

Epilogue

er of a couple of these students had an Auschwitz tattooed number on her arm. When I left for Europe in 1995 to help the Dutch commemorate the 50th anniversary of the end of World War II, a friend who was an old Wehrmacht veteran of the Russian front drove me to Montreal's Mirabel Airport for my flight to Amsterdam. On that same trip, by the way, I learned that the border-crossing rituals of many countries had disappeared. In my rented car I drove across the German-Dutch border on an autobahn at 100 kilometres an hour. No customs stop necessary!

A friend of mine in north Germany who, during the war, had been a secretary at the Luftwaffe airport at Bad Zwischenahn, and whom I came to know years later through her work in her district's military history, bore a child by one of us Canadian soldiers who occupied this area, and after a time went home. The little girl grew up, married, and gave my friend a grandchild, who eventually attended Oxford University in pursuit of her scholarly studies in French history.

This war, like those before it, supplies no answers but simply more evidence that we seem incapable of living any other way. Philosophers and historians comment endlessly on it. Karl von Clausewitz said that it was an extension of politics by other means. In John Keegan's view, "All we need to accept is that, over the course of 4,000 years of experiment and repetition, warmaking has become a habit." It has been suggested too that, as bad as war is in itself, something worse must have gone on to bring it about. It is not reasonable, I suppose, to expect that the viciousness and the urge for power that has helped our species dominate the planet will any time soon drop out of our nature. There will always be the General Pattons with us, who can say of war, "God, how I love it!"

We accept that whenever power accumulates, as in dictatorships, monsters will hatch in it. In democracy, then, surely lies a solution. Yet, the biggest democracy in the world, less than two decades after World War II, began in south-east Asia a military campaign that advanced to life-destroying actions so appalling and immoral as to leave historians still today groping with it. Perhaps democracy's only effect has been to expand the art of political seduction in order to

Chapter 22

overcome the checks and balances in a democratic society — to expand the role of private enterprise in war's process, to make it more attractive by introducing a stronger profit motive. We will try to stay out of war ourselves, yet we will sell weapons to those hatched monsters, especially if their wars and suppression benefit us economically. And in spite of the Holocaust, genocide continues. A million people are exterminated by the Khmer Rouge. We stand by during the extermination of 800,000 people in Rwanda. Ethnic groups around the world attempt daily to cleanse themselves of other ethnic groups, frequently by slaughtering them.

There were those, however, in any war, surely forming the vast majority, who, regardless of what side fate has placed them on, can be called the innocent, who obey their church and the laws of the land, and respect civil authority. Because of the shameful treatment of women in the years of World War II, war or no war, they surely best symbolize this innocence.

An example from the German side was the woman in the farmhouse whom I caught when she fainted in the midst of her smashed furniture and strewn belongings. Her husband was probably conscripted and may have been killed.

Clearly, for me, a symbol on the Dutch side was Jonanna Berdina Ariaans, a wiry little lady who, with her brother and sister, came back after the War to their destroyed farm, the one our 44th Battery had moved into during the first dark hour of November 11, 1944. I came back to see that farm with its chicken-house four times over the years, beginning with a visit during a Nijmegen stopover on a leave at war's end, and during trips to Europe later, once by my wife Jean and me. When the brother plowed up a 25-pounder shell casing, Johanna insisted I take it home. Although it had more metal in it than a Schmeisser, it went through airport security without a sound. Once she called in an English-speaking neighbour, a neighbour who helped also in our exchange of letters later on.

With the death, quite early, of her sister, and eventually her brother, she was left alone. On route to visit her during the 50th anniversary of the war's end, I stopped at a neighbour's farm on the way —

Epilogue

the home of Henk and Antoinette Janssen, whom I knew, and whose farm was once the gun position of the 22nd Battery. They told me that Jonanna, in her advanced age, was now living in an apartment in Groesbeek. The Janssen's son drove me over. She was delighted that I had come to see her, and it took some convincing to keep her from removing from her wall a large painting of the farm to give to me.

Outside the door as I was leaving, she opened her arms wide. I turned back and stepped into them, and we held one another closely for a few moments, with tears on our cheeks. This frail delicate flower of a woman, deeply religious, who had visited Lourdes, and who formed an almost mystical link that tied me to that farm, knew that we would never meet again. A friend of hers wrote me in 1998 to tell me that "in the last few months [Miss Ariaans] wished that God might let her come to him. That wish has now been fulfilled." She was 89 years old. She had died while sitting quietly reading a postcard in her apartment.

When we veterans, as guests, invaded the Netherlands in these later years, we came to realize rather chillingly how relentless the flow of time was dissolving us. Those arriving in organized tour groups were advised by the thoughtful Dutch to submit, if relevant, our names and all information concerning our pills and injections and other required medications to a specified nurse, so that these substances would be available in case of emergencies. A nurse standing by with our medication! Where are the T.A.B.T. shots and the short-arm inspections of yesteryear?

Medications and good luck have given me at least enough time to write this memoir, which I am now considering how to close. The most horrendous event of the era which encompassed that War was, of course, the Holocaust. So, I have decided to end with comments related to an anecdote told to me by a Survivor, the third whom I have come to know — the person I referred to a couple of chapters ago, who was in a slave-labour work party in Silesia when the war ended. Survivor Anita Mayer emigrated to Canada, settled with her husband in my hometown of Prescott and raised two children. Her husband died in the 1980s. She was the mother I referred to a moment ago

Chapter 22

whose two offspring attended our school. She wrote a book, *One Who Came Back*, published by Oberon Press in 1981, which is an account of her incredible experience. In the 1990s one evening she dropped in to visit, and we sat by the window, looking out on the St. Lawrence. As we talked about the war and the years since, she mentioned this anecdote.

She was sitting near the waterfront of our town on a warm summer day, waiting to witness the scheduled re-enactment of a military battle from an earlier century. Near her was a trio of youth speaking German, a language in Anita's repertoire. She struck up a conversation with the young man of the three, while his companions, two girls, were off taking pictures. They were tourists from Germany, she learned, barely out of their teens, who were travelling across Canada and just happened to be in Prescott for this occasion. With the enthusiasm of youth he asked many questions about Canada, and eventually about Anita's European connection, with her knowledge of German. Anita showed him the tattooed number on her arm, and asked, "Have you ever seen one of these?" He had not; and when she began to explain, he was amazed, and called to his two companions to come and hear the story. The three knew little or nothing about the details of the Holocaust; their parents were very young in the war and had not talked much about those years to their offspring.

When I saw the tattooed arm of that girl who reached across the table in the farmhouse in north Germany, I did not know what it was all about, for I was too close to its history. These three youth might well say that they were too far from it. Would Canadian youth have done any better? Not likely.

After 50 some years our young have a multitude of what are called wars to pick from and to treat shallowly. It has been said in many ways that if we don't study the tragedies in our history and learn from them, we are doomed to repeat them. Voices from within the camps of the Holocaust have warned us that we must be ever vigilant to see that the state of mind which made those camps possible never again be allowed to fester in our society.

Epilogue

We can't heed that warning if we forget what we are being warned about, or have never truly understood its implications in the first place.

Even before I retired from teaching in 1985, the awareness of the epoch among the generation of the time had seriously faded. At the point where the grade 10 modern history course reached World War II, I would bring to school a selection of my souvenirs to help spark interest. I found eventually that not only was student interest shifting toward the media's reprehensible enticement to enjoy the thrill of violence, but that the period of history itself — a period which contained an unparalleled human catastrophe and which crushed Western civilization to its knees for a time, and came frightfully close to keeping it there — was fading from memory. I had to explain more precisely each year the historical event that my souvenirs were all about.

"What war was that, you say?"

Endnotes

Prologue

(1) "Prompting the President," by Michael Korda. *New Yorker*, 1997, Oct. 6. "... we had to convince Reagan not to include the story [in his memoirs] about how he had been with the United States Signal Corp at the German death camps and recorded the atrocities there (a story he had told Yitzhak Shamir, bringing tears to Shamir's eyes), because it turned out that Reagan had spent the entire war in Hollywood, recruiting personnel for Army film units."

(2) Blount, Roy. "Lustily Vigilant." *Atlantic Monthly*. Dec. 1994.

Chapter 1

(3) Mowat, Farley. *The Regiment*. Toronto: McClelland & Stewart, 1955. pp. 28-35.

(4) Crowe, Jean Margaret. "Surviving the Slaughter." *Legion Magazine*. Dec. 1980. p. 16.

(5) McIntosh, Dave. "Canadian Expedition to Hong Kong." *Ottawa Journal*. Dec. 16, 1961.

(6) Stacey, C.P. *Six Years of War: the Army in Canada, Britain and the Pacific*. Ottawa: Queen's Printer, 1955. p. 490.

Chapter 3

(7) Joe Doyle, Jim Pelehos and Gerry Whitley.

(8) Shipping losses earlier were devastating and could well have brought Britain to her knees. By mid-1942, Dönitz and his men had

A Signal War

sunk 4.7 million tons of shipping. Some of their biggest successes occurred in sight of land right off the U.S. east coast. Tankers were hauling crude oil up from the Gulf of Mexico to refineries in the north. They were silhouetted against the brightly-lit coastline. In one particular night, U-boats sank eight ships inside of 12 hours. In the mid-Atlantic, convoys were being devastated by "wolf packs." Shipments to Murmansk were halted after a convoy lost 22 of its 33 ships. The crews could live only a matter of minutes in those polar waters inside the Arctic Circle.

But Allied fortune began to turn in 1943. Just weeks before the year opened, British scientists broke the German navy's Triton code by which the whole German undersea war was directed. U-boats had generally known the sailing time and route of all convoys. Also, the convoys became better protected because of increased production of escort vessels and because a few "flat-top" merchant ships were built to carry a number of planes. In addition, long-range American B-25 "Liberators" were brought into patrol service over the Atlantic. Radar and Sonar equipment was improving as well. In 1943 in May alone, Germany lost 43 submarines. They would eventually lose 25,000 men, with another 5,000 taken prisoner, which gave the U-boat crews the highest casualty rate of any branch of any service on either side in the war — 75 percent.

Canada's highest death rate among its serving branches -- perhaps not to be unexpected -- was in the merchant marine: 9.6 percent, the result of 67 of its ships going to the bottom. The death rate in our regular navy was 1.9 percent, with the loss of 24 ships. Because the merchant marine was not technically a branch of the military, its sailors were not entitled to receive military benefits after the war. One of the government's points of opposition was this: "...we are opposed to categorizing merchant seamen as veterans, which is a category well established by precedent as applying to those who served in the military during the time of war." Only after a long legal struggle did the government in 1992 eventually consent to pay — 47 years later — for those veterans still alive: about 4,500 out of 12,000 at the war's end.

(9) Fussell, Paul. "The Real War 1939-1945." *Atlantic Monthly.* August, 1989.

Chapter 5

(10) A British gun crew played a major role in securing the peninsula. The Germans were holding out in a fort-like structure, and there was no way to get at them with anything heavy. So the gunners disassembled a 3.7-inch mountain gun and re-assembled it on one of the higher floors in a building that had a view of the German strongpoint. One has to keep in mind the powerful explosive force and the formidable recoil of any piece of artillery to understand that on the first two shots the ceiling came down and the gun started to break through the floor. After the eighth round it broke through entirely and dropped to the first level. As R.W. Thompson puts it in his book, *The Eighty-Five Days* (London: Hutchinson, 1957), "The fort was demolished and so

Endnotes

was the house." The concussion inside must have been hardly bearable.

(11) In 1956, 11 years after the war, and 11 years older, I took pictures of a plain, bomb-shifted concrete bunker in an open space near the Reichstag in Berlin, because I believed, as I was told by some passerby, that it was where Hitler spent his last days. So perhaps I could have accepted as well that Esther Williams or Joan Crawford had chosen the 13th Field Regiment as her very own.

(12) On our 1956 European vacation, my wife Jean and I took a walk in St. Peter's Square so that I could point out the barracks to her. The complex was being used than as a youth hostel. By that time they must have done something about those toilets. I didn't go in to ask.

(13) White, Theodore, H., *In Search of History: A Personal Adventure*. Harper & Row, 1978.

Chapter 6

(14) Capturing the bridge over the Neder Rhine at Arnhem was to have been the last phase in the Allied scheme called Market-Garden. The attempt was a disaster, mainly because the British airborne attack dropped into the midst of a large German force that happened to be resting and refitting in the area. The British force of over 10,000 men suffered almost 8,000 casualties in its nine-day bitter struggle to take the bridge. German casualties numbered about 3,300. The force hung on desperately in the hope of being relieved by the British army moving north, which failed to reach them. Only 2,000 of the airborne troops managed to come back. They escaped over the Rhine in the dark at Oosterbeek on September 26. About 1,500 Polish paratroopers, who had landed on September 22 at Driel on the south side of the Neder Rhine about six kilometres west of Arnhem, managed by unsustainable losses to get 50 men across the river in the early morning of the next day, before accepting the hopelessness of it all and withdrawing.

Until the Rhine crossing in March the following year, Market-Garden was the largest airborne force ever assembled. It involved 5,000 planes with more than 2,500 gliders, and dropped close to 35,000 men with their equipment at the various bridges from Eindhoven to Arnhem.

(15) In 1992, the *Reader's Digest* people saw a piece on the incident, which I had written for another magazine. They bought from me and published 11 lines of the piece, and paid well. But before publishing, a representative of the Digest called at 9 o'clock one morning and grilled me on the truth of it. She was like a grand inquisitor. I had jumped out of bed to answer the phone, and was standing there stark naked. (I hadn't dressed for bed in years; all day was enough.) With a series of questions, she dragged my old mind, fuzzy with sleep, back more than 40 years. The nearest town? What direction? Date? How

A Signal War

many kilometres? Division? Regiment? Battery? Serial number? Where did you enlist? Do we have permission to check your military records. Witnesses? I gave her Whittington's name and address, and she called him. He took a bit of the inquisition, too, he told me, but he was fully dressed.

(16) In a discussion of the weapon with some students many years later in my teaching days, I mentioned this incident. A student in turn mentioned it to her veteran father. He knew all about it, including exactly where it fell — in his regiment's area.

(17) Gliders took a terrible beating in many ways. One that I read about had an especially tragic ending. Its tow-rope would not release, so apparently the towing plane let its end go, which left the glider with a rope trailing from its nose. All might have gone well, except that the rope snagged in a tree, snatched the glider out of the air and slammed it onto the ground, killing all but one aboard.

(18) It was not until years later that I learned the purpose of one of the items — a square, strapped bundle of tinfoil — that the pilot threw out when passing over us. Pilots were given it to distribute in the air to confuse the enemy's radar.

(19) My first examination of a crashed military plane was back home in Canada, before I had even joined the army. The story of the crash is especially poignant. A pilot trainee named Roland Aitken had flown down from Ottawa to Cardinal, Ontario, on the St. Lawrence river on a training run with his instructor. This was the trainee's hometown area, which he naturally wanted to "buzz," as the expression went. On a low pass over his parents' house between Cardinal and Iroquois, he caught a tree-top and crashed in his own front yard, before his mother's eyes. She was said to have been standing on the front steps. Both he and the instructor were killed. His father was at work at the Canada Starch plant. A carload of us who were employed at the plant (I worked in the cooper shop) and commuted to Prescott, drove down to the site on our way home. As with the Tempest, the motor had torn loose and continued on for some distance.

Chapter 7

(20) On a visit in 1970 to Prince Albert, Saskatchewan, home of the 44th Battery, I was told by a veteran officer of our regiment the story of another STOP order, which occurred on scheme in Britain while preparing for D-Day. He was the investigator. He told me that after he checked the calculations on the command-post drafting board and plotted on the map where those figures would send the errant round, he turned to the command-post officer and said in effect (I'll use token names), "We had better go at once to the intersection of Maple and Vine in the town of Hampstead." He was right. It was a terrible moment, he recalled. The gathered people! A dead young lady, who had just happened to be walking by!

Endnotes

Chapter 8

(21) Whitaker, W. Dennis and Shelagh Whitaker. *Rhineland: the Battle to End the War*. Toronto: Stoddart, 1989.

(22) Ibid p. 133.

(23) Gardam, John. *Ordinary Heroes*. Burnstown, ON: General Store Publishing House, 1995.

(24) The authors of *Rhineland* tell this bloody story well also — with a special intensity, for Denis Whitaker was in it as commanding officer of the Royal Highland Light Infantry. As they do often in their book, the authors include the testimony of German commanding officers.

Chapter 9

(25) The dry-cleaning remark is not that farfetched. No matter how unmerciful the war, class distinctions and privileges still held within the military of both sides, and also in what the military controlled. A case in point is the Belgian chateau of a Baroness where the North Shores made their first stop on the way from Gent to the Nijmegen Salient. She had obviously lived well all during the German occupation. She volunteered the use of her dining hall for the officers' mess, complete with dishes, silverware and her servants. She had her kitchen staff cook a number of pheasants which her gamekeeper had brought in. It would seem that the German military administration had allowed the aristocracy, and perhaps the upper class in general, to maintain their privileged status.

An air-force officer in his book says that the sergeant-pilots and officer pilots, who flew together in combat and did identical jobs, could not eat in one another's mess — thereby being deprived of an opportunity to hash over their last mission, or whatever. The officer-pilots also lived in better quarters. A former POW of the North African campaign, tells about how the Italians fed a group of their Allied prisoners who were in transit to a camp: for the officers they brought food from the Italian officers' mess, while the other ranks received obviously inferior fare — even though all ranks were sitting together. The prisoners deliberately combined the food to make it all the same.

I have a copy of a 1918 World War I Christmas dinner menu for the officers' mess, which was found among the belongings of my father-in-law who was a Canadian officer in that War. Martini cocktails were followed by oyster stew which was followed by all the traditional Christmas fare plus asparagus, accompanied by a red burgundy wine and champagne. Port was served with the plum pudding and mince pie. Liqueurs with the coffee and tea. One might wonder what was on the menu for the bottom ranks. The Geneva Convention specifies a

A Signal War

superior mess arrangement for commissioned officers, even if they should be prisoners of war.

Sometimes special treatment has a clearly understandable motive. In the Schelde Pocket fighting, a certain part of the city of Assenede in Belgium near the Dutch border north of Gent is said to have been spared from bombardment because a brewery was believed to be operating there. Heidelberg is alleged to have missed the fate of other German cities through the intervention of Churchill, who was fond of this place where he had spent holidays.

(26) Emmott, Norman. *One Foot on the Ground*. Toronto: Lugus Publications, 1992, p.93.

(27) Ellis, John. *The Sharp End: the Fighting Man In World War 2*. Toronto: Lugus Publications, 1992, p.93

Chapter 10

(28) There is no mention of the term "Blockbuster" in the stapled 30-page packet that the military made available to the troops very shortly after the war. It calls the entire campaign Operation Veritable. The packet consists of eight by 14-inch off-white wartime paper on which was typed, single-spaced (with a fair number of typos) and then apparently reproduced on a Gestetner, a concise outline of the "Campaign in North-West Europe, 6 June 1944 - 8 May 1945," as it was titled, "a Review by Brig. C.C. Mann, CBE, DSO." Obviously the military wanted us to be educated about what we had just been a part of — a gesture with considerable merit to it, it seems to me, for there is no question about our ignorance at the bottom if I was any example. It was the first time I ever knew anything about the set-up of Canadian army divisions and their brigades, even my own, or of very few battalions beyond those we of the 13th Field Regiment directly supported. A real gung-ho soldier! The outline included a schematic diagram of each division, with the name of every battalion (regiment) and of all supporting units such as artillery.

Chapter 11

(29) My main sources for the story of the Hochwald Gap have been Denis and Shelagh Whitaker's book *Rhineland*, previously mentioned, and also G.L. Cassidy's *Warpath: from Tilly-la-Campagne to the Kusten Canal*. Markham, ON: Paperbacks Ltd., 1980.

(30) John A. English, in his book *The Canadian Army and the Normandy Campaign: a Study of Failure in High Command* (New York: Praeger, 1991), says that Simonds was bitter because Montgomery chose Crerar to head the Canadian army instead of himself, who had better experience and qualifications, although his younger age was against him. It was said, too, that Crerar was a friend of Colonel James Ralston, Canada's Minister of Defence.

Endnotes

Crerar seemed jealous of Simonds' professional ability, and appeared to be bent on irritating him at every opportunity, an example of which would be a particularly "bizarre, picayune incident," as English calls it, wherein Crerar, during the Italian Campaign, sent an officer to get into and examine and take interior measurements of Simonds' mobile office and living quarters, an act which angered Simonds who, on discovering the trespasser, ordered him out. Crerar claimed that this reaction put Simonds' emotional stability and his loyalty to his commander in question, which could affect his professional abilities. All of this, along with complaints about others as well, Crerar took to Montgomery, who was also getting other generals' complaints about Crerar.

The haggling lasted into Normandy, but the exasperated Montgomery had no one else to take Crerar's place. Crerar tried to get a particular British general under him removed, but Montgomery refused, because the general was a good man. Yet Crerar insisted on keeping another general who was under him, General Rod Keller, Commander of the 3rd Canadian Division, in spite of complaints (about his drinking problem, for one thing) coming in. The Keller problem was solved, however, when the Americans bombed the Canadian 3rd Division in France. The general was one of the evacuated wounded. (This turn of events brings to mind John Kenneth Galbraith's remark about Field Marshal Kitchener of World War 1, who went down with the British cruiser Hampshire in 1916: the War Office's "regret over the loss of the ship at sea was considerably tempered by the simultaneous loss of Kitchener.")

English quotes from a Montgomery letter to a colleague in the War Office: "I fear [Crerar] thinks he is a good soldier, and he was determined to show it the very moment he took over command at 1200 hrs 23 July. He made his first mistake at 1205 hrs; and his second after lunch." In reading about these squabbles, what stands out is Montgomery's commendable diplomacy in dealing with them. He took out valuable time to listen, to mediate and to soothe Crerar and those he had upset, so they would help him get on with the war.

Chapter 12

(31) That proposal reminds me of a shocking, and revealing, statement by Arthur Currie, former leader of the Canadian corps in the World War I. When he returned home, the shadow of a military incident followed him. He had ordered an attack on Mons in the early morning of November 11, 1918, when he allegedly knew that an armistice had been arranged and would be officially declared at 1100 hrs. His professed ignorance of the armistice was astounding, given his rank and position. Finally, when a Port Hope, Ontario, newspaper put the accusation in writing, Currie sued for libel. After he had laid the libel charge, he gave an interview to a newspaper. As he spoke of how he felt at the war's end while watching Canadian troops marching away — stirring him, no doubt, with the pounding steel of their

A Signal War

boots — the newspaper quoted him as saying, "By God, I'd like to see them at the Bosch again."

By God, yes, and add to the German casualties and to that Canadian figure of 60,000 dead and 175,000 wounded, a higher rate of per capita casualties than any other allied country in WW I. In Toronto stands a statue to the man.

(32) Lavender, Emerson and Norman Sheffe. *The Evaders*. Toronto: McGraw-Hill Ryerson, 1992.

(33) Whitaker, W. Denis and Shelagh Whitaker. Rhineland: the Battle to End the War. Toronto: Stoddart, 1989.

Chapter 13

(34) Air losses throughout the war had been consistently terrible. Decades later I read a report on one of the war's outstanding bombers, the British Lancaster. It claims that over 50 percent of the total manufactured were either shot down or otherwise damaged. A particularly disturbing example of what these and other heavy bombers faced is the 779-plane raid on Nuremberg in which almost 100 planes were lost, with 545 airmen killed. Over 40 years later in an interview, one of the survivors of the raid, no doubt speaking for all air-crew survivors, remarked that "To a man we felt that Bomber Command headquarters was being uncommonly generous with our lives." (Dennis Foley. "Through Hell in a Halifax." *Ottawa Citizen*, March 30, 1993, p.B4.)

Chapter 14

(35) In 1993, an RCAF veteran told me in a letter of his purchase of a book that has a brief sketch of every Canadian Air Force member, some 17,000 of them, who died while serving -- a horrendous toll that represents close to 37 percent of the total of all Canadian military losses, even though the Air Force in the war represented only a quarter of Canada's forces. I gave him several names to look up. He obliged and wrote back. Something in the information about George Miller grabbed me: WO 2 ... air gunner ... shot down over Holland March 12, 1943 ... age 23 ... buried in RC churchyard in Beek, Prov. Gelderland.

(36) Years before our ground troops arrived, the Netherlands had been burying Canadian airmen. In the big province of Friesland alone, according to figures I was given by a Frisian, 91 RCAF men crashed and died, out of a total of 622 aircraft. Here in Gelderland province, the Dutch couple who took me to Beek churchyard also drove me over to a churchyard in nearby Kilder to see the graves of six more airmen, four of them Canadian. (The other Canadian in George's crew, G.W. Sellers, rests with George in Beek.)

Endnotes

(37) Some 10 years after learning about George's grave in Beek, another RCAF veteran and former schoolmate, Carman Brown, sent me a seven-page story in Dutch, which had been drawn to his attention because George Miller's name and the name of our town appeared in it. A Dutch lady, Mary Vanderzyde, kindly did the translation for us. It is by the Dutch writer Hennie Freriks, and is an historical account, in the form of a tragic drama, written from three points of view and titled "Flight EF 330: F.T.R. (Failed to Return)." The writer happened to pick this plane, a Short Stirling bomber in which George was a gunner. He tells of the plane's and the crew's preparation in England for the flight, and of its mission. He tells of the preparation in the Netherlands of the night fighter Messerschmitt BF 110 and its crew. He outlines the BF 110's shooting down of Flight EF 330 on its return from its mission. And he unfolds the tragedy of the Dutch family on the ground — innocent bystanders.

(38) On our 1956 visit to Europe, my wife Jean and I stopped in Wehl. The big tree was still there, next to the schoolhouse, just as I had remembered it; but the land had long forgotten my digging. On my visit to the town in 1995 in my rented car, I dropped into a small restaurant-tavern combination on the main street for a sandwich and beer, and got talking to the English speaking owner. I gave him my story and pointed from the window to the intersection where I thought the tank got hit — a point near where a church comes out to the edge of the street. On the tavern side he took me to the table of a local who wanted to meet me. He could speak no English, but the owner interpreted. It turned out that as a young teenager he saw the tank struck. He was watching from the basement window. Before I left, he smiled and made a correction in my memory of where the tank was. "He says," the owner interpreted, "that you are one block out." I was pleased that my old memory could even be that close.

I struck a mother-lode of information when the tavern owner directed me to the residence of Mr. H.M. Bles, an English-speaking longtime citizen of the district, who had a good knowledge of the war's movements over the area. For example, he had corresponded with and had been visited by — family and all — the troop commander of the Shermans that came into Wehl on that April day. The commander's name was Haddon, he told me, and his troop had been the tanks of the Sherbrooke Fusiliers of Montreal.

It was Mr. and Mrs. Bles who took me in their car to the graves at Beek and Kilder, and then to spots in Wehl and on surrounding farms. In Wehl there was a tree where my memory said one should be, but it was too young to be my tree. And a large modern building sat in place of the school. Mr. Bles showed me the farm where he and his family had lived when the war passed by, and told about how they came out of the cellar with his father waving a tablecloth when the Germans had left and our infantry could be seen approaching. My host, a young boy at the time, had been hit by shrapnel from our shelling or perhaps by a bullet. The infantry put him in a Jeep and rushed him all the way to a hospital in Nijmegen, which no doubt saved his life. His skull had been broken. He bent over to show me the ugly scar along a valley in

A Signal War

the top of his head. At one of the farms he took me to, the farmer told of the terrifying sight of three Germans burned to death by a Wasp flame-thrower.

(39) I attended the 1988 reunion of the 13th Field Regiment, in Red Deer, Alberta. Ike Thompson was there, 43 years later and still able to drink. I would never have recognized him, although I guessed by the missing arm. He died in 1996.

Chapter 15

(40) It was in the Frisian city of Leeuwarden in 1782 that the decision was made to recognize the United States, that new country in North America; and it was a Frisian, Peter Stuyvesant, who was the founder of New York City — a couple of small items from what is no doubt a long and proud Frisian history.

Chapter 16

(41) Wolff, Leon. *In Flanders Fields*. New York: Viking Press, 1958. p.35

Chapter 17

(42) Stacey, C.P. *The Victory Campaign: the Operations in North-West Europe 1944-1945*. Queen's Printer, 1960. p.584.

(43) It is surely worth mentioning for the sake of giving due credit to the Swedish citizens who, three months earlier in the middle of the Dutch winter of starvation, had put together a shipload of food, which arrived in the port of Delfzijl on January 28, 1945.

(44) If Montgomery had gotten what he wished, the 4th Division's last days would have been quite different, for he wanted the Division to be attached to his British force to help in the attack on Bremen. Crerar declined because he wanted to keep the Canadians together in closing out the War.

(45) At some point earlier, a few of our vehicles came into flooded soggy ground because the determined, relentless Poles had dumped a great quantity of baled hay into a water course, perhaps a creek or drainage canal. They did it to get their troops across smartly and push forward rather than wait for a section of Bailey bridge. What had happened to their homeland no doubt gave them this seemingly untiring impatience. It showed as well in that part of their Division that had advanced to Astederfeld. Ignoring the general order not to fire unless fired upon, they shelled continuously the German territory in front of them until the last minute of the war.

Endnotes

Chapter 18

(46) I have met only one North Shore veteran in my post-military years, and it was some three decades later. My sister and brother-in-law, Gert and Jim Dunn (RCAF veteran), brought to our farm one Sunday afternoon a paraplegic from the veterans' hospital in Ste. Anne de Bellevue, Quebec. His name was Clarence (Mac) McLaughlin. Had our experiences intertwined at times from the Schelde on? No, he told me, for he had been shot in the spine within an hour after coming ashore on D-Day. He was 22 years old, and had been in a wheelchair ever since.

When they promised to visit our farm on other Sundays, I got prepared by constructing on the front of an old car chassis a low platform to accommodate a wheelchair. With our tractor behind, Mac on the front, and others comfortable on the chassis seats, we spent many pleasant afternoons moving through the beautiful trails in our woods, at about two kilometres an hour, and finding various spots for our picnic lunch. He eventually moved to the new Parkwood Hospital veterans' wing in London, Ontario, where I visited him in 1987. I had forgotten exactly what year (1992) he had died, so in 2001 I phoned the hospital to find out. They gave me the run-around, telling me, that they do not keep records very far back and couldn't help me. Lest we forget! I found the date from another source.

(47) Rumpf, Hans. *The Bombing of Germany*. Trans. Edward Fitzgerald. London: Frederick Muller, 1963. p.206.

(48) Bollen, Hen and Paul Vroemen. *The End: of Five Years of Terror in Holland*. Zaltbommel: Europese Bibliotheek, 1990.

(49) At least our war's protocol had some improvement over that of medieval times, when you had to be careful about the rank of those whom you killed. History says that the poor common soldier who from the ramparts of a French fortress at Calais picked off Richard the Lionheart with an arrow, as he took a canter around its walls during the British siege, was skinned alive and had his hide draped from the ramparts to show how contrite the French command was at such a violation of military etiquette.

(50) Eaton's and Simpson's were the two major mail-order and department store chains in Canada.

Chapter 19

(51) Continuously reinforced hate over centuries can express itself very strangely. When Hitler in his underground quarters in Berlin shot himself on April 30, 1945, the prime minister of Ireland at the time, Eamon Da Valera, called on the German legation here in Dublin to offer condolences on behalf of the Irish people on the death of

Germany's Führer. Earlier, in the middle of the war, 1943, the Irish Press, which had the largest circulation in the country, told its readers that "there is no kind of oppression visited on any minority in Europe which [Irish nationalists] have not also endured." The German writer Heinrich Böll, who was travelling in Ireland sometime in 1950, found people who still believed that Germany's wartime atrocities were simply British propaganda. With the plethora of Holocaust revisionists throughout the West still plying their wares some 50 years later, Ireland's tedious blindness back then doesn't seem to be too exceptional.

Chapter 20

(52) The dark side of Canadian behaviour while stationed in the Netherlands had a lingering effect, which I became aware of some 40 years after the war. I mentioned earlier in Chapter 15 the story of the two Chaudière men who went on patrol into Zwolle, where the one got shot but the other made contact with the city's underground. In 1993, Hugh McVicar, the Essex Scottish veteran whom I mentioned elsewhere, told me in our correspondence that he was stationed in Zwolle after the war, and by coincidence was billeted with one Frits Kuipers who turned out to be the underground leader whom the Chaudiere man, Private Leo Major by name, had contacted. In 1968 Kuipers visited the McVicar's here in Islington; and he had come with a mission, which in McVicar's words was this. "On behalf of Zwolle City Council he was to find [the Chaudière veteran] Leo Major, to ensure Leo's appearance in Zwolle in April of 1970 to be honoured in the 25th Anniversary of [the city's] liberation." No problem, surely! For such a fine cause, the DVA (Department of Veterans' Affairs) will help locate him. Well, not really!

The Department refused. Apparently all sorts of innocent-sounding reasons were being given by European parties to track down veterans for, as one can imagine, paternity suits, robbery, rape, spousal abandonment and the like. McVicar told me that, fortunately, he had a contact with a high-ranking officer in the Salvation Army's Bureau of Missing Persons, who was a friend of a DVA official, who called another DVA official in Montreal, who eventually arranged for both parties to be rigorously questioned separately, the result of which finally brought the two men together for the first time since that fateful day in the war. Major accepted the Dutch city's invitation. Accompanied by his wife, he was honoured by the citizens of Zwolle, and met Dutch Queen Juliana, who also attended. A happy ending!

(53) Cassidy, G.L. *Warpath: from Tilly-la-Campagne to the Kusten Canal*. Markham, ON: Paperjacks, Ltd., 1980. pp.373-374.

(54) One of the writers for the paper, who did a column called "Current Comment," was a soldier named Bernard Wand. I remember him, too, conducting a class in the CAOF school that had been set up. A decade or so later the professor who walked into my philosophy class at Carleton University to deliver the lecture was Bernard Wand.

Endnotes

He didn't remember me, of course, for he was either a university graduate or well on his way when he entered the army, and as a consequence travelled with a different set in the CAOF. He came to a couple of student/faculty parties that Jean and I held at our house in Ottawa in the 1950s, and we reminisced about those occupation days.

(55) Lavender, Emerson and Norman Sheffe. *The Evaders.* Toronto:McGraw-Hill Ryerson, 1992. p.177.

Chapter 21

(56) The Canadian war brides who were on his ship were to remain segregated in a specified area of deck and accommodations, but a number of them were wandering afield and carrying out some loin-baring unfaithfulness among the lifeboats and rigging. The ship's command announced by loudspeaker that soldiers caught in the women's area would be placed on charge, and that women found outside their boundary would not be allowed to disembark and would be returned to Britain. Whittington said that when the ship docked, the command announced the order of disembarkation, and made it a point to say that a number of the war brides would be compelled to stay on board and would be going back with the ship. Knowing the military, we agreed that the ship's authorities probably kept their word.

(57) On a late evening in 1993, I was watching a long-retired movie director being interviewed on TV. He told a story about how the script of one of the extravaganzas he directed years ago called for an ocean liner to blow up and sink. The producers heard that Japan had bought an old one cheap for scrap, so off they went to buy it back. He said the old hulk was called the *Isle de France*. Inasmuch as a few of the hometown boys either went to war or returned on that ship, I wrote to our local paper, *The Prescott Journal*, about this discovery. I said that when the fellow mentioned the ship's name, I slopped my beer down the side of my rocking chair. If we had only known about her retirement, I suggested, we grateful former passengers, with memories of throwing up over her railing, could have bought her by pooling our clothing allowances, and anchored her in the St. Lawrence in front of the town, where she could be used for shuffle-board tournaments, livestock shows and the like.

Bibliography

Abella, Irving and Harold Troper. "The line must be drawn somewhere: Canada and Jewish Refugees, 1933-9." *Canadian Historical Review*. Vol. 60, No.2, 1979.

Allan, Ralph. "Was Kurt Meyer Guilty?" *Maclean's*. Feb. 1, 1950, pp. 9, 47-49.

Anderson, Omer. (A piece on Kurt Meyer.) *Weekend Magazine*. Vol. 7, No. 5, 1950.

Bailey, Ronald H. *Prisoners of War*. Time-Life Books, 1981. pp. 173-176.

Barrett, W.W. *The History of 13 Canadian Field Regiment Royal Canadian Artillery 1940-1945*. No publisher nor date given. Made available to each member of the Regiment in 1946.

Bird, Will R.. *North Shore (New Brunswick) Regiment*. Brunswick Press, 1963.

Blount, Roy. "Lustily Vigilant." *Atlantic Monthly*. Dec. 1994.

Bollen, Hen and Paul Vroemen. *The End: of Five Years of Terror in Holland*. Zaltbommel: Europese Bibliotheek, 1990.

Byers, A.R., ed.. *The Canadians at War 1939-1945*. Montreal: Reader's Digest Assoc., 1986.

Carlson, Norm. "30 Rounds Later." *Legion Magazine*. April, 1994.

Cassidy, G.L.. *Warpath: from Tilly-la-Campagne to the Kusten Canal*. Markham, ON, Paperjacks, Ltd., 1980.

Bibliography

Charles, John. "Confessions of a Military Historian." *New Internationalist.* Sept.,1993, pp. 22-23.

Coffey, Thomas M. *Decision over Schweinfurt: the US 8th Air Force Battle for Daylight Bombing.* New York: David McKay, 1977.

Copp, Terry. "Battle Exhaustion in WW II." (Part 19 in series "Canadian Military History in Perspective.") *Legion Magazine.* Jan./Feb., 1998, pp. 40-42.

Copp, Terry and Robert Vogel. *Maple Leaf Route: Victory.* Alma, ON: published by Maple Leaf Route, 1988.

Cronin, Fergus. "The Rumor that Killed a General." *Maclean's.* May 12, 1956.

Crowe, Jean Margaret. "Surviving the Slaughter." *Legion Magazine.* Dec., 1980.

Donat, Alexander. *The Holocaust Kingdom.* New York: Holocaust Library, 1978.

Dunne, John Gregory. "Virtual Patriotism." *New Yorker.* Nov. 16, 1998.

Edmonds, Alan. "Return to the Killing Ground: 25 Years after Dieppe." *Maclean's,* July, 1967.

Ellis, John. *The Sharp End: The Fighting Man in World War II.* New York: Scribner's, 1980.

Elstob, Peter. *Battle of the Reichwald.* New York: Ballantine Books, 1970.

Emmott, Norman. *One Foot on the Ground.* Toronto: Lugus publications, 1992.

English, John A.. *The Canadian Army and the Normandy Campaign: a Study of Failure in High Command.* New York: Praeger, 1991.

Foley, Dennis. "Through Hell in a Halifax." *Ottawa Citizen*, March 30, 1993, p. B4.

Fotheringham, Allan. "Tuned out and turned off." *Maclean's.* Nov. 21, 1988, p. 64.

A Signal War

Fussell, Paul. "The Real War 1939-1945." *Atlantic Monthly*. August, 1989.

Galbraith, John Kenneth. *A Journey through Economic Time*. Boston: Houghton Mifflin, 1994.

Gardam, John. *Ordinary Heroes*. Burnstown, ON: General Story Publishing House,1995.

Keegan, John. "D-Day: Being There." *Sunday Times*. June 3, 1984, pp. 33-34.

Keegan, John. *Six Armies in Normandy: from D-Day to the Liberation of Paris*. New York: Viking Press, 1982.

Kennedy, David M. "Victory at Sea." *Atlantic Monthly*. March 1999, pp. 51-76.

Knoke, Heinz. *I Flew for the Führer*. London: Evans, 1953.

Lavender, Emerson and Norman Sheffe. *The Evaders*. Toronto:McGraw-Hill Ryerson,1992.

Mayer, Anita. *One Who Came Back*. Oberon Press, 1981.

McIntosh, Dave. *High Blue Battle*. Toronto: Stoddart, 1990.

McIntosh, Dave. "Canadian Expedition to Hong Kong." *Ottawa Journal*. Dec. 16, 1961.

McWhinney, Edward. "The Firing Squad Case: Have we swept it under the rug?" *The Globe and Mail*. Nov. 4, 1966.

Milberry, Larry. *Sixty Years: the RCAF and CF Air Command 1924-1984*. Toronto: Canav Books, 1984.

Morrow, Lance. "Chronicling a Filthy 4,000-Year-Old Habit. Time. Dec. 13, 1993.

Mowat, Farley. The Regiment. Toronto: McClelland & Stewart, 1955.

North Shore (New Brunswick) Regiment. War Diary: March 23 through April 1, 1945.National Archives of Canada, Ottawa.

Bibliography

Onderwater, Hans. *Memories of a Miracle*. [Re: food drop.] Rotterdam: Ad. Donker,1995.

Robertson, Heather. *A Terrible Beauty: the Art of Canada at War*. Lorimer, 1977.

Rumpf, Hans. *The Bombing of Germany*. Trans. Edward Fitzgerald. London: Frederick Muller, 1963.

Ryan, Cornelius. *A Bridge Too Far*. New York: Fawcett Popular Library, 1974.

Stacey, C.P.. *Six Years of War: the Army in Canada, Britain and the Pacific*. Ottawa: Queen's Printers, 1955.

Stacey, C.P.. *The Victory Campaign: the Operations in North-West Europe 1944-1945*. Ottawa: Queen's Printer, 1960.

Thompson, R.W.. *Battle for the Rhine*. New York: Ballantine Books, 1959.

Not attributed. *The Eighty-Five Days*. London: Hutchinson, 1957.

Villa, Brian Loring. *Unauthorized Action: Mountbatten and the Dieppe Raid*. Toronto: Oxford University Press, 1989.

Whitaker, W. Dennis and Shelagh. *Rhineland: the Battle to End the War*. Toronto: Stoddart, 1989.

White, Theodore H.. *In Search of History: A Personal Adventure*. Harper & Row, 1978.

Wilson-Smith, Anthony. "The Unsung Seamen." *Maclean's*. July 6, 1972.

Wolff, Leon. *In Flanders Fields*. New York: Viking Press, 1958, p.35.

Wright, Michael, ed.. *The World at Arms*. London: Reader's Digest Assoc, Ltd., 1989.

Index

A

Aalten: 286.
Achterwehl: 209.
Aldershot: 33, 34, 39.
Algonguin Regiment: 46, 144, 151, 153, 263, 284.
Alkmaar: 279.
Almen: 209.
Alpon: 154.
Ambrosius, Johanna: 130, 136-7, 139.
Amersfoort: 261.
Amsterdam: 242, 278, 298, 361.
Antionette, Marie: 291.
Antwerp: 44, 56-7, 65, 82.
Apeldoorn: 258, 276, 295.
Argyle and Sutherland Highlanders Regiment: 144, 153.
Ariaans, Johanna Berdina: 362-3.
Arnhem: 66, Battle of: see Endnote #14; 73, 81, 88, 189, 234, 259, 262.
Assen: 295.
Astederfeld: 263.
Attlee, Clement: 305.
Aufsluitdijke: 237-9, 278-9.
Aurich: 265, 267-8, 273, 298, 321, 330.
Auschwitz: 338, 340, 361.

Aymans, Josef: 136.

B

Baak: 209, 233.
Badoglio, Marshal: 9.
Bad Zwischenahn: 262-3, 361.
Bagband: 266-7, 270-3.
Balbergerwald: 145-9, 153, 155, 172, 182.
Bangor: 348.
Bantford. Alex: 328.
Barley, Ainsley: 84, 89, 90.
Barneveld: 262.
Barrett, Lieutenant W.W.: 58.
Barriefield: 21.
Base Censor: see Green Envelopes.
Batteries: 22nd: 67, 92, 95, 123, 129, 238, 249, 254, 363.
    44th: 45, 47, 52, 59, 67, 84, 123, 200, 209, 237; CAOF: 295, 309-10, 328, 362.
    78th: 146, 149, 153, 328.
    56th Canadian Anti-Tank: 118.
Battle Exhaustion: 120-21.
Batz, Hauptmann: 142.
Beck, Rainer: 282, 284.
Bedburg: 119.
Beek (near Nijmegen): 72, 76, 81, 97-8, 106.

Index

Beek (grave of George Miller): 205-07, 266; see also Endnotes #35, #36, #37.
Beethoven: 336.
Belfast: 305-06, 308.
Berchtesgaden:194.
Berg en Dal: 72, 76, 78, 106, 111, 104.
Bergen-Belsen: 321.
Berlin: 187, 310.
Bernhardt, Prince of the Netherlands: 219, 280.
Beurling, Flying Officer George, "Buzz": 143.
Beverwijk: 279.
Biccum, Jack: 243.
Bienen: 193-94, 196, 198.
Bingum: 251, 254.
Bird, Will R.:60, 234.
Black (roommate at Jever airbase): 340.
Black Watch Regiment (British): 192.
Blaskowitz, General Johannes: 280-81.
Bles, H.M.: see Endnote # 38.
Boivin, Leo: 17.
Bollen, Hen: 280.
Bolsward: 237.
Borden: 31-3, 39, 41.
Boer War: 256.
Boswell, James: 348.
Braakman Inlet: 45.
Bradford: 37.
Brantford: 21.
Bremen: 204, 315, 319, 344.
Bremerhaven: 344.
Brest: 2.
Brereton, General Lewis: 190.
Breskens: 44, 57.
Brinkum: 266.
British Broadcasting Corporation (BBC): 268.
Brockville: 23-5, 353-54.
Broda, Turk:17, 22.

Brooke, Field-Marshal Sir Allen: 152, 190.
Brown, Cecil: 353.
Brown, Connie: 17, 19.
Brunshof: 137.
Brussels: 289, 291-92, 305.
Bunde: 249, 253.
Burchell, Merton: 298.
Buswell, Sergeant Roy (signals sergeant): 49, 129-30, 133, 138, 244, 246, 308.

C

Caen: 63
Calais: 305, 309.
Calgary Highlanders Regiment: 103
Caligula: 240.
Cameron Highlanders Regiment: 238.
Campbell, Captain A.L.: 247, 250-51, 253, 255, 268, 270.
Canadian Grenadier Guards Regiment: 144-45, 150.
Canadian Scottish Regiment: 112.
Capone, Al: 40.
Cardinal: 3, 5, 28, 232, 301.
Carleton University: 272.
Carter, Bud, 13th Field Regiment Quartermaster: 44, 45.
Causeway: see Aufsluitdijke.
Charles, Bonnie Prince: 346.
Chaudiere Regiment (Le Regiment de la Chaudiere): 127, 129, 146, 149, 153, 200-02, 208-09, 213, 233, 236-38, 247, 250, 253, 267.
Chennault, General Claire: 63.
Chicago: 217.
Churchill, Prime Minister Winston: 4, 152, 190, 274.
Clausewitz, Karl von: 361.
Clay, Pat: 328.
Clemenceau, George: 291.
Clyde River: 30, 33, 248.
Collison, Stan: 355.

385

Index

Cornwall: 23, 354.
Cosens, Sergeant Aubrey, V.C.: 128-29.
Crerar, General H.D.G.: 89, 102-03, 152, 287.
Culloden: 346.
Cumberland, Lord: 346.
Cuxhaven: 344.

D

Dale: 286.
Danson, Barney: 238.
Danzig: 19.
D'Assargues, Peter: 346.
Davis, Bette: 17.
De Lemmer: 238.
Delfzijl: 262.
Delmenhorst: 344.
Den Heuvel: 103.
Deventer: 233, 276.
Diefenbaker, John: 283.
Dieppe: 151, 276, 282, 346.
Ditzumer Verlaat: 253.
Doesburg: 209.
Dollart: 247.
Donat, Alexander: 339.
Dorchester: 330.
Dorfer, Bruno: 282, 284.
Dornick: 199, 200.
Dover: 305, 309.
Doyle, Joe: see Endnote #7.
Drugs: 121-22.
Dublin: 307.
Duffelward: 105.
Dunfermline: 329.
Dunkalk: 307.
Dunkirk: 2, 41.
Dunn, Jim & Gertrude: see Endnote #46.

E

Eberding, General Kurt: 54.

Ede: 276.
Edinburgh: 329-30, 341.
Eefde: 179.
Eem River: 258.
Eindhoven: 286.
Eisenhower, General Ike: 190, 306.
Elb River: 204.
Elizabeth II, Queen: 1.
Elliot, Bill: 347.
Ellis, John: 122.
Elstob, Peter: 179.
Elten: 202.
Emden: 205, 254-55, 262, 265.
Emerson, Faye: 60.
Emmerich: 104-05, 198-202, 205.
Emo: 298.
Ems River: 246, 250, 253, 255, 262, 264-67.
Ems-Jade Canal: 296.
Enschede: 108.
Essame, Major-General Hubert: 110.
Essen: 206.
Essex Scottish Regiment: 114, 132, 136-37, 145-46, 154, 284.
Evinrude Outboard Motors: 188-89.
Exe River: 36, 38.
Exeter: 34, 36.
Exmorra: 237.
Exmouth: 38.

F

Farnborough: 33, 345.
Faust: 355.
15th Panzer Grenadiers: 193-94.
1st Canadian Parachute Battalion: 190.
1st Hussars: 134, 145.
1st Polish Armoured Division: 243-45, 261-63, 265-67, 330; see also Endnote #45.
Flynn, Errol: 196.
Fort Gary Horse Guards Regiment: 114.

Index

Fort William: 348.
Foster, Brigadier Harry: 331.
Foulkes, General Charles: 280-81.
Fraser, Mr.: 346-47.
Friesland: 235-36, 241.
Friesoythe: 263.
Fussell, Paul: 331.

G

Galland, General Adolf: 90.
Geldern: 152.
Gent: 42, 55, 57, 59, 61-2, 64, 154, 240.
George VI, King: 1, 274, 305.
Gershwin, George: 20.
Gessner, Ernst-Wilhelm: 266.
Glasgow: 347-48.
Goch: 111-13, 123, 127, 136.
Goethe: 355.
Gordon, Major J.N.: 197.
Gorredijk: 239, 274, 278.
Göttern: 137.
Grabstede: 263.
Grebbe River: 258, 262.
Green envelopes: 180-81, 357.
Greenland: 30.
Greenock: 30-1, 348.
Grenadier Guards: see Canadian Grenadier Guards.
Groesbeek: 66, 70, 72, 74, 78, 81, 87, 89-90, 93, 117, 259, 263.
Groningen: 243, 262, 276, 322.
Grootenhuis, John te: 286.

H

Haarlem: 278.
Haddon, tank commander: see Endnote #38.
Hague, The: see >s-Gravenhage.
Haig, Field-Marshall Douglas: 257.
Halifax: 26, 352, 354.
Hamb: 152.
Hamburg: 204, 310.
Hannover: 204.
Harderwijk: 262.
Hardijus, Hector: 62.
Harlingen: 239.
Harris, Air Chief Marshal Sir Arthur, "Bomber": 121, 190. Harrison, Ab: 53, 97, 106-07, 110, 115, 131-34, 139, 147-48, 179, 191, 195-97, 201, 210, 213, 218, 232, 239, 270, 287-88, 294, 306, 360.
Hartmann, Oberleutnant Eric: 142.
Harwich: 328, 341.
Heerenveen: 235, 237, 239, 243.
Heidelberg: 283.
Heino: 233.
Helensburgh: 348.
Hellyer, Paul: 283.
Hesel: 265-66.
Hess, Rudolf: 108.
Heydrich, Reinhard: 172.
Heyst: 45, 54.
Hickey, Major R.M.: 232.
Highland Light Infantry Regiment: 105, 188, 192, 194, 196, 239, 264.
Hilversum: 287.
Hitler, Adolf: 4, 5, 89, 141, 172, 217, 265, 290, 294, 350.
Hoch Elten: 202.
Hochwald: 145, 148, 151, 284.
Hochwald Gap: 143-51.
Hoek van Holland: 328, 330.
Hollen: 129, 135.
Holman, Ken: 33.
Hong Kong: 6, 7.
Horrocks, Lieutenant-General Brian: 98, 110, 152.
Horsford, Frank: 36.
Horsford, Mr. and Mrs. (in Devonshire, England): 37-9.
Hunter, Norm: 288.
Hüthem: 201.
Hyman, Mr.: 346-48.

387

Index

I

Ijssel Meer: 237, 258, 262, 278.
Ijssel River: 209, 217-18, 233, 235.
Inkrum: 263.
Innis, Carl: 6.
Inverness: 345-47.
Iroquois: 354.

J

Jacobs, G.J.: 286.
Janssen, Henk and Antoinette: 363.
Jever: 310, 325, 327-28, 330. 332, 336-37, 341, 344.
Johnson, Ben: 341.
Johnson, Dr. Samuel: 348.
Johnstown: 5, 25.
Joppe: 233.
Joure: 235.

K

Kael, Pauline: vi.
Kalkar: 111-13, 123, 127-28, 136, 152.
Kaye, Danny: 18.
Keaton, Buster: 18.
Keegan, John: 218, 361.
Kekerdom: 106.
Kelly, Leila: 358.
Keppeln: 129-30, 133-40, 197.
Kesselring, Field-Marshal Albert: 265.
Kilder: 207, 266.
King, Mackenzie: 338.
Kingston: 8, 12, 13, 21, 23, 35, 179, 299, 343, 357.
Kirchborgum: 250-51.
Kirkby, Don: 25, 33.
Kirkby, Lloyd: 329.
Kirkland Lake: 18.
Kitching, General George: 280.
Kleve: 103, 105, 110-11, 115-17, 155, 168, 174-77, 181-82, 184, 195, 233, 295, 312, 351.

Knocke-sur-Mer: 54.
Koning, Hans: 236.
Koudum: 237.
Küsten Canal: 262-63.

L

Laag-Keppel: 208.
Lake Superior Regiment: 144-45, 150.
Lamoureux, Major C.R.: 249.
Larne: 305.
Laurenburg: 204.
Leeds: 37.
Leer: 253-55, 263, 265-66, 276, 295.
Leeuwarden: 243.
Leitz, Ernst: 78.
Leopold Canal: 45.
Leuth: 106.
Lincoln and Welland Regiment: 144, 153.
Lippens, Henk: 241, 278.
Loga: 264.
London: 4, 32, 34, 36, 39, 65, 66, 142, 305, 308, 344-46, 349-50, 357.
Louis XVI: 291.
Louisendorf: 113, 119, 123.
Lourdes: 363.
Lovat, Lord: 346-47.
Lübeck: 311.
Lunteren: 276-77, 291-94.
Lympstone: 36, 182.

M

Maas River: 98, 103, 113, 127.
Mackay: 30, 31.
Macon: 313.
Makkum: 237, 238.
Maldegem: 45.
Malmedy: 331.
Manchester: 348.
Mannheim: 336, 343.
Marleen. Lili: 351.

Index

Marx Groucho: 304.
Matachewan: 18.
Mayer, Anita: 363-64.
McCool, Brian: 282, 331.
McCormick: 170.
McGill University: 283.
McIntosh, Dave: 9.
McLaughlin, Clarence (Mac): see Endnote #46.
McVicar, Hugh: 136-37.
Meppel: 233-34.
Meppen: 262.
Meyer, General Kurt: 330-32.
Meyers, George: 121, 133-35, 172, 184, 250, 252, 288.
Miller, George: 206-07.
Millingen (Holland): 106-07, 111.
Millingen (Germany): 194, 196-98.
Milwaukee: 217.
"Moaning Minnie": 147, 194.
Montesquieu, Baron de: 121, 360.
Montgomery, Field-Marshal Bernard: 7, 110, 126, 152, 190, 205, 328.
Montreal: 23, 198, 352, 361.
Mooshof: 128-29, 135.
Mowat, Farley: 2.
Moyland Wood: 111-13, 117, 119, 127, 151, 202, 276.
Mussert, Anton: 293-94.
Mussolini, Benito: 5, 9, 264.

N

Naples: 40.
Napoleon (Bonaparte): 42, 290.
Nattrass, E.C.: 239-40, 242.
Naula, Tina: 242.
New York: 327.
Niagara Falls: 21.
Nieuwe-Pekela: 244.
Nieuwe-Schans: 276.
Nijmegen: 64, 66, 71-74, 76, 80-81, 83-86, 88, 90, 97-98, 115, 154-55, 174, 184, 206, 291, 305, 309, 351.

Neuenburg: 303.
North Bay: 33.
North Nova Scotia Highlanders Regiment: 54, 105, 193-94.
North Shore (New Brunswick) Regiment: 45, 50, 52-54, 60, 66, 74, 76-79, 81, 91, 123, 127,129, 132-33, 139-40, 146-47, 149-50, 153, 155, 171-72, 177, 183-86, 192-93, 194-202, 207-09, 212-214, 216, 232, 234, 237, 244-48, 250-52, 255, 264-68, 270-72.
Nuremberg: 204.

O

Odessa: 339.
Oldenburg: 205, 262, 295, 299-300, 304, 309, 330, 336.
Oostburg: 47, 63.
Orwell, George: 294.
Osnabrück: 325, 330.
Ostend: 41, 42, 62.
Ostersander: 268.
Ostrander, Colonel C.R.: 271-73.
Ottawa: 1, 8, 24, 249.
Ottawa River: 12.
Owens, Jesse: 314, 341.

P

Papenburg: 263.
Paris: 2, 21, 289-92.
Parker, Major: 134.
Patton, Lieutenant-General George: 204-05, 361.
Pearl Harbour: 6.
Pelehos, Jim: see Endnote #7.
Petawawa: 12, 20-22, 25, 178.
Peterson, Junior: 345, 349-50, 357.
Peterson, Louie: 43.
Pettem, Allen: 298.
Picadilly: 34-35, 349.
Pingjum: 238.
Polish Division: see 1st Polish

389

Index

Armoured Division.
Piper, Allen: 14.
Pius XII, Pope: 340.
Place, Merwin: 310.
Plymouth: 2, 38.
Prague: 273.
Prescott: 3, 23-24, 300, 328-29, 342, 345, 347, 351, 353-54, 357-58, 363-64.
Prince Albert: 59, 288.
Princess Patricia's Canadian Light Infantry (PPCLI) Regiment: 173.
Putten: 262.

Q

Queen's Own Rifles Regiment: 111, 127-28, 146, 153, 200-02, 207-09, 219, 238, 247, 253. 267.
Queen's Own Camerons of Canada Regiment: 114.
Queensferry: 329.

R

Rastede: 262.
Rauter, General Hans: 259.
Raycroft, Donnie: 25.
Raycroft. Glenn: 25, 335.
Raycroft, Jean: v, 14, 362; Endnote #38.
Reagan, Ronald: i; see also Endnote #1.
Red Cross, Canadian: 177.
Red Deer: 59, 61.
Rees: 42, 93, 185, 187-88, 191-92, 200, 205.
Regiment de la Chaudière, Le: see Chaudière Regiment.
Regiment de Maisonneuve, Le: see Maisonneuve Regiment.
Regina Rifles Regiment: 112, 207.
Renfrew: 12.
Rhede: 244.
Rheinberg: 153.

Rhine River: 81, 97-98, 102, 104, 107, 117, 119, 127, 136, 144, 151, 153, 155, 182-83, 185, 192-93, 200-01, 204-05, 235.
Ridgway, General Matthew: 190.
Roer River: 111, 119, 152, 175.
Rogers, Will: 21.
Rommel, Field-Marshal Erwin: 5, 126.
Rooke, Mrs.: 1, 2, 354.
Ross, Jack: 347.
Ross Rifle: 188.
Rotterdam: 261, 281, 323.
Rowley, Colonel John: 133, 196.
Royal Hamilton Light Infantry Regiment: 114, 146, 154.
Royal Regiment of Canada: 114, 282.
Royal Winnipeg Rifles Regiment: 112-13.
Rumpf, Hans: 275.
Rundstedt. Field-Marshal Gerd von: 89.
Ryan, Cornelius: 66, 122.

S

St. Anna ter Muiden: 53.
St. Lawrence: 5, 25, 298, 364.
St. Paul: 217.
Salisbury Plain: 32.
Sande: 332-33.
Schettens: 237-39.
Schlemm, General Alfred: 142, 144, 180, 275.
Scott, Bud: 345.
Seeley, Graham: 41.
Seyss-Inquart, Arthur: 258.
s-Gravenhage: 260, 286, 292.
Shaw, Oliver: 50-51, 62, 67-69, 73, 82, 84, 87, 98-92, 94, 99-100, 104, 109-11, 116-17, 119, 129-34, 140, 171, 173, 175, 183-84, 189, 191, 194-96, 201, 206, 210-13, 215-16, 217-18, 239, 244, 253, 265, 270,

Index

277, 287-88, 294, 312, 360.
sHeerenberg: 205, 286.
Shentow, David: 321.
Sherbrooke Fusiliers Tank Regiment: 113, 154, 238.
Shilo: 67.
Sidney, Sir Philip: 232.
Siegfried Line: 66, 84, 113, 117, 143, 152.
Simonds, General Guy: 98, 112, 154, 276.
Simpson, General William: 190.
Skorzeny, Otto: 9.
Sluis: 52, 53, 139.
Smith, Art: 342.
Smith, Johnny: 43
Smith, L.K. "Smitty": 87, 216, 291-92.
Smiths Falls: 5.
Sneek: 237-39.
Sonsbeck: 149, 152.
South Alberta Tank Regiment: 144.
Southampton: 41, 350.
Speer, Albert: 290.
Speldrop: 192.
Stacey, Colonel C.P.: ii, iii, 6, 152, 258, 344.
Stalin, Joseph: 301-02.
Stalingrad: 4, 7.
Staveren: 237.
Steenwijk: 235.
Sten Gun; its flaws: 172-73, 270.
Stilwell, General Joseph: 64.
Stormont, Dundas and Glengary Highlanders Regiment: 105.
Stranraer: 305, 308.
Streicher, Julius: 142.
Swastika: 18, 130, 275.

T

Tanks: 125-26.
Tannenhausen: 321, 332.
Taylor, A.J.P.: ii, iii, vi.

The Hague: see s-Gravenhage.
3rd Canadian Medium Artillery Regiment: 238.
13th Royal Canadian Field Artillery Regiment (See also Batteries.): 44, 52, 57-59, 97, 110, 123, 146-47, 205, 207, 239, 263-64, 270, 272;
CAOF: 295, 310.
Thompson, Captain: 46.
Thompson, Sergeant Ike: 209. see Endnote #39
Tilston, Major Fred, V.C.: 145-46.
Tito: 40.
Tobruk: 327.
Toronto: 23, 116, 352-53.
Toronto Scottish Regiment: 233.
Trevor, Claire: 11.
Trudeau, Pierre: 238.

U

Ubbergen: 72.
Uedem: 128, 134-36, 140-43, 148, 181, 199.
Urquhart, General Robert: 172.
Utah Beach: 39.
Utrecht: 261, 277, 287, 322.

V

Vanderzyde, John: 260, 261.
Varel: 324.
Veen: 153, 272.
Venlo: 152.
Verrieres Ridge: 151, 202, 276.
Versailles: 290-91.
Victor Emmanuel III, King of Italy: 9.
Vielstadt: 315.
Viereck, George Silvester: 337.
Vietnam: 281.
Vokes, General Chris: 330, 344.
V-1 and V-2 (statistics): 65-66, 69-70.
Vroeman, Paul: 280.
Voorburg: 260.

Index

W

Wadina: 288.
Wageningen: 280.
Warbeyen: 200.
Waugh: 313.
Webb, Tip: 25.
Weener: 244-45, 247-50, 253, 255, 263, 276.
Wehl: 207-09.
Werra, Franz von: 5.
Wesel: 102, 127, 136, 151, 153, 186, 189-90.
Weser River: 255, 262, 344.
Westerloog: 273.
Westerstede: 263.
Weynert: 351.
Wezepe: 233.
Whitaker, W. Denis & Shelagh Whitaker: 112, 154.
Whitley, Gerry: see Endnote #7.
Whitley: 345, 350-51.
Whitney, Bud: 169.
Whitney, Jim: 300.
Whittington, Elmer: iv, 51, 64, 67-68, 77, 80, 85, 92, 94, 96, 110, 116, 131-32, 139, 141, 144, 171, 173-74, 184, 210, 287, 351, 359-60.
Wiesmoor: 266.
Wilhelmina, Queen of the Netherlands: 259, 324.
Wilhelmshaven: 205, 255, 263, 275, 295, 304, 310, 313, 327, 332, 340, 342.
Wiesel, Elli: 284.
Wijthmen: 233.
Wilson, Woodrow: 291.
Winnipeg: 23.
Winschoten: 243, 276.
Wissel: 152, 182, 183.
Wittmund: 273, 332, 340.
Woensdrecht: 56-57.
Wolvega: 235.
Wons: 328.

Woodstock: 20, 21.
Workum: 237.
Wyler: 76-77, 80, 98, 103, 105-08, 110, 115, 119, 334.

X

Xanten: 136, 143, 152-54, 188, 190, 272.

Y

Yarmouth: 25.

Z

Zandpol: 106.
Zangen, General Gustav von: 57.
Zeddam: 205.
Zeebrugge: 54.
Zeelst: 286.
Zeist: 277, 284, 287, 296.
Zetel: 295, 298-99, 309-10, 314, 332.
Zuidzande: 49.
Zutphen: 179, 209; capture of: 212-232; 233, 245.
Zwolle: 233, 295.
Zyfflich: 105.

About the Author

John Raycroft was born in Cardinal, Ontario in 1923 and moved to Prescott, Ontario as a boy, growing up there during the Depression. He worked as a farmhand and cooper (barrel maker) before joining the Canadian Army in 1943 at age 18, serving in the Third Canadian Division as part of a signals forward line crew in the campaign to liberate the Netherlands. He served in Germany after the war as part of the Canadian Army of Occupation before returning in 1946 to Canada.

After the war, Mr. Raycroft worked as an electrician and powerhouse operator with Ontario Hydro before going back to school and earning a Bachelor of Arts degree from Carleton University in 1957. Mr. Raycroft began teaching high school in 1959 and retired as librarian at South Grenville District High School in Prescott after 26 years.

A Signal War is Mr. Raycroft's second book. In 1999, Mr. Raycroft published Never Smile Before Christmas (Legas), a memoir and critique of education based on his experiences as a high school teacher.

To learn more about this and other books from Babblefish Press
contact
Babblefish Press
Box 633
Prescott, Ontario, K0E 1T0
www.babblefishpress.ca

Also by John Raycroft

Never Smile Before Christmas

A memoir of John Raycroft's 26 years of teaching, *Never Smile Before Christmas* (Legas) was written in the form of a letter to his former students, but is of interest to anyone who cares about education — where it has been and where it is headed.

If you have ever wondered about the occult process of marking and grading students, or had doubts about the value of humiliation as an incentive to learn, or if you believe that the same rules of ethics and the same means of earning respect should apply to both student and teacher, then this book will be a revelation.

Never Smile Before Christmas is in one sense a short history of the evolution of post-war education policies illustrated by amusing and often shocking anecdotes about the life and conflicts within the walls of an Ontario high school. But more than that, it is the account of the battle between two conflicting views of the purpose of education.

For older readers, the conflicts described will often reflect their own experiences — for a younger generation, some of the incidents from the tumultuous 1960's and 70's will simply be beyond belief.

A behind-the-scenes account that manages to be both informative and entertaining, Mr. Raycroft's book reveals much about the past and serves as a warning about the future of an education system once again in crisis.